AUTHENTIC TRANSCRIPTIONS WITH NOTES AND TABLATURE

AVENGED SEVENFOLD

Waking the Fallen

Music transcriptions by Pete Billmann, Jeff Jacobson and David Stocker

ISBN 978-1-61780-426-7

In Australia Contact:
Hal Leonard Australia Pty. Ltd.
4 Lentara Court
Cheltenham, Victoria, 3192 Australia
Email: ausadmin@halleonard.com.au

Visit Hal Leonard Online at
www.halleonard.com

Waking the Fallen (Intro)

Words and Music by Matthew Sanders, James Sullivan, Brian Haner, Jr. and Zachary Baker

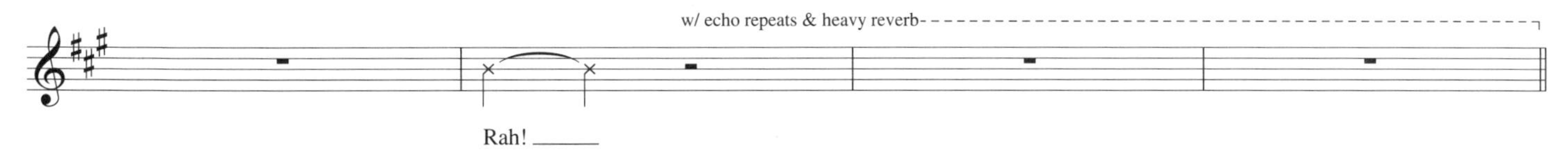
Gtr. 1: w/ Rhy. Fig. 1
w/ echo repeats & heavy reverb
Rah!

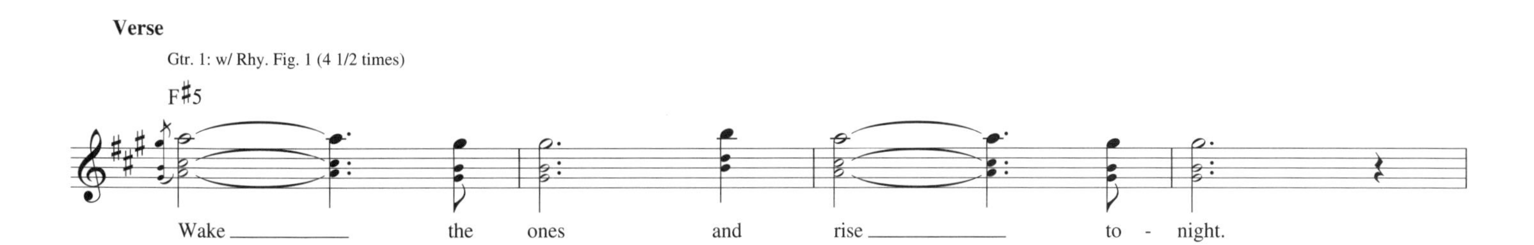
Verse
Gtr. 1: w/ Rhy. Fig. 1 (4 1/2 times)
F♯5
Wake the ones and rise to - night.

Fall - en souls, we shine so bright.

Rise now and ev - er, leave your mem - 'ries.

Rise now and ev - er,

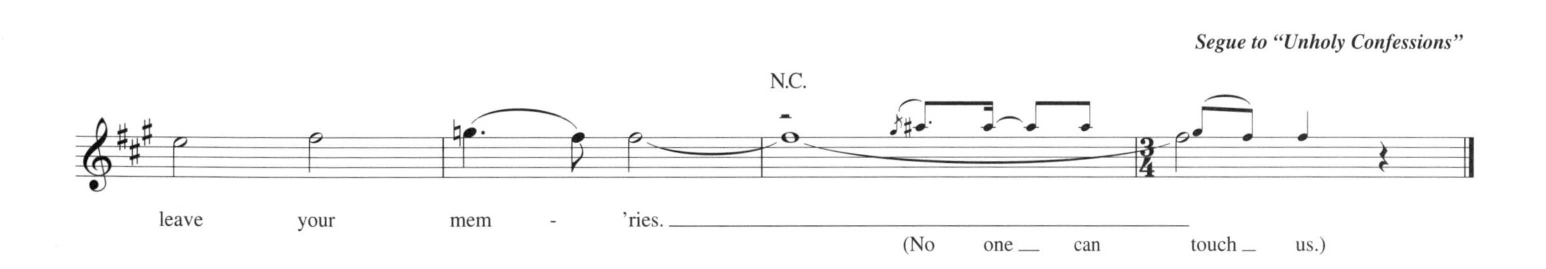
Segue to "Unholy Confessions"
N.C.
leave your mem - 'ries.
(No one can touch us.)

Unholy Confessions

Words and Music by Matthew Sanders, James Sullivan, Brian Haner, Jr. and Zachary Baker

4.
Verse
End double-time feel
Half-time feel
B♭5
N.C.
A5
D5
Screamed: 1. "I'll try."
Gtr. 1
Gtr. 3 (dist.)
Gtr. 1 divisi
Rhy. Fig. 1
P.M.
Gtr. 2
Gtr. 4 (dist.)
Gtr. 2 divisi
B♭5
C5
She said as he walked a - way. "Try not to lose
Riff C
End Riff C
End Rhy. Fig. 1
Riff C1
End Riff C1
Gtrs. 1 & 2: w/ Rhy. Fig. 1
Gtrs. 3 & 4: w/ Riffs C & C1
D5
B♭5
C5
you." Two vi - brant hearts could change.

D5
Bb5
C5
Noth - ing tears the be - ing more than de - cep - tion. Un - masked fear.
Gtrs. 1 & 2
P.M.
Gtrs. 3 & 4: w/ Riffs C & C1
D5
"I'll be here wait - ing,"
Interlude
Bb5
C5
D5
N.C.
test - ed and se - cure.
(Ah.)
Rhy. Fig. 2
End Rhy. Fig. 2
Gtrs. 1 & 2: w/ Rhy. Fig. 2

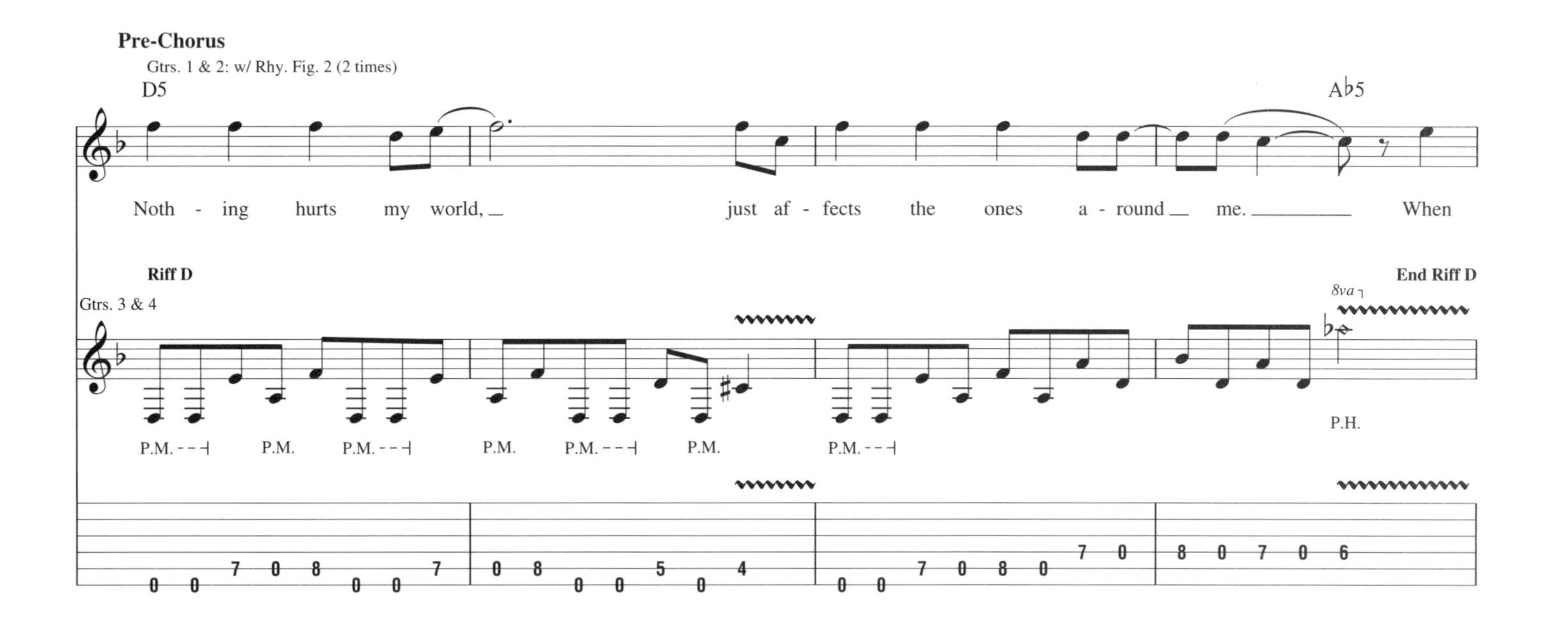
Pre-Chorus
Gtrs. 1 & 2: w/ Rhy. Fig. 2 (2 times)
D5
A♭5
Noth - ing hurts my world, just af - fects the ones a - round me. When
Riff D
Gtrs. 3 & 4
End Riff D
8va
P.M.
P.H.

Gtrs. 3 & 4: w/ Riff D
D5
A♭5
sin's deep in my blood, you'll be the one to fall! "I

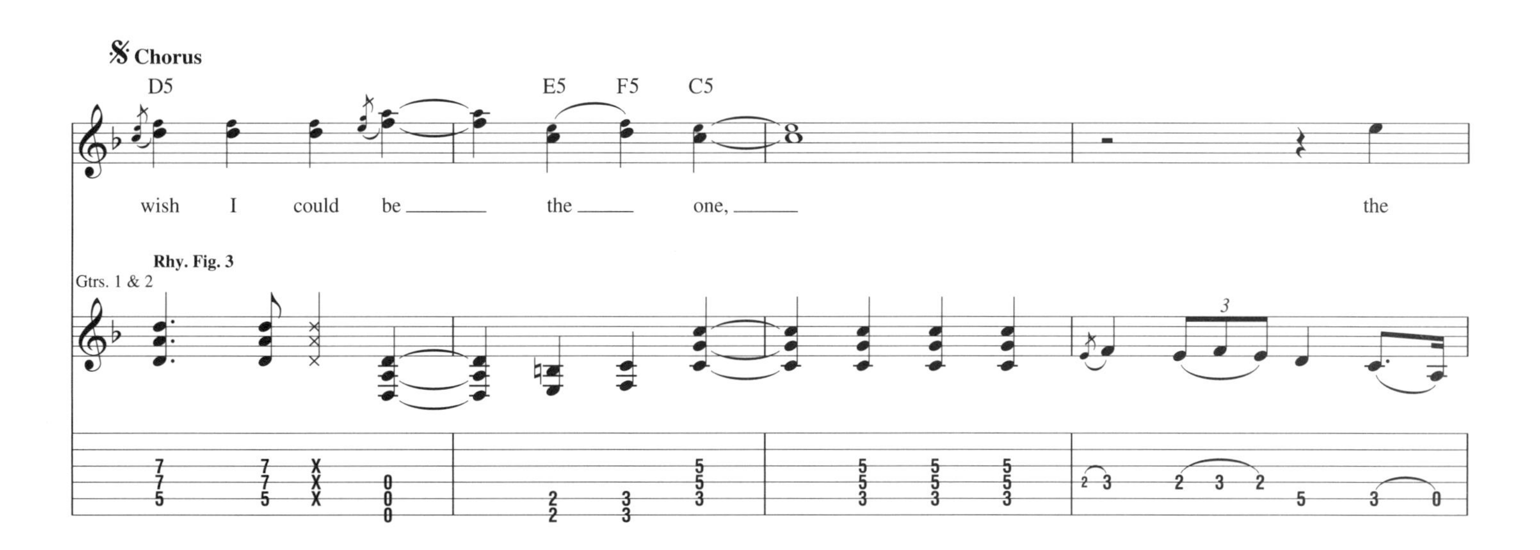
Chorus
D5
E5
F5
C5
wish I could be the one, the
Rhy. Fig. 3
Gtrs. 1 & 2

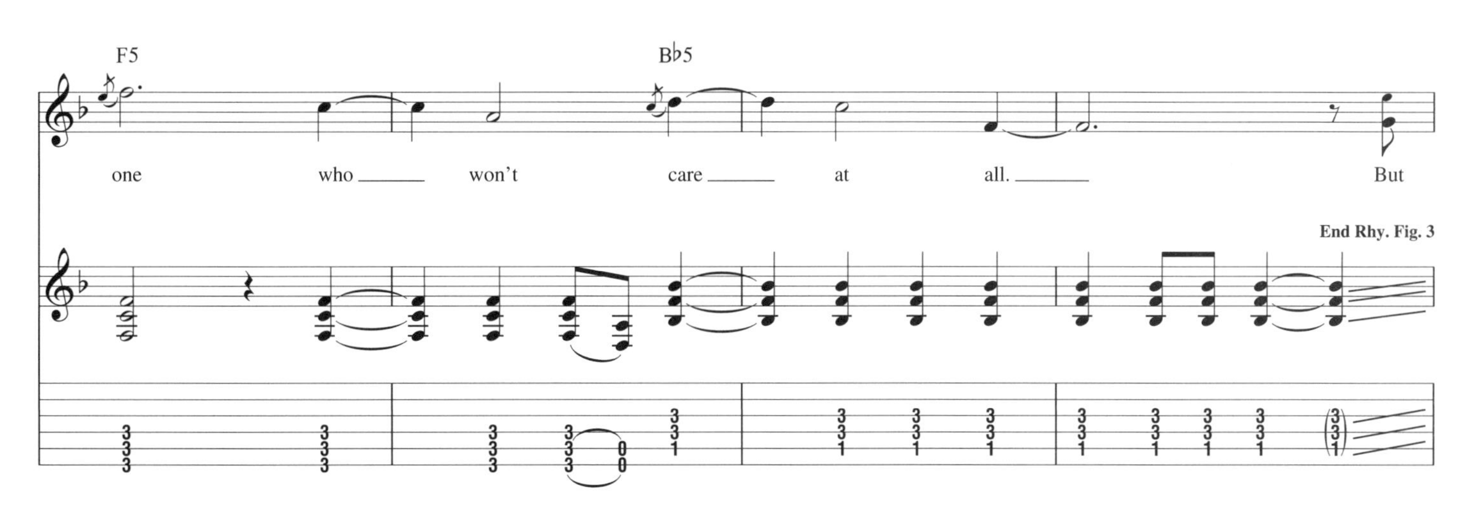
F5
B♭5
one who won't care at all. But
End Rhy. Fig. 3

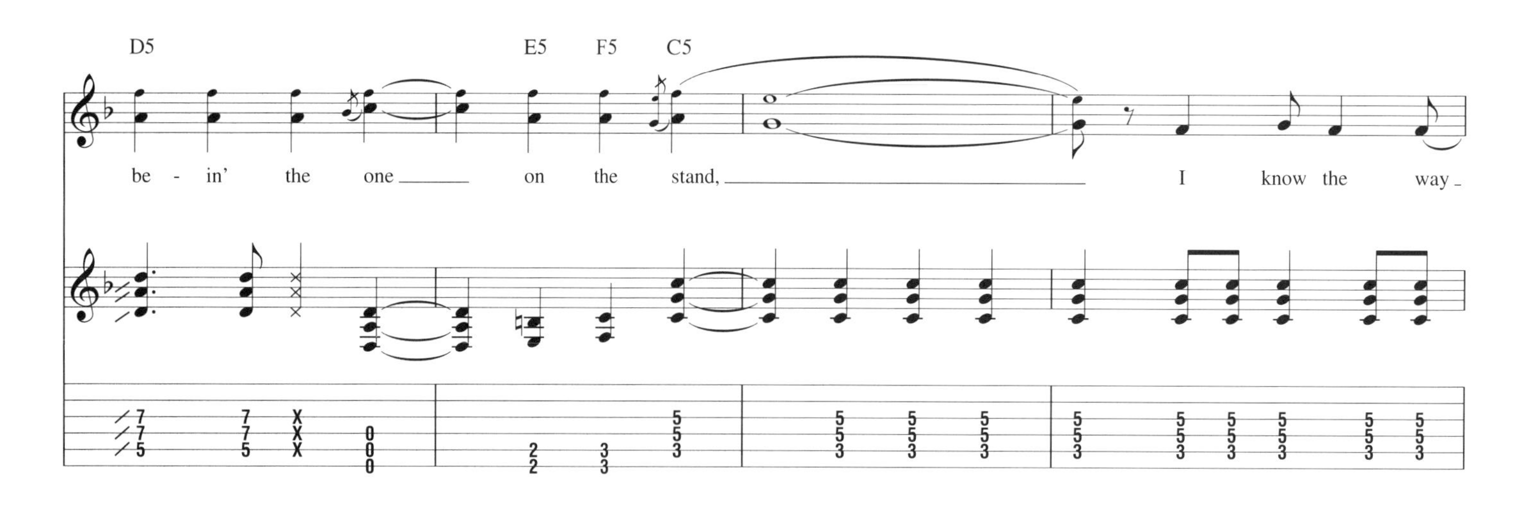
D5
E5 F5 C5
be - in' the one on the stand,
I know the way

F5
G5
Dm/F
to go, no one's guid - in' me.
When

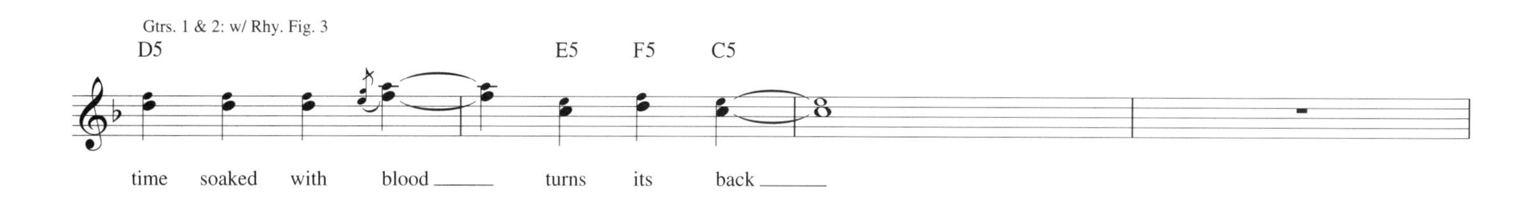
Gtrs. 1 & 2: w/ Rhy. Fig. 3
D5
E5 F5 C5
time soaked with blood turns its back

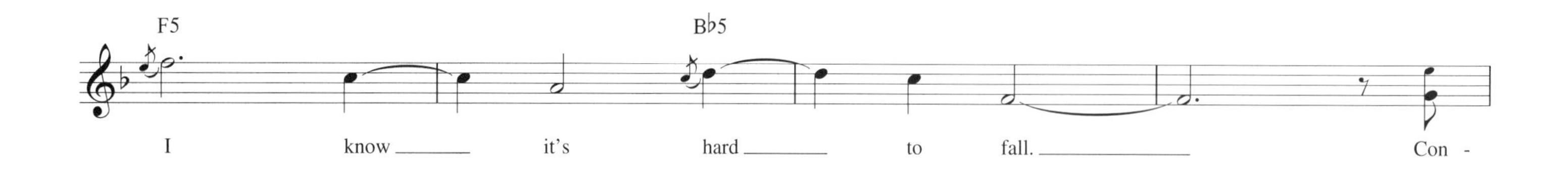
F5
B♭5
I know it's hard to fall.
Con -

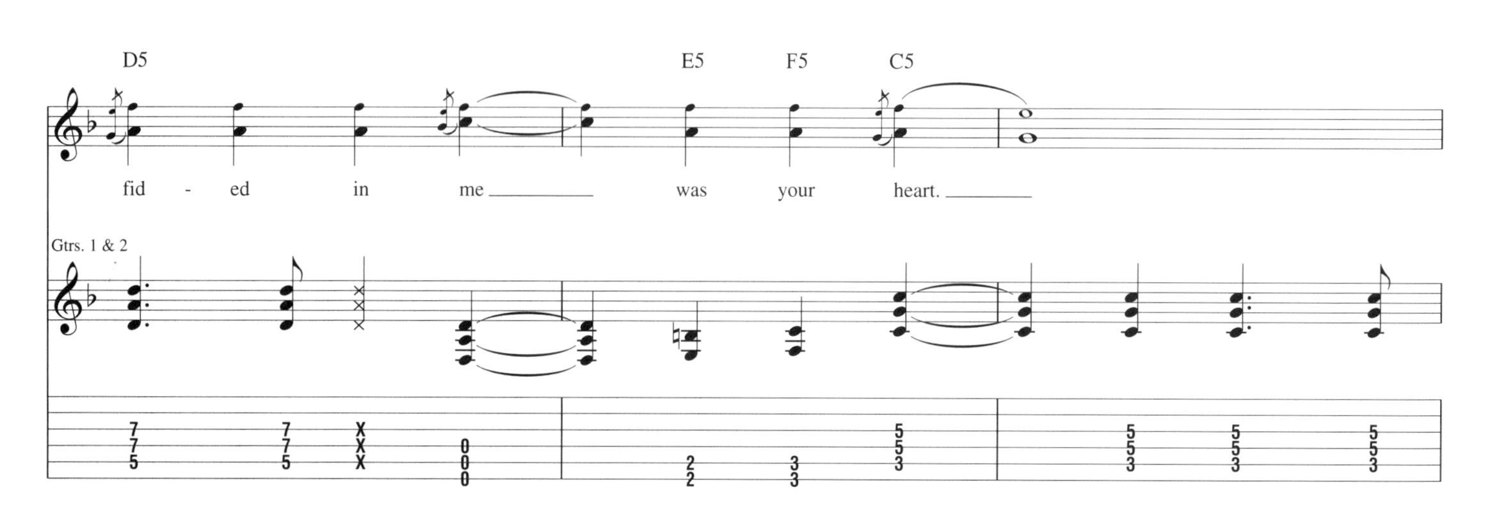
D5
E5 F5 C5
fid - ed in me was your heart.
Gtrs. 1 & 2

To Coda
F5
I know it's hurt - in' you, but it's
G5
Dm/F
kill - in' me."
Interlude
Dm
Gtr. 1
Gtr. 2
A7
B♭
D♭
C
B♭

1.
2.
A
Aadd♭13
Aadd♭13
Gtr. 1: w/ Riff A (1 1/2 times)
D5
Gtr. 2
B♭5
A5
D5
B♭5
N.C.
Gtrs. 1 & 2
A5
N.C.
End half-time feel
P.M.
Bridge
Double-time feel
Gtrs. 1 & 2: w/ Riffs A & B (4 times)
D5
B♭5
A5
Screamed: Noth - ing will last in this life, our time is spent con - struct - ing.
D5
B♭5
A5
Now you're per - fect - ing a world meant to sin.
D5
B♭5
A5
Con - strict your hands a - round me, squeeze till I can - not breathe.
D5
B♭5
A5
End double-time feel
This air tastes dead in - side me. Con - tri - bute to our

Half-time feel
D5
Break all your prom - is - es,...
plague.
...tear down this stead - fast wall.
Rhy. Fig. 4
Gtrs. 1 & 2
End Rhy. Fig. 4
P.M.
Gtrs. 1 & 2: w/ Rhy. Fig. 4
Re - straints are use - less here.
Tast - ing sal - va - tion's near.
Interlude
D5 C♯5 D5 C5 B5 B♭5 D5 A5 D5 A♭5 G5
*Gtrs. 1 & 2
*Composite arrangement
D5 C♯5 D5 C5 B5 B♭5 D5 A5 D5 A♭5 G5
P.M.
Gtrs. 1 & 2: w/ Rhy. Fig. 2 (2 times)
D5
Ah.
Pre-Chorus
Gtrs. 1 & 2: w/ Rhy. Fig. 2 (2 times)
Gtrs. 3 & 4: w/ Riff D (2 times)
D5
A♭5
Noth - ing hurts my world, just af - fects the ones a - round me. When

D5
Ab5
sin's deep in my blood, you'll be the one to fall!
Interlude
Gtrs. 1 & 2: w/ Rhy. Fig. 2
D5
Riff E
G5
D5
G5
End Riff E
*Gtrs. 3 & 4
grad. bend
grad. bend
*Composite arrangement
D5 G5 A5 D5 G5 A5 D5 G5 D5 F5 D5 Em A
D.S. al Coda
I
Gtrs. 1–4
Gtrs. 2 & 4
Gtrs. 1 & 3
divisi
Coda
G5
Dm/F
kill - in' me."
Gtrs. 1 & 2
Outro
Gtrs. 1 & 2: w/ Rhy. Fig. 2
Gtrs. 3 & 4: w/ Riff E (4 times)
D5
G5
D5
G5
Ah.
D5
G5
D5
G5
D5 N.C.
Gtrs. 1 & 2
Play 3 times
Gtrs. 1–4
P.M.

Chapter Four

Words and Music by Matthew Sanders, James Sullivan, Brian Haner, Jr. and Zachary Baker

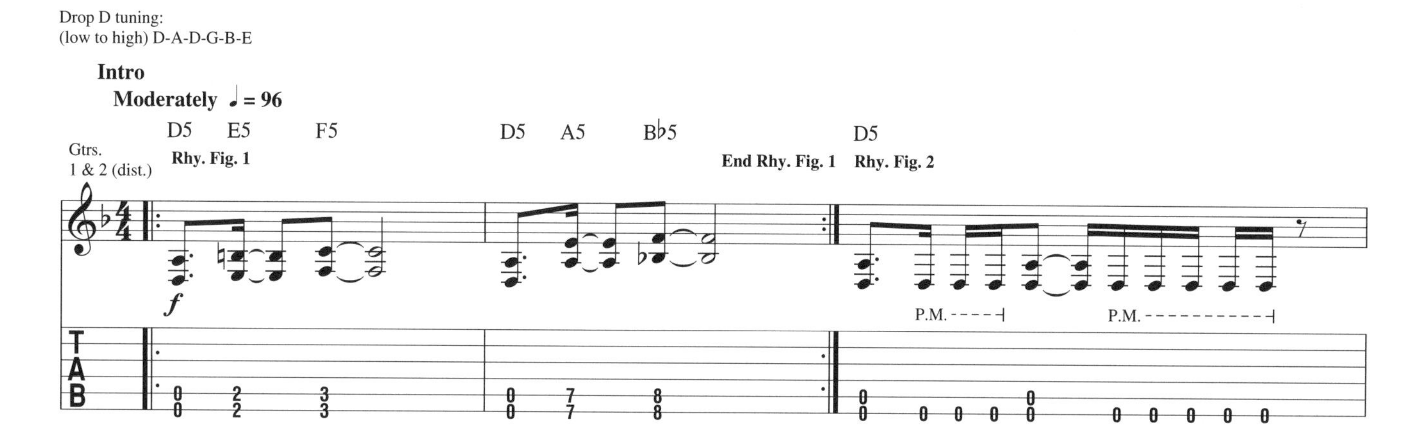

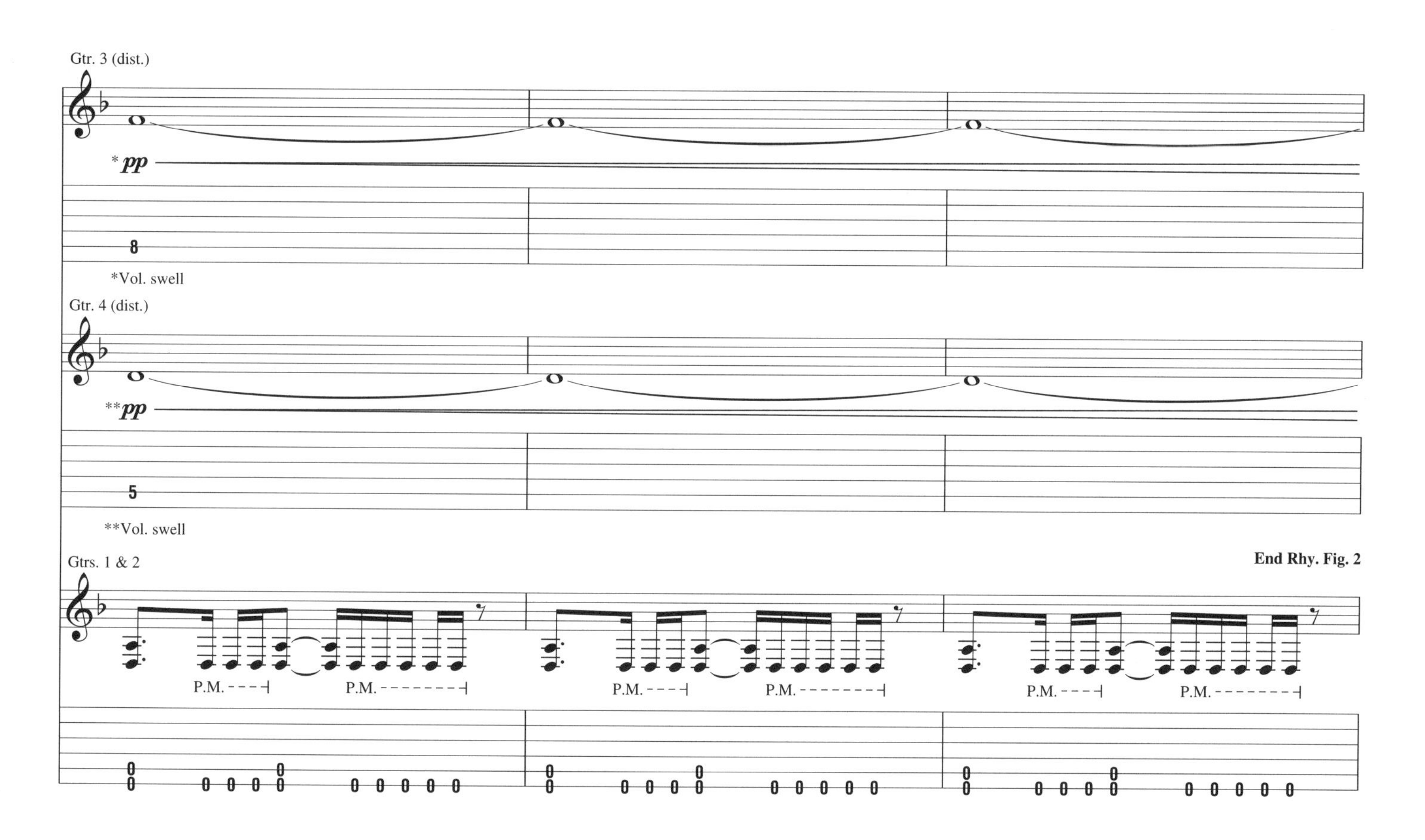

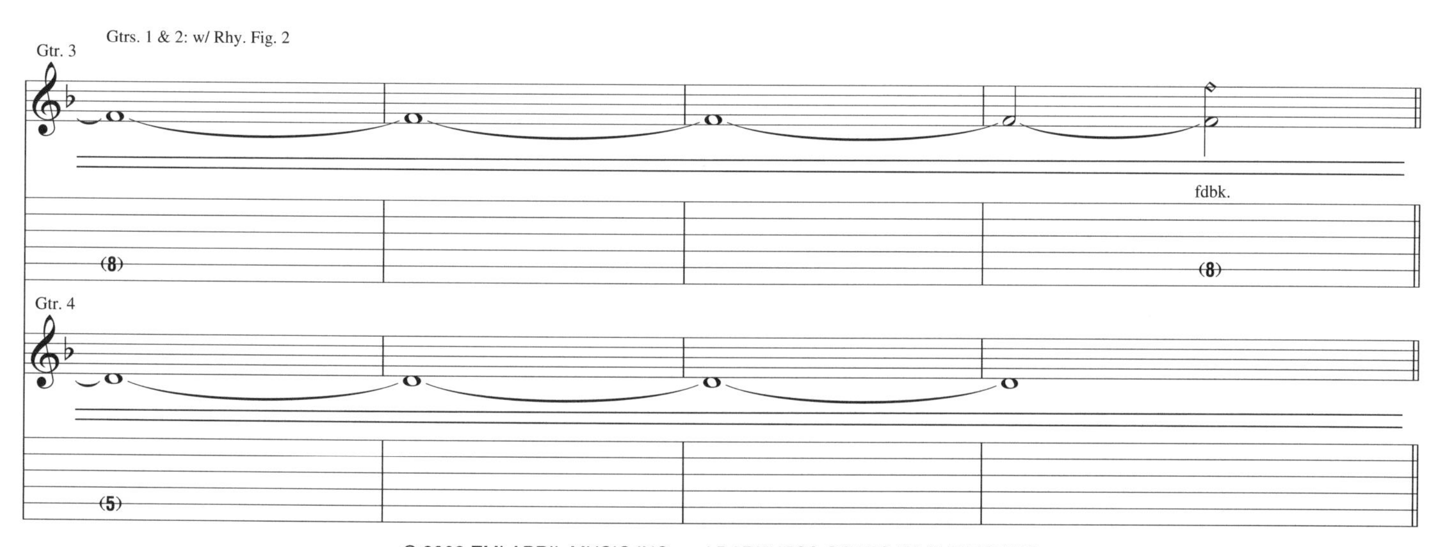

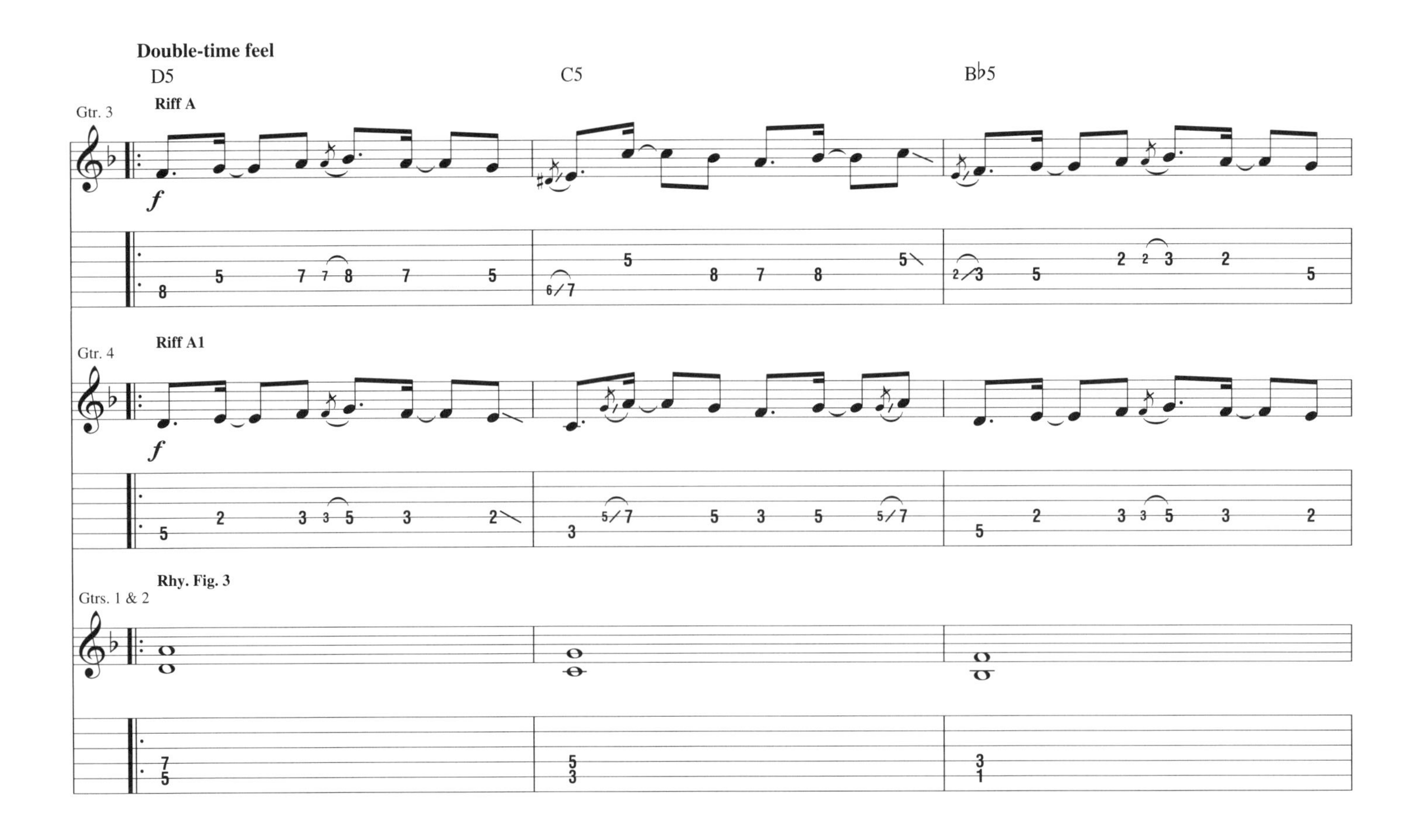

Double-time feel
D5
C5
B♭5
Gtr. 3
Riff A
Gtr. 4
Riff A1
Rhy. Fig. 3
Gtrs. 1 & 2

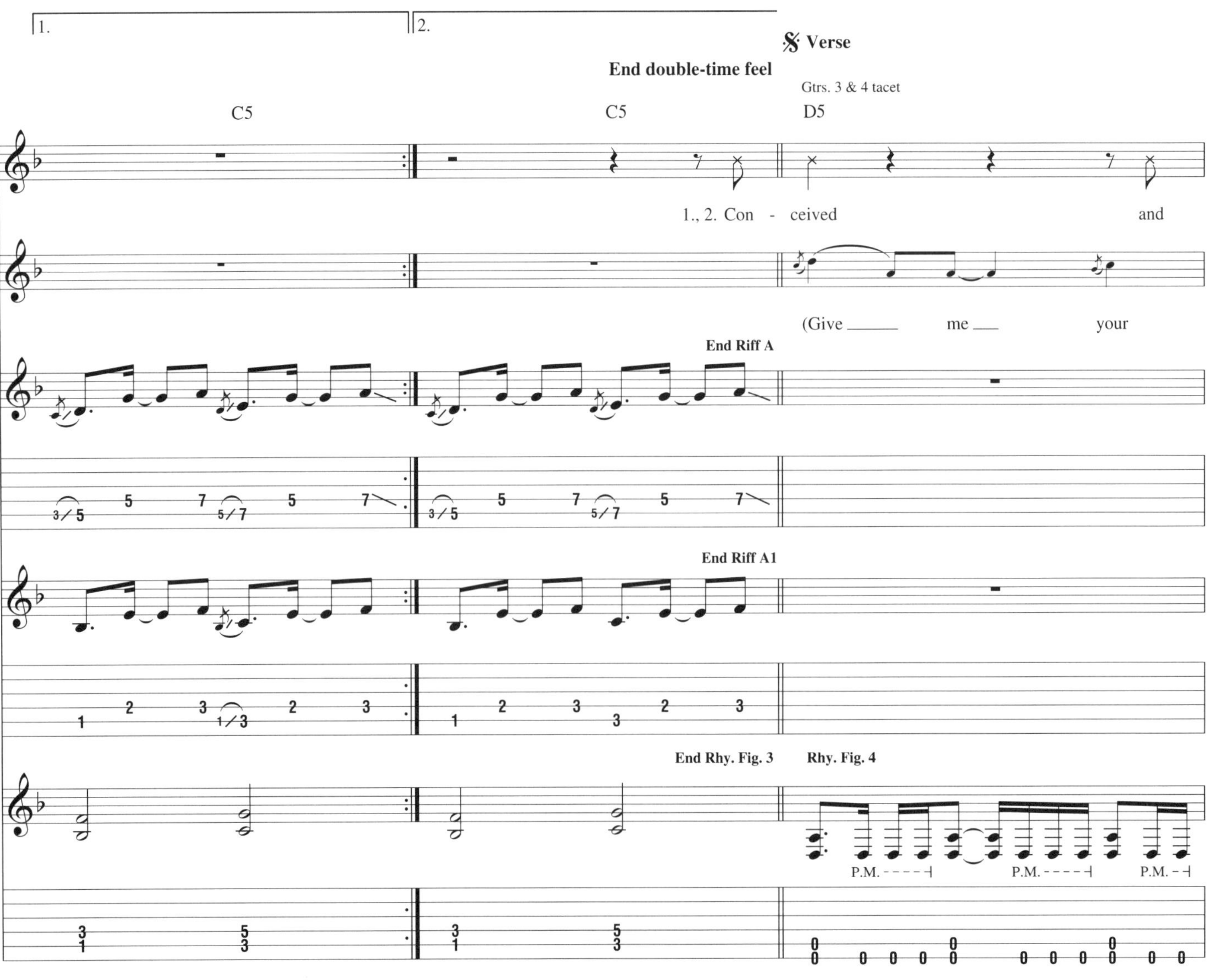

1.
2.
Verse
End double-time feel
Gtrs. 3 & 4 tacet
C5
C5
D5
1., 2. Con - ceived and
(Give me your
End Riff A
End Riff A1
End Rhy. Fig. 3
Rhy. Fig. 4
P.M.

F5 C/E Bb5 F5 C/E
born was one of light.
hand, blood is spilled and man will fol - low.
Gtrs. 1 & 2
End Rhy. Fig. 4
P.M.

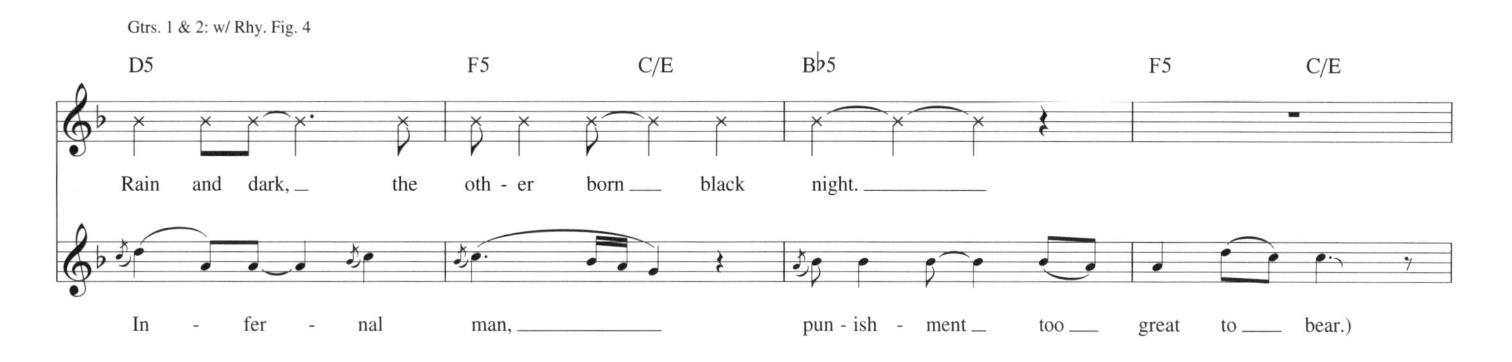

Gtrs. 1 & 2: w/ Rhy. Fig. 4
D5 F5 C/E Bb5 F5 C/E
Rain and dark, the oth - er born black night.
In - fer - nal man, pun - ish - ment too great to bear.)

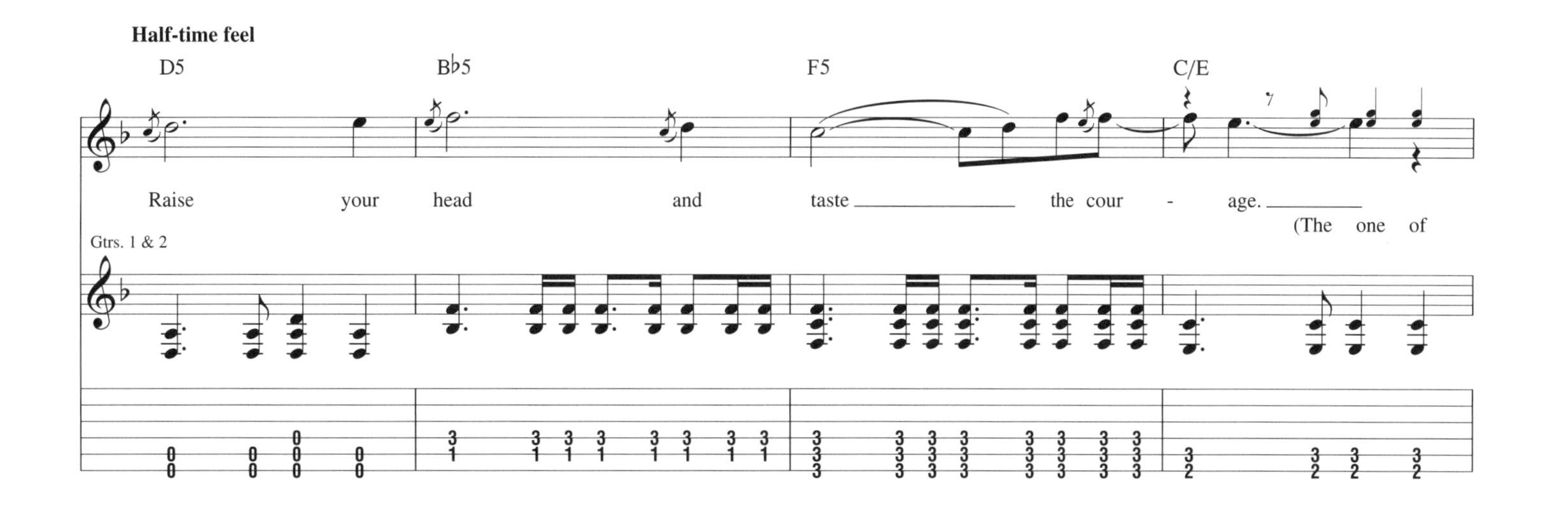

Half-time feel
D5 Bb5 F5 C/E
Raise your head and taste the cour - age.
(The one of
Gtrs. 1 & 2

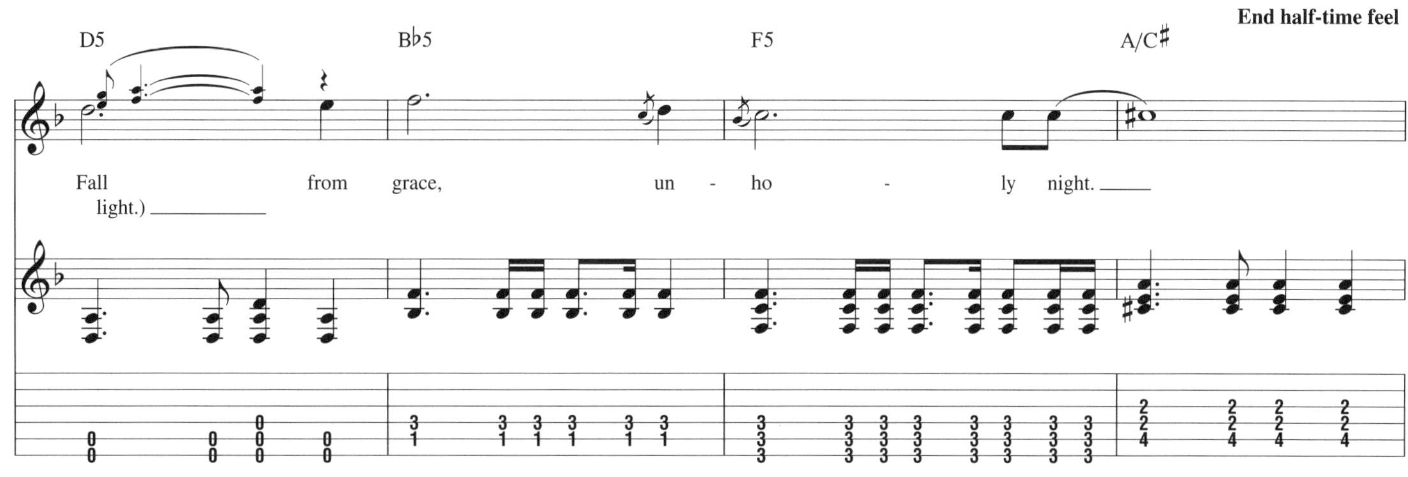

End half-time feel
D5 Bb5 F5 A/C#
Fall from grace, un - ho - ly night.
light.)

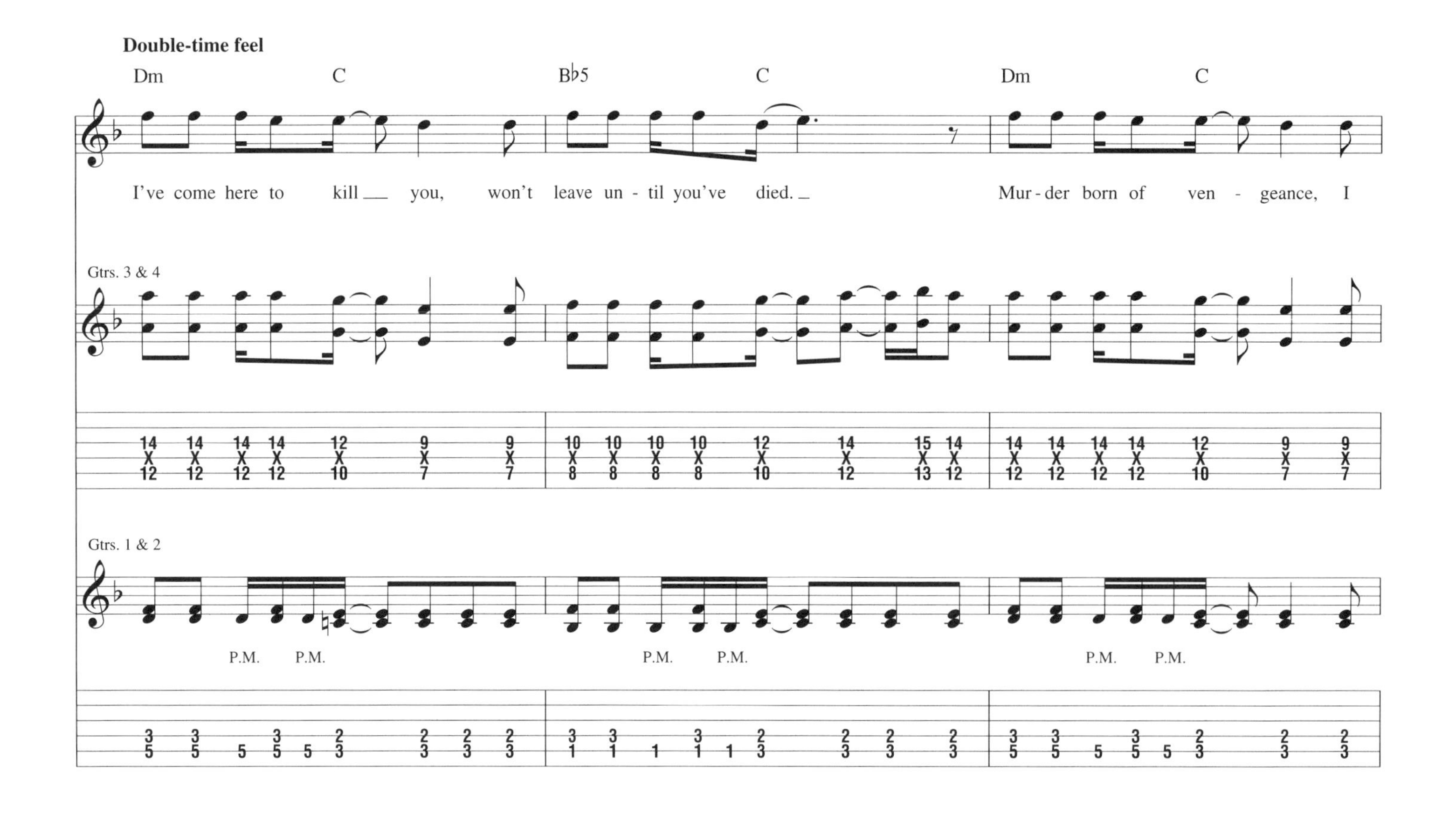
Double-time feel
Dm
C
B♭5
C
Dm
C
I've come here to kill __ you, won't leave un - til you've died. _
Mur - der born of ven - geance, I
Gtrs. 3 & 4
Gtrs. 1 & 2
P.M.
P.M.
P.M.
P.M.
P.M.
P.M.

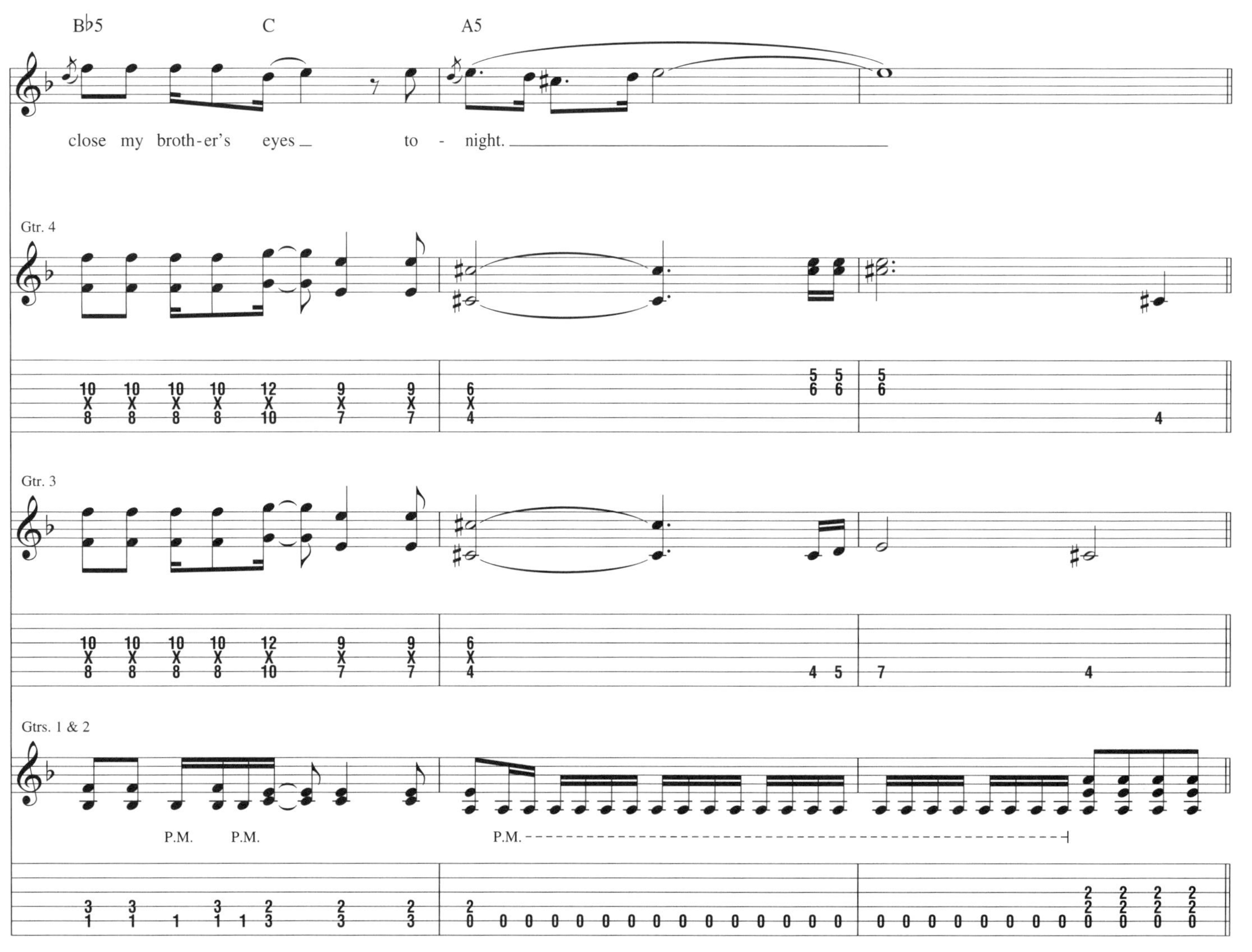
B♭5
C
A5
close my broth - er's eyes _ to - night.
Gtr. 4
Gtr. 3
Gtrs. 1 & 2
P.M.
P.M.
P.M.

Interlude
1.
3rd time, To Coda
D5
C5
B♭5
C5
D5
C5
B♭5
2.
D.S. al Coda
End double-time feel
C5
D5
C5
B♭5
C5
2. Con -

Coda
D5
C5
B♭5
C5
It's

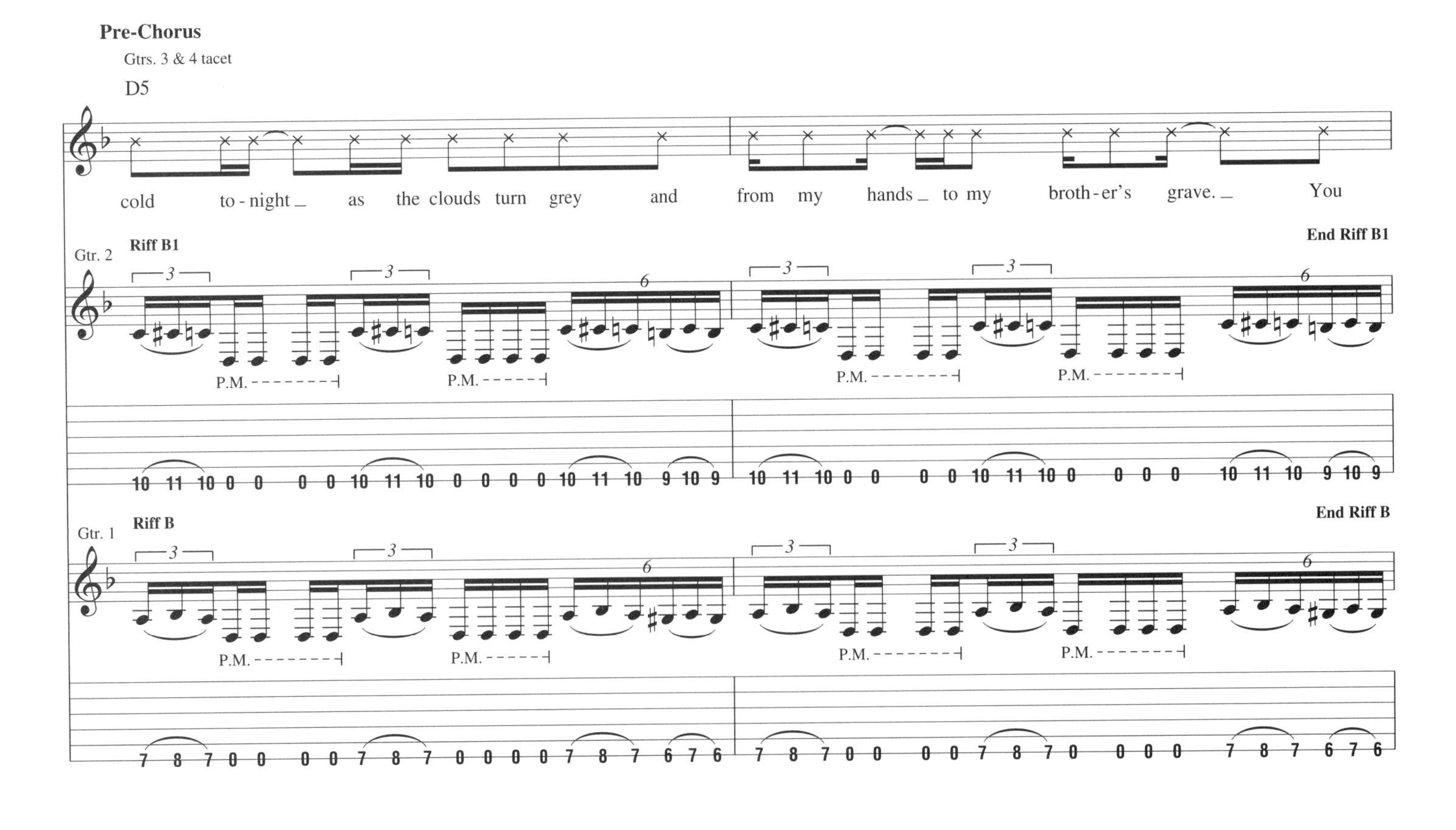
Pre-Chorus
Gtrs. 3 & 4 tacet
D5
cold to-night as the clouds turn grey and from my hands to my broth-er's grave. You
Gtr. 2
Riff B1
End Riff B1
P.M.
Gtr. 1
Riff B
End Riff B
P.M.

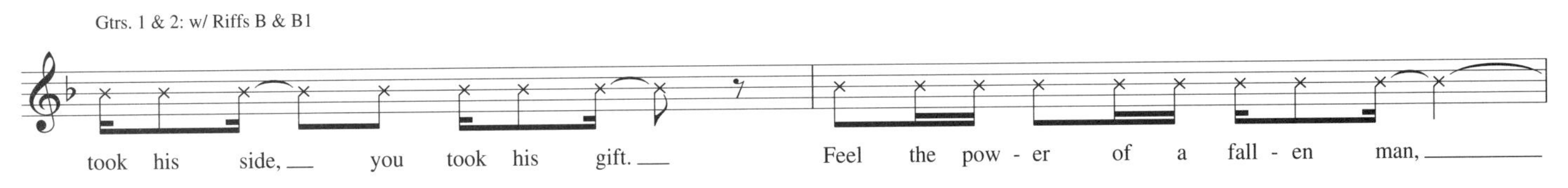
Gtrs. 1 & 2: w/ Riffs B & B1
took his side, you took his gift. Feel the pow-er of a fall-en man,

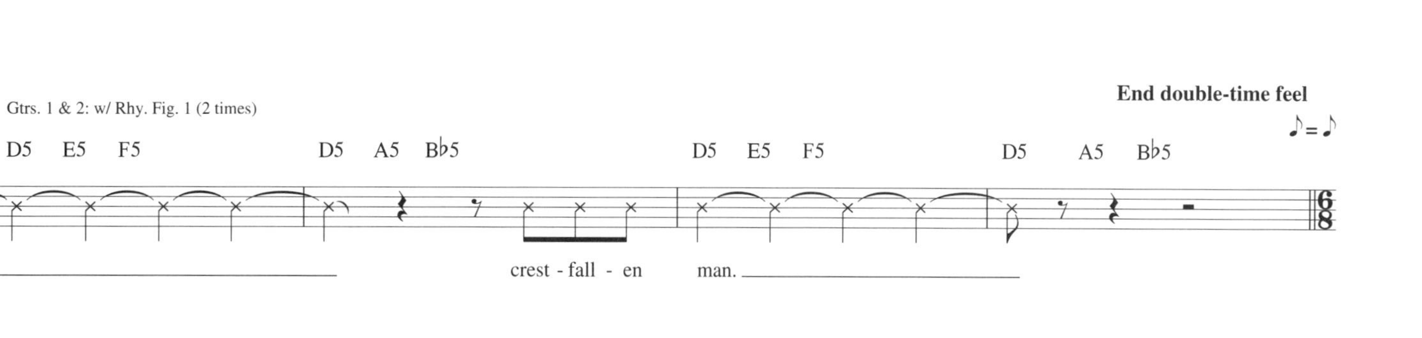
Gtrs. 1 & 2: w/ Rhy. Fig. 1 (2 times)
End double-time feel
D5 E5 F5 D5 A5 B♭5 D5 E5 F5 D5 A5 B♭5
crest - fall - en man.

Chorus
D5 A5 G5 A5 B♭5 Dm/F A/E
Far a - way in this land I must go, out of the site of the
Gtrs. 1 & 2
Rhy. Fig. 5
End Rhy. Fig. 5

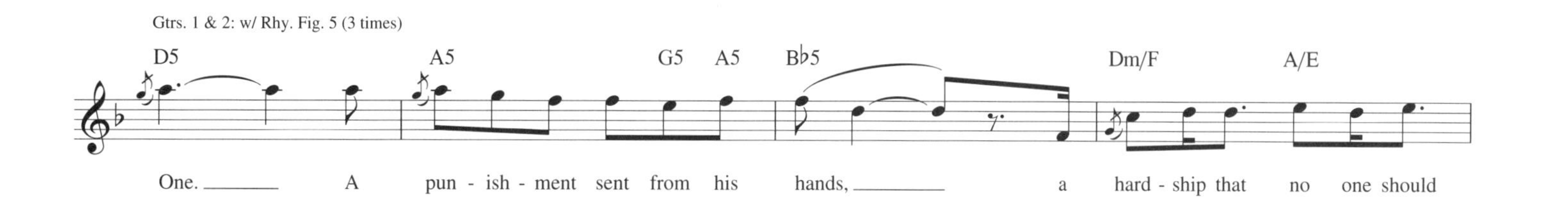
Gtrs. 1 & 2: w/ Rhy. Fig. 5 (3 times)
D5 A5 G5 A5 B♭5 Dm/F A/E
One. A pun - ish - ment sent from his hands, a hard - ship that no one should

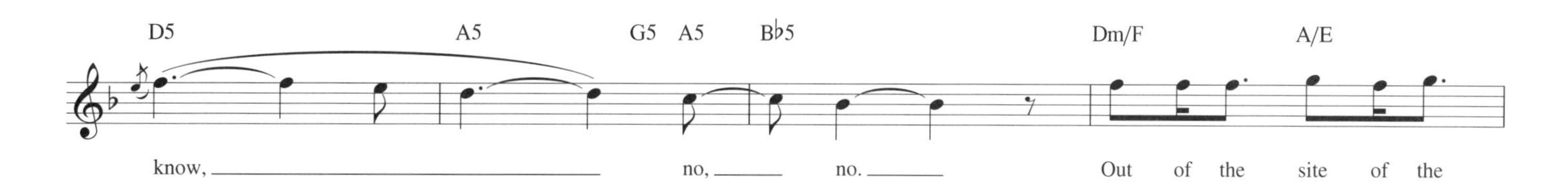
D5 A5 G5 A5 B♭5 Dm/F A/E
know, no, no. Out of the site of the

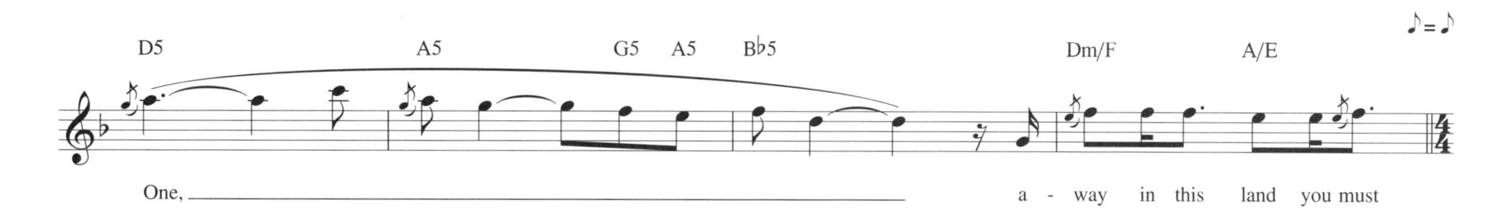
D5 A5 G5 A5 B♭5 Dm/F A/E
One, a - way in this land you must

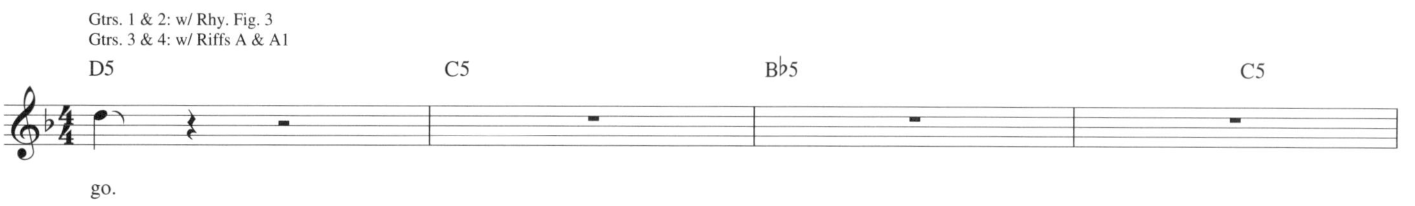
Interlude
Double-time feel
Gtrs. 1 & 2: w/ Rhy. Fig. 3
Gtrs. 3 & 4: w/ Riffs A & A1
D5 C5 B♭5 C5
go.

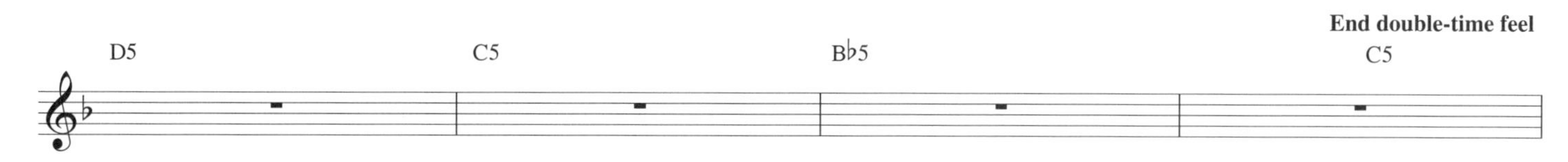
End double-time feel
D5 C5 B♭5 C5

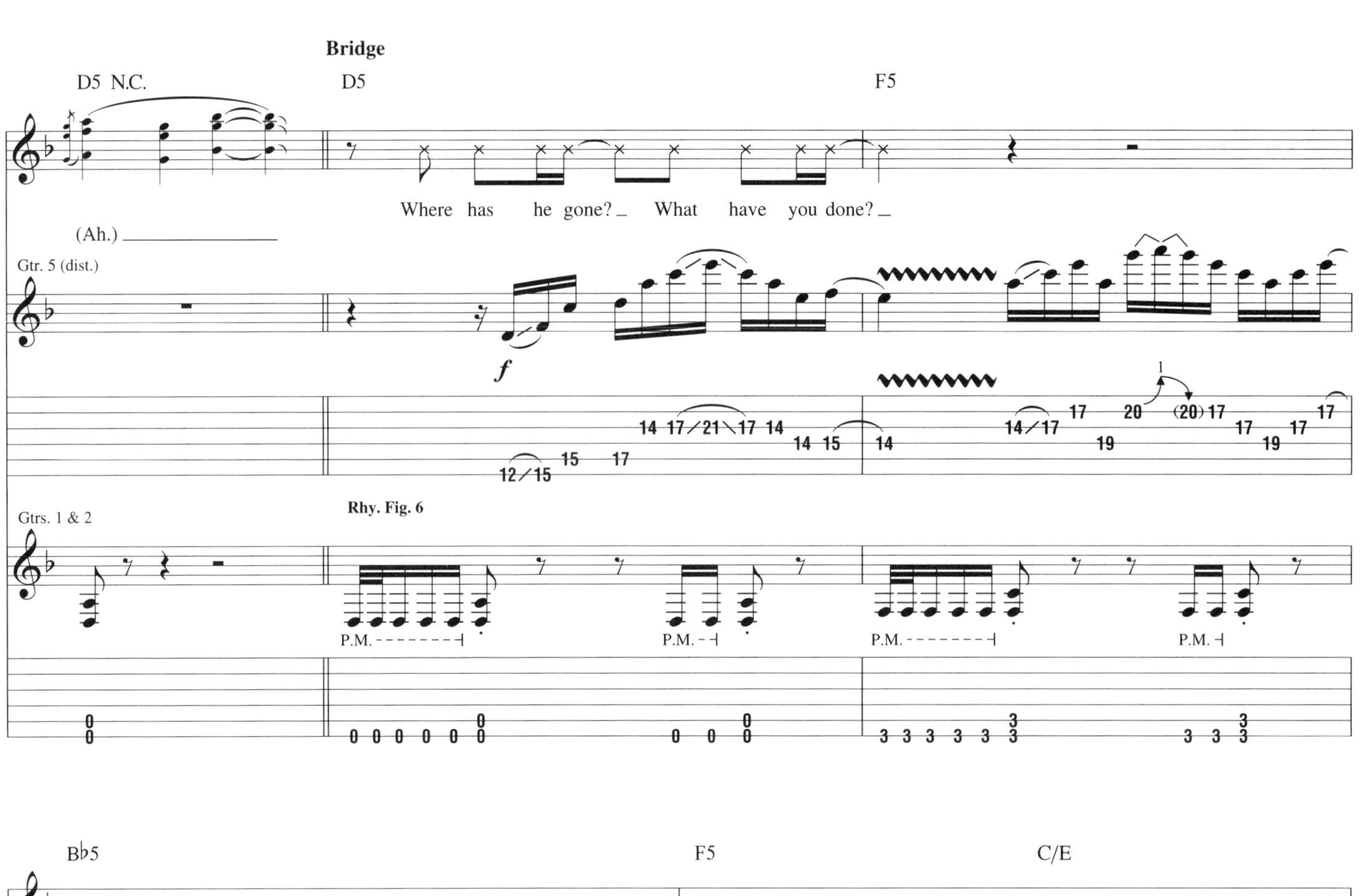
Bridge
D5 N.C.
D5
F5
Where has he gone? What have you done?
(Ah.)
Gtr. 5 (dist.)
Gtrs. 1 & 2
Rhy. Fig. 6
P.M.

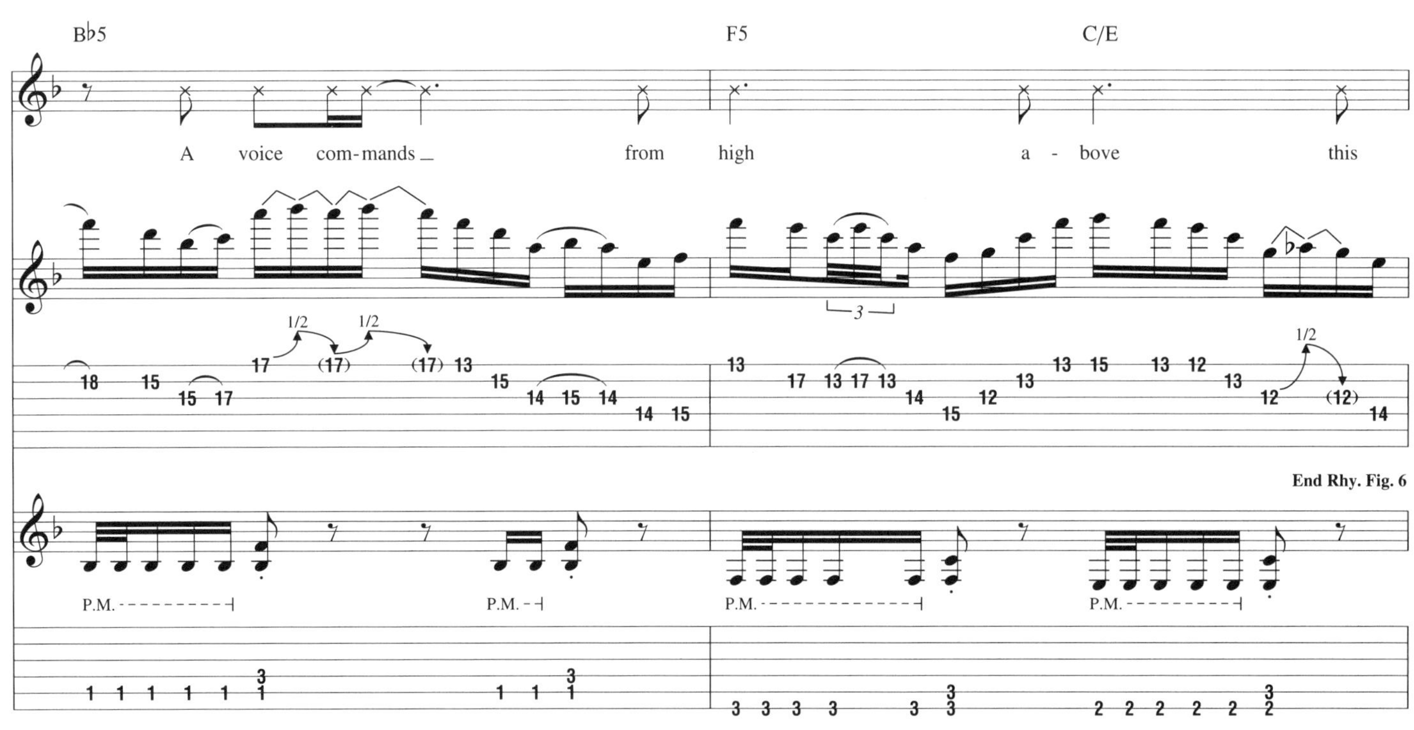
B♭5
F5
C/E
A voice com-mands from high a - bove this
End Rhy. Fig. 6
P.M.

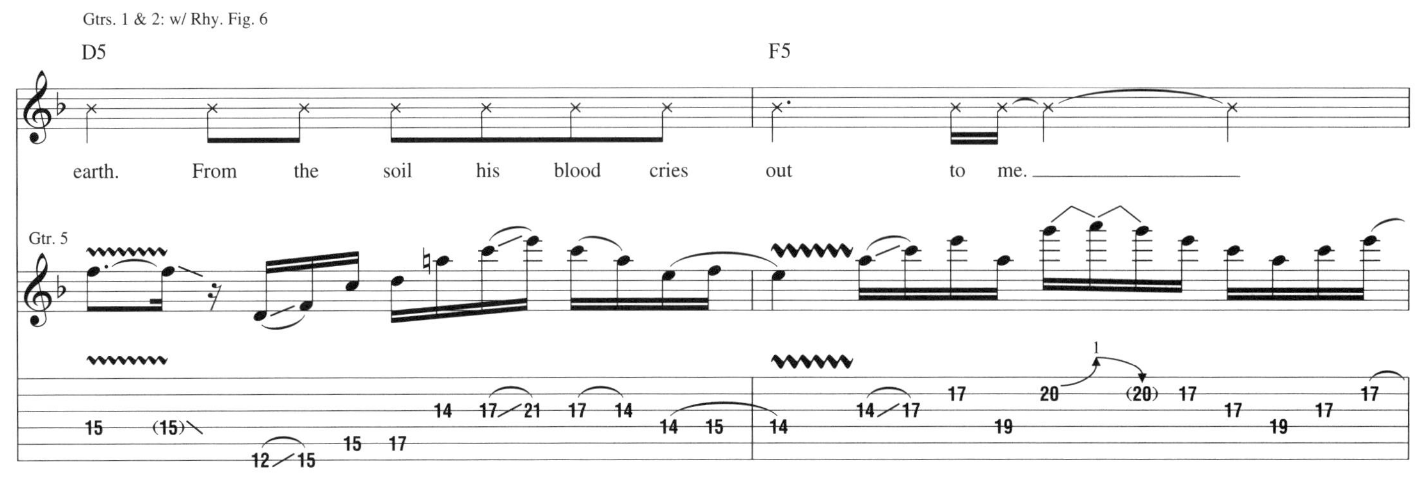
Gtrs. 1 & 2: w/ Rhy. Fig. 6
D5
F5
earth. From the soil his blood cries out to me.
Gtr. 5

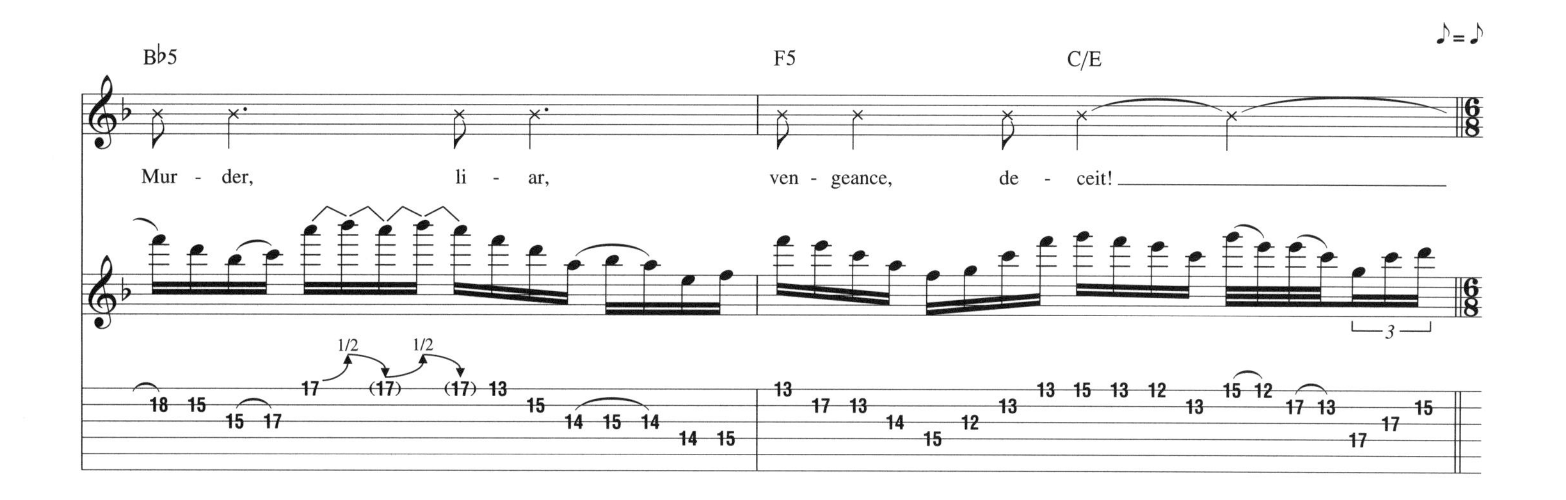
B♭5
F5
C/E
Mur - der, li - ar, ven - geance, de - ceit!
1/2
1/2

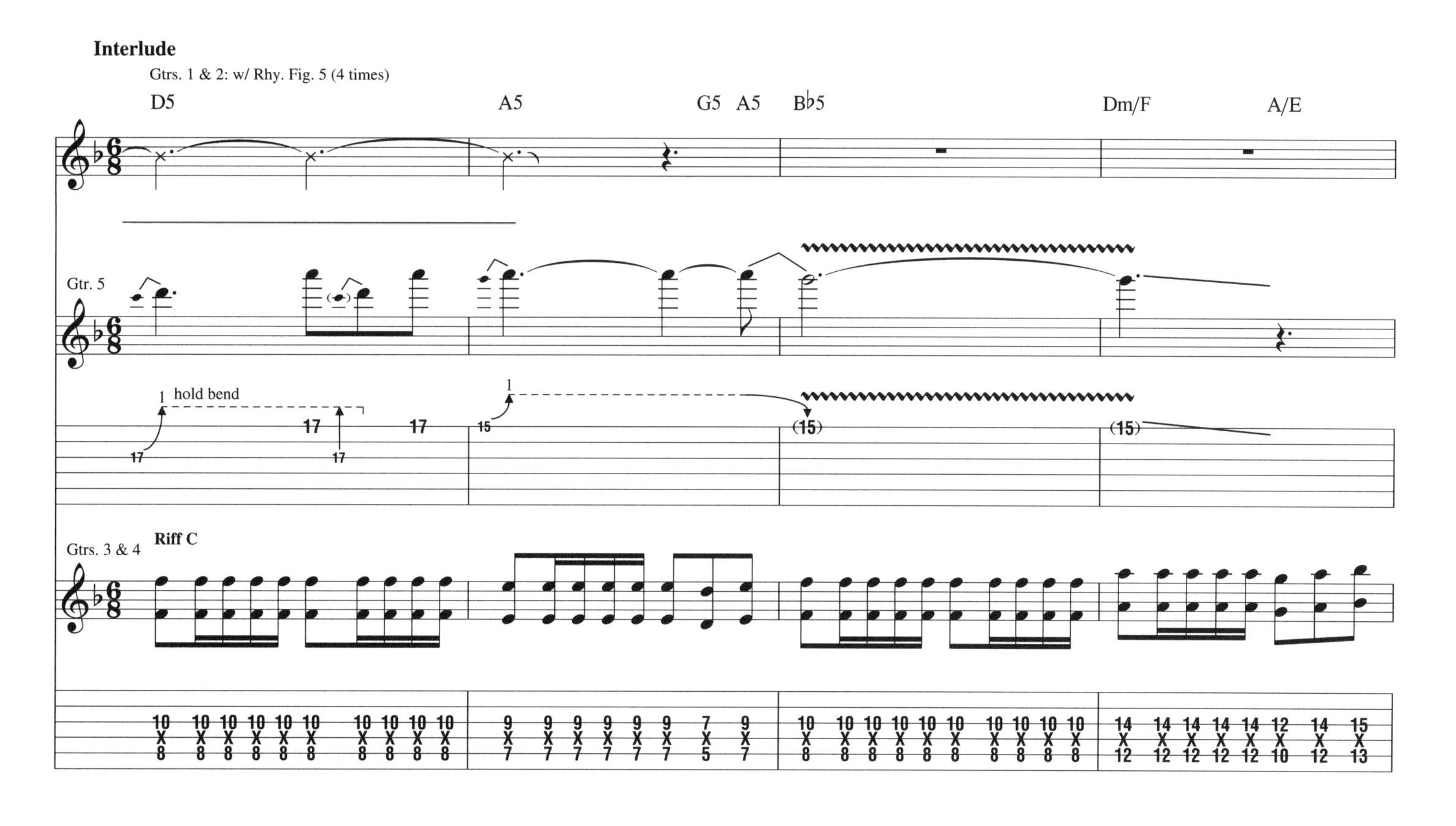
Interlude
Gtrs. 1 & 2: w/ Rhy. Fig. 5 (4 times)
D5
A5
G5 A5
B♭5
Dm/F
A/E
Gtr. 5
hold bend
Gtrs. 3 & 4
Riff C

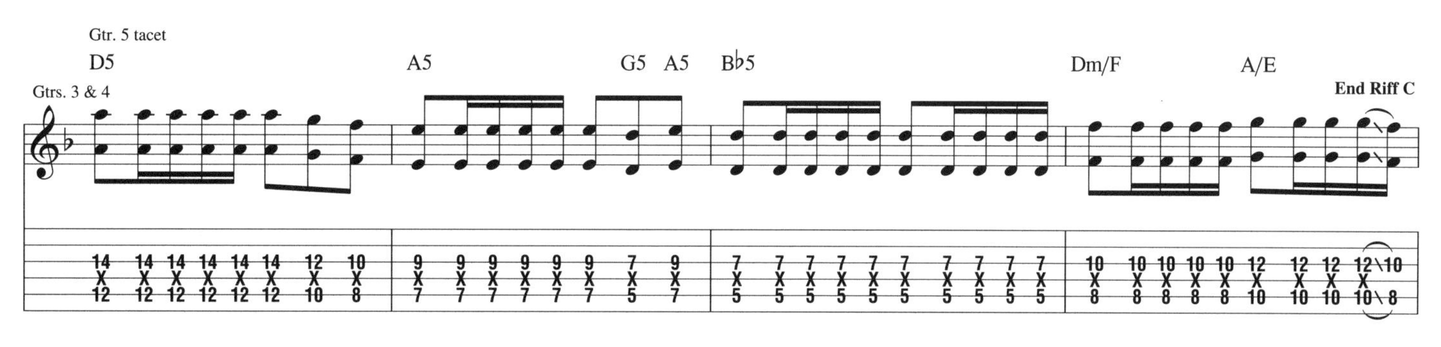
Gtr. 5 tacet
D5
A5
G5 A5
B♭5
Dm/F
A/E
Gtrs. 3 & 4
End Riff C

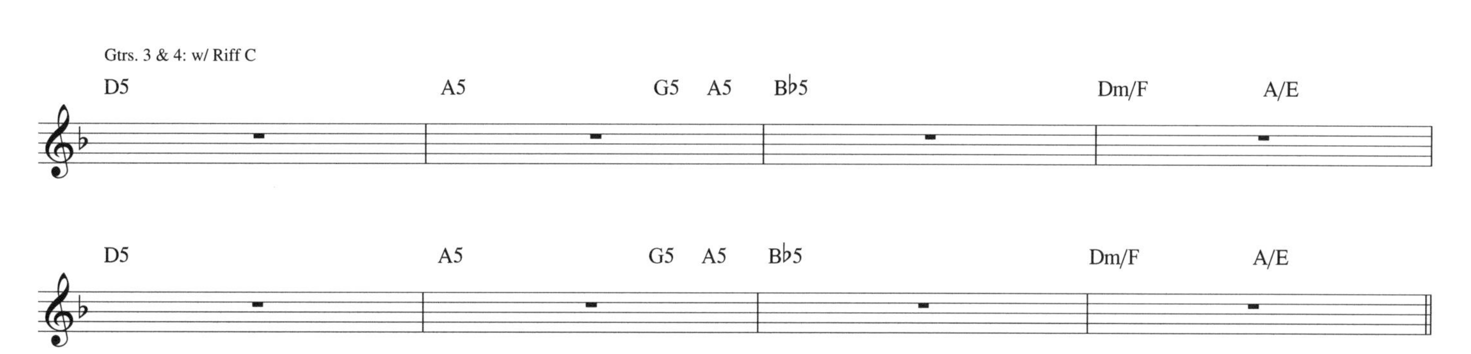
Gtrs. 3 & 4: w/ Riff C
D5
A5
G5 A5
B♭5
Dm/F
A/E
D5
A5
G5 A5
B♭5
Dm/F
A/E

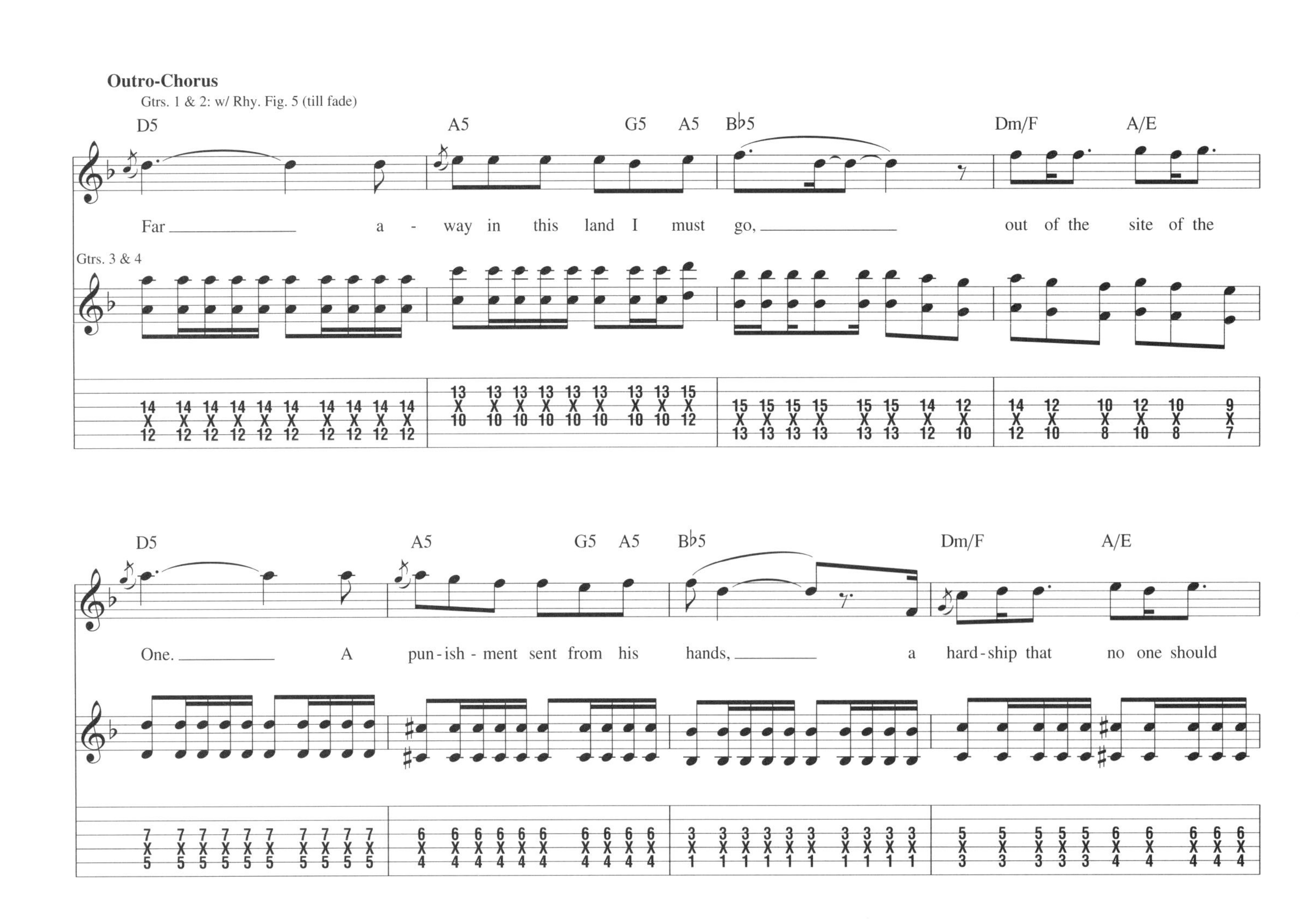
Outro-Chorus
Gtrs. 1 & 2: w/ Rhy. Fig. 5 (till fade)
D5 A5 G5 A5 B♭5 Dm/F A/E
Far a - way in this land I must go, out of the site of the
Gtrs. 3 & 4
D5 A5 G5 A5 B♭5 Dm/F A/E
One. A pun-ish - ment sent from his hands, a hard-ship that no one should

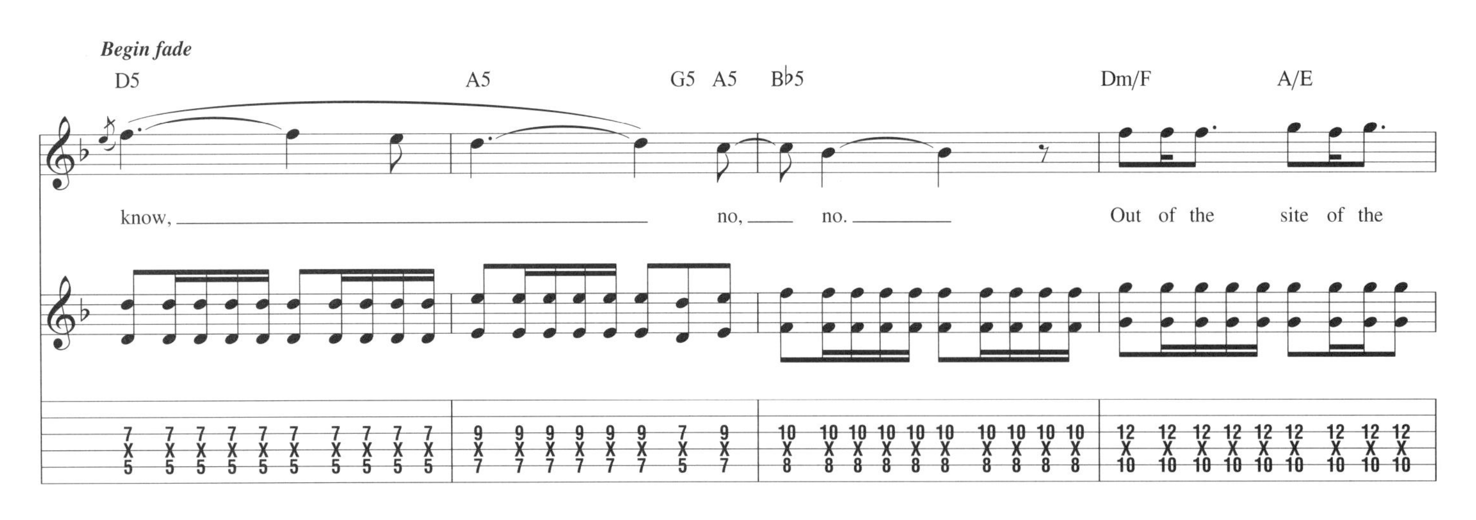
Begin fade
D5 A5 G5 A5 B♭5 Dm/F A/E
know, no, no. Out of the site of the

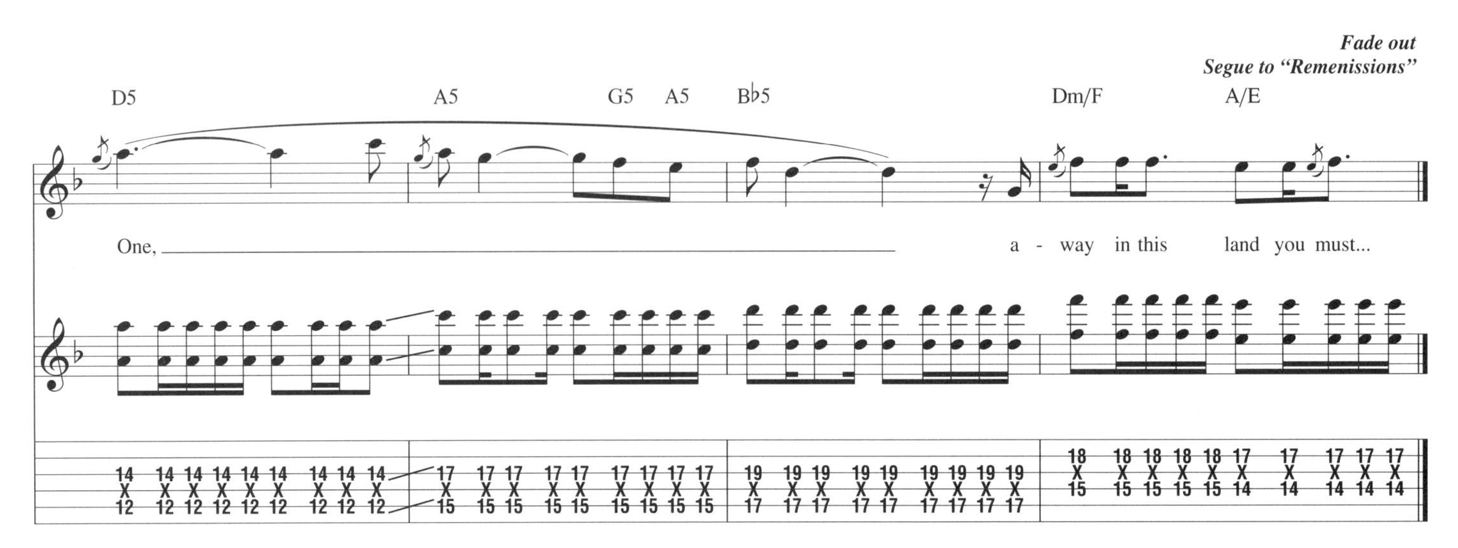
Fade out
Segue to "Remenissions"
D5 A5 G5 A5 B♭5 Dm/F A/E
One, a - way in this land you must...

Remenissions

Words and Music by Matthew Sanders, James Sullivan, Brian Haner, Jr. and Zachary Baker

Drop D tuning:
(low to high) D-A-D-G-B-E

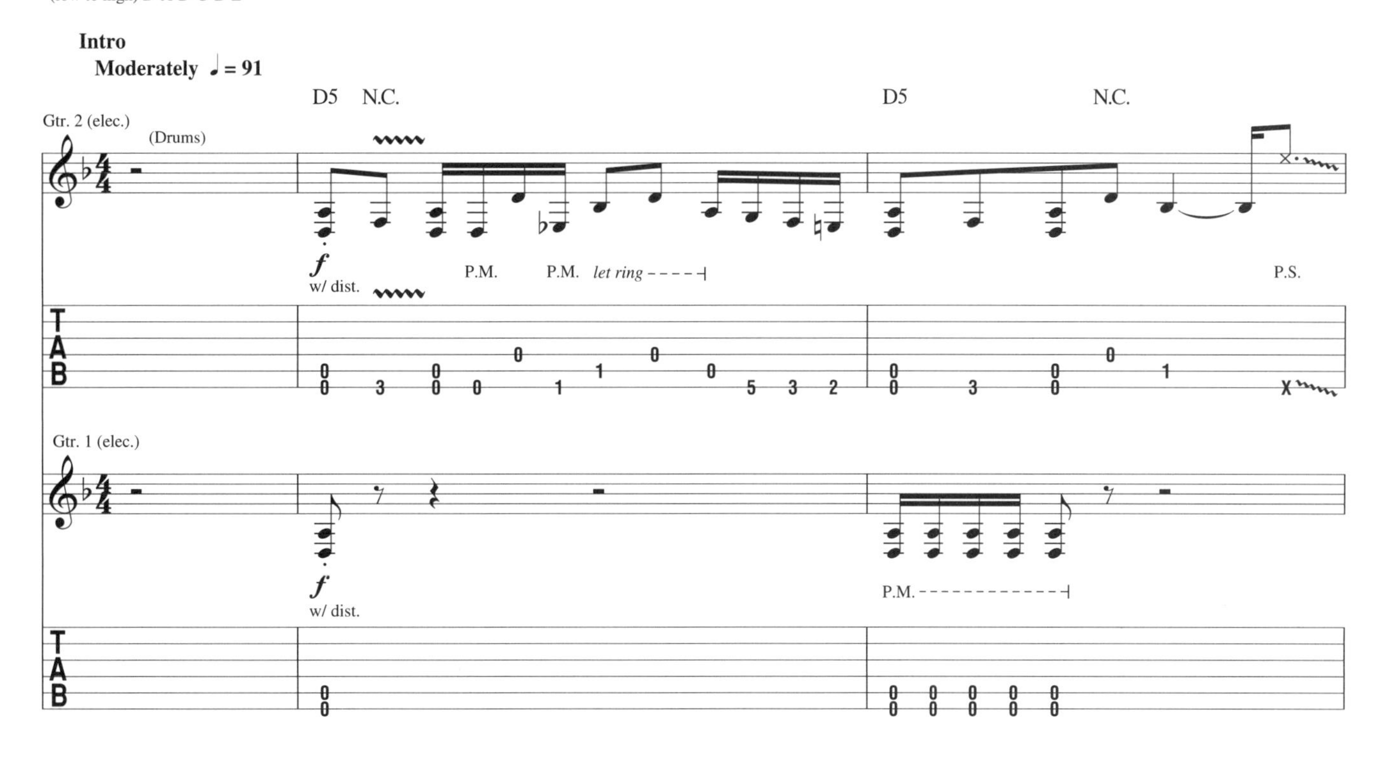

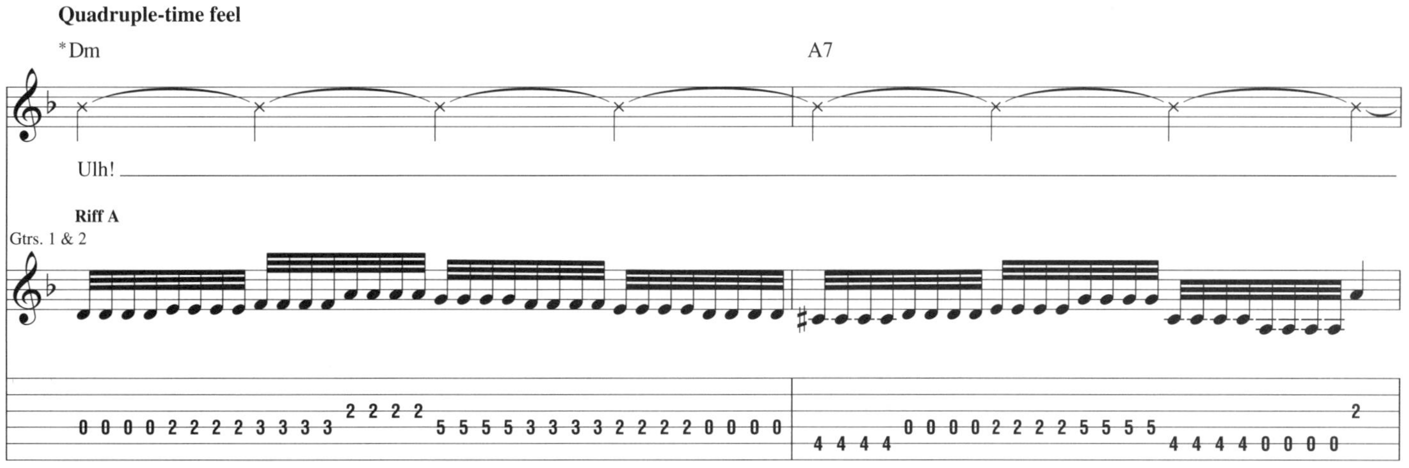

*Chord symbols reflect implied harmony.

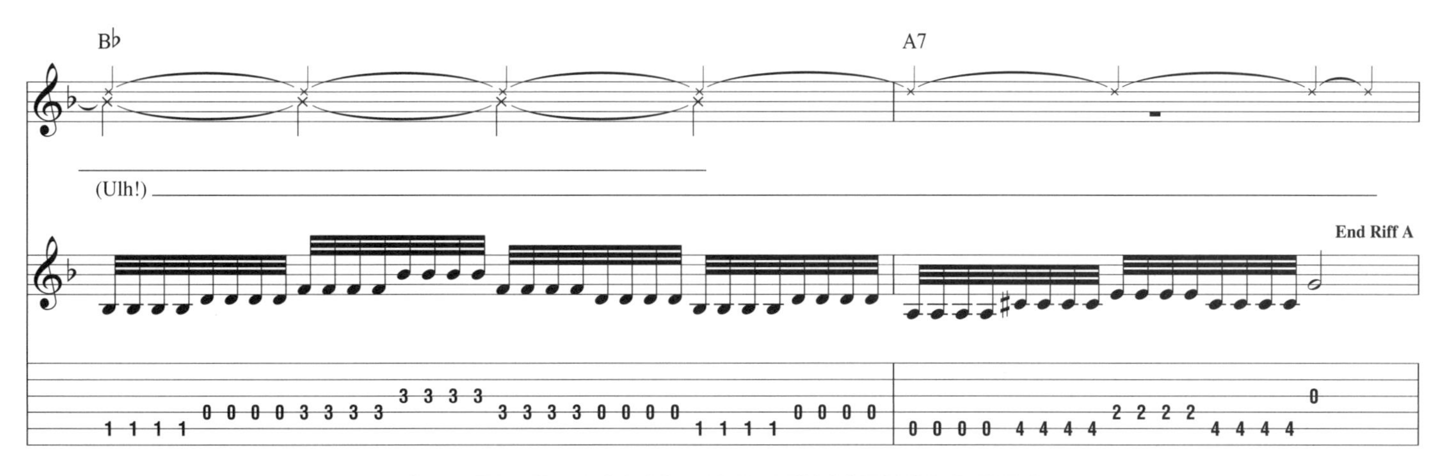

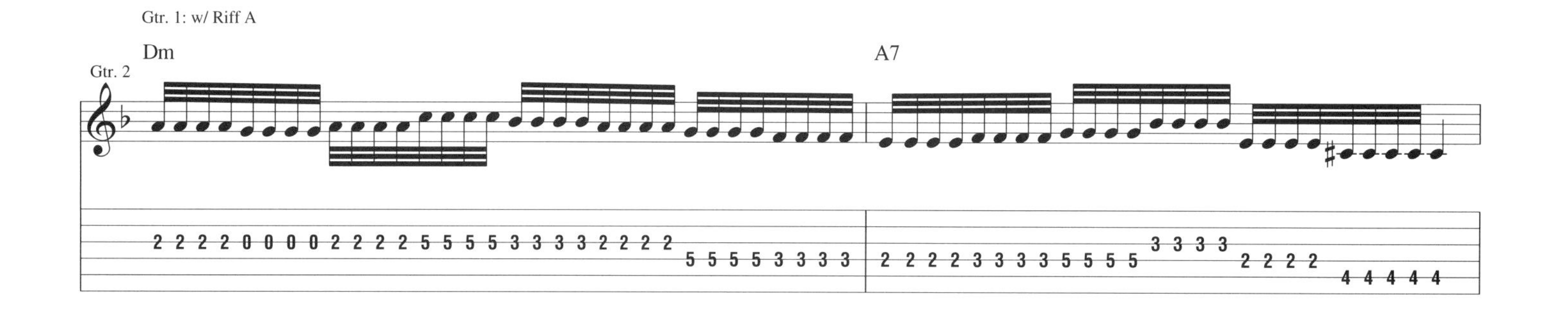
Gtr. 1: w/ Riff A
Dm
A7
Gtr. 2

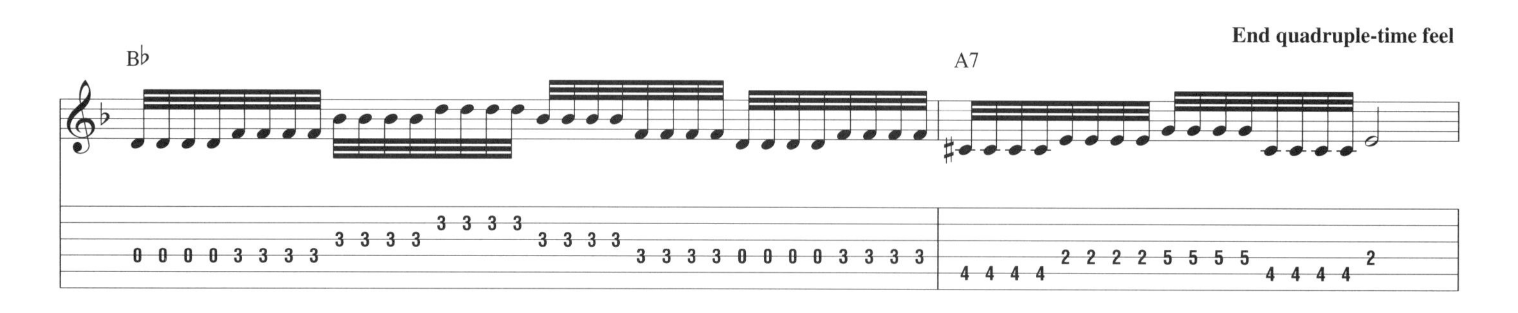
B♭
End quadruple-time feel
A7

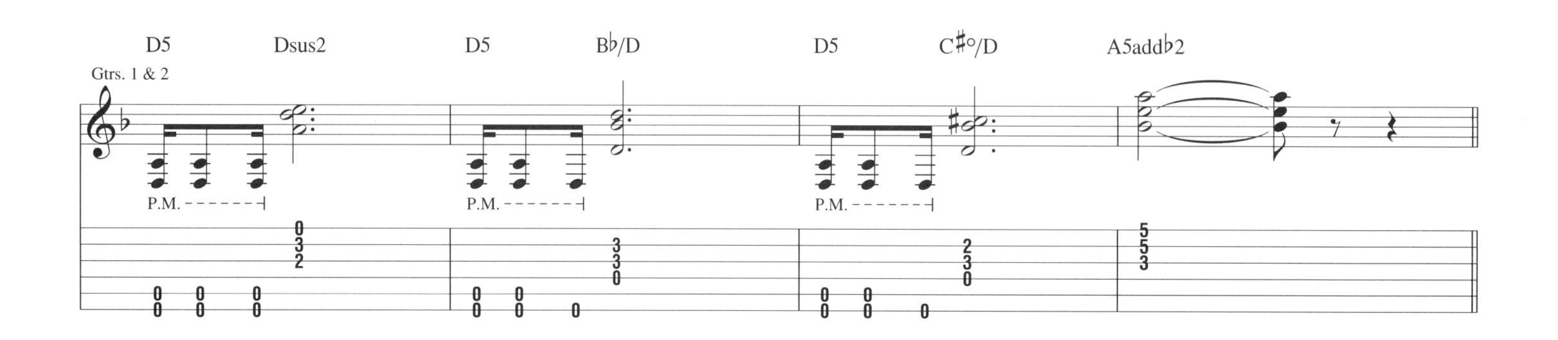
D5 Dsus2 D5 B♭/D D5 C♯°/D A5add♭2
Gtrs. 1 & 2
P.M.

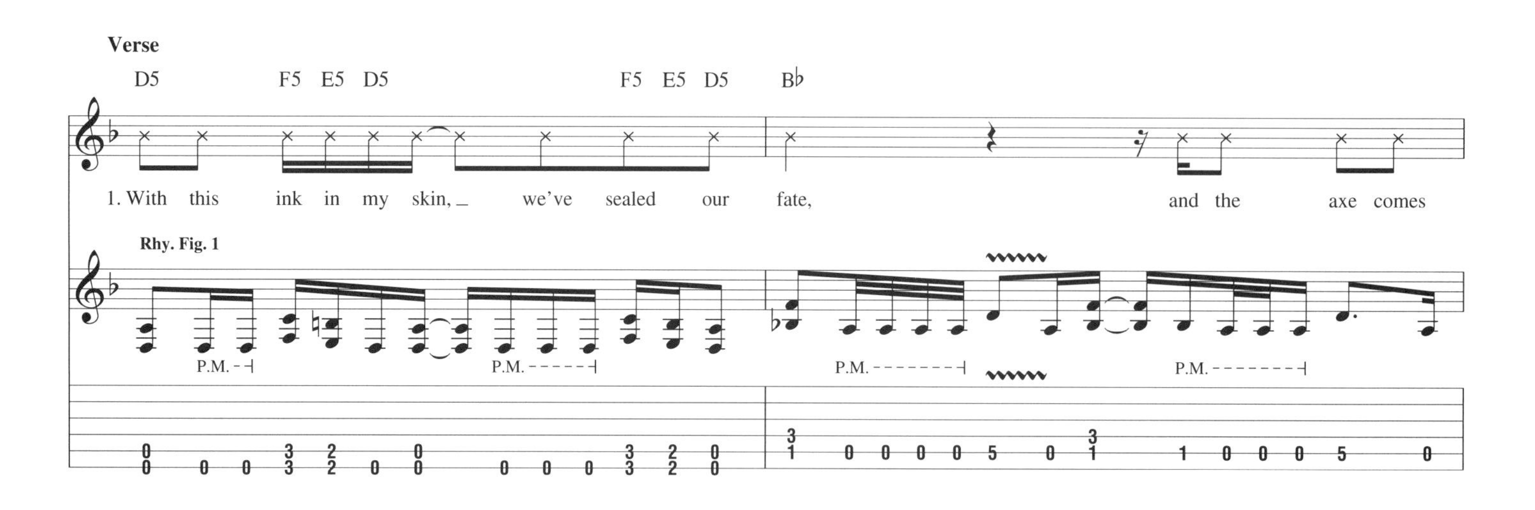
Verse
D5 F5 E5 D5 F5 E5 D5 B♭
1. With this ink in my skin, we've sealed our fate, and the axe comes
Rhy. Fig. 1
P.M.

C B♭5 G5 C5 A5
ear - ly. So, what does that mat - ter?
(On - ly nat - 'ral - ly.)
End Rhy. Fig. 1
P.M.

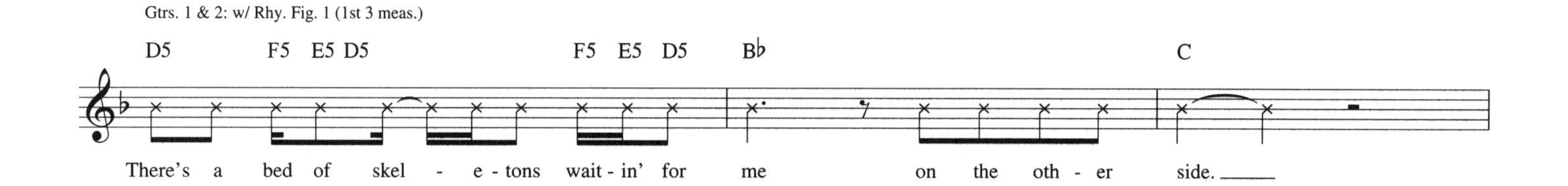
Gtrs. 1 & 2: w/ Rhy. Fig. 1 (1st 3 meas.)
D5 F5 E5 D5 F5 E5 D5 B♭ C
There's a bed of skel - e - tons wait - in' for me on the oth - er side.

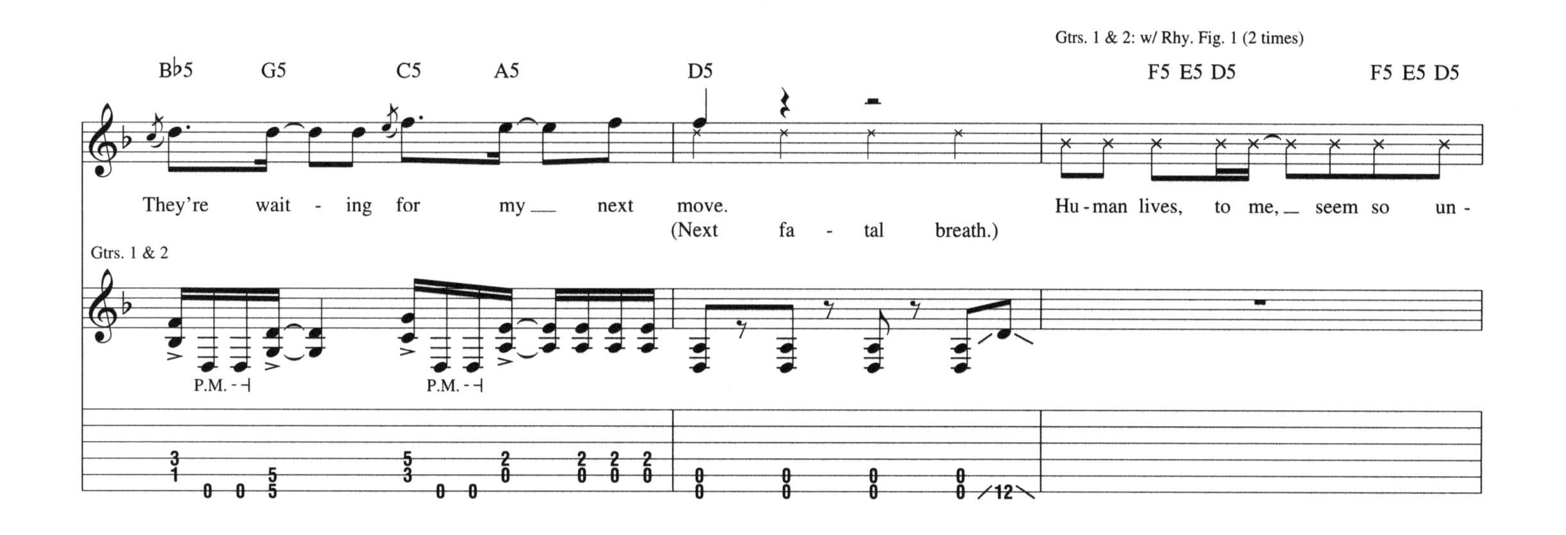
Gtrs. 1 & 2: w/ Rhy. Fig. 1 (2 times)
B♭5 G5 C5 A5 D5 F5 E5 D5 F5 E5 D5
They're wait - ing for my next move. Hu - man lives, to me, seem so un -
(Next fa - tal breath.)
Gtrs. 1 & 2
P.M.
P.M.

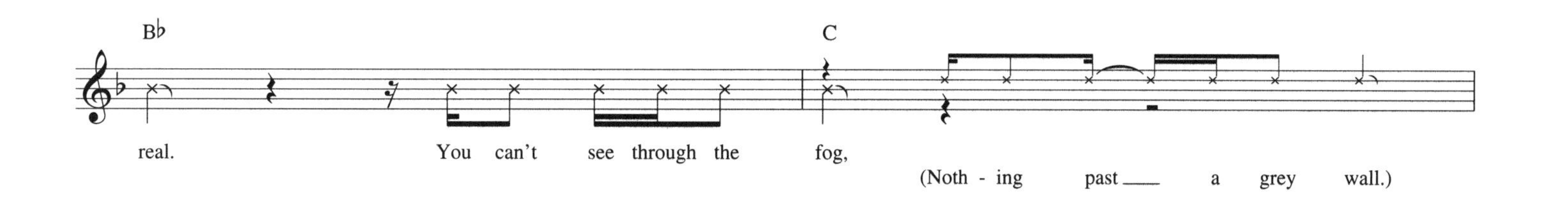
B♭ C
real. You can't see through the fog,
(Noth - ing past a grey wall.)

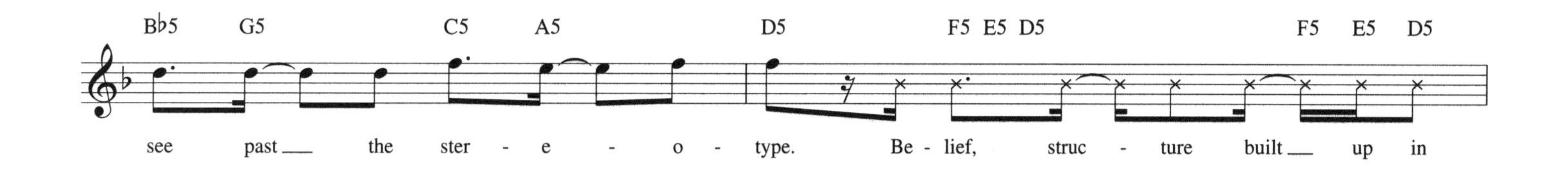
B♭5 G5 C5 A5 D5 F5 E5 D5 F5 E5 D5
see past the ster - e - o - type. Be - lief, struc - ture built up in

B♭ C B♭5 G5 C5 A5
you. I'll tear you down and the one who cre - at - ed

Interlude

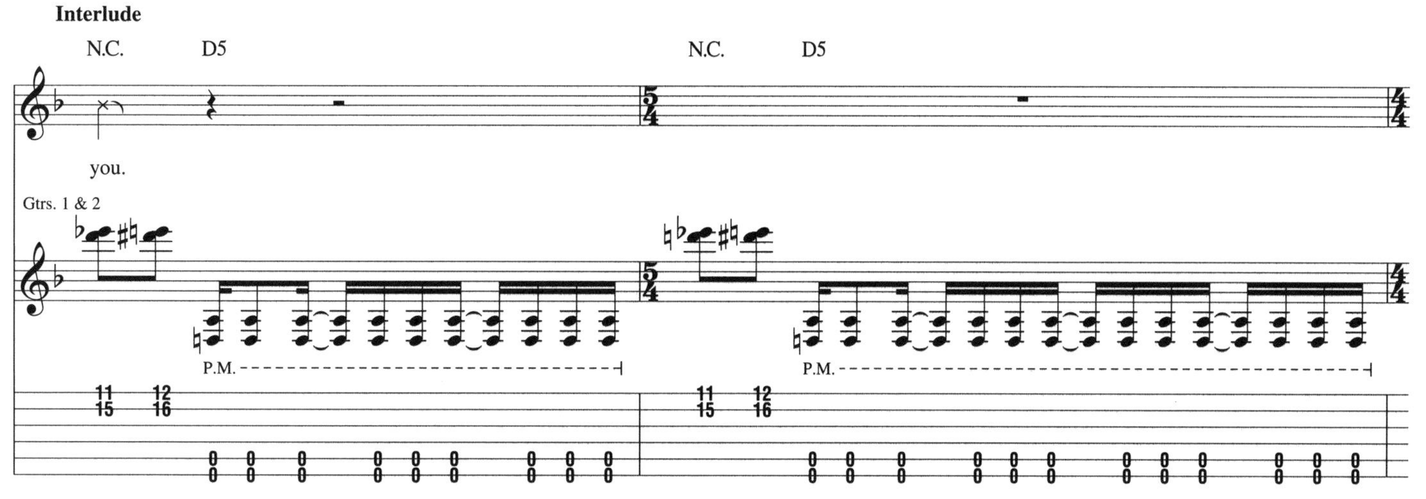
N.C. D5 N.C. D5
you.
Gtrs. 1 & 2
P.M.
P.M.

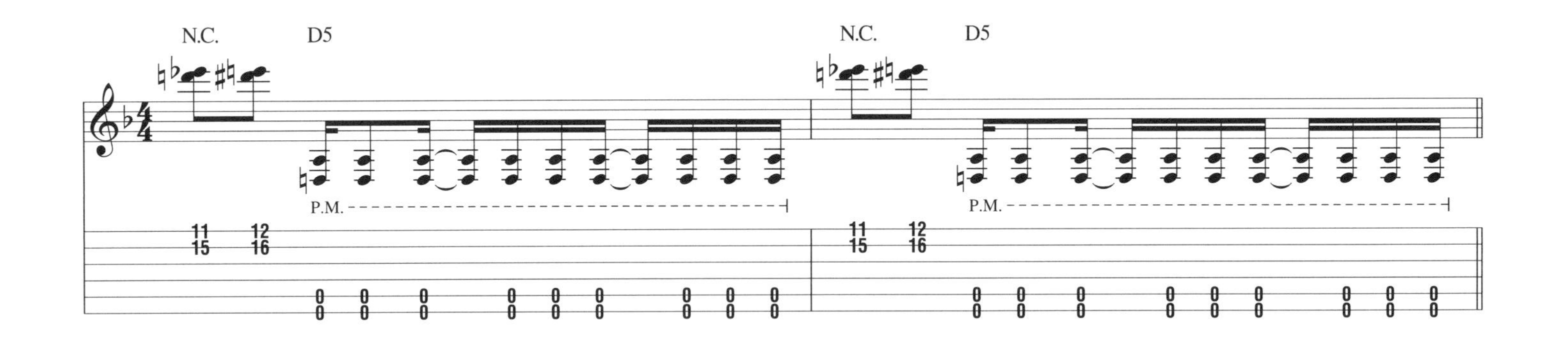
N.C.
D5
N.C.
D5
P.M.
P.M.
11 12
15 16
11 12
15 16

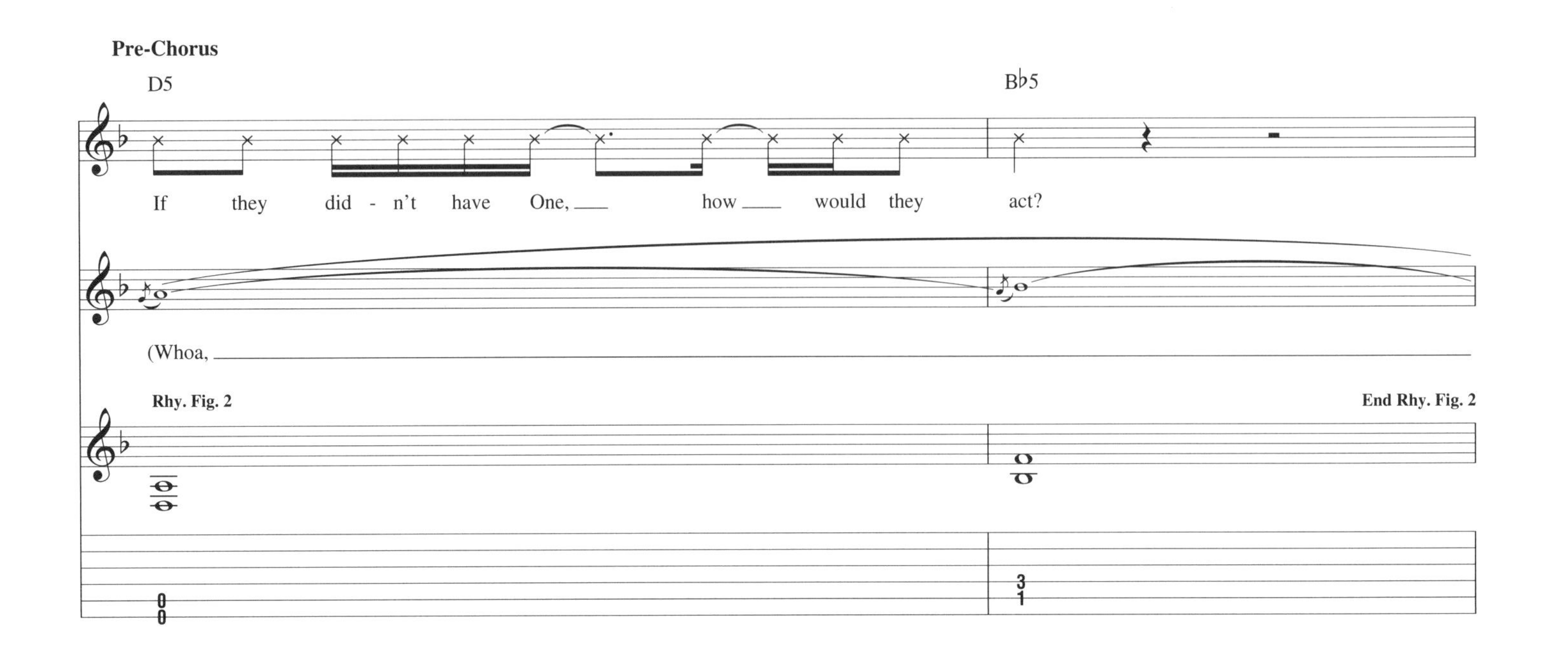
Pre-Chorus
D5
Bb5
If they did - n't have One, how would they act?
(Whoa,
Rhy. Fig. 2
End Rhy. Fig. 2

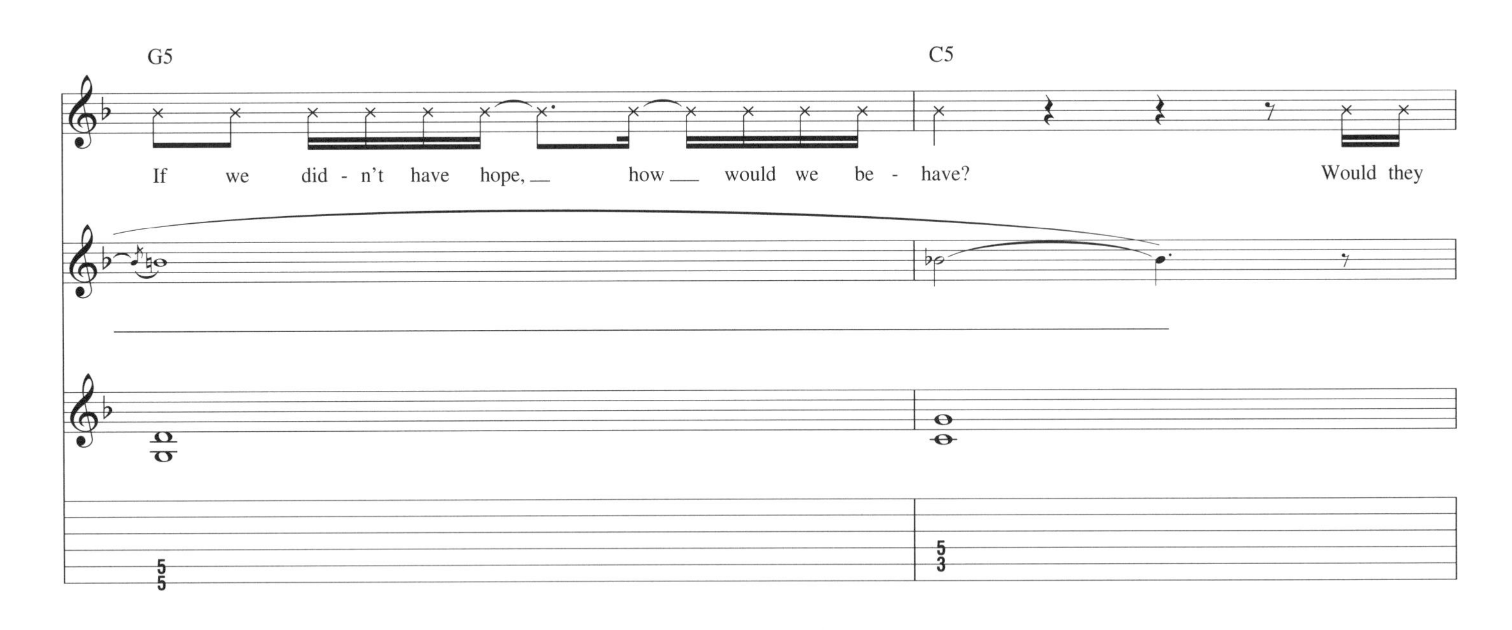
G5
C5
If we did - n't have hope, how would we be - have? Would they

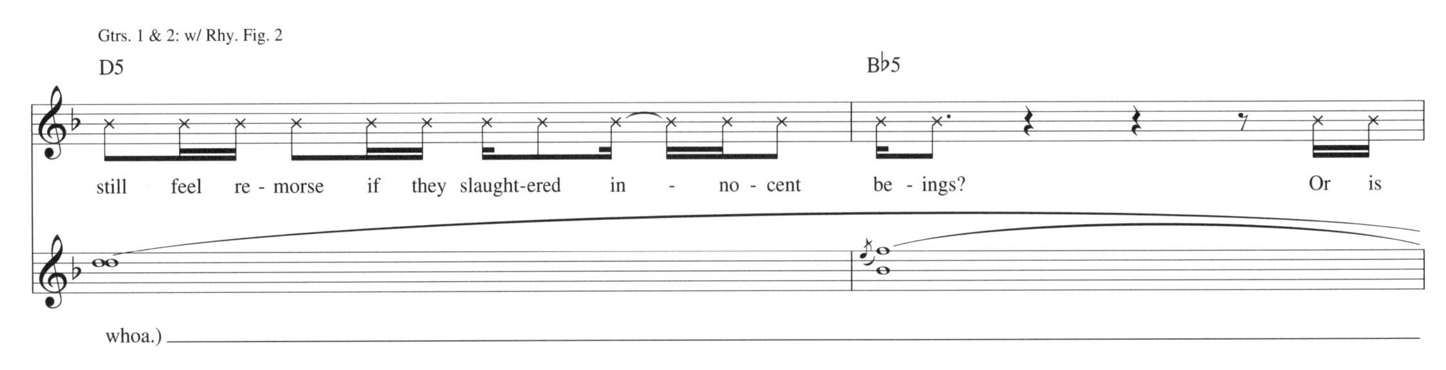
Gtrs. 1 & 2: w/ Rhy. Fig. 2
D5
Bb5
still feel re - morse if they slaught-ered in - no - cent be - ings? Or is
whoa.)

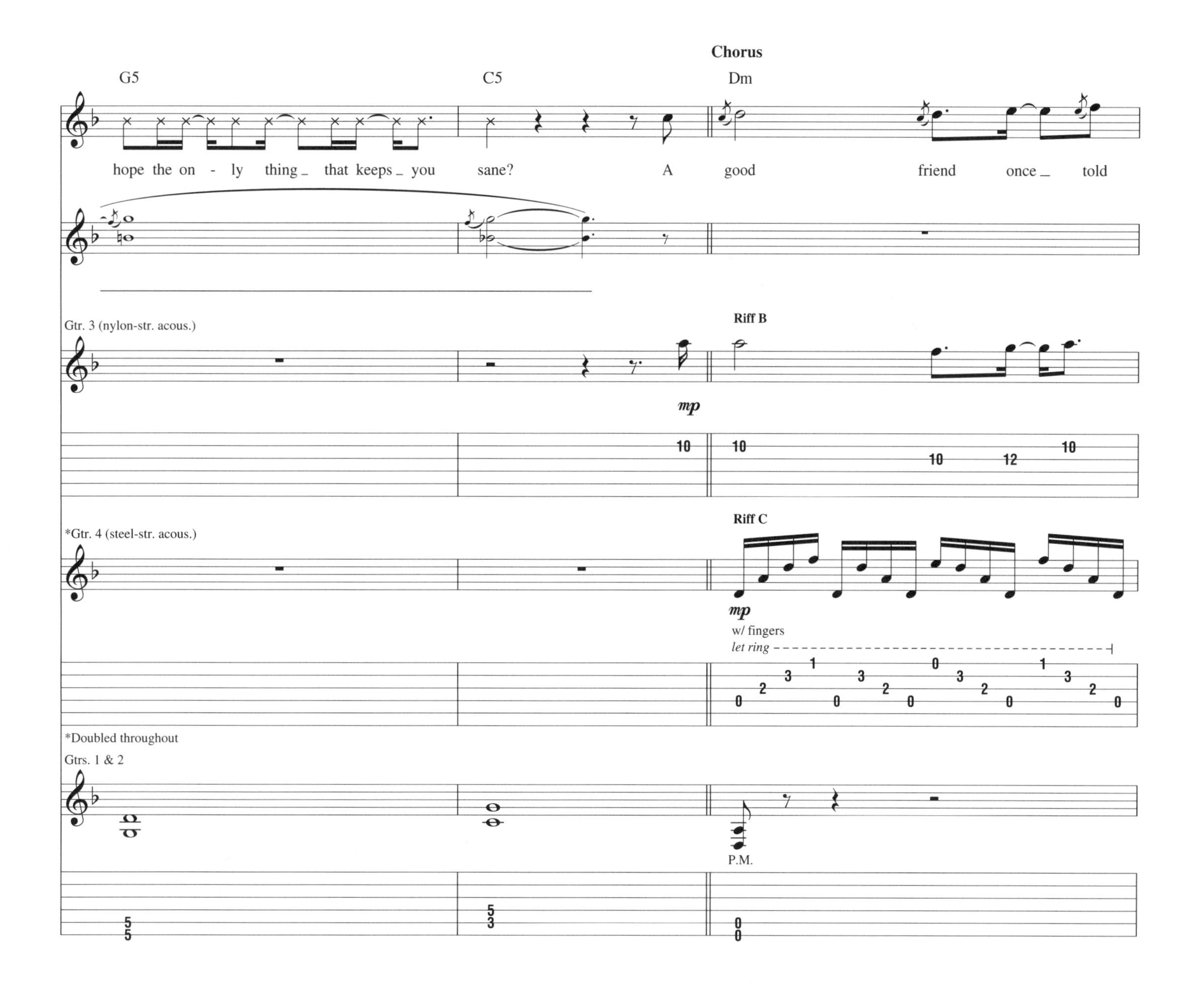
Chorus
G5
C5
Dm
hope the on - ly thing that keeps you sane? A good friend once told
Gtr. 3 (nylon-str. acous.)
Riff B
mp
*Gtr. 4 (steel-str. acous.)
Riff C
mp
w/ fingers
let ring
*Doubled throughout
Gtrs. 1 & 2
P.M.

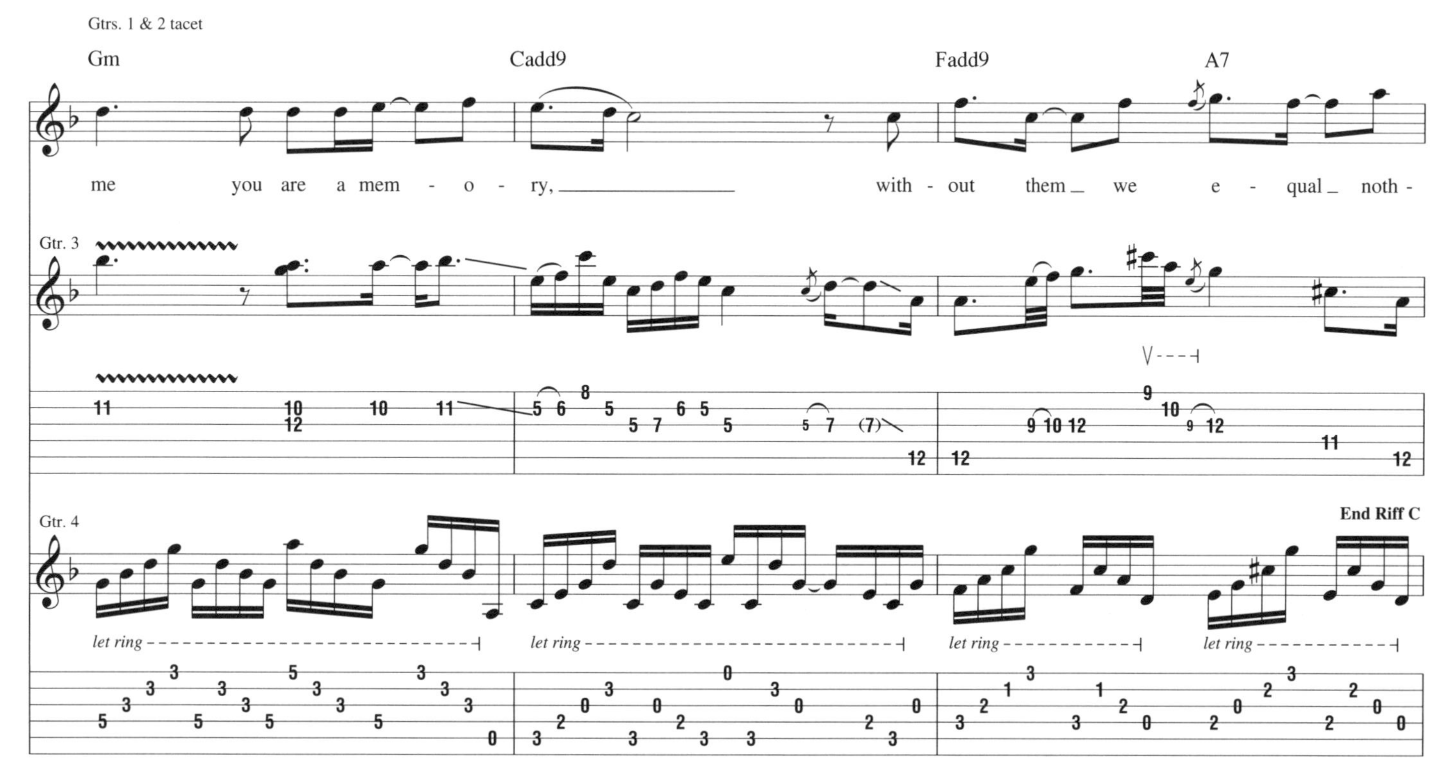
Gtrs. 1 & 2 tacet
Gm
Cadd9
Fadd9
A7
me you are a mem - o - ry, with - out them we e - qual noth -
Gtr. 3
Gtr. 4
let ring
End Riff C

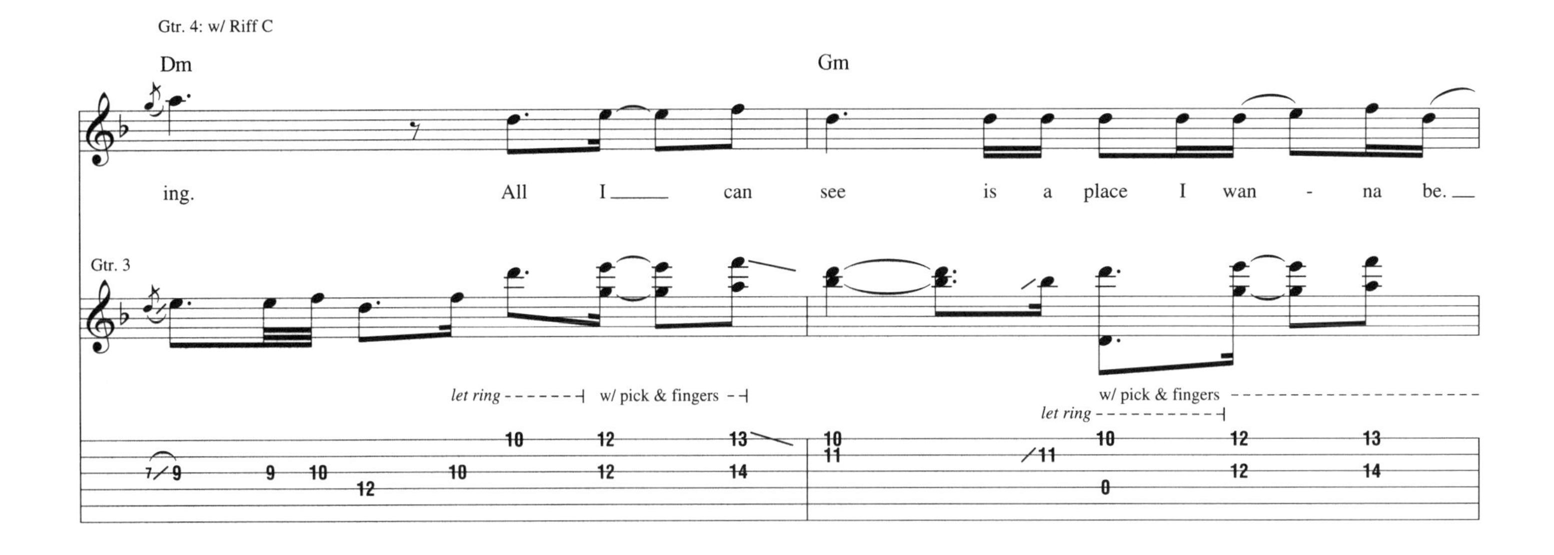
Gtr. 4: w/ Riff C
Dm
Gm
ing. All I can see is a place I wan - na be.
Gtr. 3
let ring
w/ pick & fingers
w/ pick & fingers
let ring

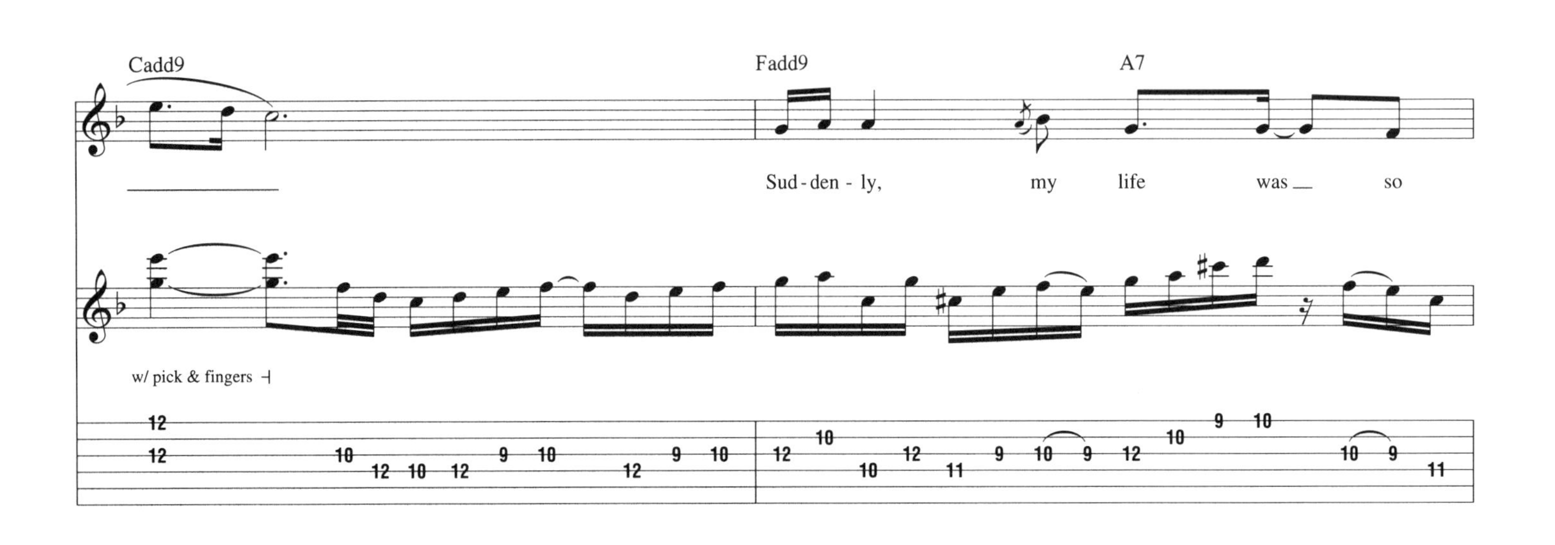
Cadd9
Fadd9
A7
Sud - den - ly, my life was so
w/ pick & fingers

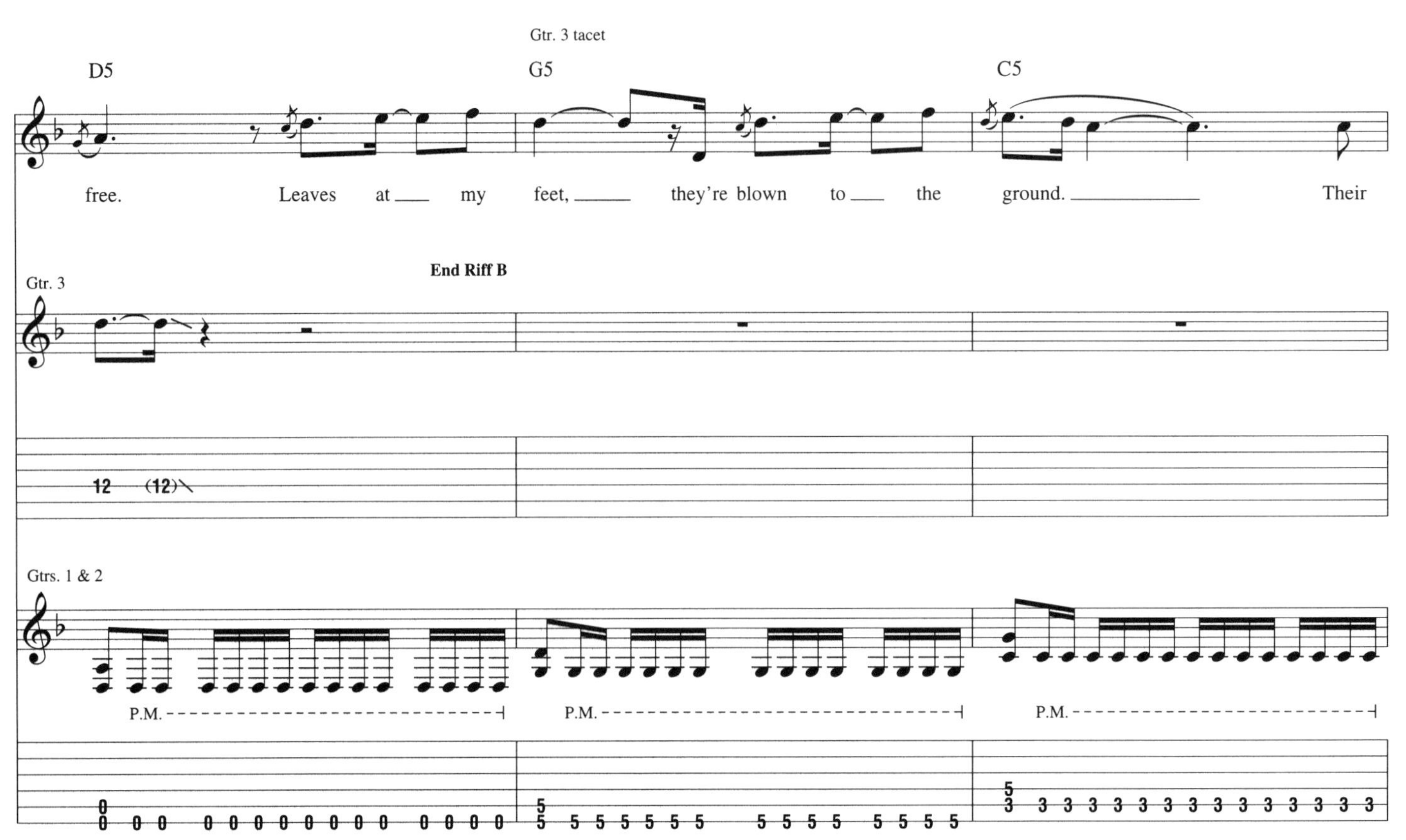
Gtr. 3 tacet
D5
G5
C5
free. Leaves at my feet, they're blown to the ground. Their
End Riff B
Gtr. 3
Gtrs. 1 & 2
P.M.
P.M.
P.M.

F5 A5 D5
ech - oes are reach - ing my ears. Night's com - in'
Gtrs. 1 & 2
P.M.
G5 C5
fast, the sun's go - in' down, but
B♭5 C5 D5 B♭5 C5
keep a - way from me. Keep a - way from
Quadruple-time feel
Dm B♭5 C5 F5 C/E
me, keep a - way from
(Oh, it's hard to keep me in this

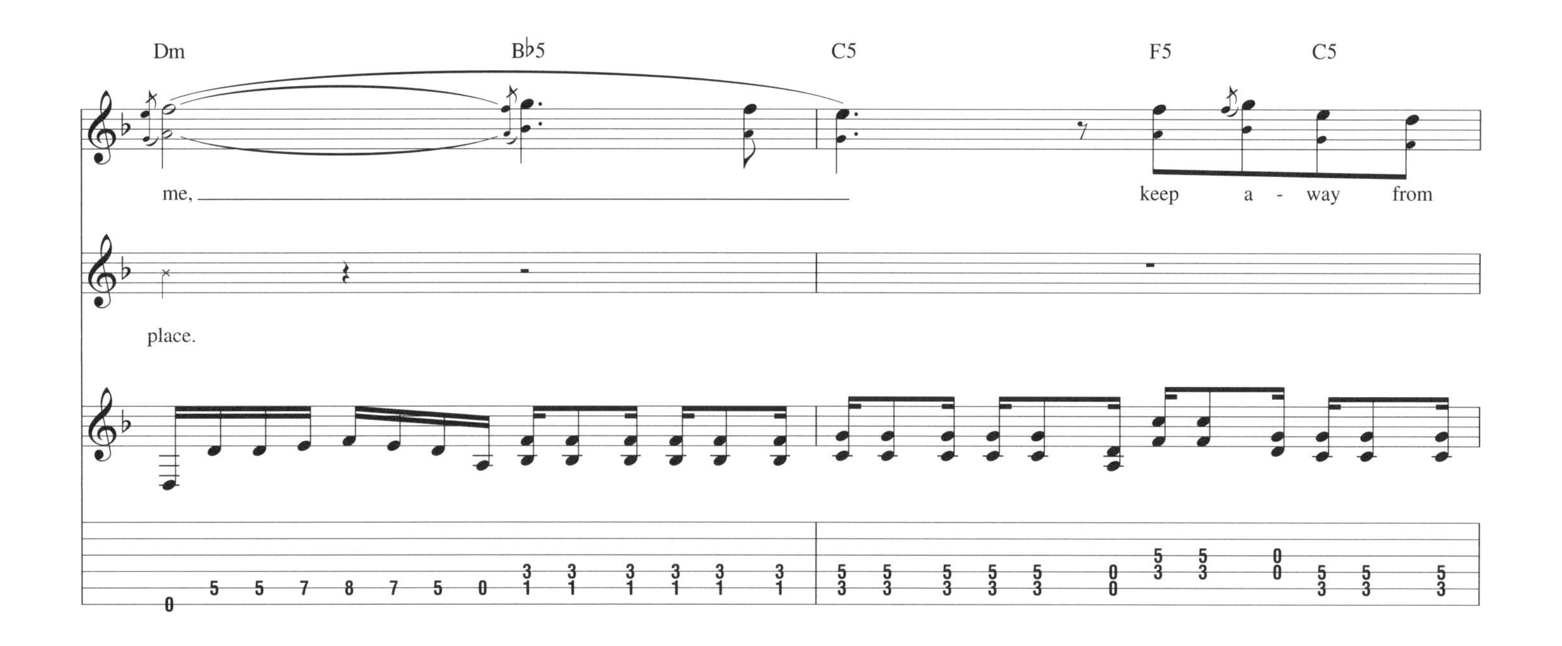
Dm
B♭5
C5
F5
C5
me, ___
keep a - way from
place.

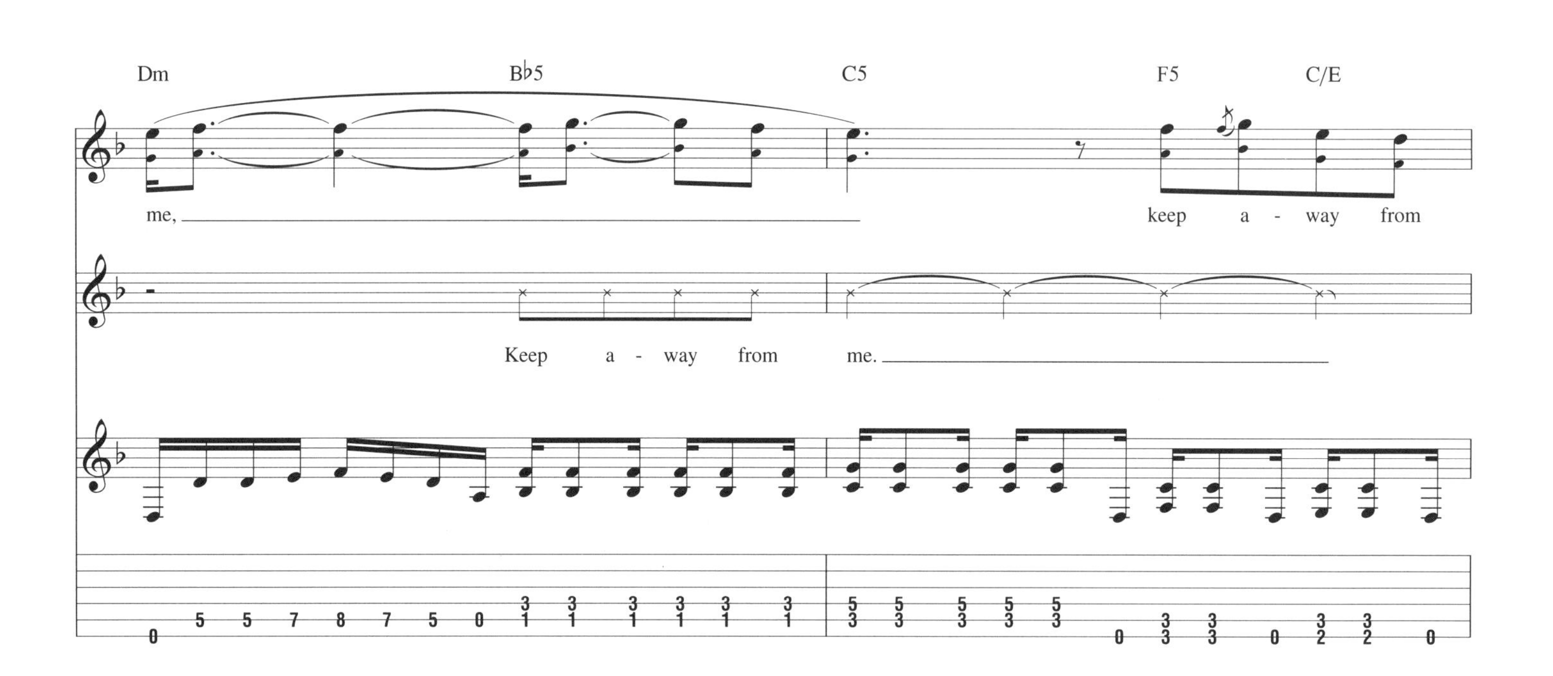
Dm
B♭5
C5
F5
C/E
me, ___
keep a - way from
Keep a - way from me. ___

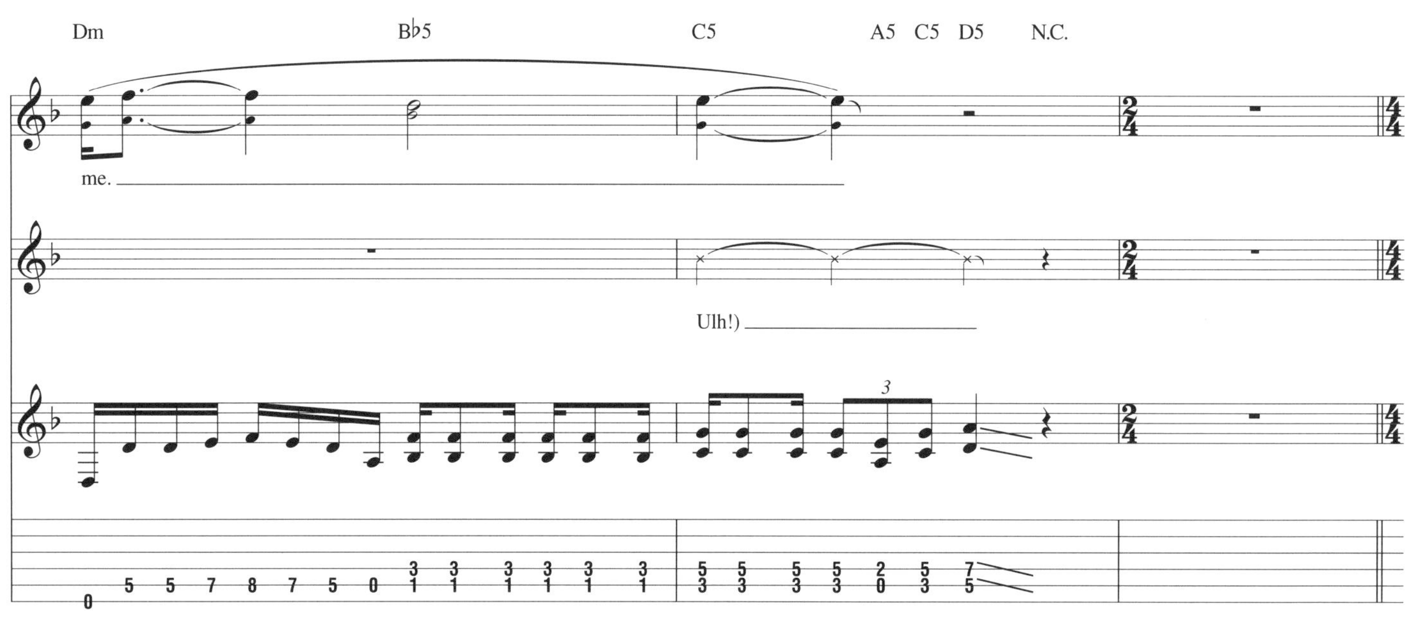
Dm
B♭5
C5
A5 C5 D5
N.C.
me. ___
Ulh!) ___

Bridge

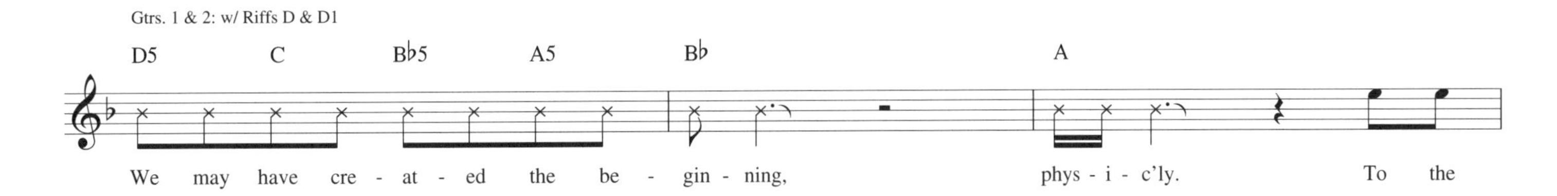

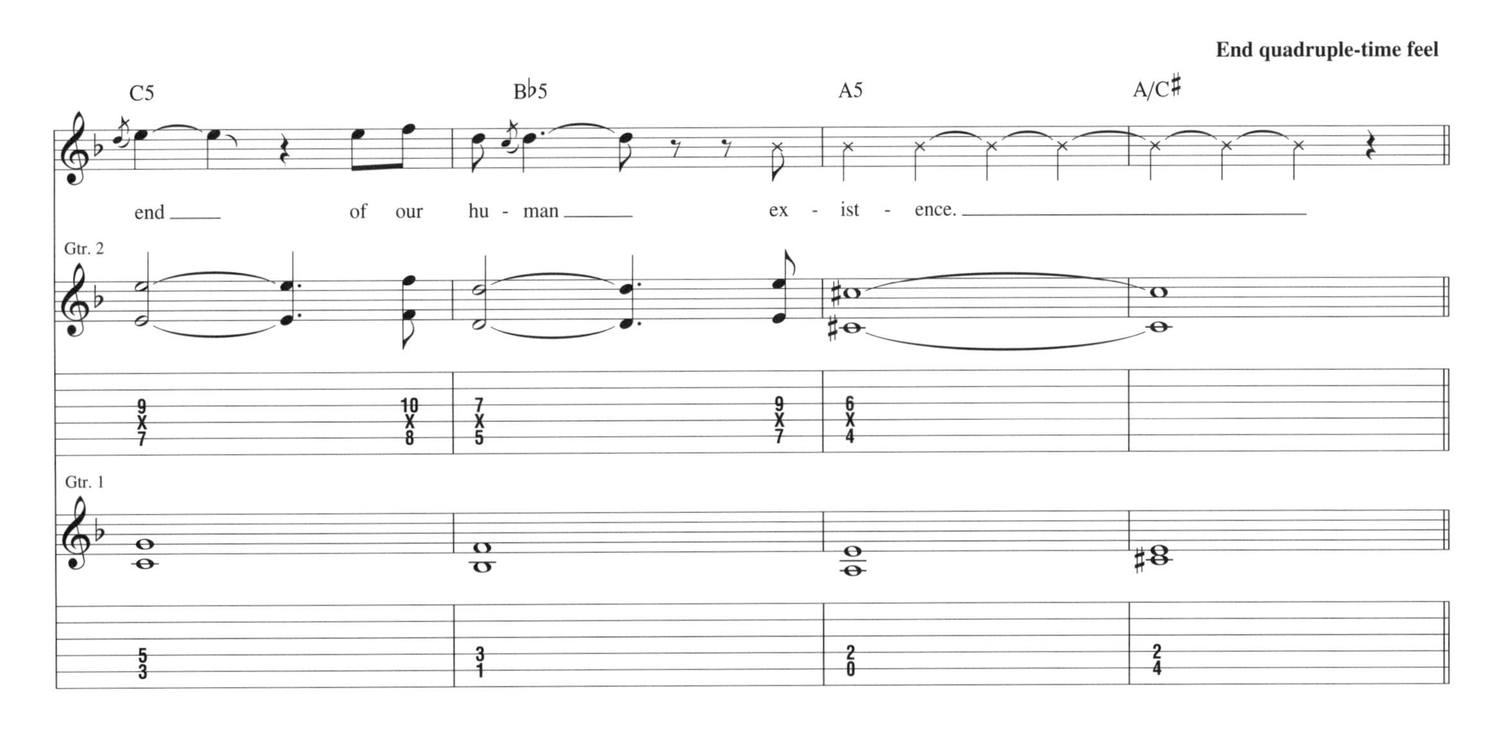

Interlude

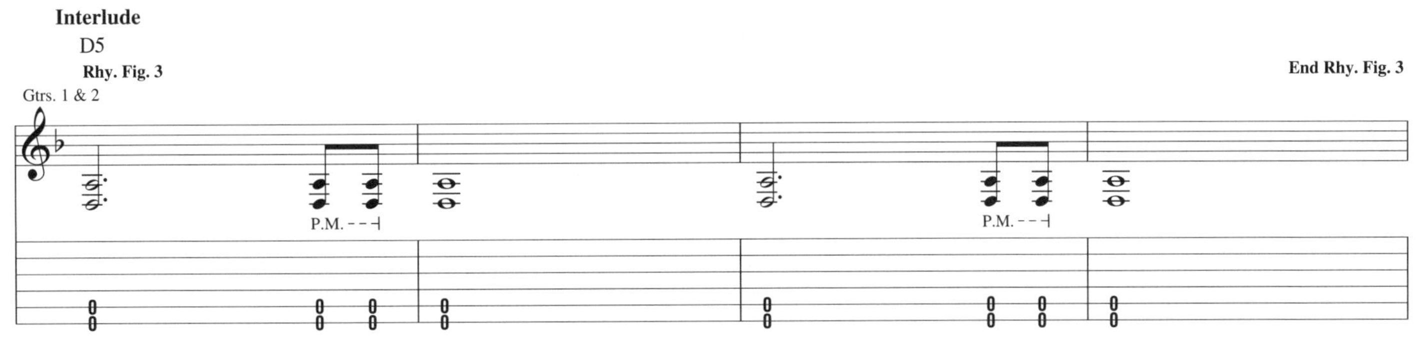

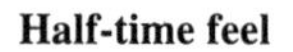

Half-time feel

Bridge

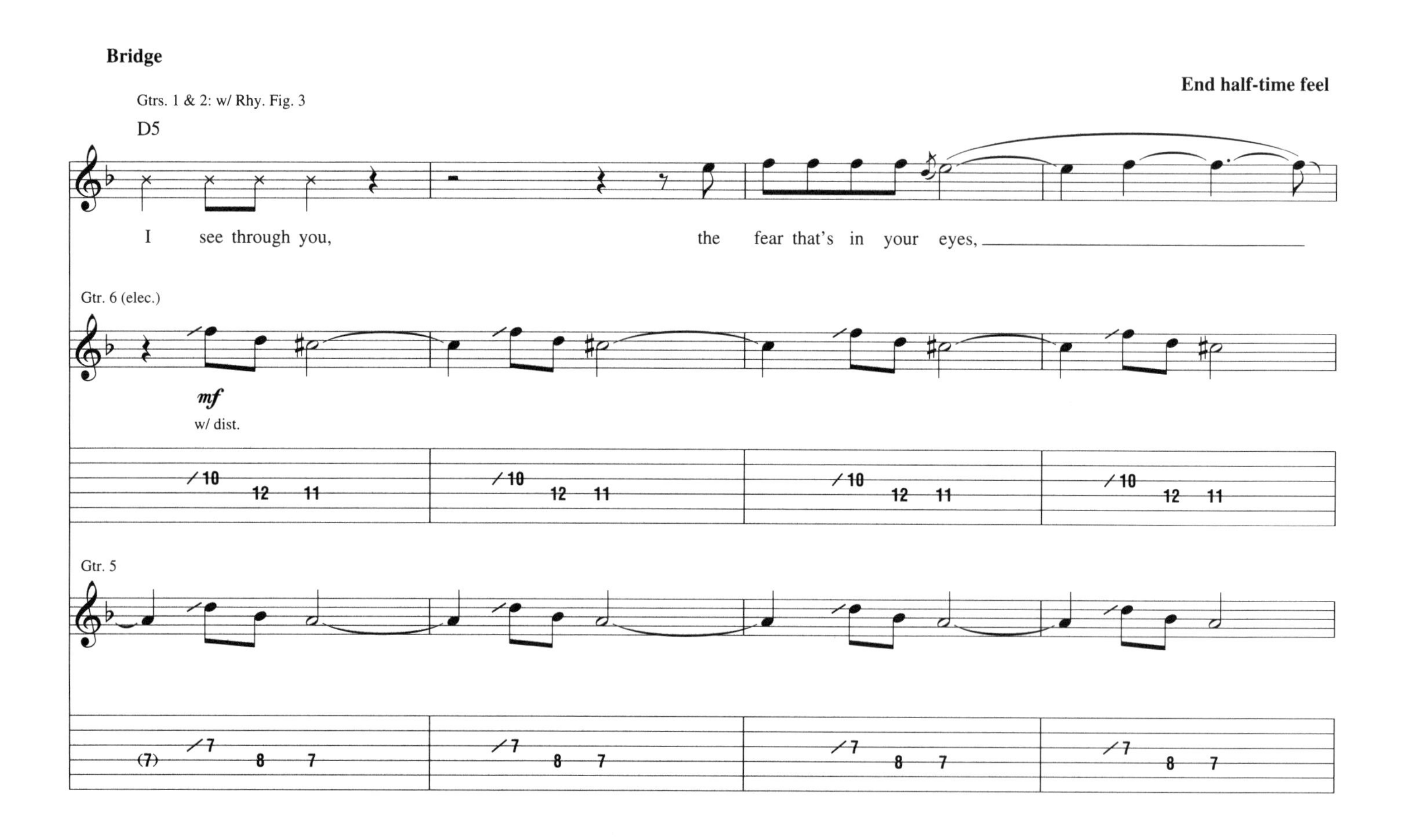

Guitar Solo
D5
B♭5
Gtr. 5
Gtr. 6
Rhy. Fig. 4
Gtrs. 1 & 2
P.M.
C5
F5
C/E
End Rhy. Fig. 4

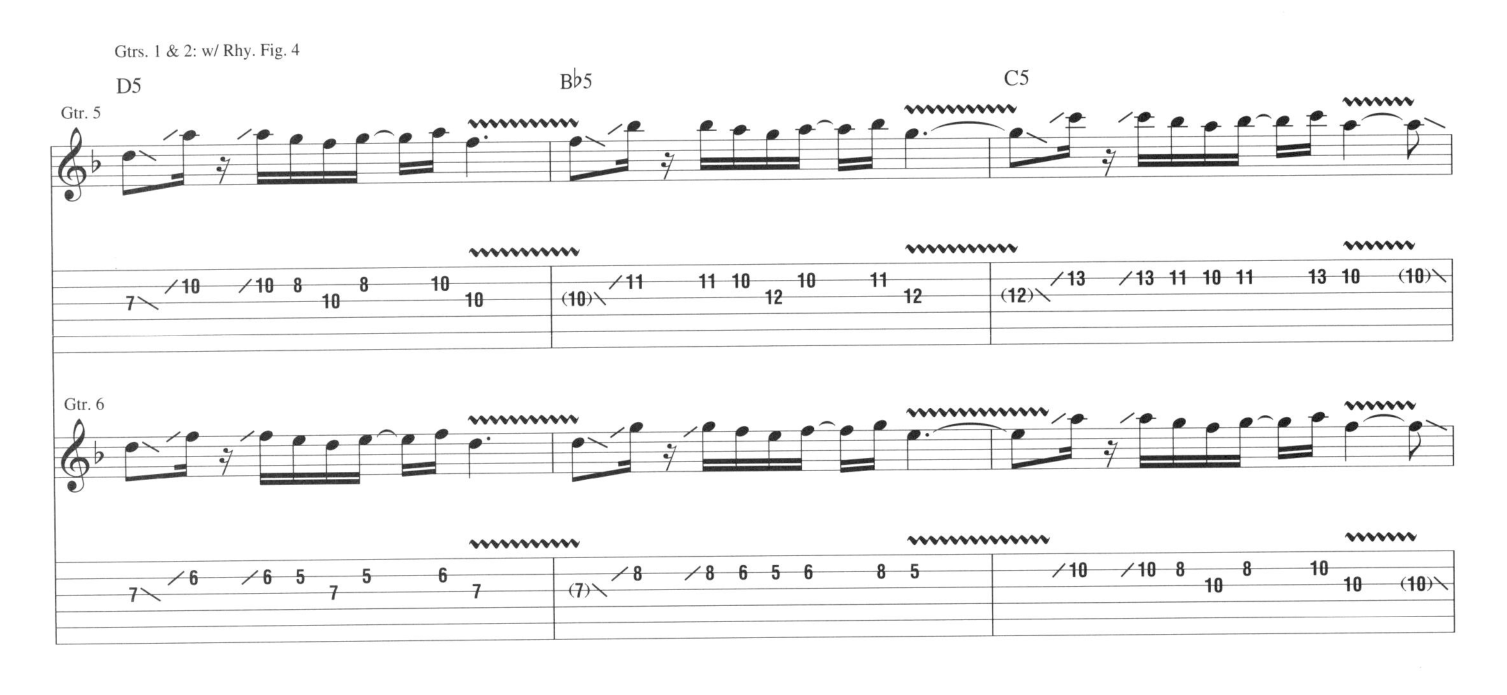
Gtrs. 1 & 2: w/ Rhy. Fig. 4
D5
B♭5
C5
Gtr. 5
Gtr. 6

Chorus
Gtr. 3: w/ Riff B
Gtrs. 5 & 6 tacet
F5
C/E
D5
G5
A good friend once _ told me we are a mem - o -
Gtrs. 5 & 6
Rhy. Fig 5
Gtrs. 1 & 2
(cont. on upper staff)

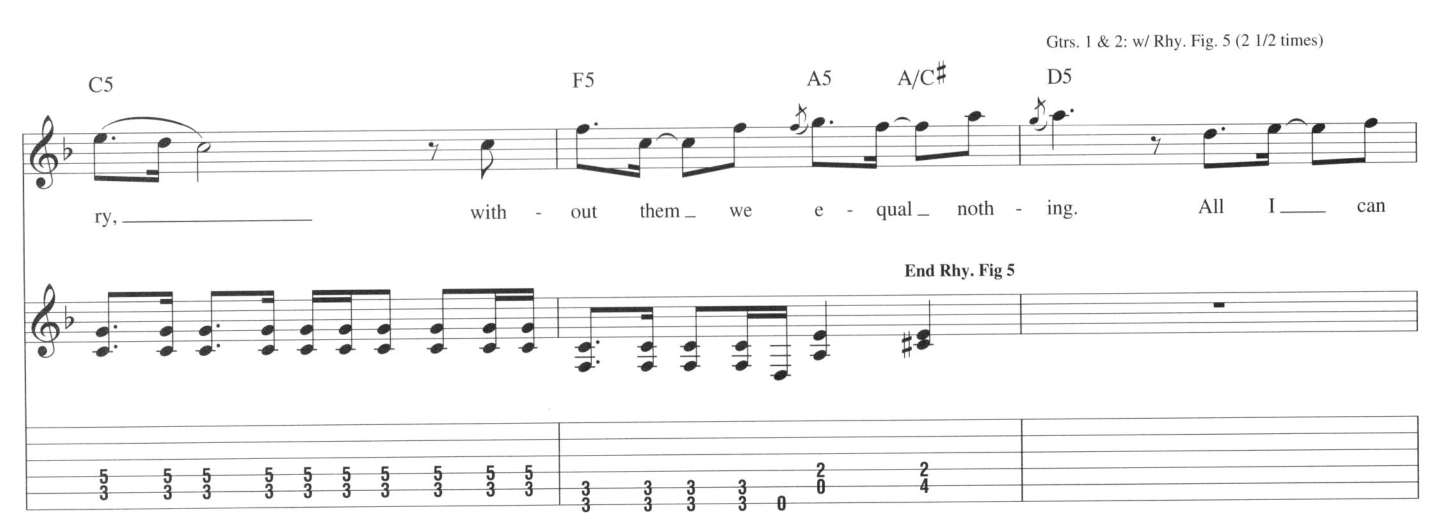
Gtrs. 1 & 2: w/ Rhy. Fig. 5 (2 1/2 times)
C5
F5
A5
A/C♯
D5
ry, with - out them _ we e - qual _ noth - ing. All I _ can
End Rhy. Fig 5

G5
C5
F5
A5
A/C♯
see is a place I wan - na be.
Time - less, my life was so

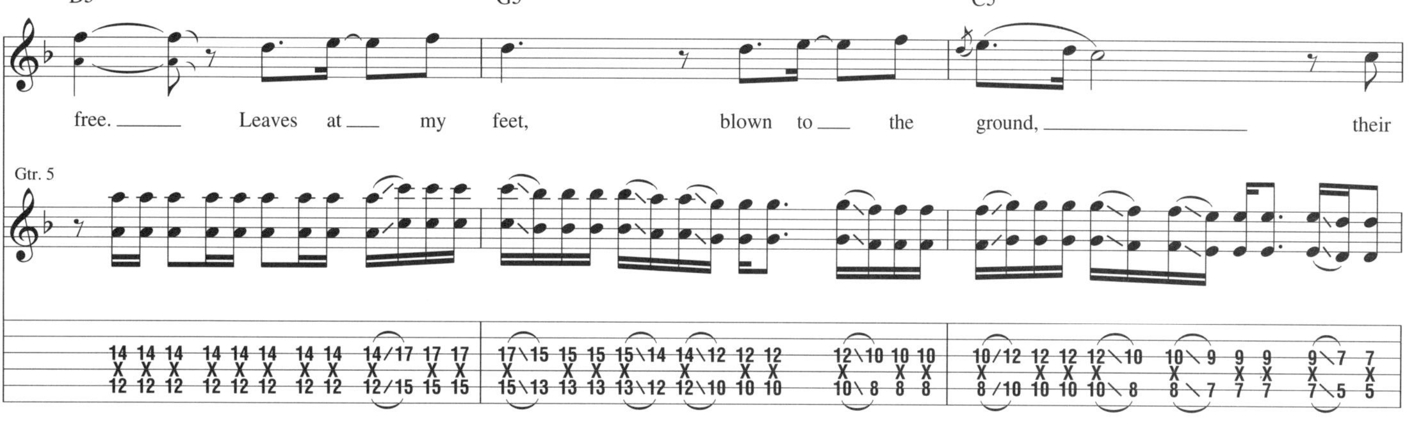
D5
G5
C5
free. Leaves at my feet, blown to the ground, their
Gtr. 5

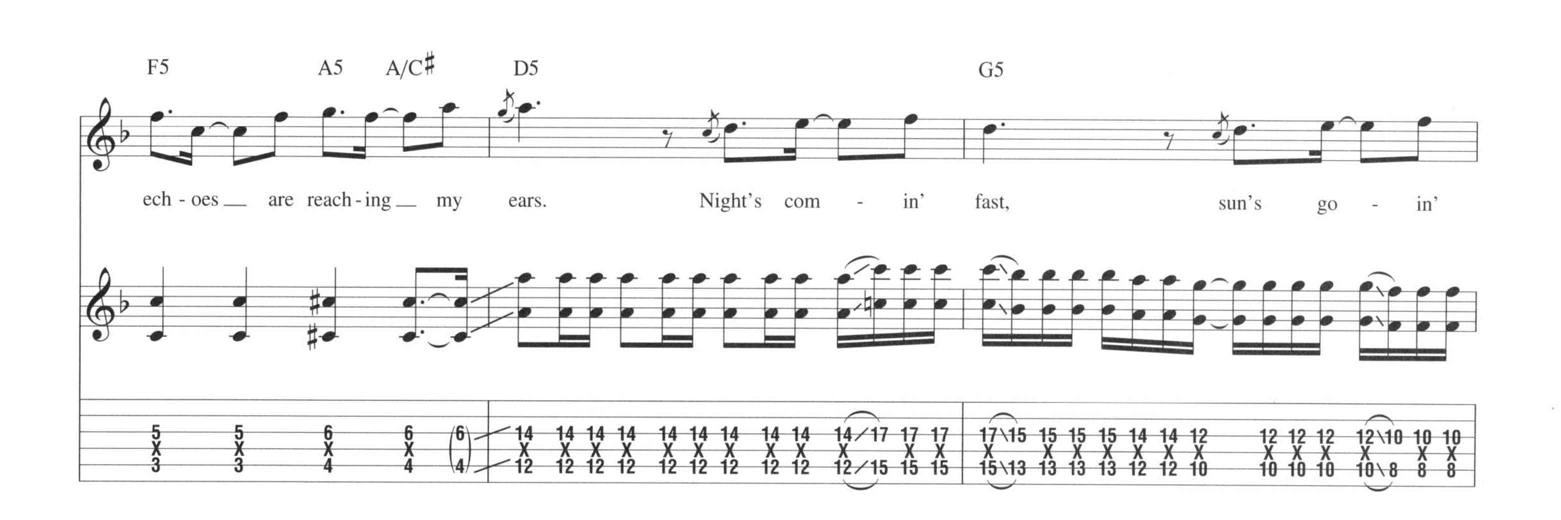
F5
A5
A/C♯
D5
G5
ech - oes are reach - ing my ears. Night's com - in' fast, sun's go - in'

C5
A5
Gtr. 5 tacet
E♭5
down, con - fused. I don't know the
Gtr. 5
Gtrs. 1 & 2
P.M.

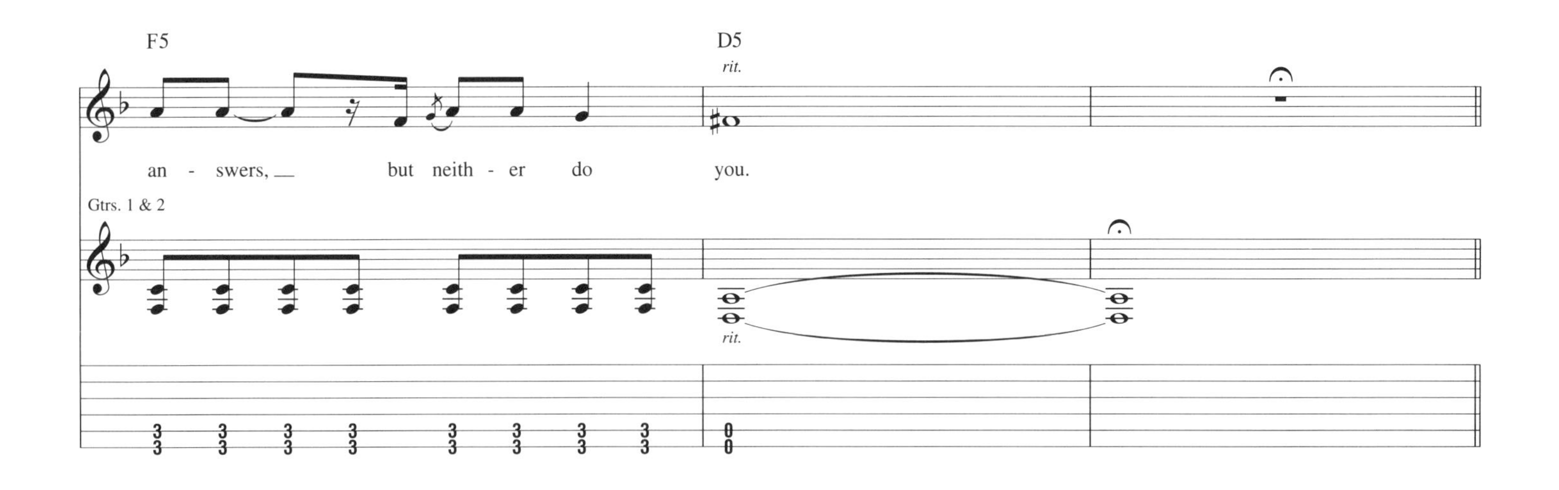

Outro

Faster ♩ = 130

Half-time feel

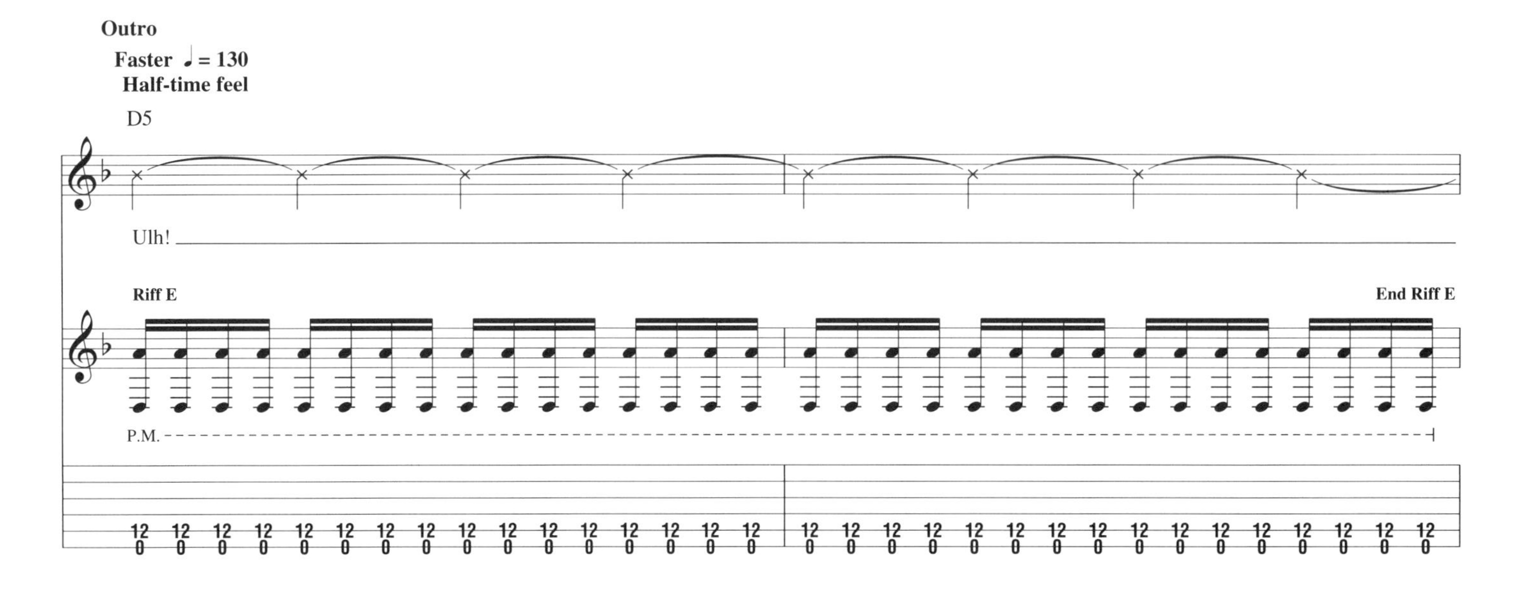

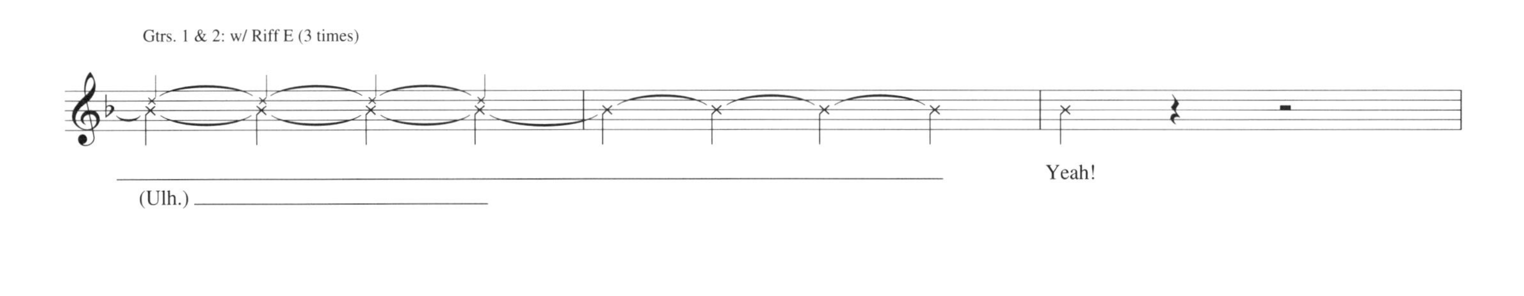

Begin fade

Play 4 times & fade

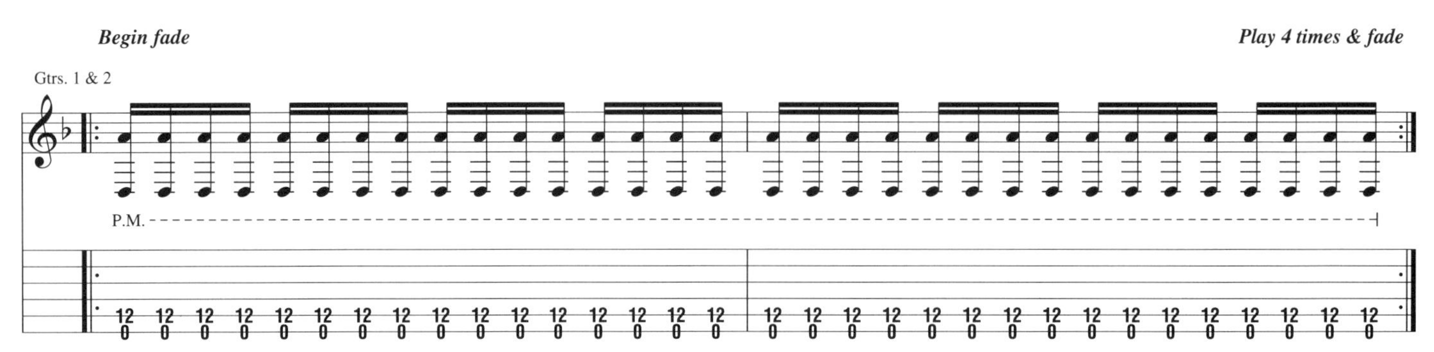

Desecrate Through Reverence

Words and Music by Matthew Sanders, James Sullivan, Brian Haner, Jr. and Zachary Baker

Drop D tuning:
(low to high) D-A-D-G-B-E

*Chord symbols reflect implied harmony.

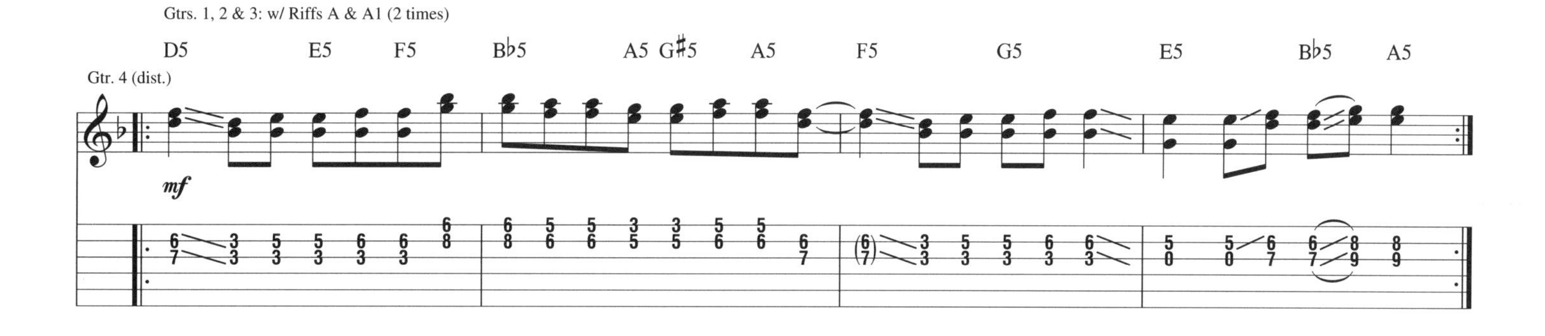

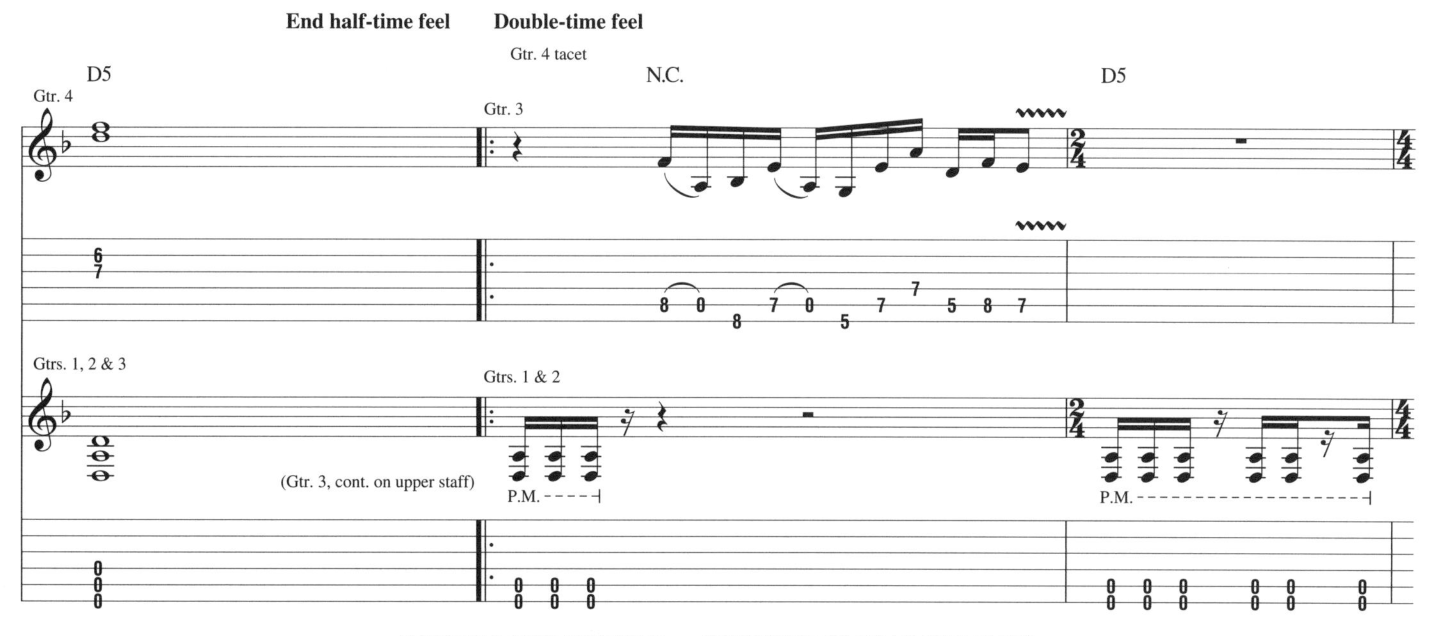

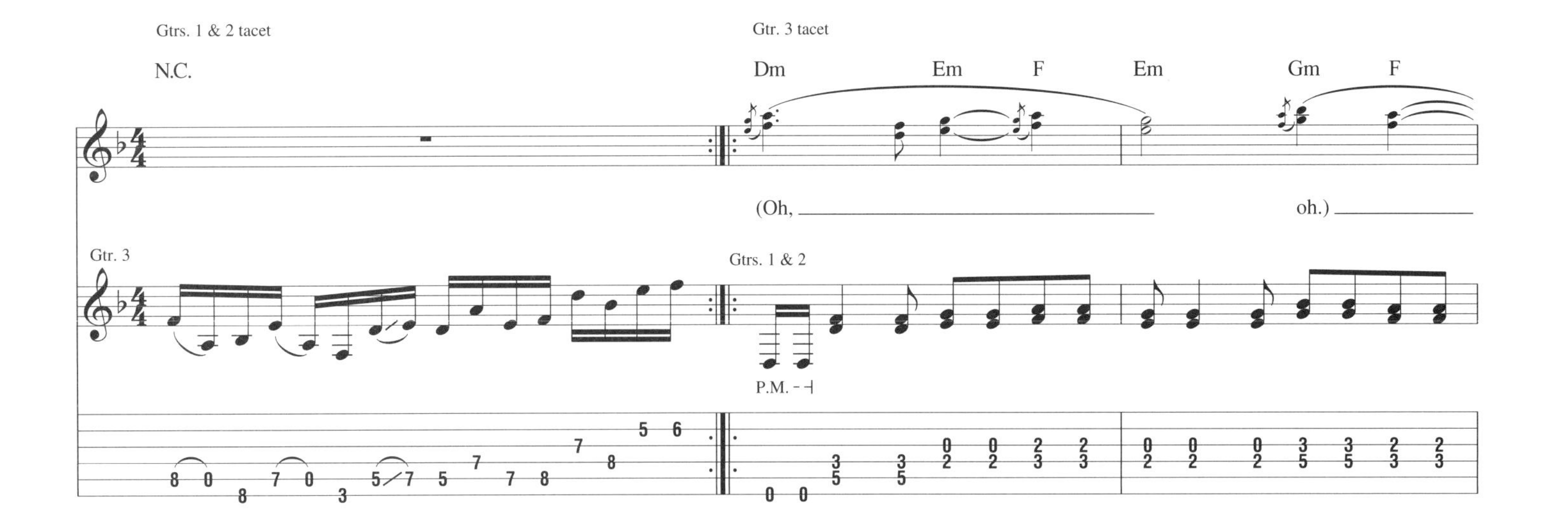
Gtrs. 1 & 2 tacet
N.C.
Gtr. 3 tacet
Dm
Em
F
Em
Gm
F
(Oh,
oh.)
Gtr. 3
Gtrs. 1 & 2
P.M.

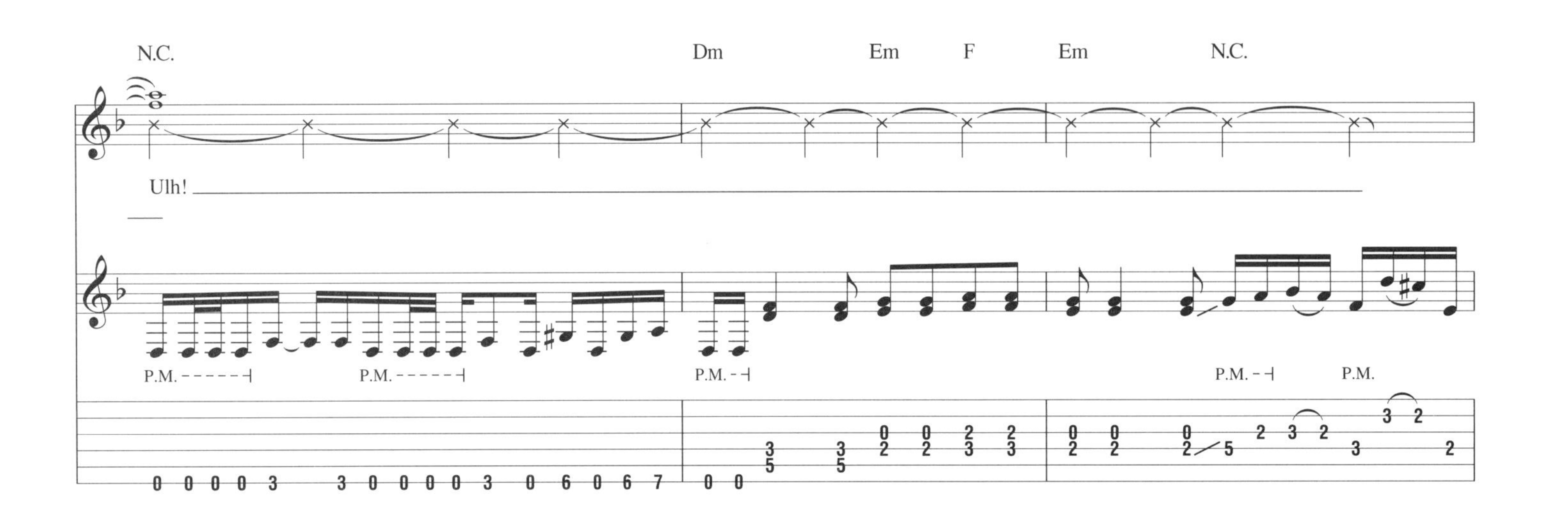
N.C.
Dm
Em
F
Em
N.C.
Ulh!
P.M.
P.M.
P.M.
P.M.
P.M.

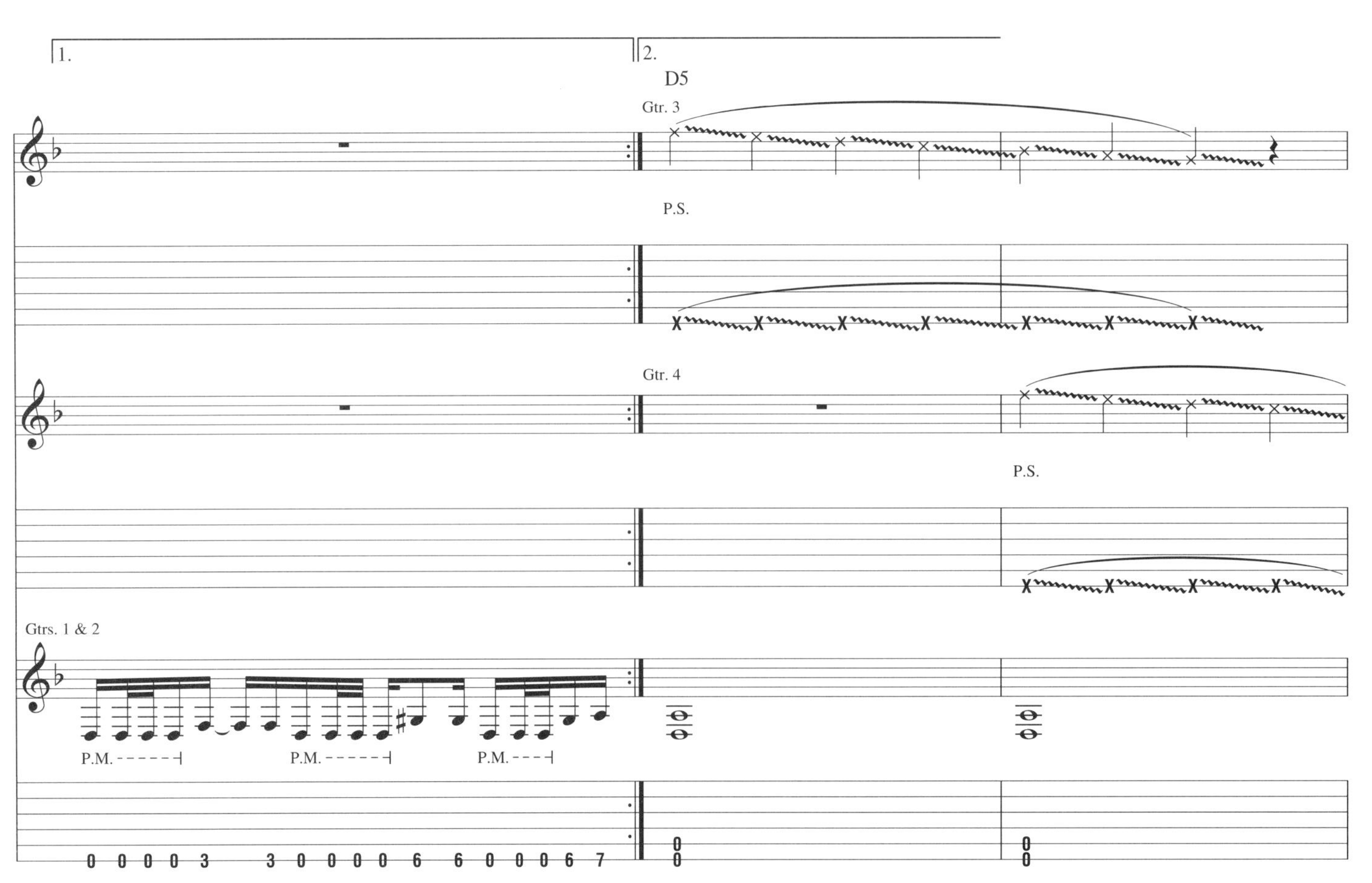
1.
2.
D5
Gtr. 3
P.S.
Gtr. 4
P.S.
Gtrs. 1 & 2
P.M.
P.M.
P.M.

End double-time feel

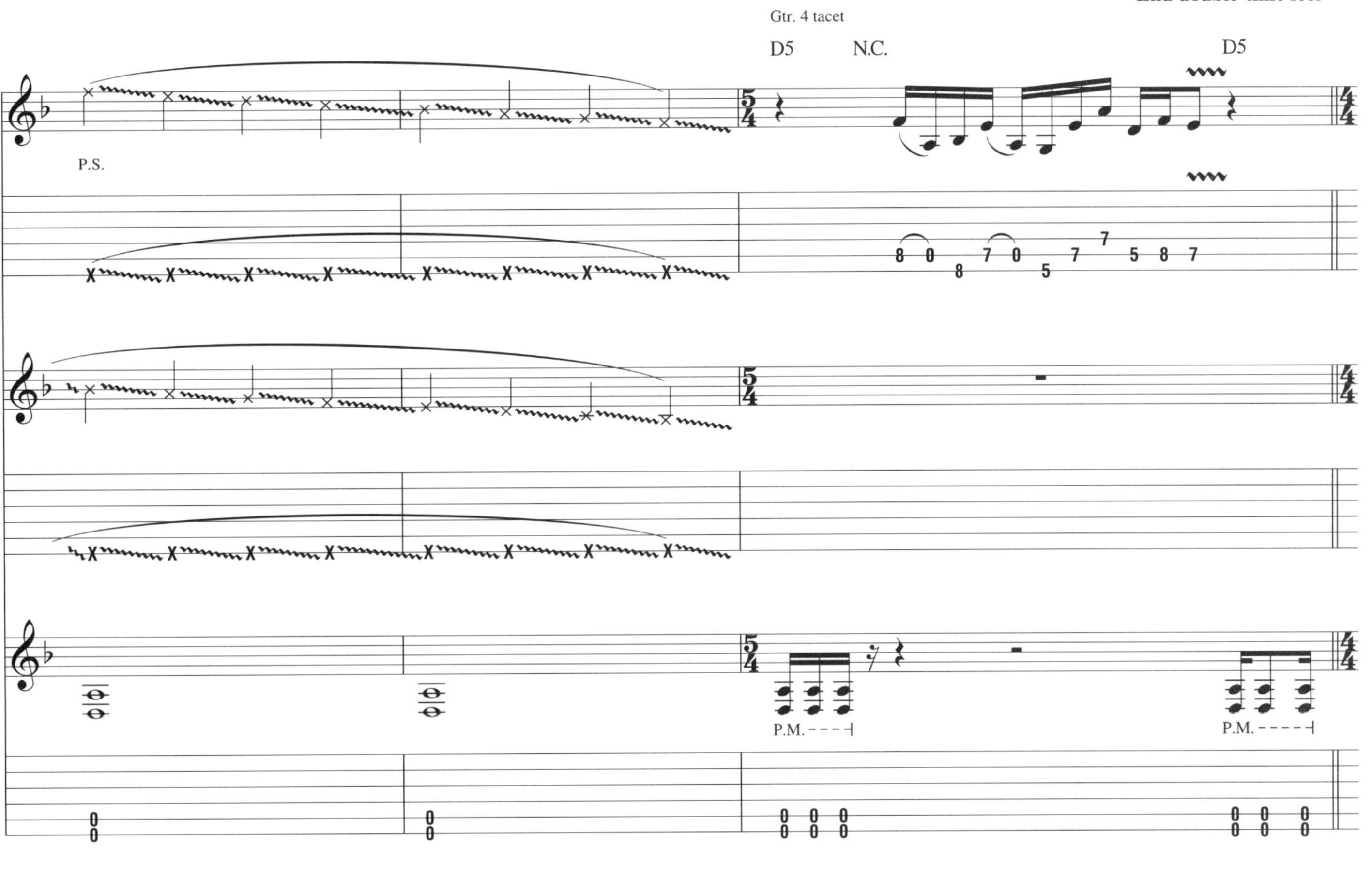
Gtr. 4 tacet
D5
N.C.
D5
P.S.
P.M.
P.M.

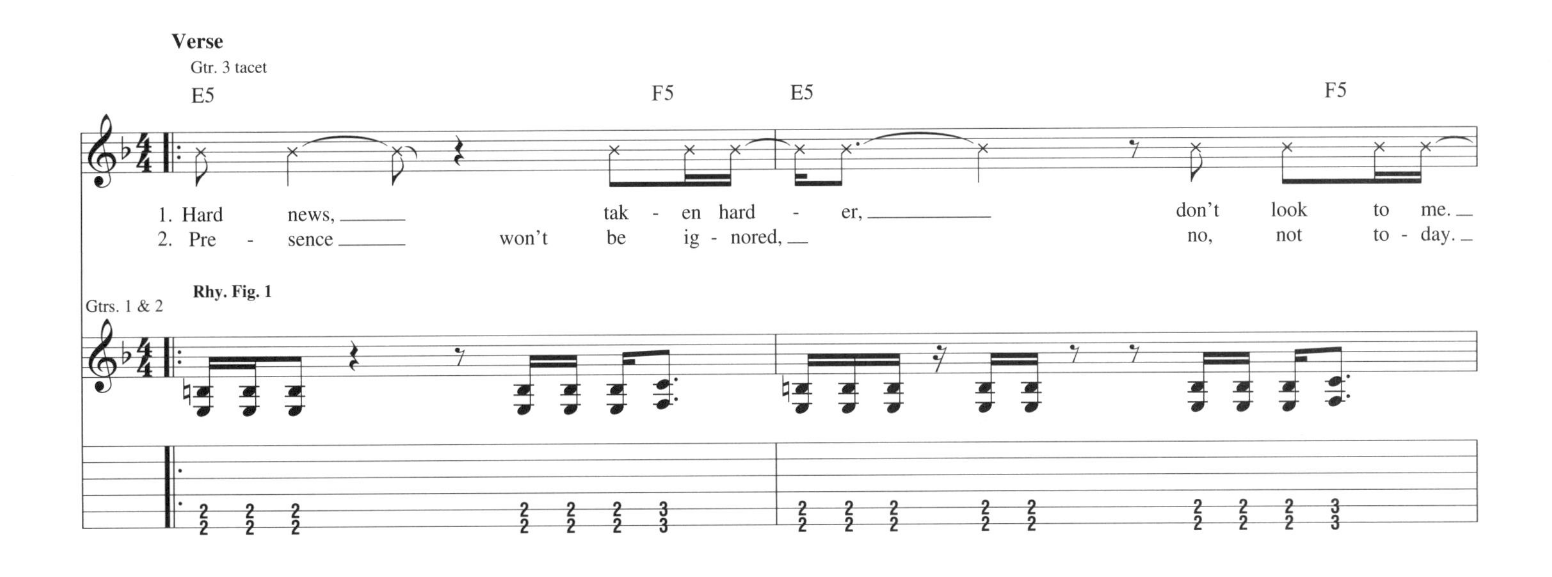
Verse
Gtr. 3 tacet
E5
F5
E5
F5
1. Hard news, tak - en hard - er, don't look to me.
2. Pre - sence won't be ig - nored, no, not to - day.
Rhy. Fig. 1
Gtrs. 1 & 2

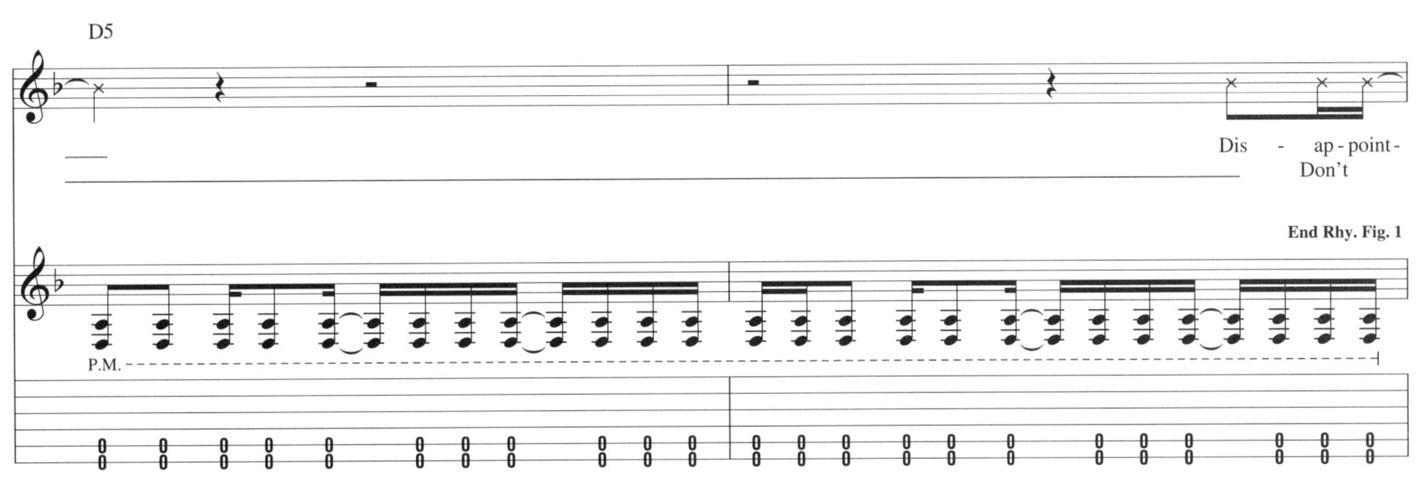
D5
Dis - ap - point -
Don't
End Rhy. Fig. 1
P.M.

Gtrs. 1 & 2: w/ Rhy. Fig. 1
E5
F5
E5
F5
- ed, we don't a - gree, I don't need your
walk in my di - rec - tion; turn the oth - er
D5
praise.
way.
(Don't look my way for help, from the be - gin - ning you came to me.)
Ask - ing ques -
Gtrs. 1 & 2: w/ Rhy. Fig. 1 (1st meas., 2 times)
E5
F5
E5
F5
Nev - er asked you to like me, I don't need your
- tions, pre - de - ter - mined an - swers, you won't find them
Gtr. 6 (dist.)
f
18
Gtr. 5 (dist.)
f
16
Gtrs. 1 & 2: w/ Rhy. Fig. 1 (last 2 meas.)
Gtrs. 5 & 6 tacet
D5
praise. (Won't play your games.) Look
here. (We don't want your o - pin - ion.) And I don't want
E5
F5
E5
F5
D5
down on me, spit in my face. You're noth - ing to me,
you, I won't let you think. Com - pro - mise is near,
Gtrs. 1 & 2

N.C.
D5
not to me.
'cause it's not near.
P.M.
N.C.
Chorus
Double-time feel
Dm/F
A/E
Dm/F D5
Gm/B♭
B♭5
C
Csus4 D5
Dark - ened eyes you'll see, there is no hope, no sav - ior in me.
Rhy. Fig. 2
End Rhy. Fig. 2
(Don't look this way, don't breathe this way, don't stare this way an - y - more.)
Riff B
End Riff B

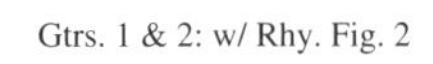
Gtrs. 1 & 2: w/ Rhy. Fig. 2

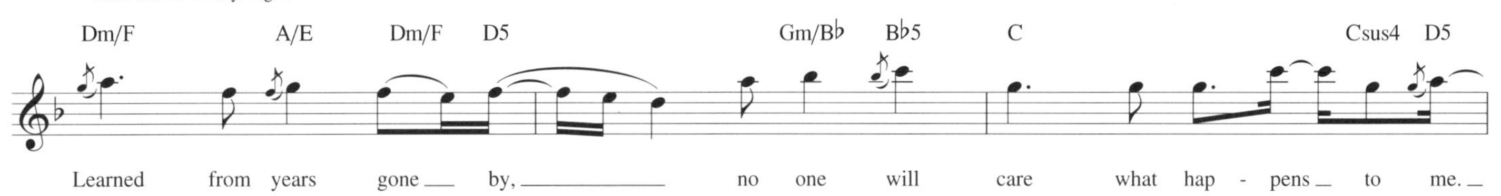
Dm/F A/E Dm/F D5 Gm/B♭ B♭5 C Csus4 D5
Learned from years gone by, no one will care what hap - pens to me.

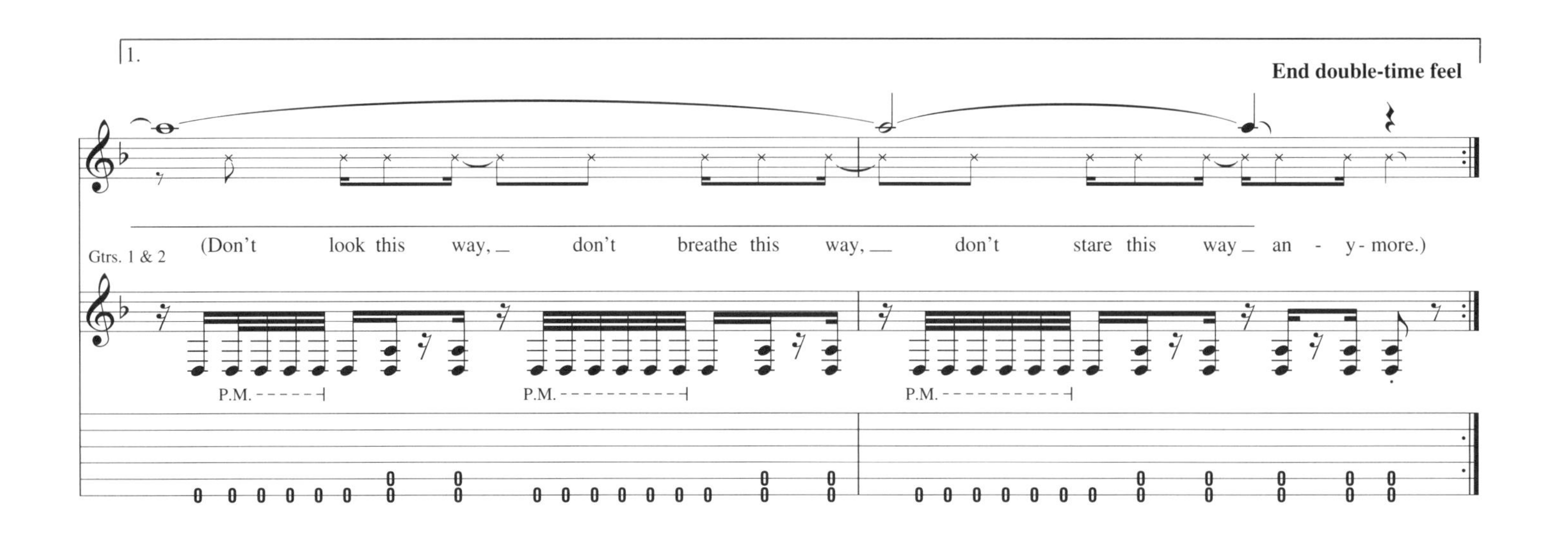
1.
End double-time feel
(Don't look this way, don't breathe this way, don't stare this way an - y - more.)
Gtrs. 1 & 2
P.M.
P.M.
P.M.

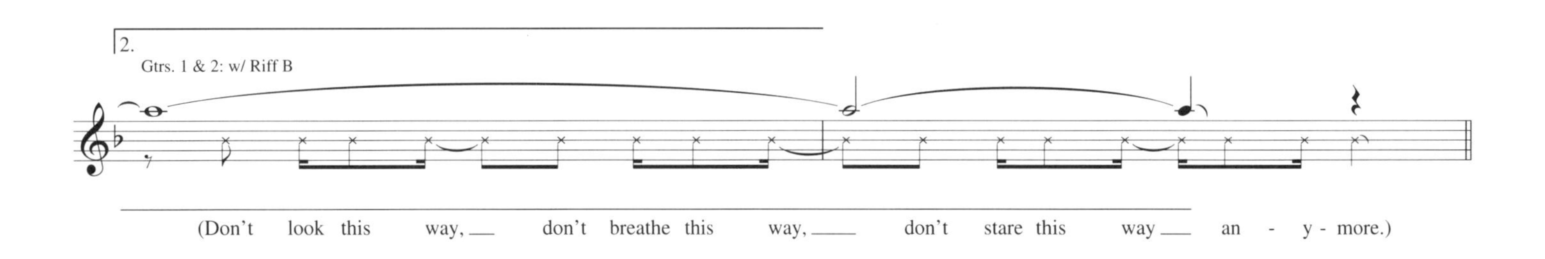
2.
Gtrs. 1 & 2: w/ Riff B
(Don't look this way, don't breathe this way, don't stare this way an - y - more.)

Guitar Solo

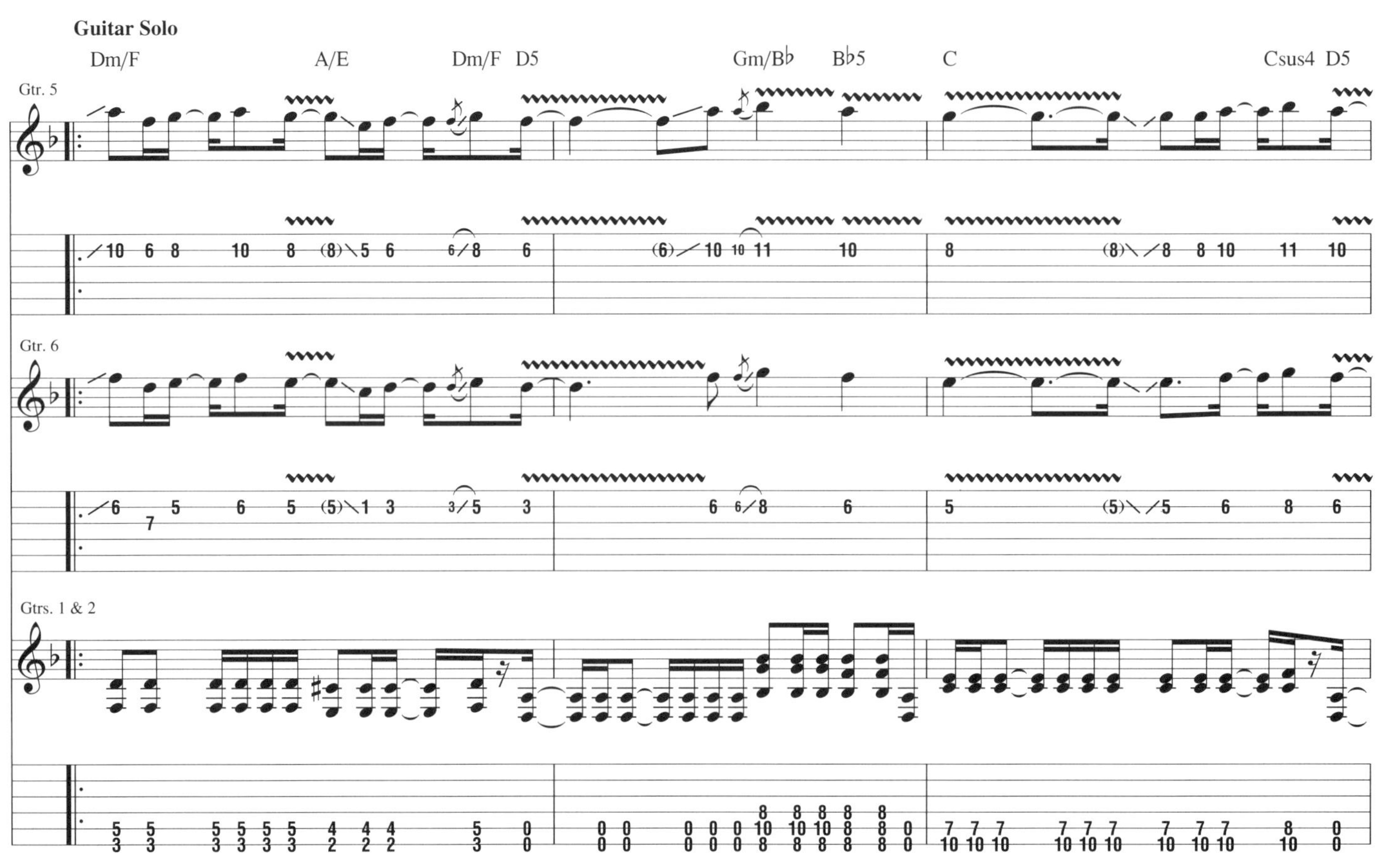
Dm/F A/E Dm/F D5 Gm/B♭ B♭5 C Csus4 D5
Gtr. 5
Gtr. 6
Gtrs. 1 & 2

2nd time, End double-time feel
B♭5
C5
Bridge
Half-time feel
Gtrs. 5 & 6 tacet
Dm
Gtrs. 1 & 2: w/ Riffs C & C1 (3 times)
I'm a - lone in here. No more feel - ings, killed my
Gtr. 1
Riff C
End Riff C
P.M.
Gtr. 2
Riff C1
End Riff C1
fears. Don't ask, you'll nev - er know. You're
End half-time feel
left be - hind, I'll be ex - posed.

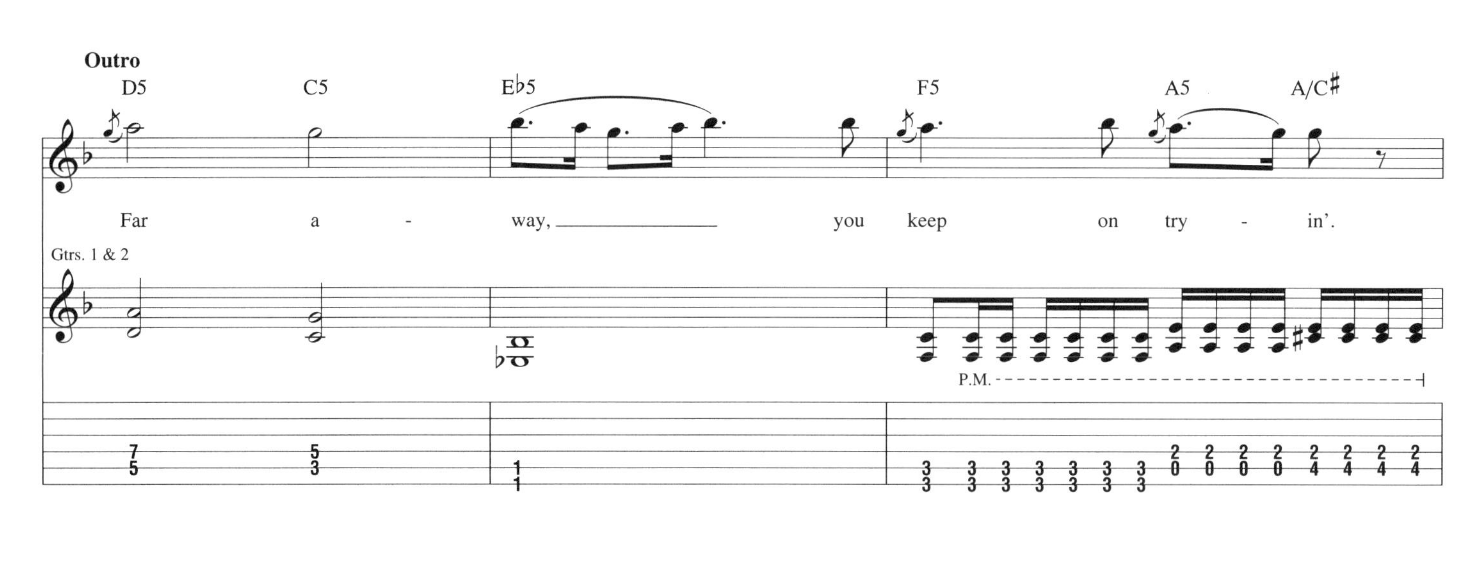
Outro
D5
C5
E♭5
F5
A5
A/C♯
Far a - way, you keep on try - in'.
Gtrs. 1 & 2
P.M.

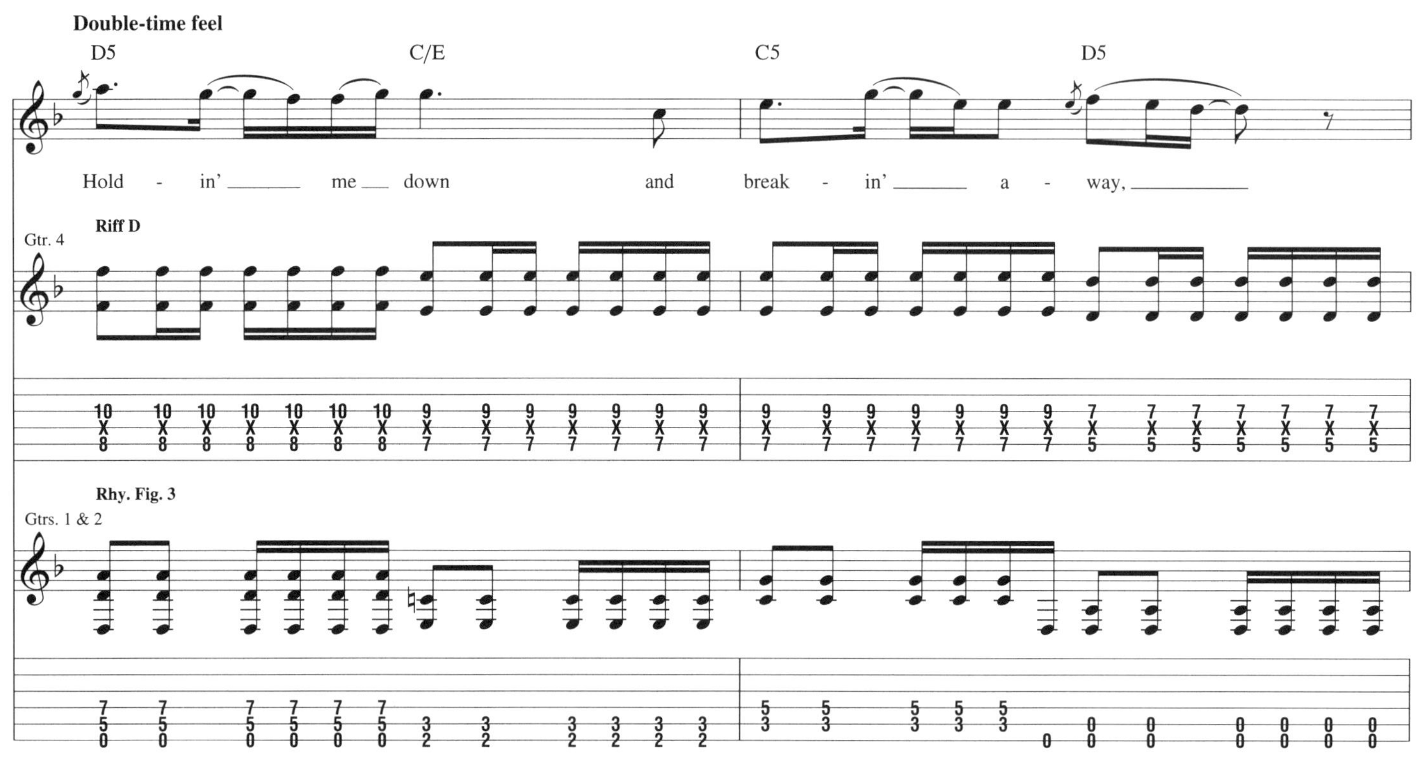
Double-time feel
D5
C/E
C5
D5
Hold - in' me down and break - in' a - way,
Riff D
Gtr. 4
Rhy. Fig. 3
Gtrs. 1 & 2

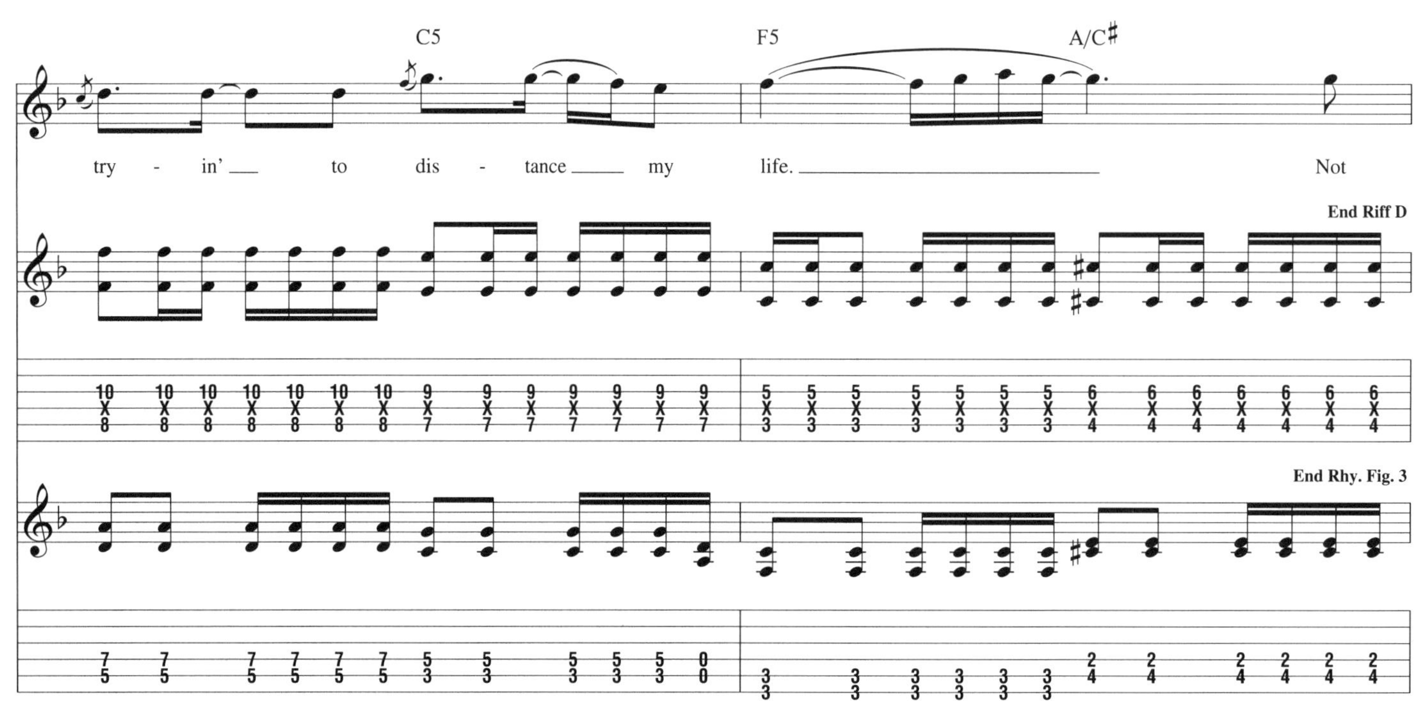
C5
F5
A/C♯
try - in' to dis - tance my life. Not
End Riff D
End Rhy. Fig. 3

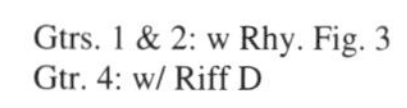
Gtrs. 1 & 2: w Rhy. Fig. 3
Gtr. 4: w/ Riff D

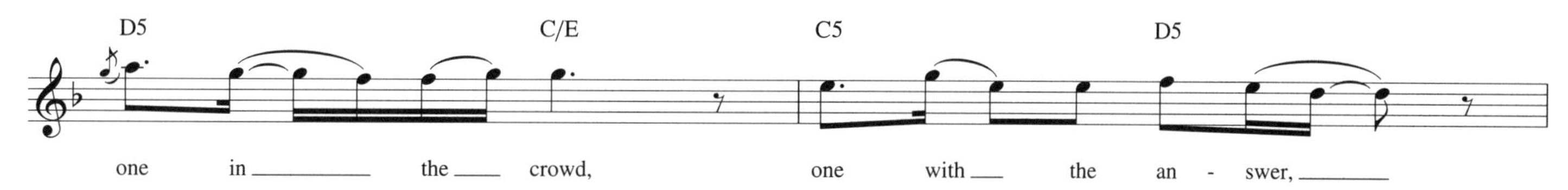
D5
C/E
C5
D5
one in the crowd, one with the an - swer,

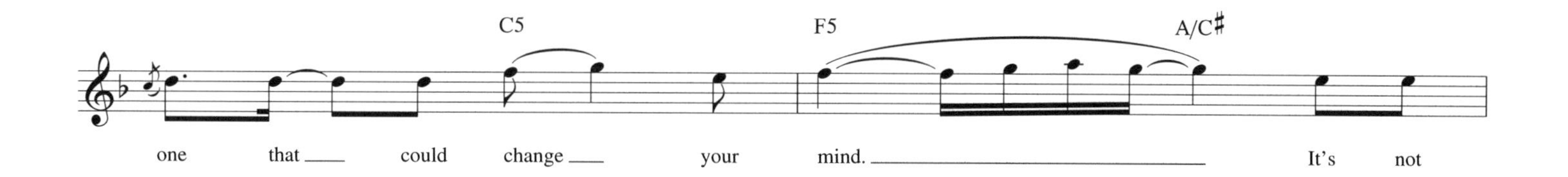
C5
F5
A/C♯
one that could change your mind. It's not

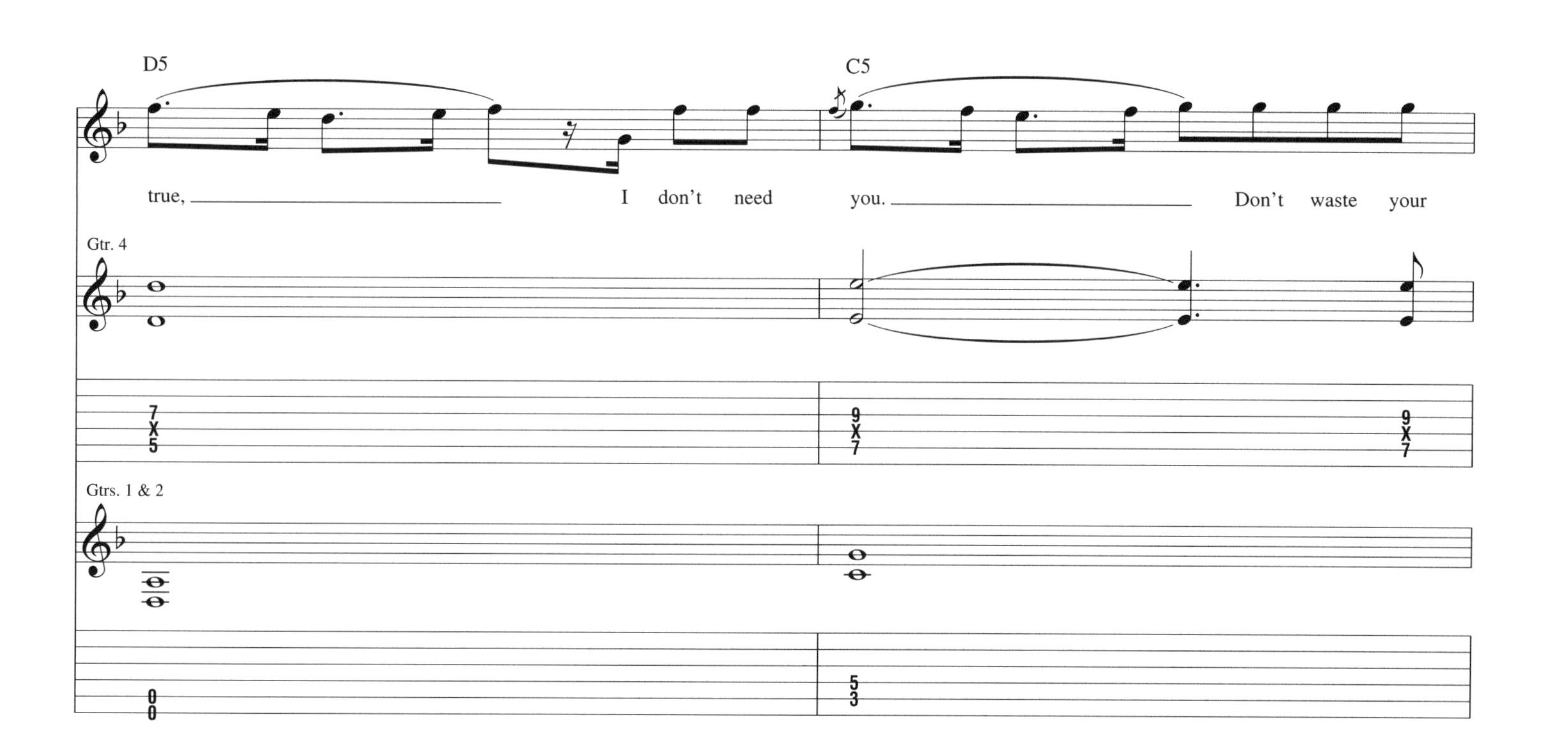
D5
C5
true, I don't need you. Don't waste your
Gtr. 4
Gtrs. 1 & 2

B♭5
F5
A/C♯
time, and don't waste mine. I'm not your

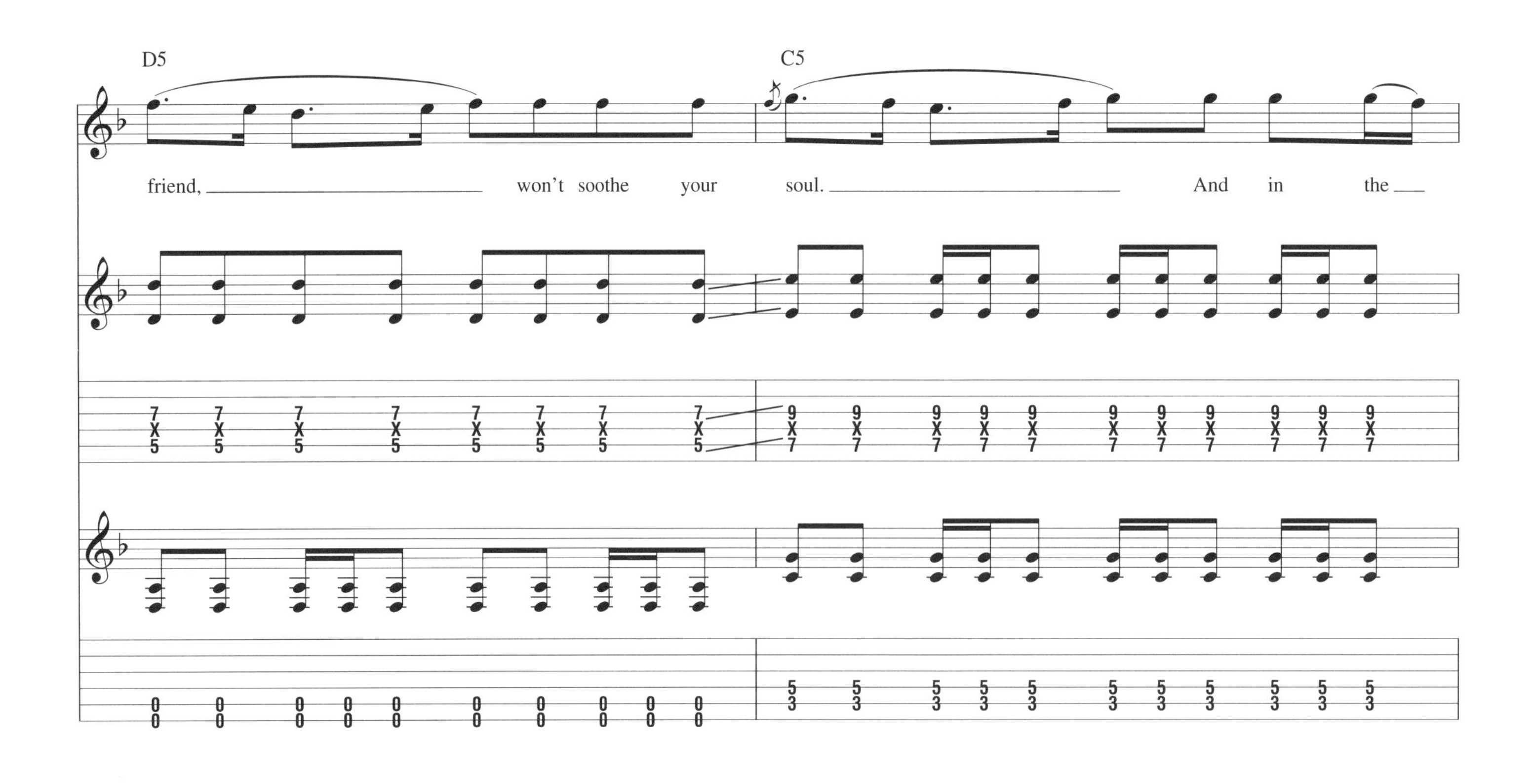
D5
C5
friend, won't soothe your soul. And in the

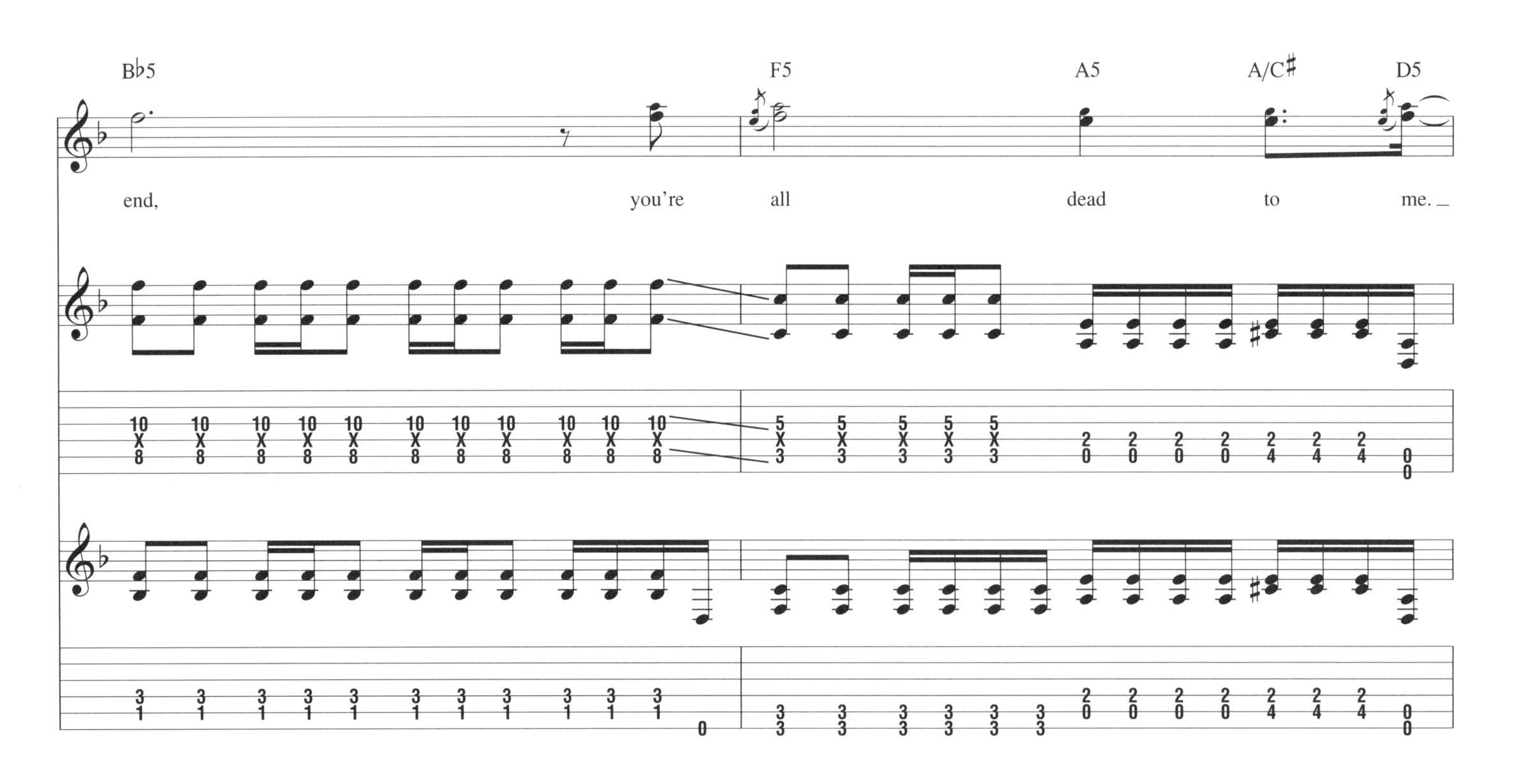
B♭5
F5
A5
A/C♯
D5
end, you're all dead to me.

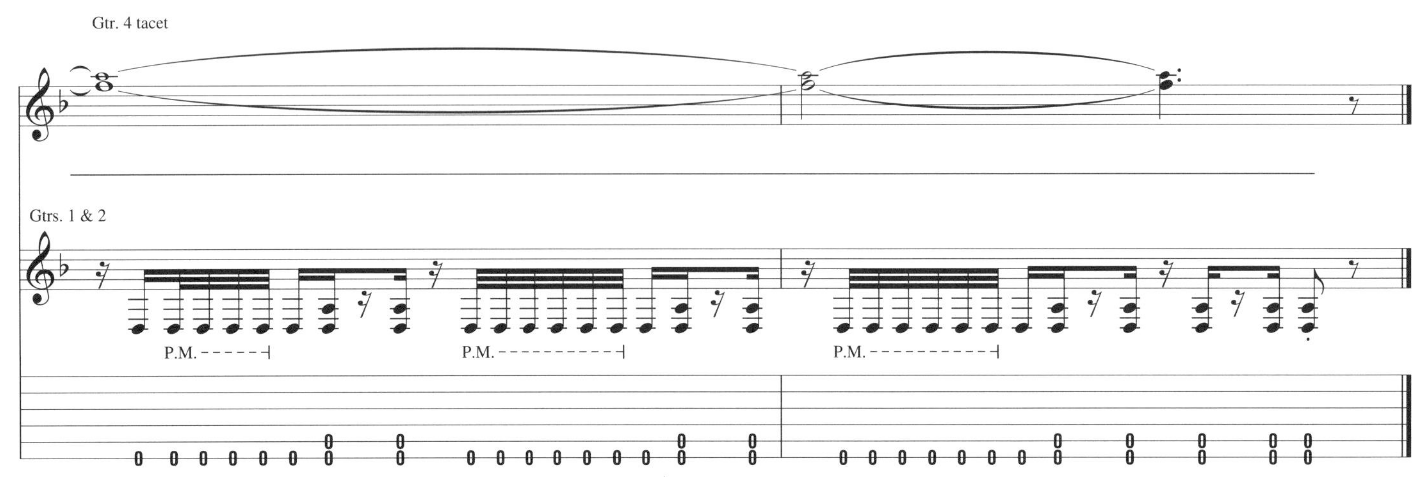
Gtr. 4 tacet
Gtrs. 1 & 2
P.M.
P.M.
P.M.

Eternal Rest

Words and Music by Matthew Sanders, James Sullivan, Brian Haner, Jr. and Zachary Baker

Drop D tuning:
(low to high) D-A-D-G-B-E

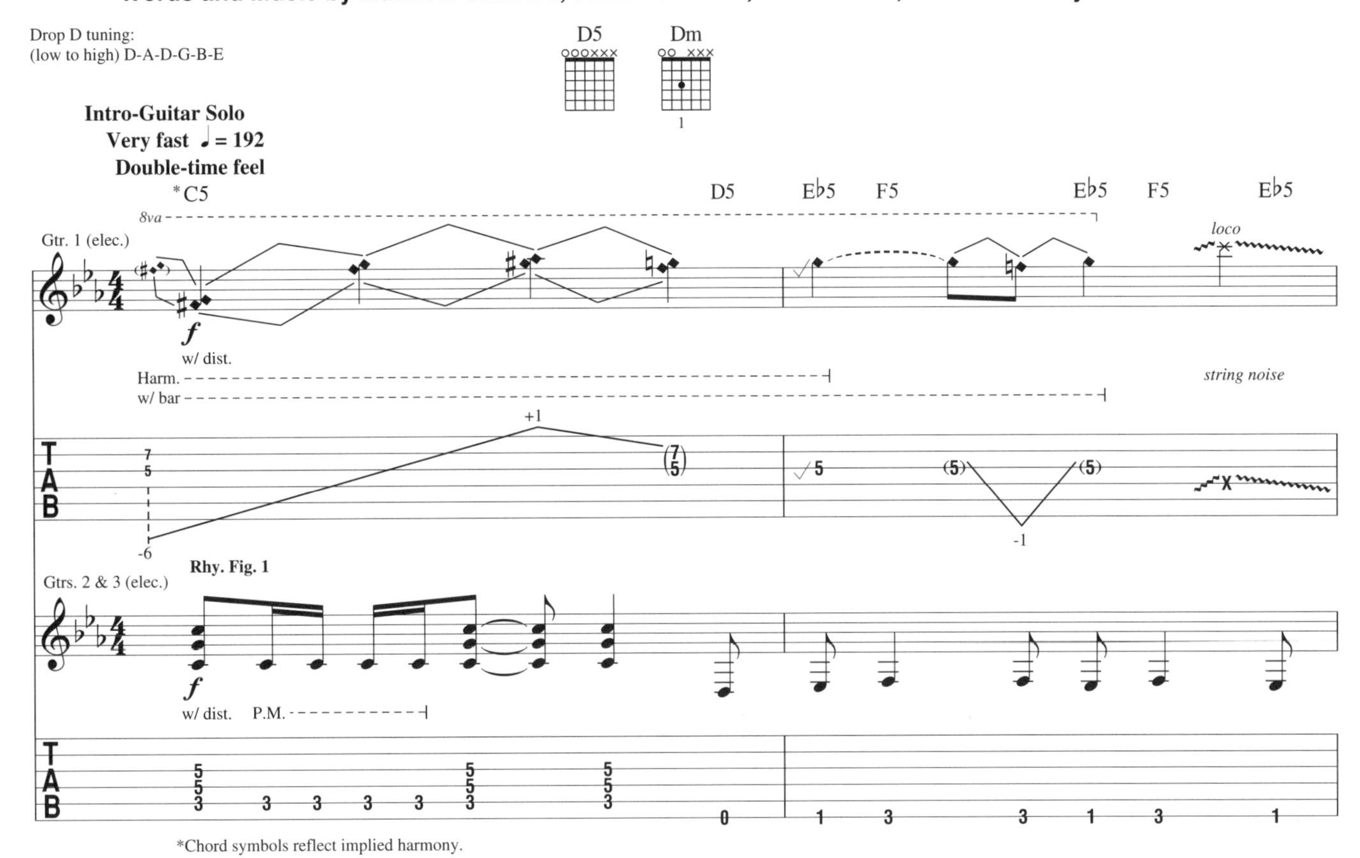

*Chord symbols reflect implied harmony.

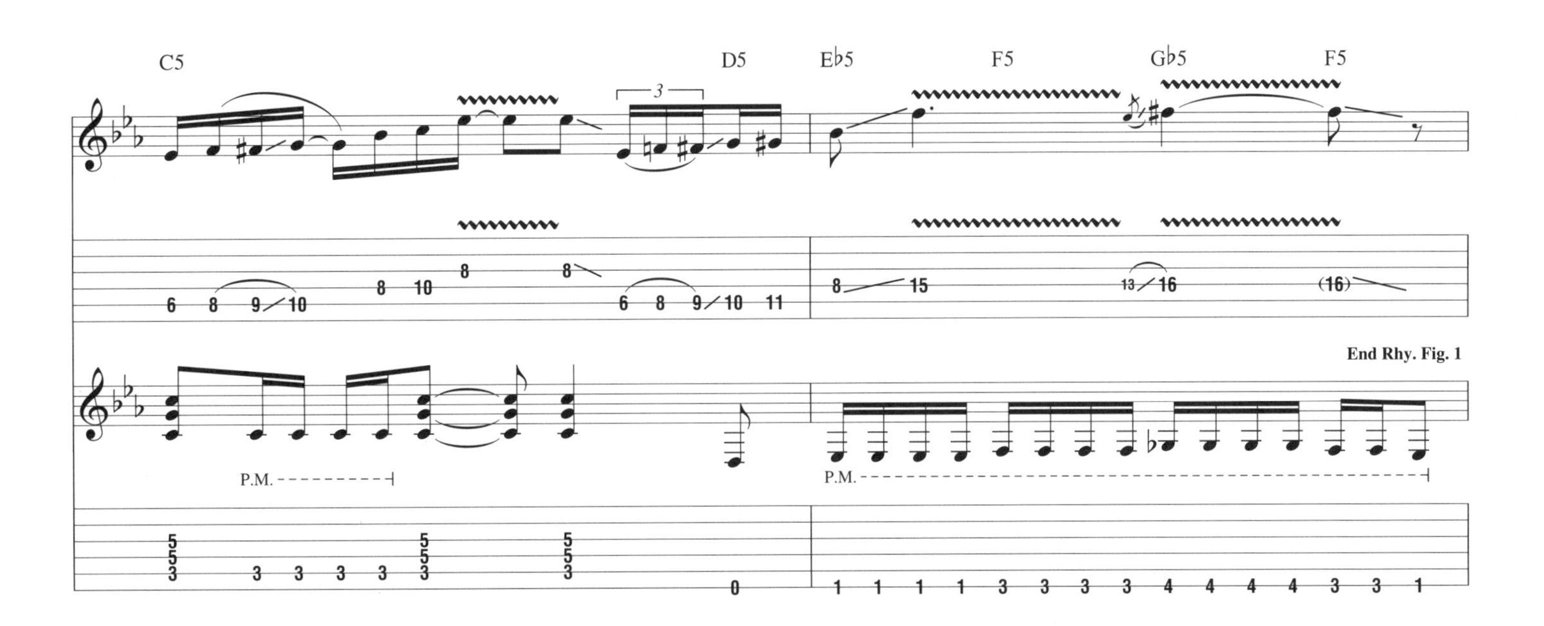

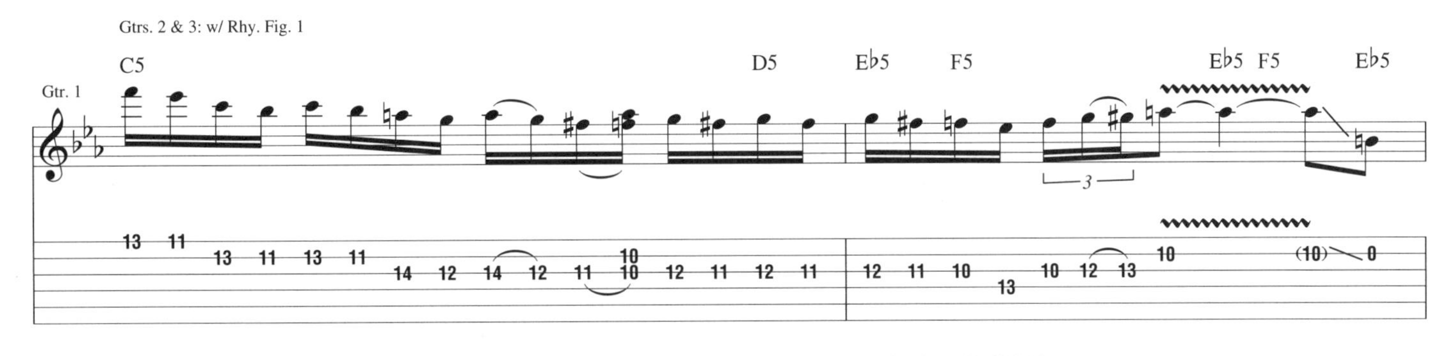

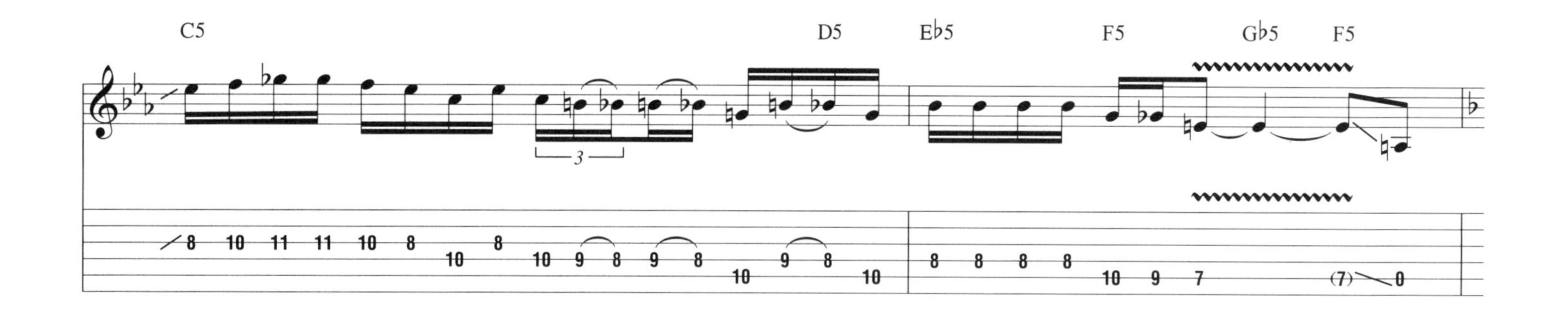
C5
D5
E♭5
F5
G♭5
F5

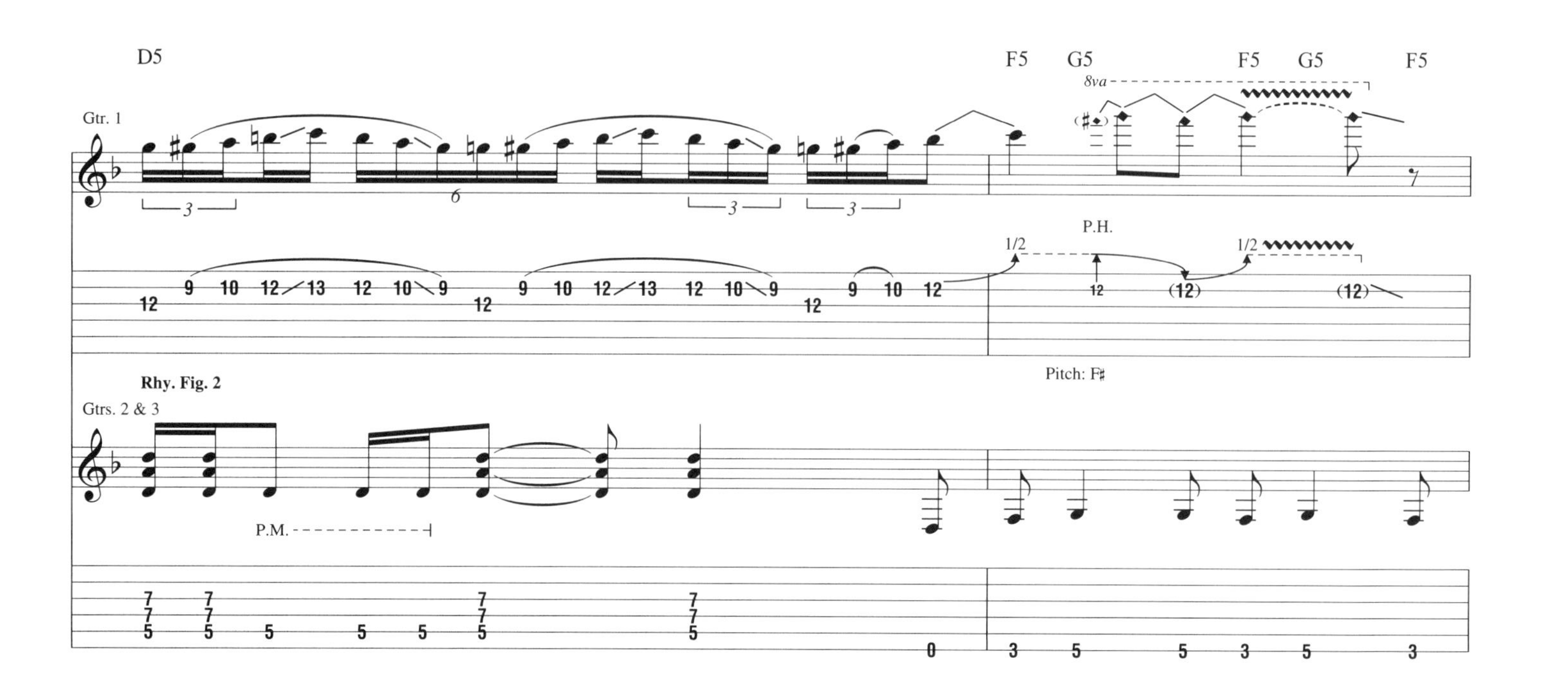
D5
F5
G5
F5
G5
F5
8va
Gtr. 1
P.H.
Pitch: F♯
Rhy. Fig. 2
Gtrs. 2 & 3
P.M.

D5
F5
G5
A♭5
G5
F5
loco
End Rhy. Fig. 2
P.M.
P.M.

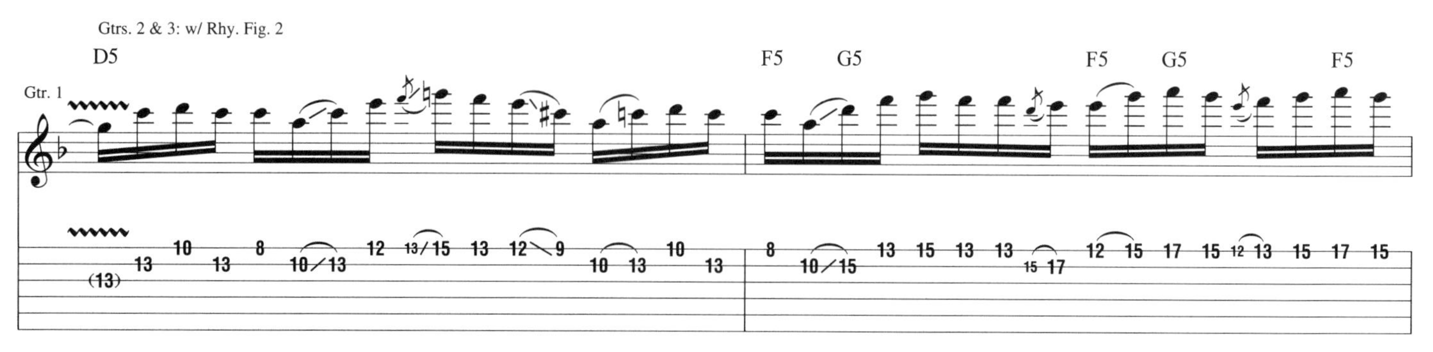
Gtrs. 2 & 3: w/ Rhy. Fig. 2
D5
F5
G5
F5
G5
F5
Gtr. 1

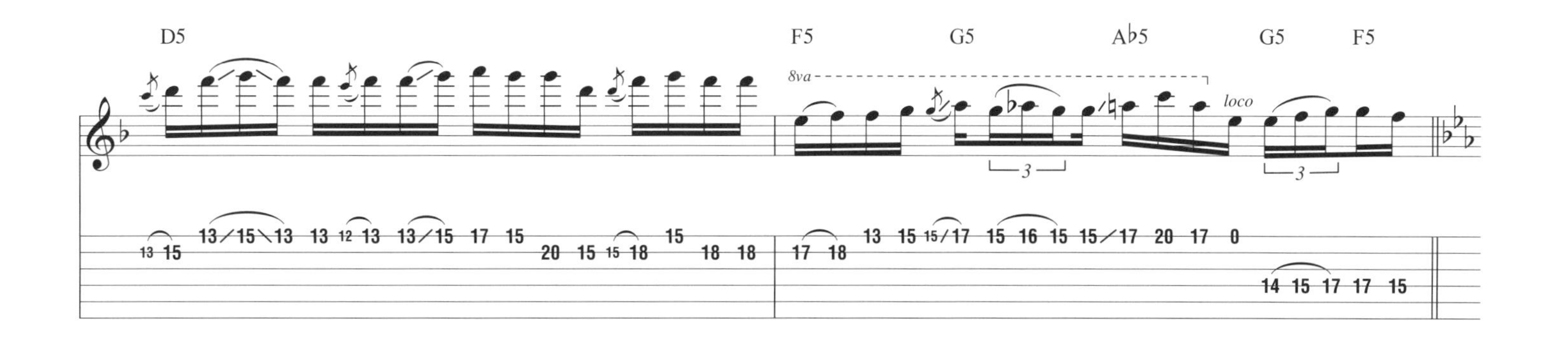
D5
F5
G5
A♭5
G5
F5
8va
loco
13 15 13⁄15⁄13 13 12 13 13⁄15 17 15 20 15 15 18 15 18 18
17 18 13 15 15⁄17 15 16 15 15⁄17 20 17 0
14 15 17 17 15

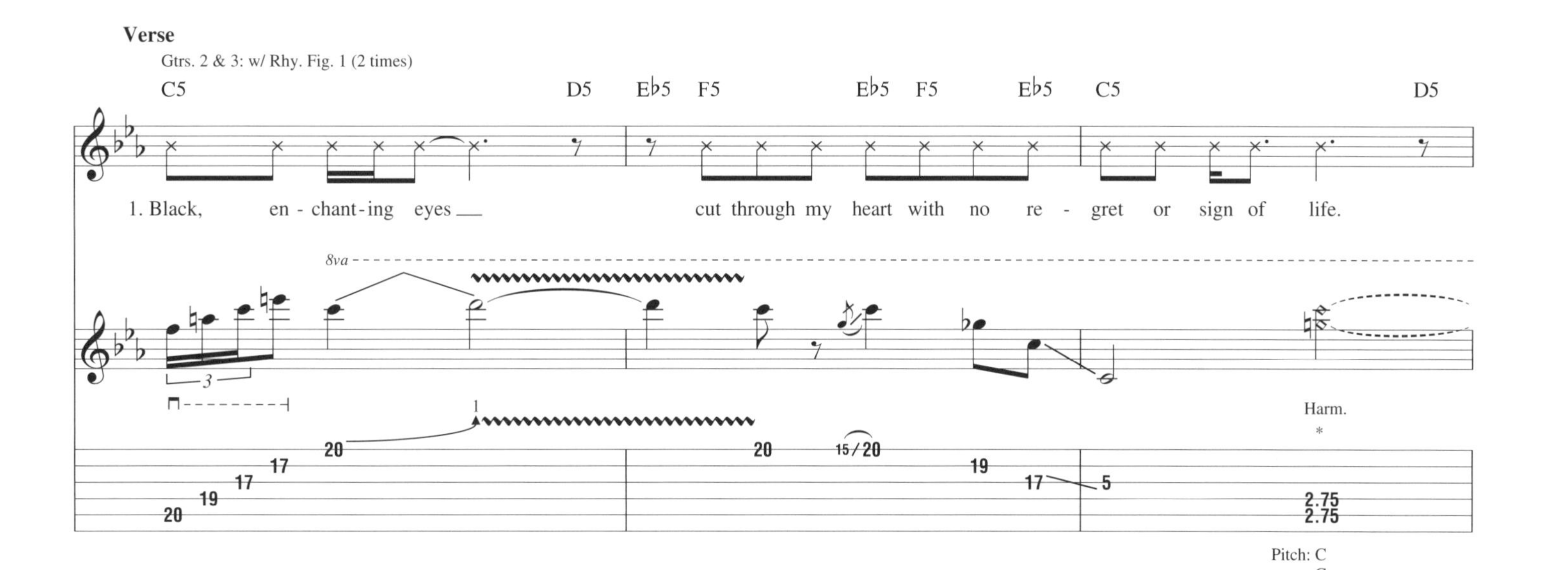
Verse
Gtrs. 2 & 3: w/ Rhy. Fig. 1 (2 times)
C5
D5
E♭5
F5
E♭5
F5
E♭5
C5
D5
1. Black, en - chant - ing eyes __ cut through my heart with no re - gret or sign of life.
8va
Harm.
*
20 19 17 17 20
20 15⁄20 19 17 5
2.75
2.75
Pitch: C
G
*Harmonic located three-fourths the distance between the 2nd & 3rd frets.

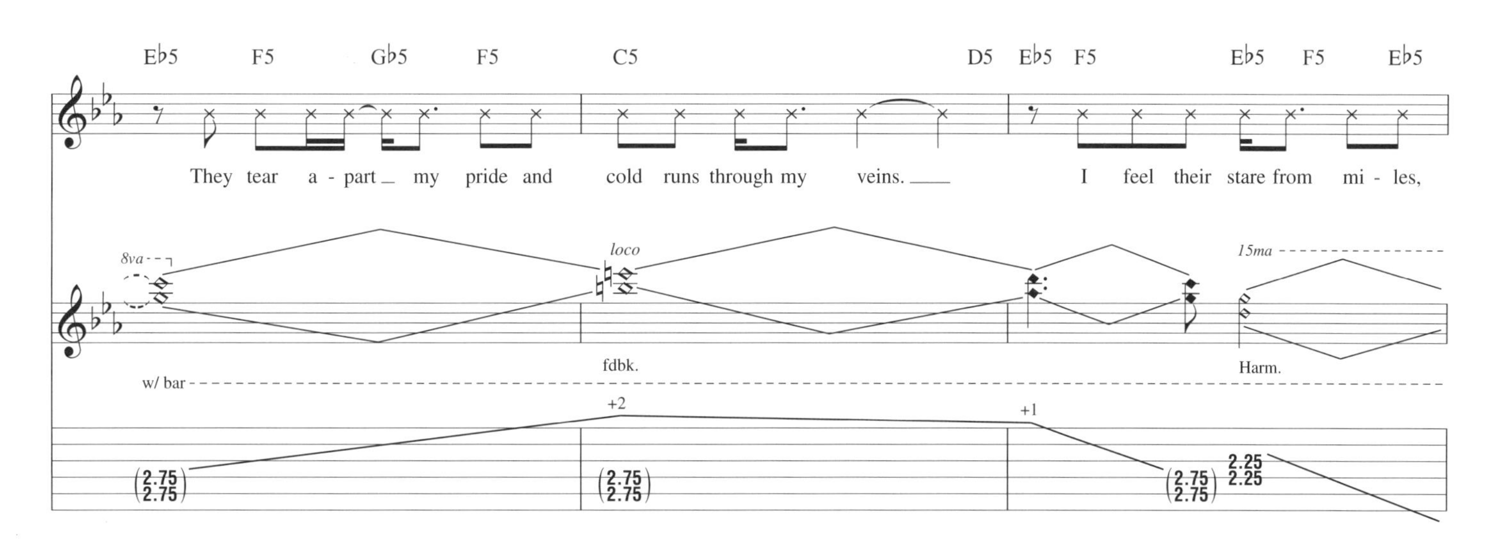
E♭5
F5
G♭5
F5
C5
D5
E♭5
F5
E♭5
F5
E♭5
They tear a - part __ my pride and cold runs through my veins. ____ I feel their stare from mi - les,
8va
loco
15ma
fdbk.
Harm.
w/ bar
+2
+1
(2.75)
(2.75)
(2.75)
(2.75)
(2.75)
(2.75)
2.25
2.25

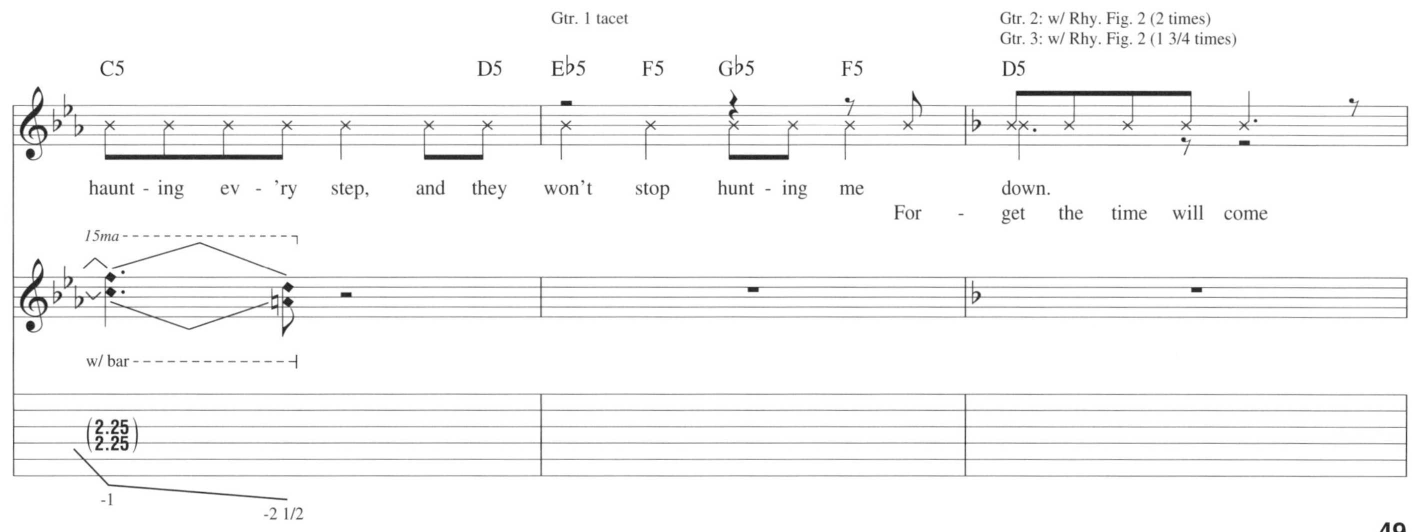
Gtr. 1 tacet
Gtr. 2: w/ Rhy. Fig. 2 (2 times)
Gtr. 3: w/ Rhy. Fig. 2 (1 3/4 times)
C5
D5
E♭5
F5
G♭5
F5
D5
haunt - ing ev - 'ry step, and they won't stop hunt - ing me down.
For - get the time will come
15ma
w/ bar
(2.25)
(2.25)
-1
-2 1/2

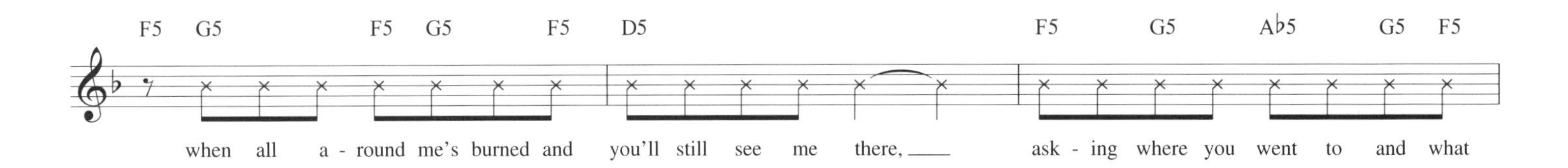
F5 G5 F5 G5 F5 D5 F5 G5 A♭5 G5 F5
when all a - round me's burned and you'll still see me there,
ask - ing where you went to and what

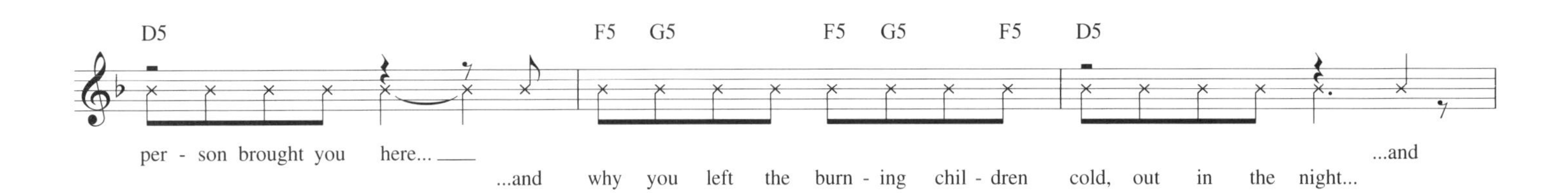
D5 F5 G5 F5 G5 F5 D5
per - son brought you here...
...and why you left the burn - ing chil - dren cold, out in the night...
...and

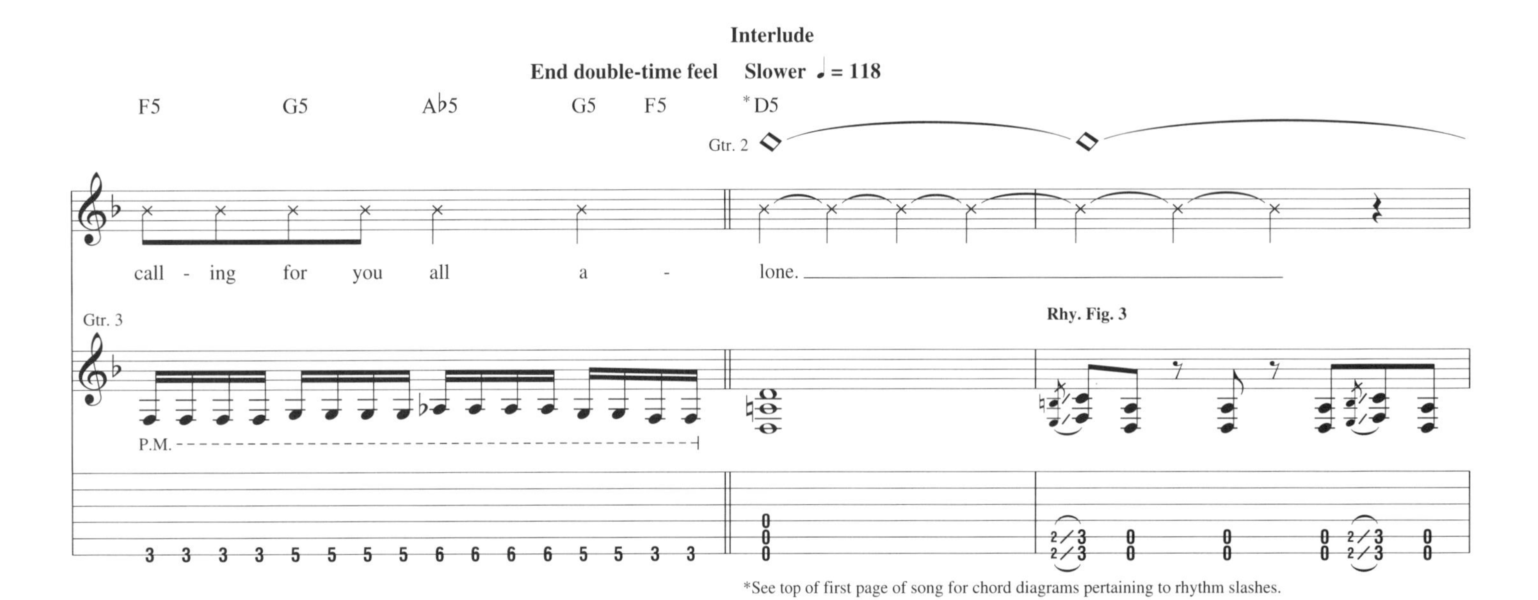
Interlude
End double-time feel
Slower ♩ = 118
F5 G5 A♭5 G5 F5 *D5
Gtr. 2
call - ing for you all a - lone.
Gtr. 3
Rhy. Fig. 3
P.M.
*See top of first page of song for chord diagrams pertaining to rhythm slashes.

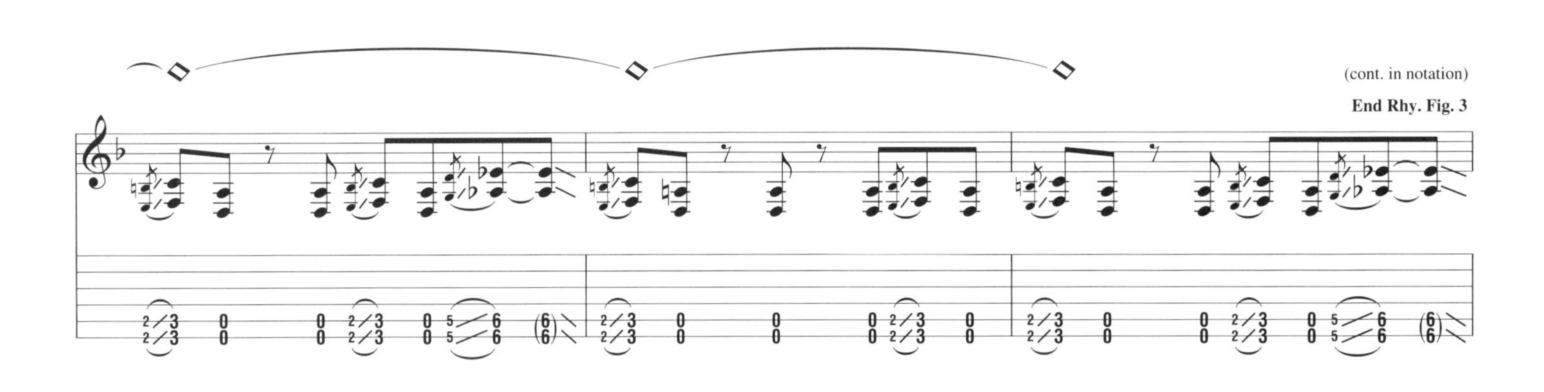
(cont. in notation)
End Rhy. Fig. 3

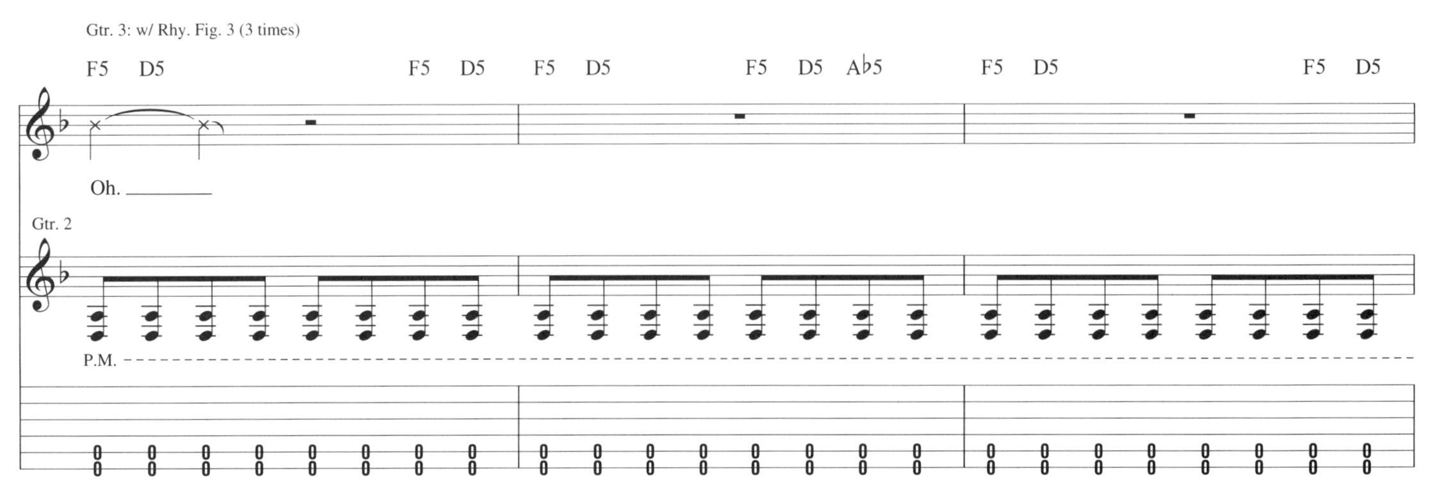
Gtr. 3: w/ Rhy. Fig. 3 (3 times)
F5 D5 F5 D5 F5 D5 F5 D5 A♭5 F5 D5 F5 D5
Oh.
Gtr. 2
P.M.

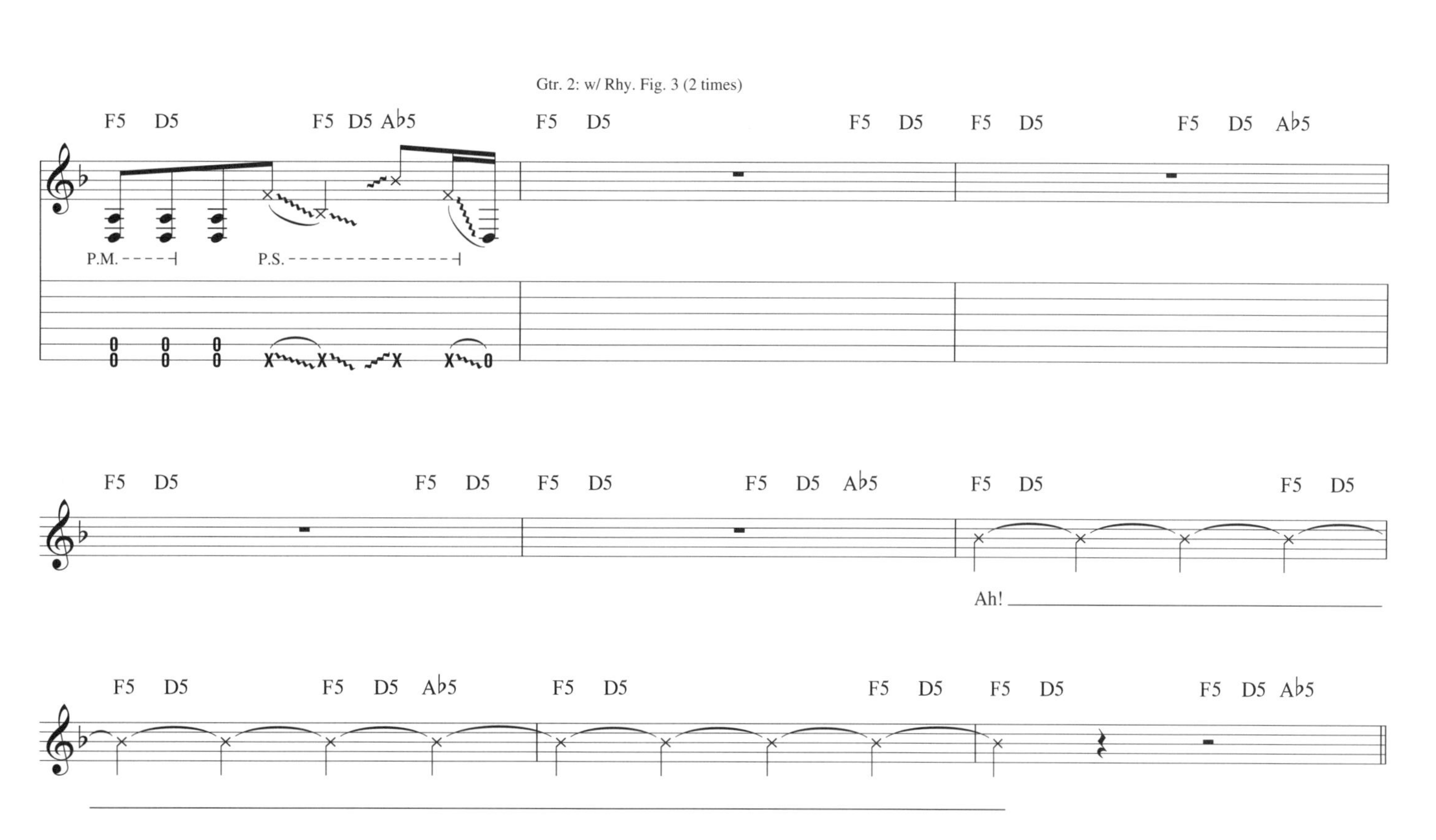
Gtr. 2: w/ Rhy. Fig. 3 (2 times)
F5 D5 F5 D5 A♭5 F5 D5 F5 D5 F5 D5 F5 D5 A♭5
P.M.
P.S.
F5 D5 F5 D5 F5 D5 F5 D5 A♭5 F5 D5 F5 D5
Ah!
F5 D5 F5 D5 A♭5 F5 D5 F5 D5 F5 D5 F5 D5 A♭5

Verse
2nd time, Bkgd. Voc.: w/ Voc. Fig. 1
D5 G5 D5 F5 D5 F5 G5
2., 4. Dark in their hearts, I can feel it burn in - side of me.
Rhy. Fig. 4
Gtrs. 2 & 3
End Rhy. Fig. 4
P.M.
0 0 5 0 3 0 3 5

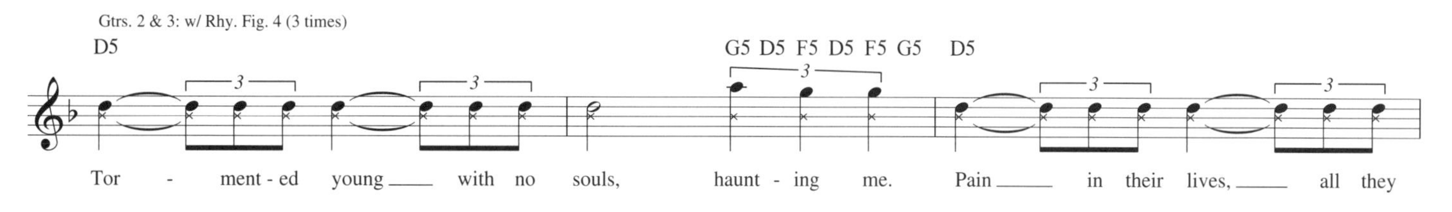
Gtrs. 2 & 3: w/ Rhy. Fig. 4 (3 times)
D5 G5 D5 F5 D5 F5 G5 D5
Tor - ment - ed young with no souls, haunt - ing me. Pain in their lives, all they

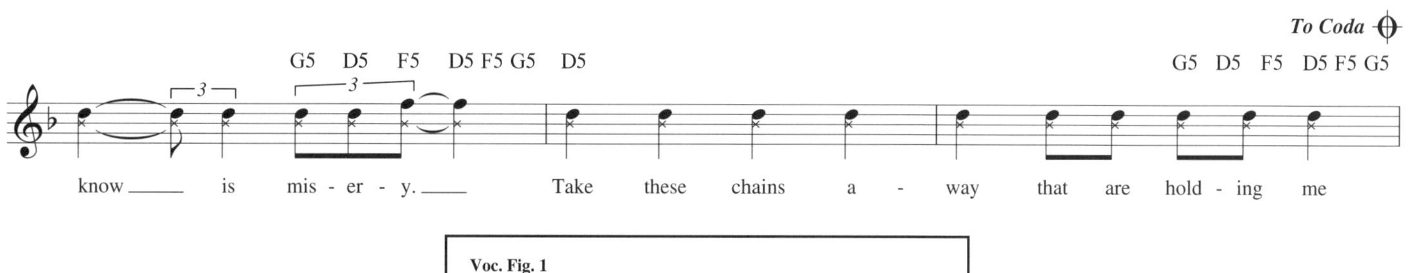
To Coda
G5 D5 F5 D5 F5 G5 D5 G5 D5 F5 D5 F5 G5
know is mis - er - y. Take these chains a - way that are hold - ing me

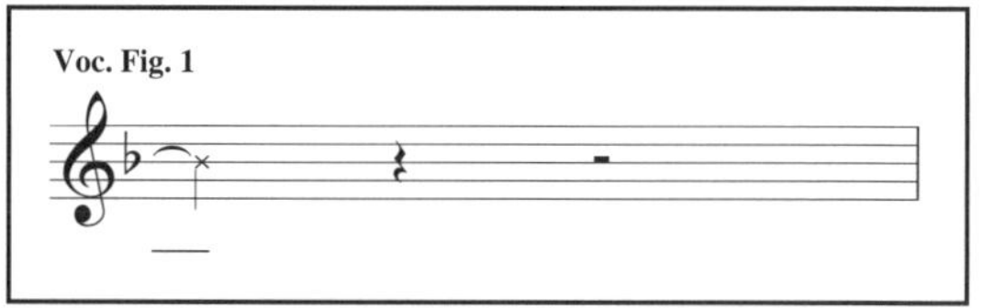
Voc. Fig. 1

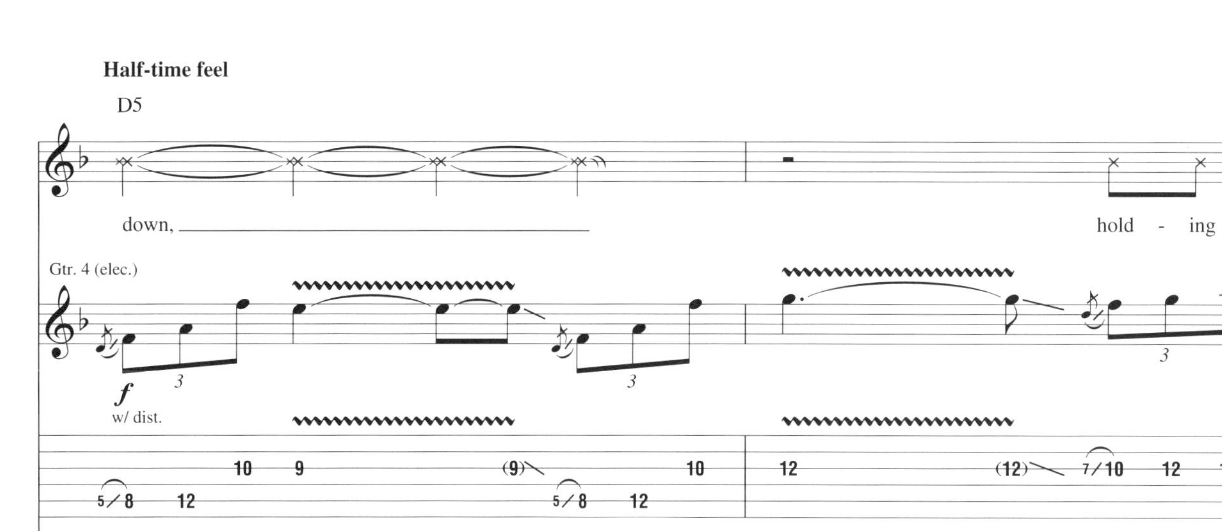
Half-time feel
D5
down,
hold - ing me
Gtr. 4 (elec.)
w/ dist.

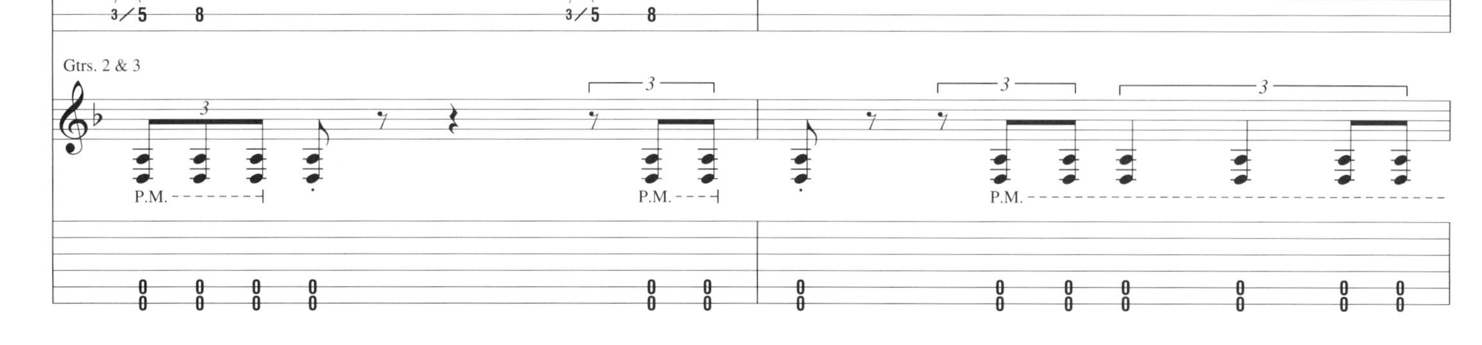
Gtr. 5 (elec.)
w/ dist.
Gtrs. 2 & 3
P.M.

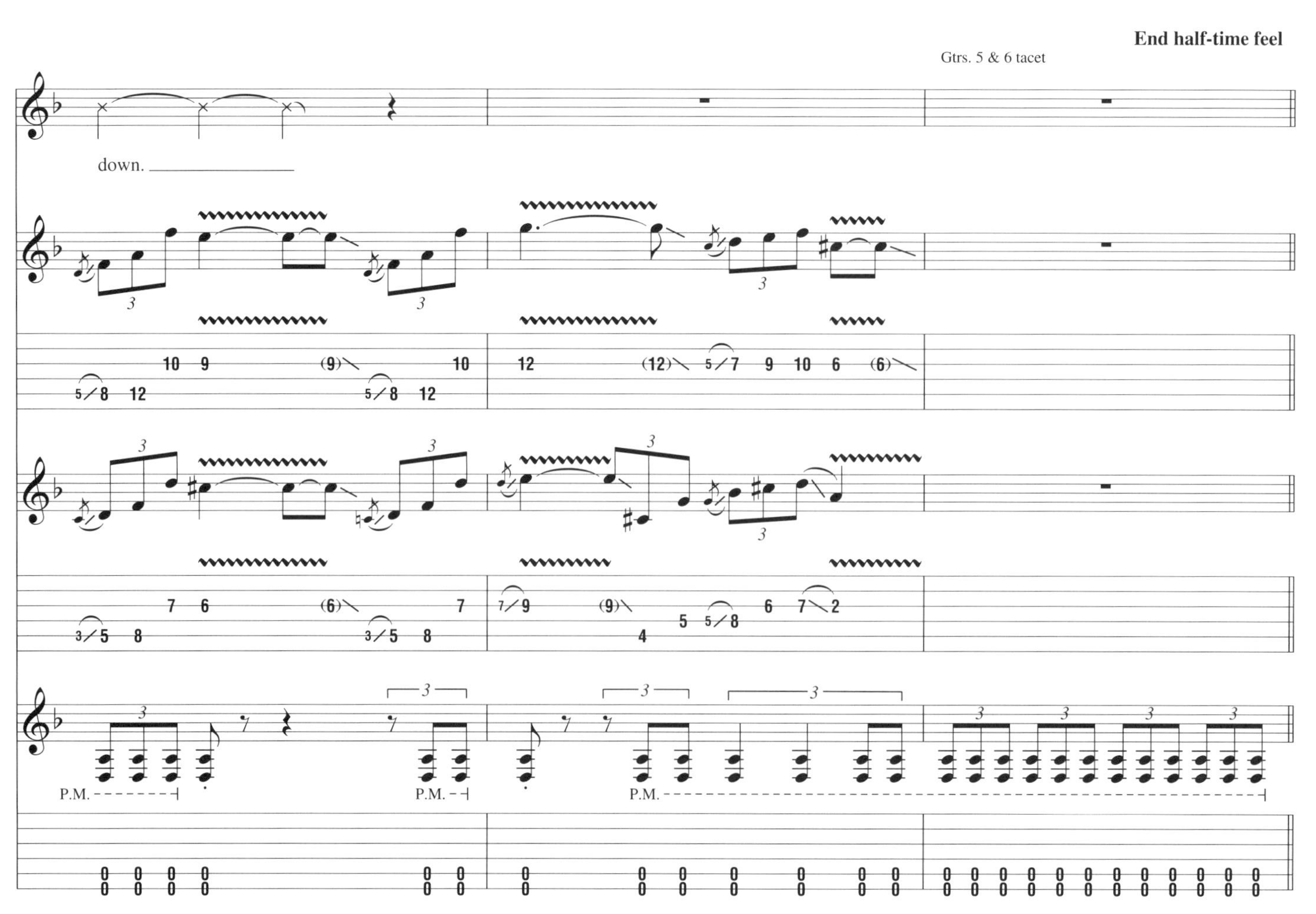
End half-time feel
Gtrs. 5 & 6 tacet
down.
P.M.

Verse
Double-time feel
D5
E°
D5/A
A5
3. They'll find you a - lone, your des - p'rate and vil - lain - ous
Riff A
Gtrs. 2 & 3
P.M.
A/E
Dm/F
D°/A♭
Eadd♯9/G♯
ways.
Turn - ing their hearts in - to stone, they seek more than
End Riff A
Gtrs. 2 & 3: w/ Riff A
venge - ance.
Look in their eyes, your pain is their sat - is -
fac - tion.
Look in their eyes and see the dark - ness take
Chorus
Dm/F
A7/E
C♯m/E
hold.
I'm con - trolled by fate.
(Wait - ing for,
Gtrs. 2 & 3

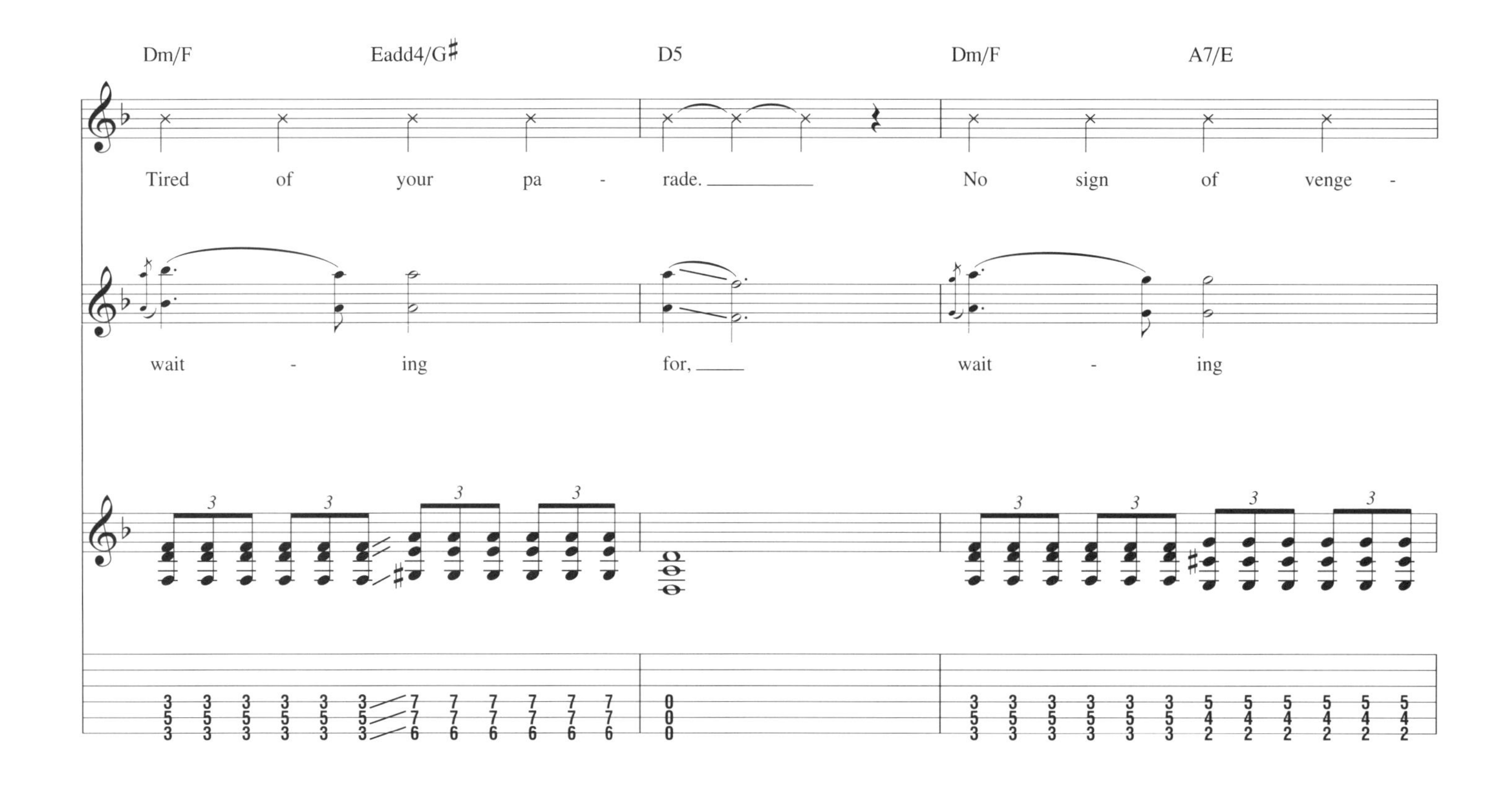
Dm/F
Eadd4/G♯
D5
Dm/F
A7/E
Tired of your pa - rade.
No sign of venge -
wait - ing for,
wait - ing

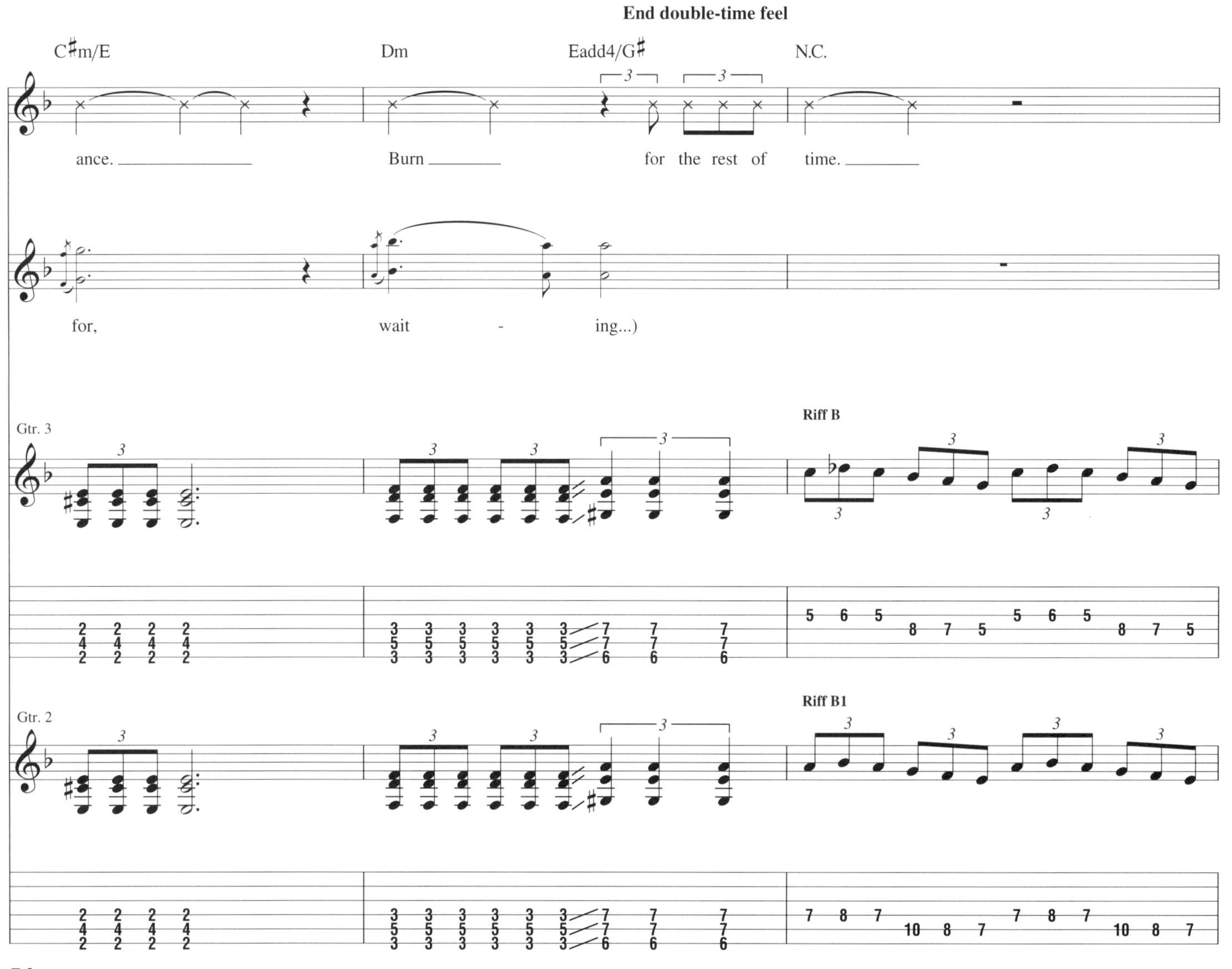
End double-time feel
C♯m/E
Dm
Eadd4/G♯
N.C.
ance.
Burn
for the rest of
time.
for,
wait - ing...)
Gtr. 3
Riff B
Gtr. 2
Riff B1

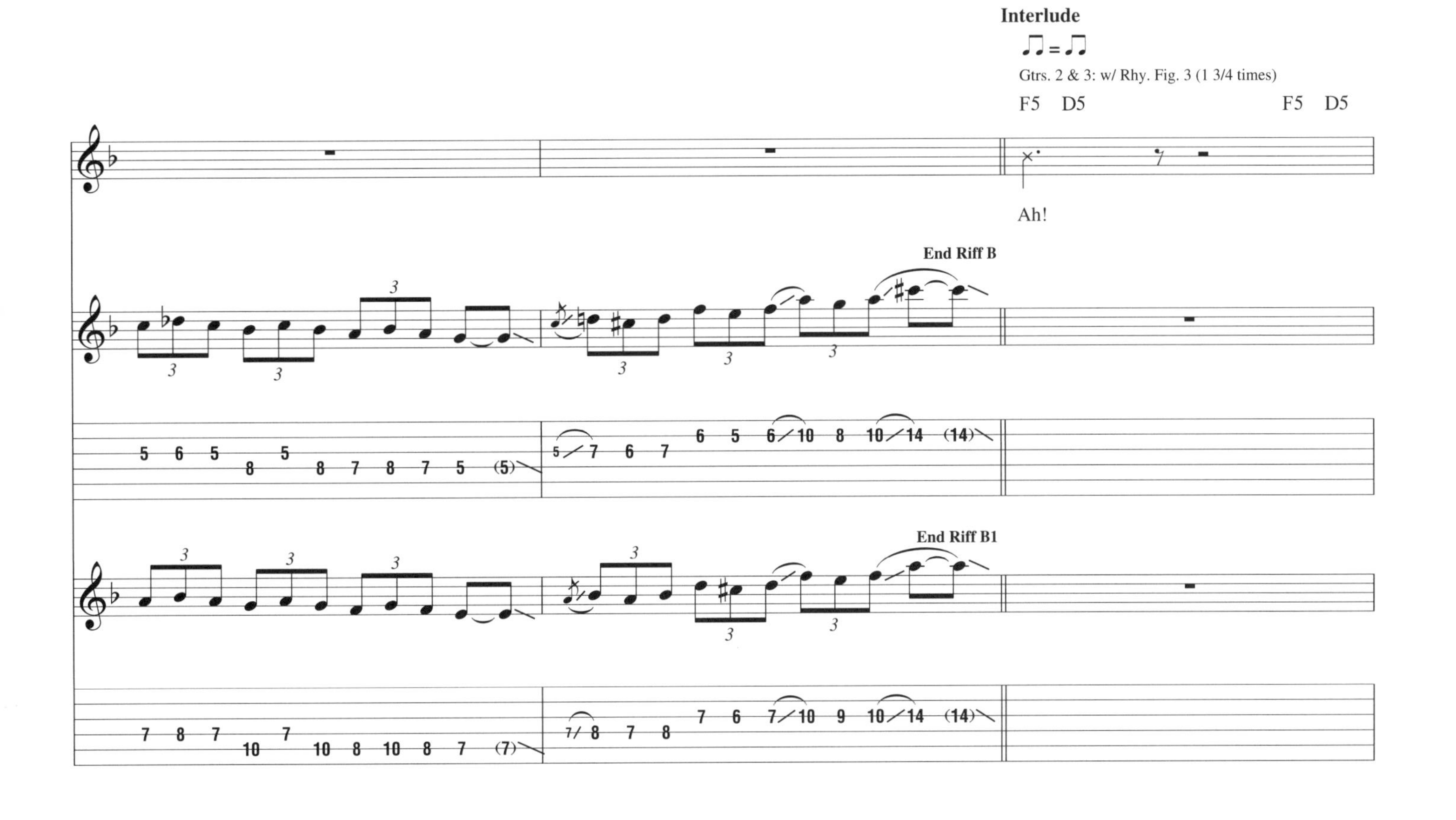
Interlude
Gtrs. 2 & 3: w/ Rhy. Fig. 3 (1 3/4 times)
F5 D5 F5 D5
Ah!
End Riff B
End Riff B1

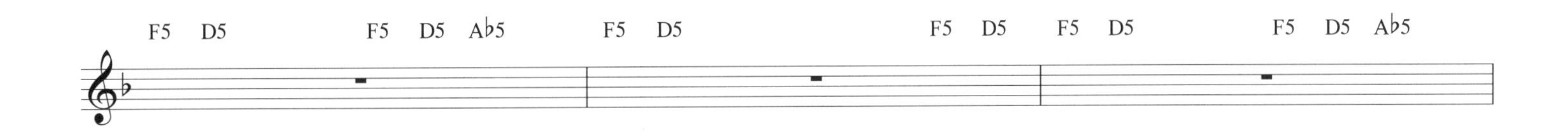
F5 D5 F5 D5 A♭5 F5 D5 F5 D5 F5 D5 F5 D5 A♭5

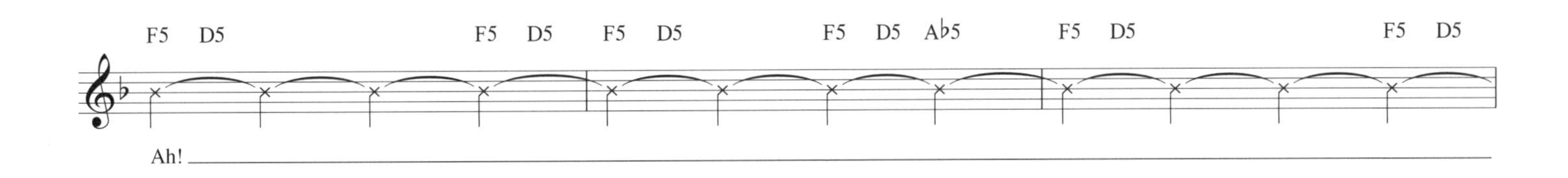
F5 D5 F5 D5 F5 D5 F5 D5 A♭5 F5 D5 F5 D5
Ah!

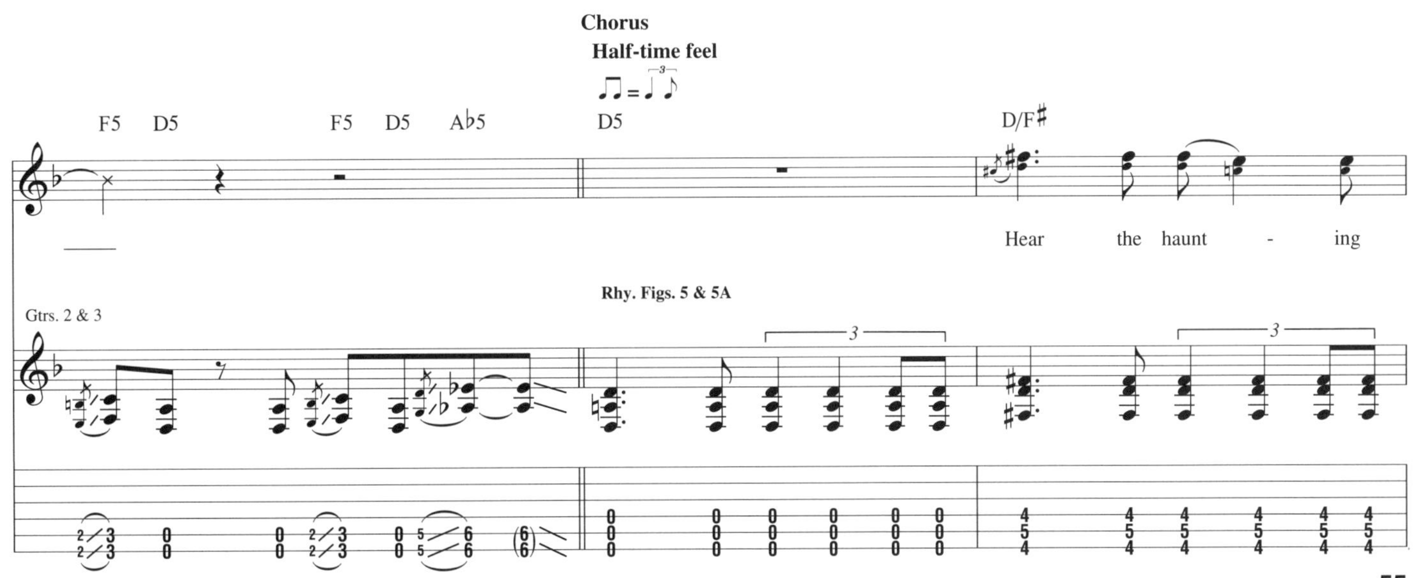
Chorus
Half-time feel
F5 D5 F5 D5 A♭5 D5 D/F♯
Hear the haunt - ing
Gtrs. 2 & 3
Rhy. Figs. 5 & 5A

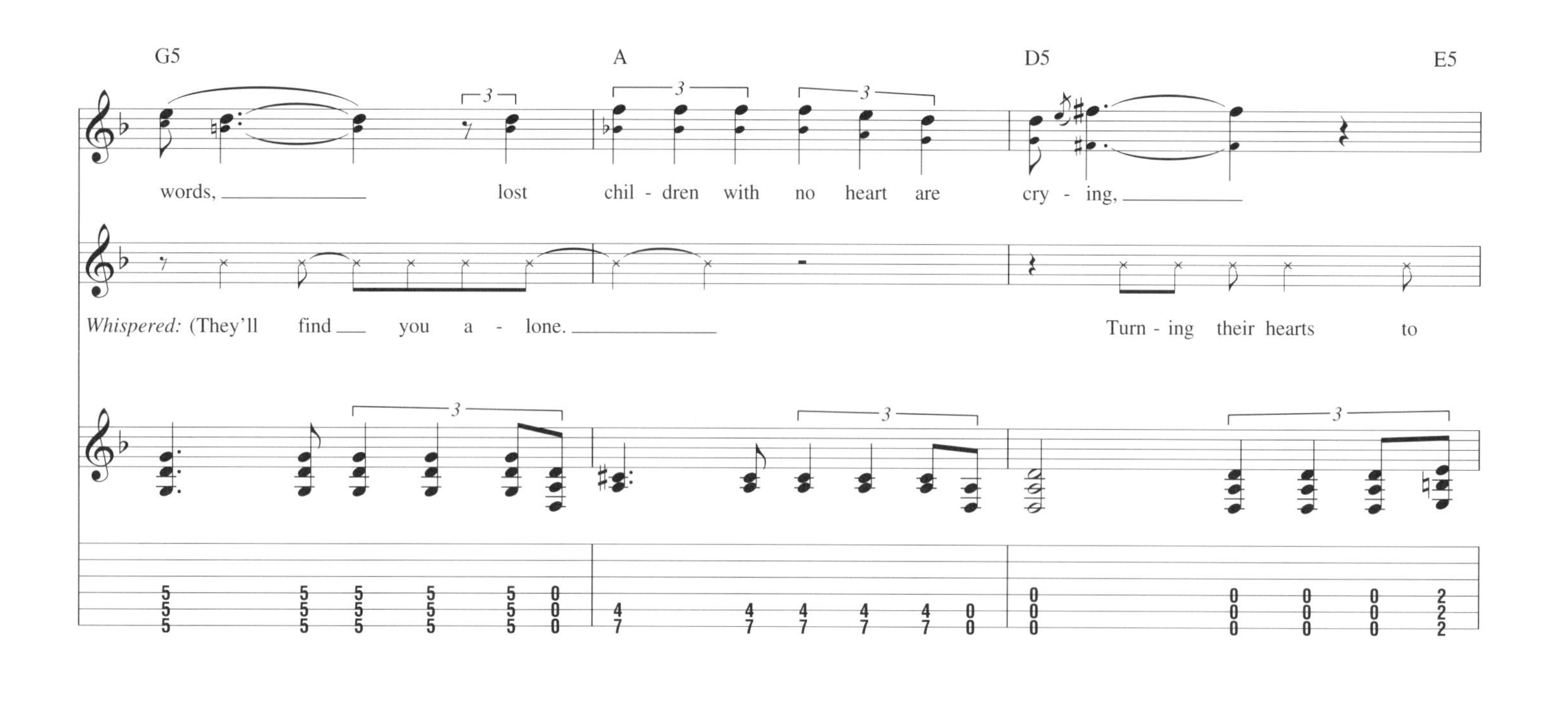
G5
A
D5
E5
words, lost chil - dren with no heart are cry - ing,
Whispered: (They'll find you a - lone. Turn - ing their hearts to

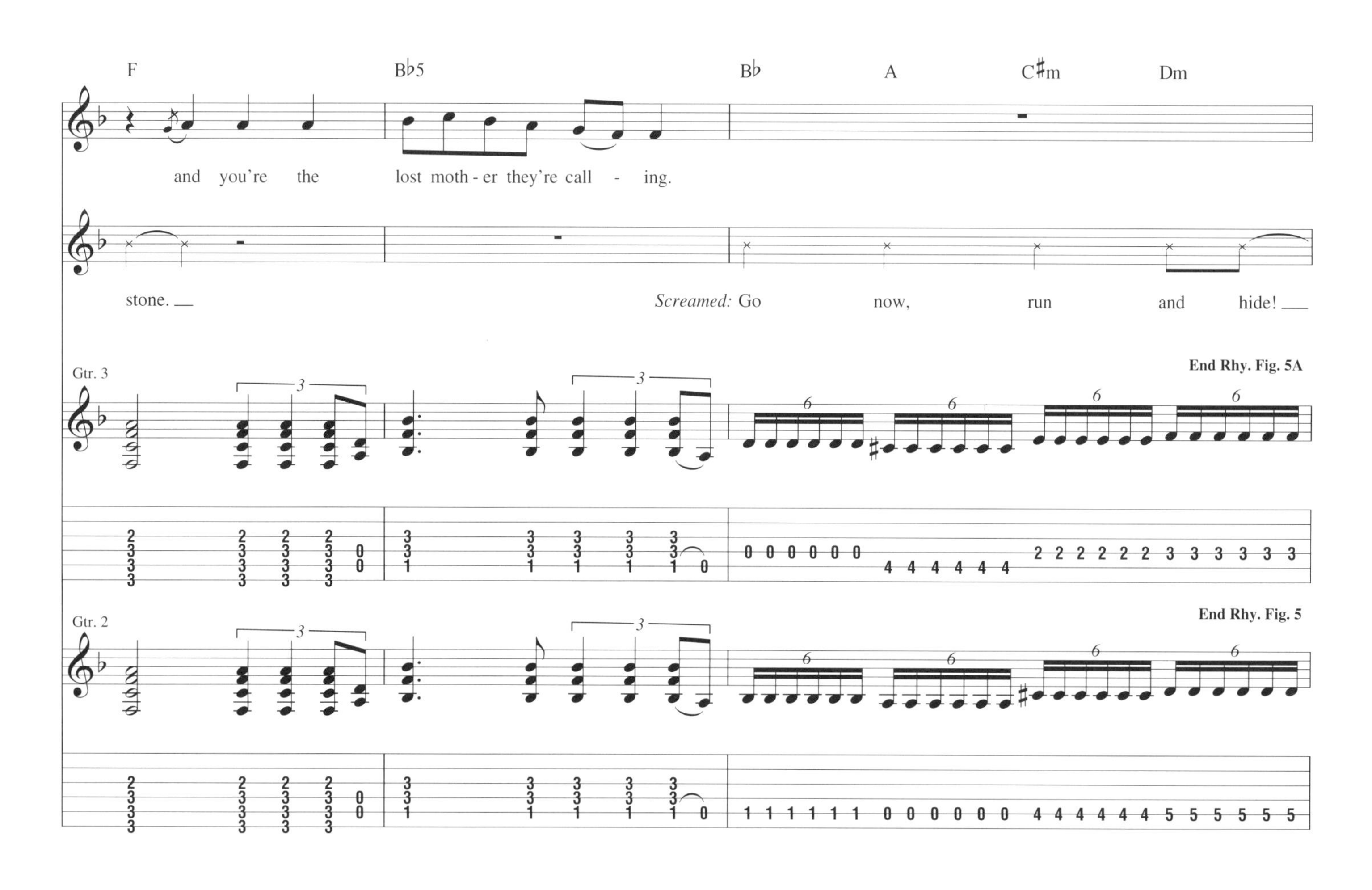
F
B♭5
B♭
A
C♯m
Dm
and you're the lost moth - er they're call - ing.
stone.
Screamed: Go now, run and hide!
Gtr. 3
End Rhy. Fig. 5A
Gtr. 2
End Rhy. Fig. 5

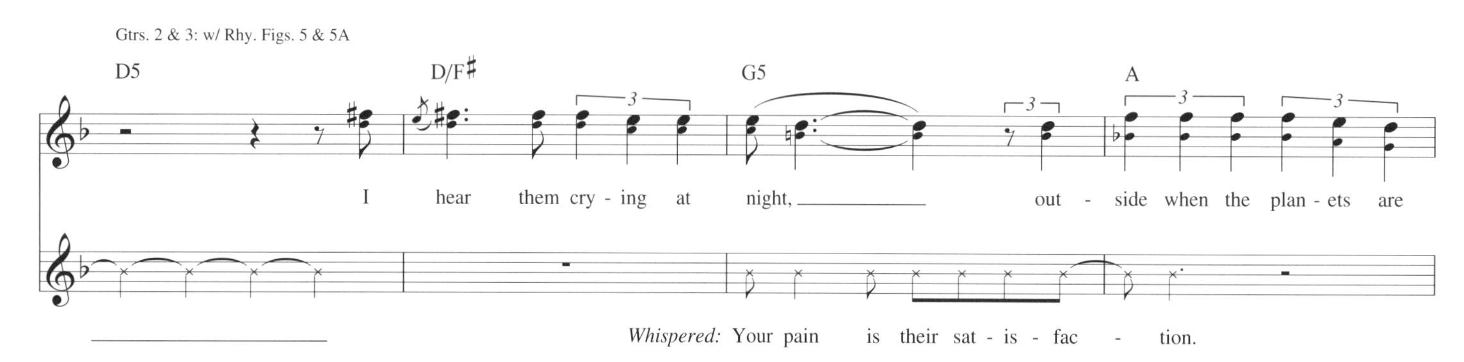
Gtrs. 2 & 3: w/ Rhy. Figs. 5 & 5A
D5
D/F♯
G5
A
I hear them cry - ing at night, out - side when the plan - ets are
Whispered: Your pain is their sat - is - fac - tion.

D.S. al Coda
End half-time feel
D5
E5 F
B♭5
B♭ A C♯m Dm
fall - ing.
They want to feel and know you hear them.
For the rest of time.
Go now, run and hide.)

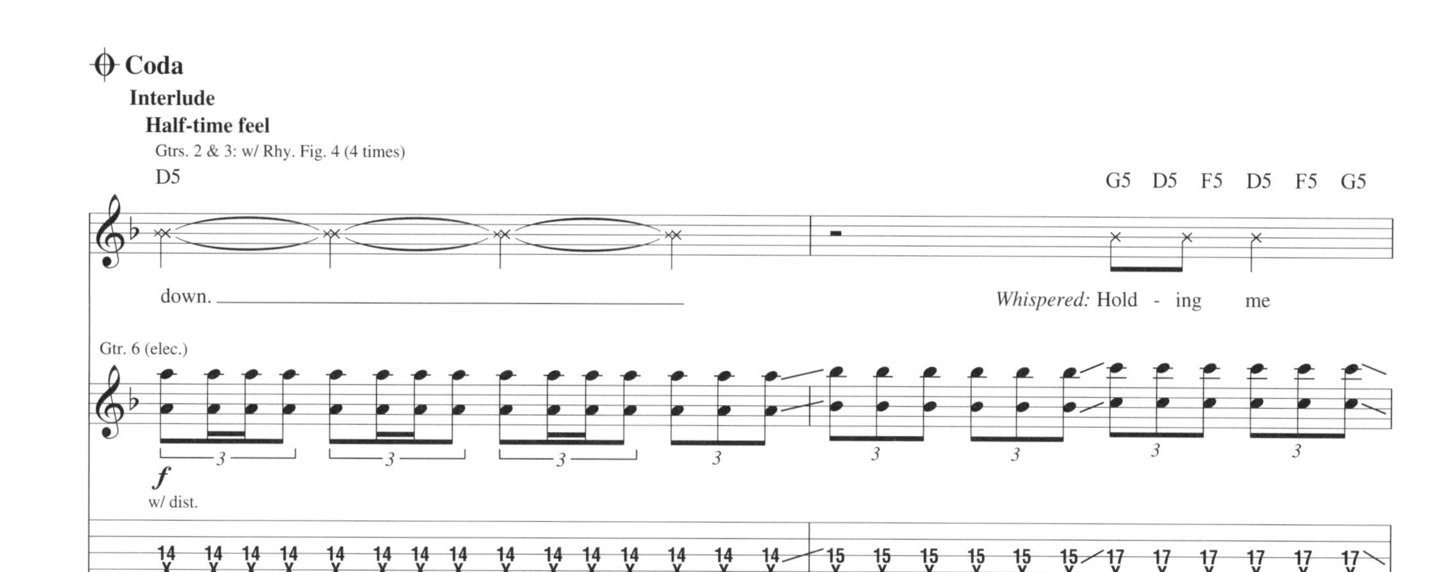
Coda
Interlude
Half-time feel
Gtrs. 2 & 3: w/ Rhy. Fig. 4 (4 times)
D5
G5 D5 F5 D5 F5 G5
down.
Whispered: Hold - ing me
Gtr. 6 (elec.)
f
w/ dist.

D5
G5 D5 F5 D5 F5 G5 D5
down.
Screamed: Hold - ing,

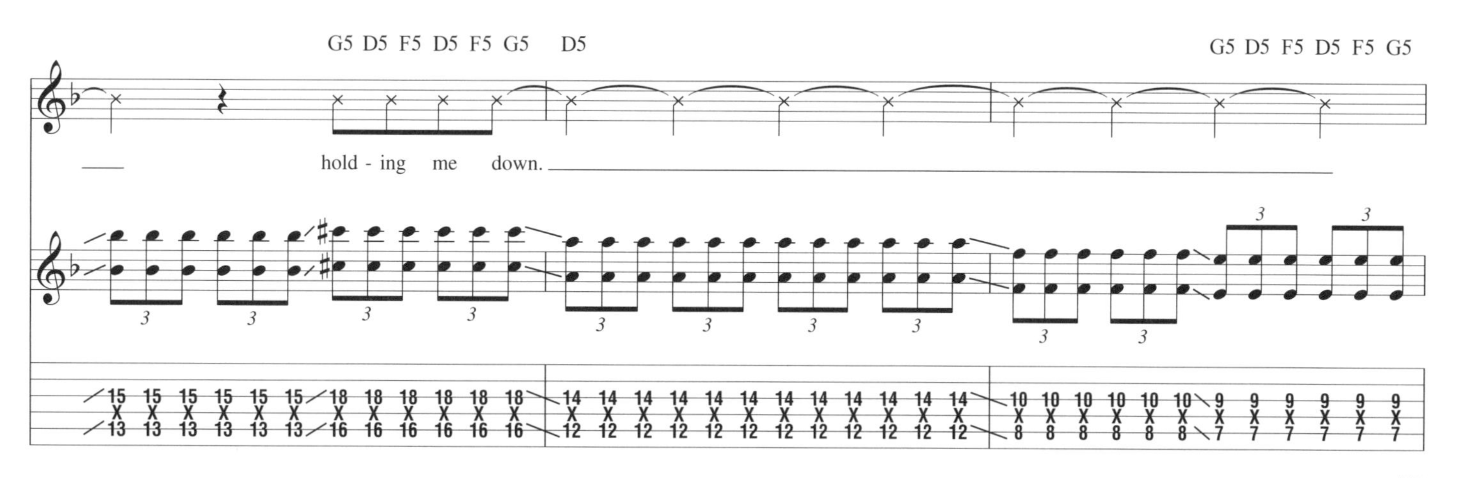
G5 D5 F5 D5 F5 G5 D5
G5 D5 F5 D5 F5 G5
hold - ing me down.

Gtr. 2: w/ Riff B
Gtr. 3: w/ Riff B1
Gtr. 6 tacet

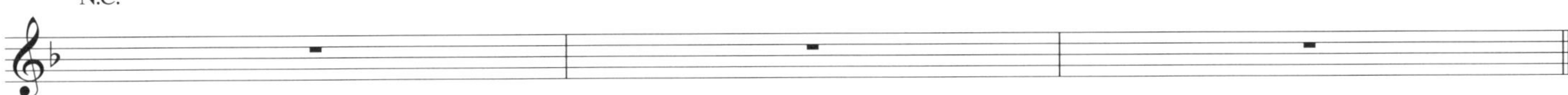

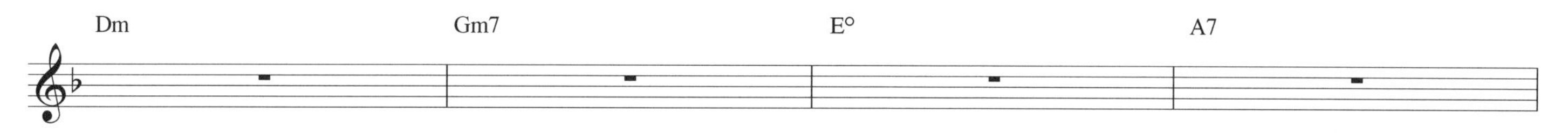
Gtrs. 2, 3 & 7: w/ Riffs C, C1 & C2 (3 times)
Dm
Gm7
E°
A7

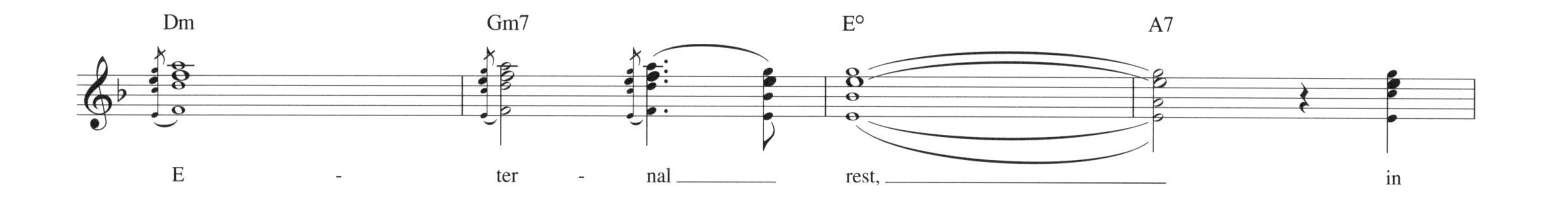
Dm
Gm7
E°
A7
E - ter - nal rest, in

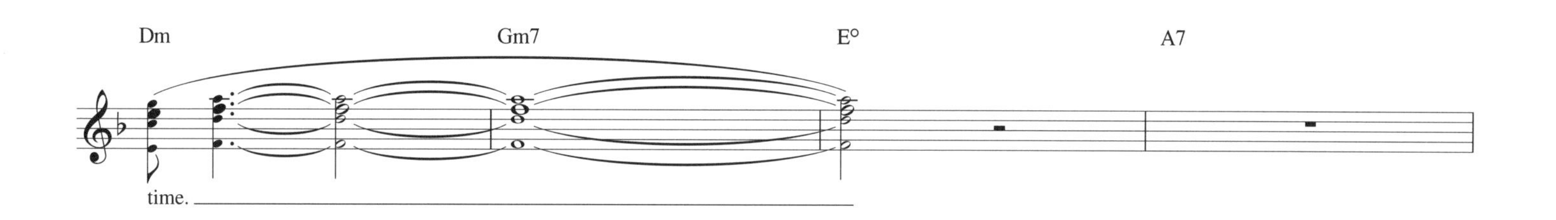
Dm
Gm7
E°
A7
time.

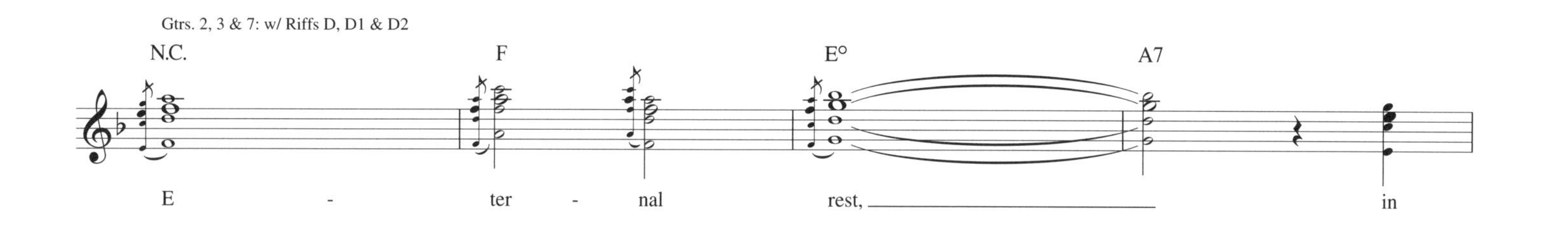
Gtrs. 2, 3 & 7: w/ Riffs D, D1 & D2
N.C.
F
E°
A7
E - ter - nal rest, in

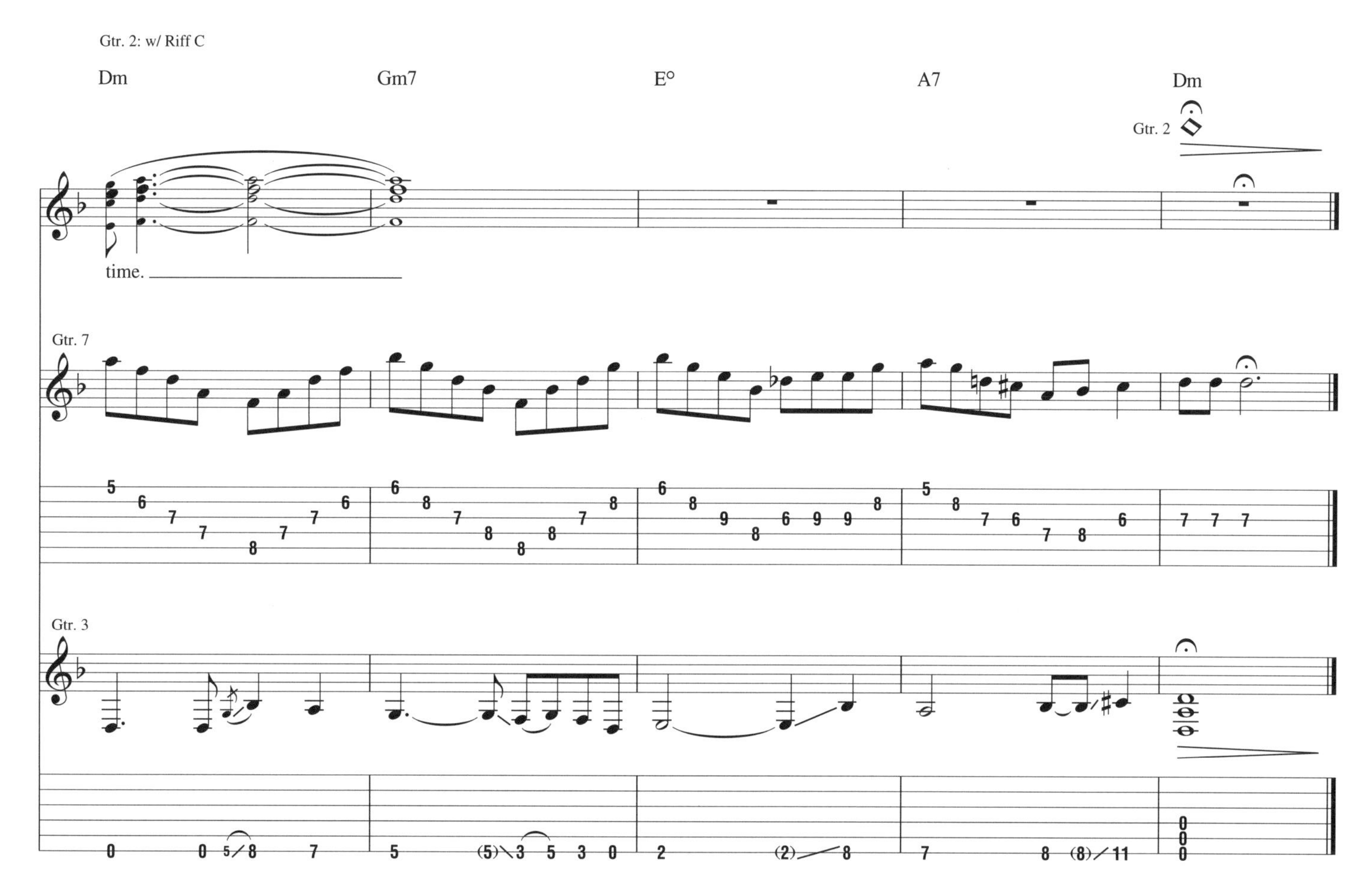
Gtr. 2: w/ Riff C
Dm
Gm7
E°
A7
Dm
Gtr. 2
time.
Gtr. 7
Gtr. 3

Second Heartbeat

Words and Music by Matthew Sanders, James Sullivan, Brian Haner, Jr. and Zachary Baker

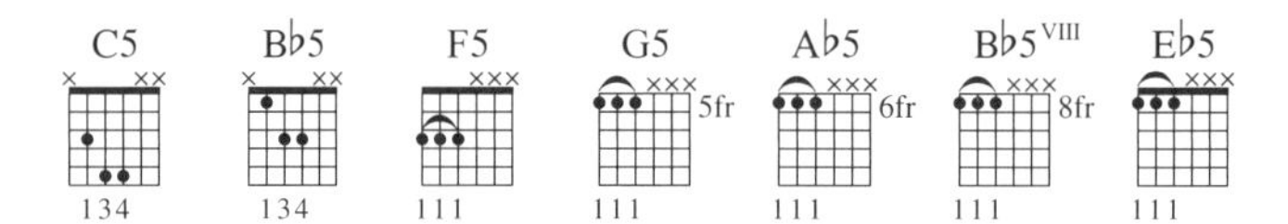

Gtrs. 1-7: Drop D tuning:
(low to high) D-A-D-G-B-E

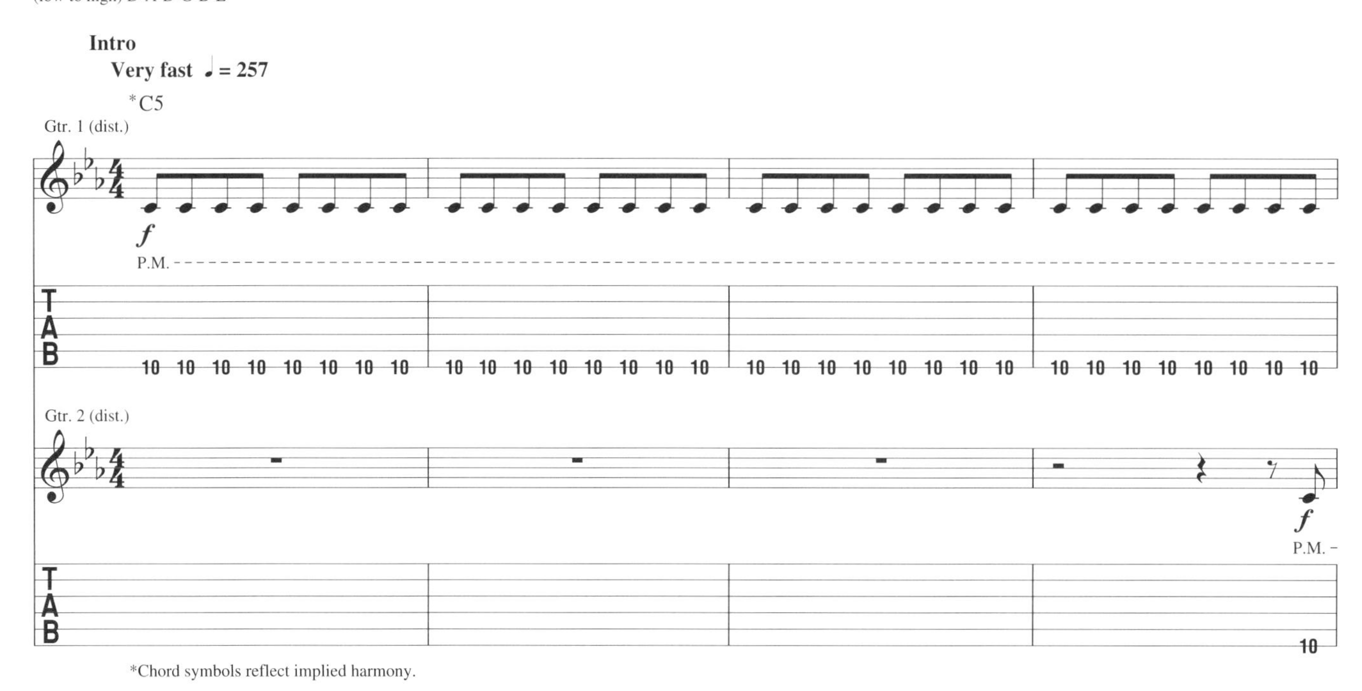

*Chord symbols reflect implied harmony.

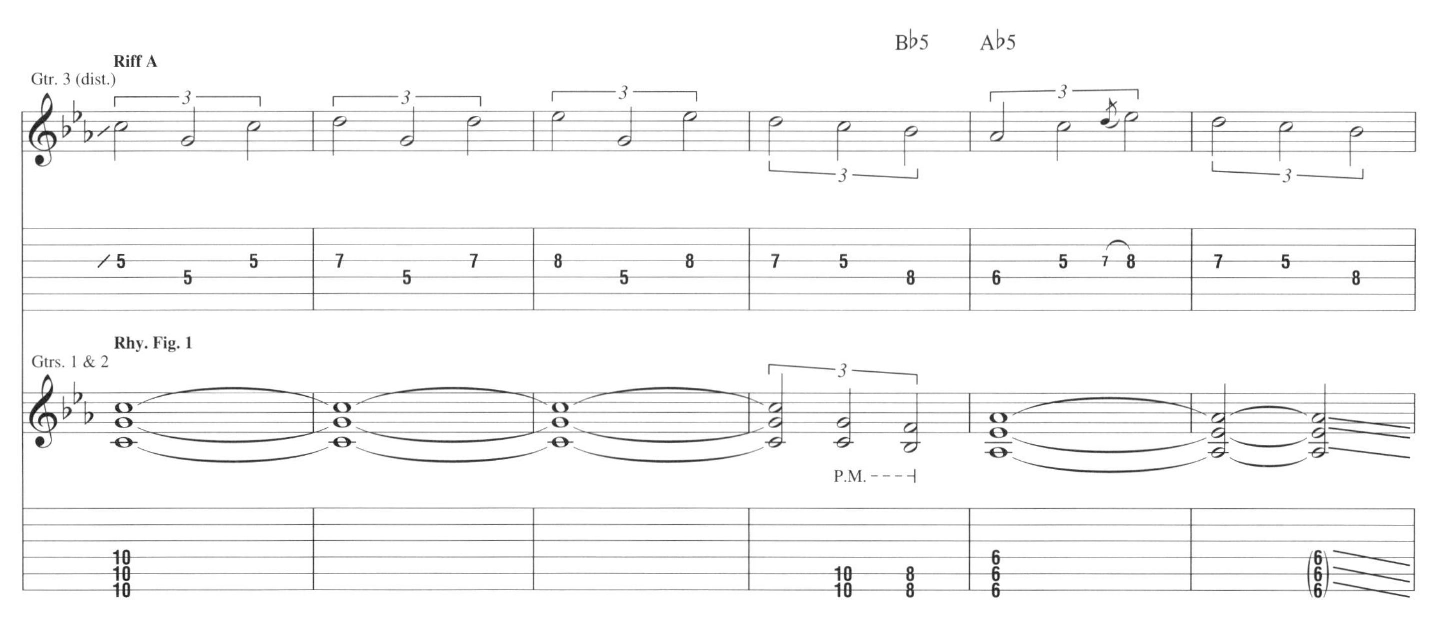

Gtrs. 1 & 2: w/ Rhy. Fig. 1
Gtr. 3: w/ Riff A
F5
G5
C5
End Riff A
Gtr. 4 (dist.)
End Rhy. Fig. 1

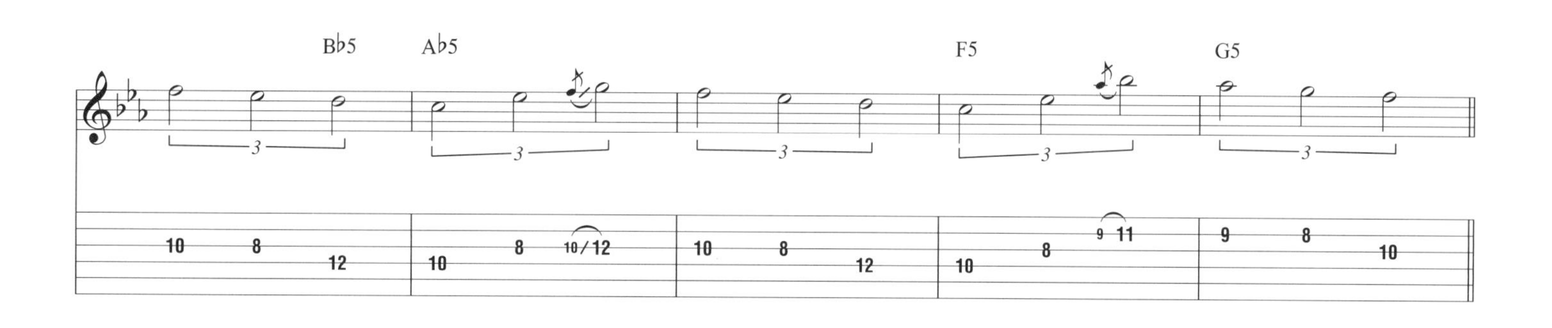
B♭5
A♭5
F5
G5

C5
Gtr. 4
Riff B1
Gtr. 3
Riff B
Gtrs. 1 & 2
P.M.

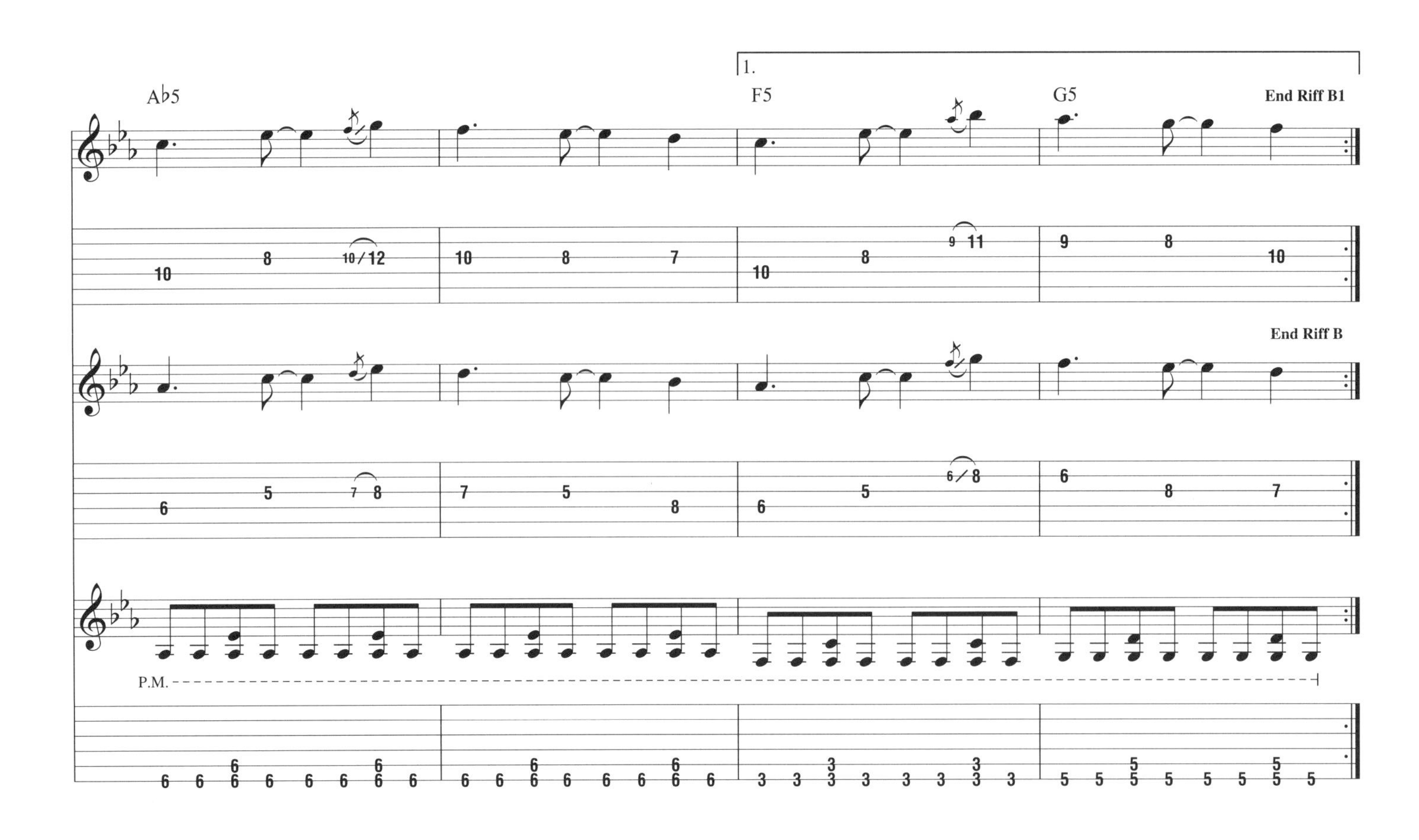
1.
A♭5
F5
G5
End Riff B1
End Riff B
P.M.

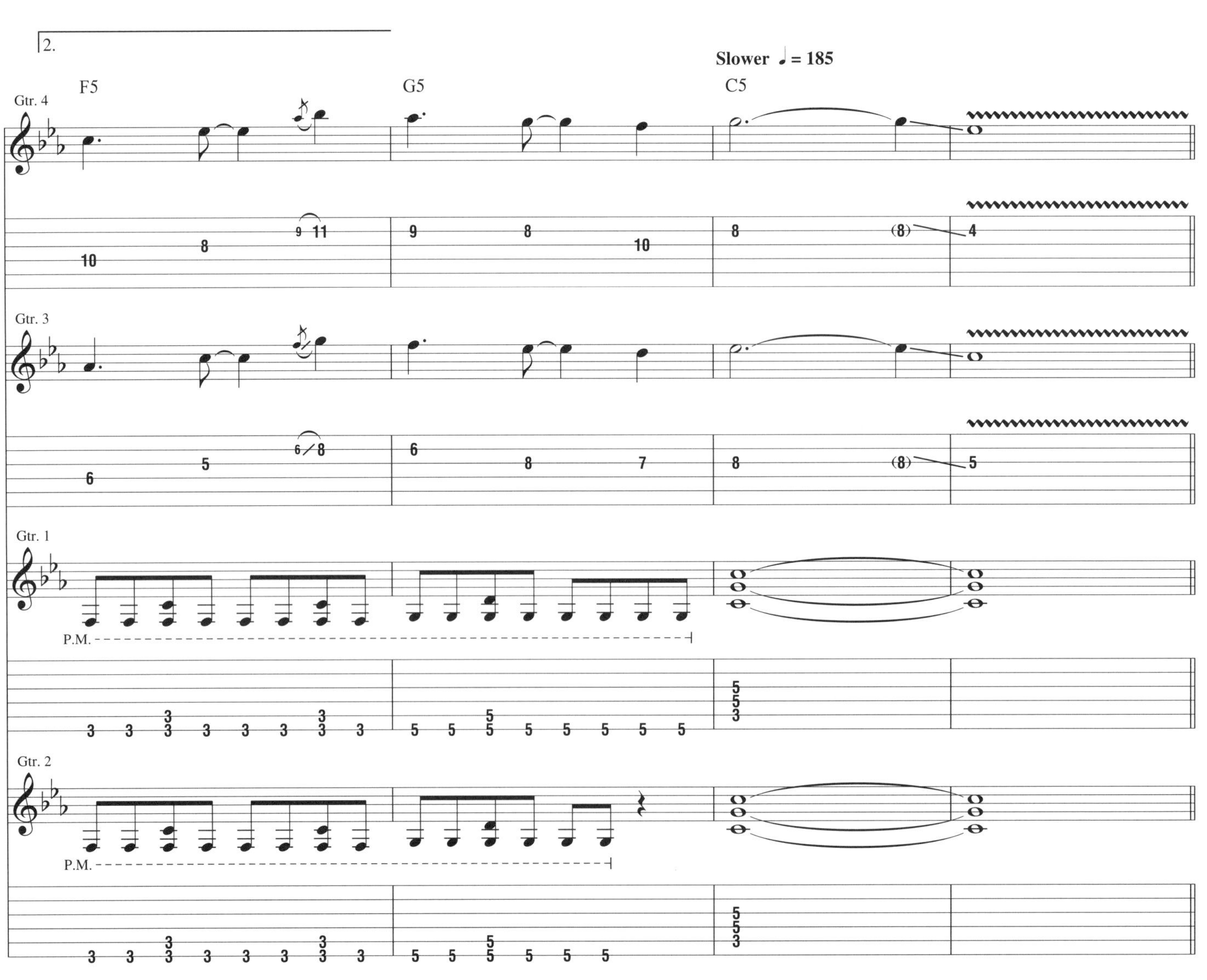
2.
Slower ♩ = 185
F5
G5
C5
Gtr. 4
Gtr. 3
Gtr. 1
P.M.
Gtr. 2
P.M.

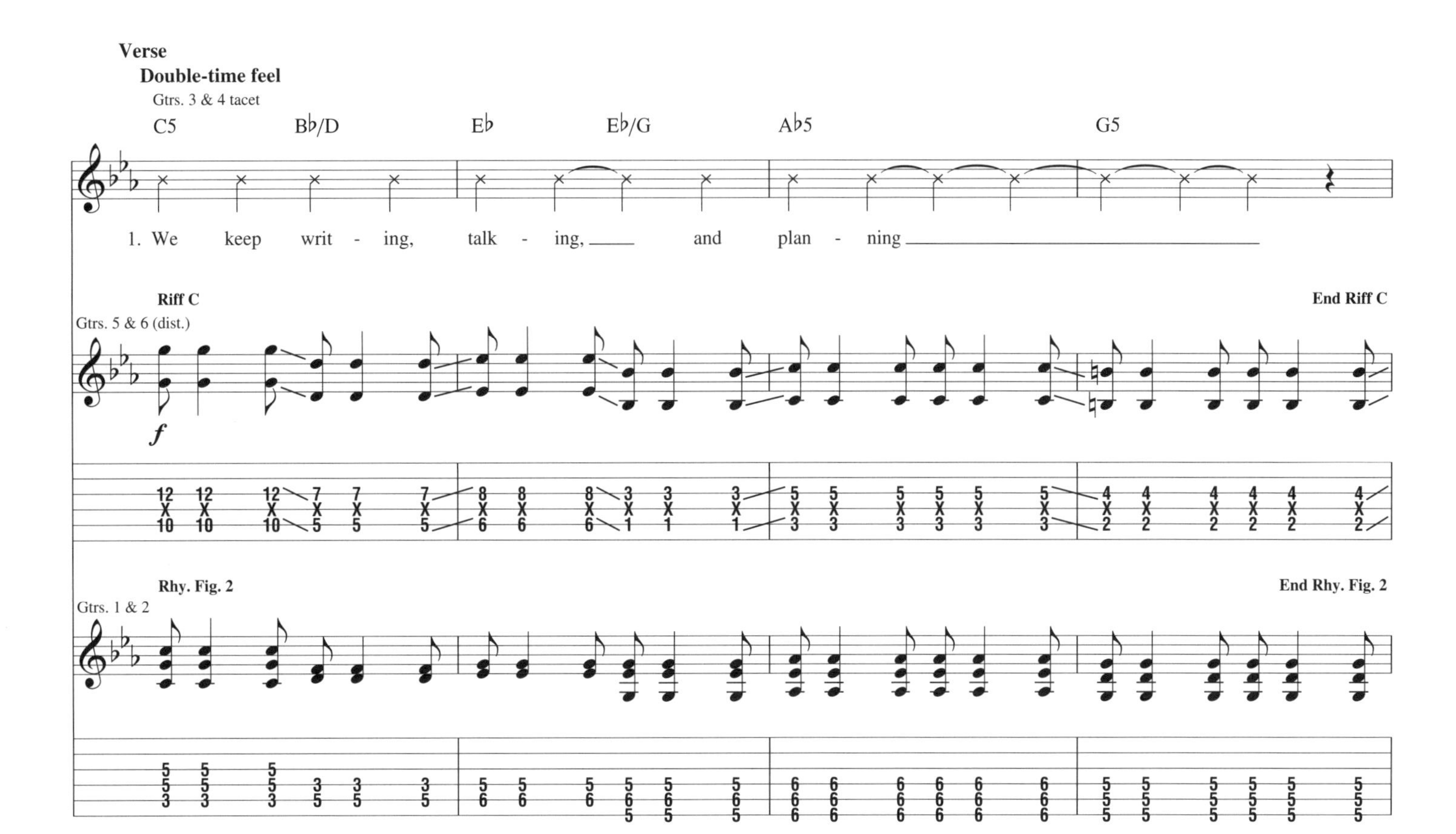
Verse
Double-time feel
Gtrs. 3 & 4 tacet
C5
B♭/D
E♭
E♭/G
A♭5
G5
1. We keep writ - ing, talk - ing, and plan - ning
Riff C
End Riff C
Gtrs. 5 & 6 (dist.)
Rhy. Fig. 2
End Rhy. Fig. 2
Gtrs. 1 & 2

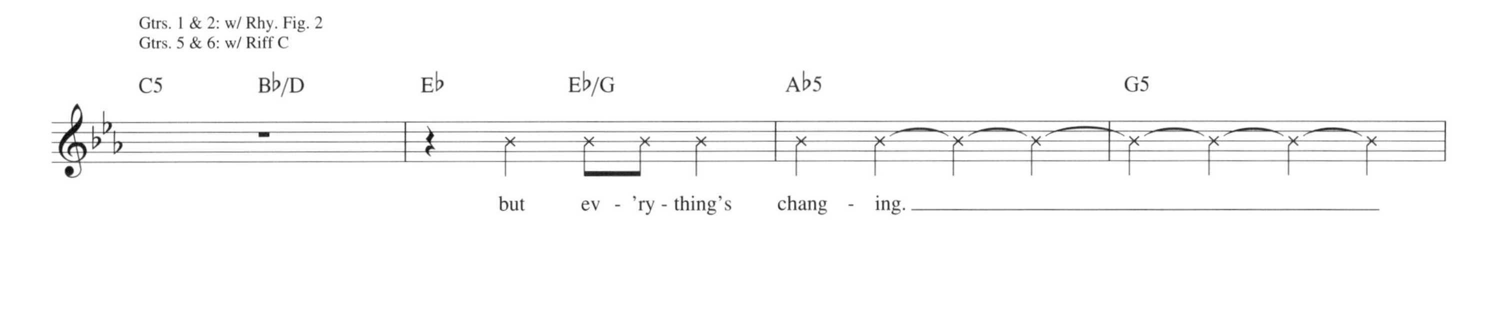
Gtrs. 1 & 2: w/ Rhy. Fig. 2
Gtrs. 5 & 6: w/ Riff C
C5
B♭/D
E♭
E♭/G
A♭5
G5
but ev - 'ry - thing's chang - ing.

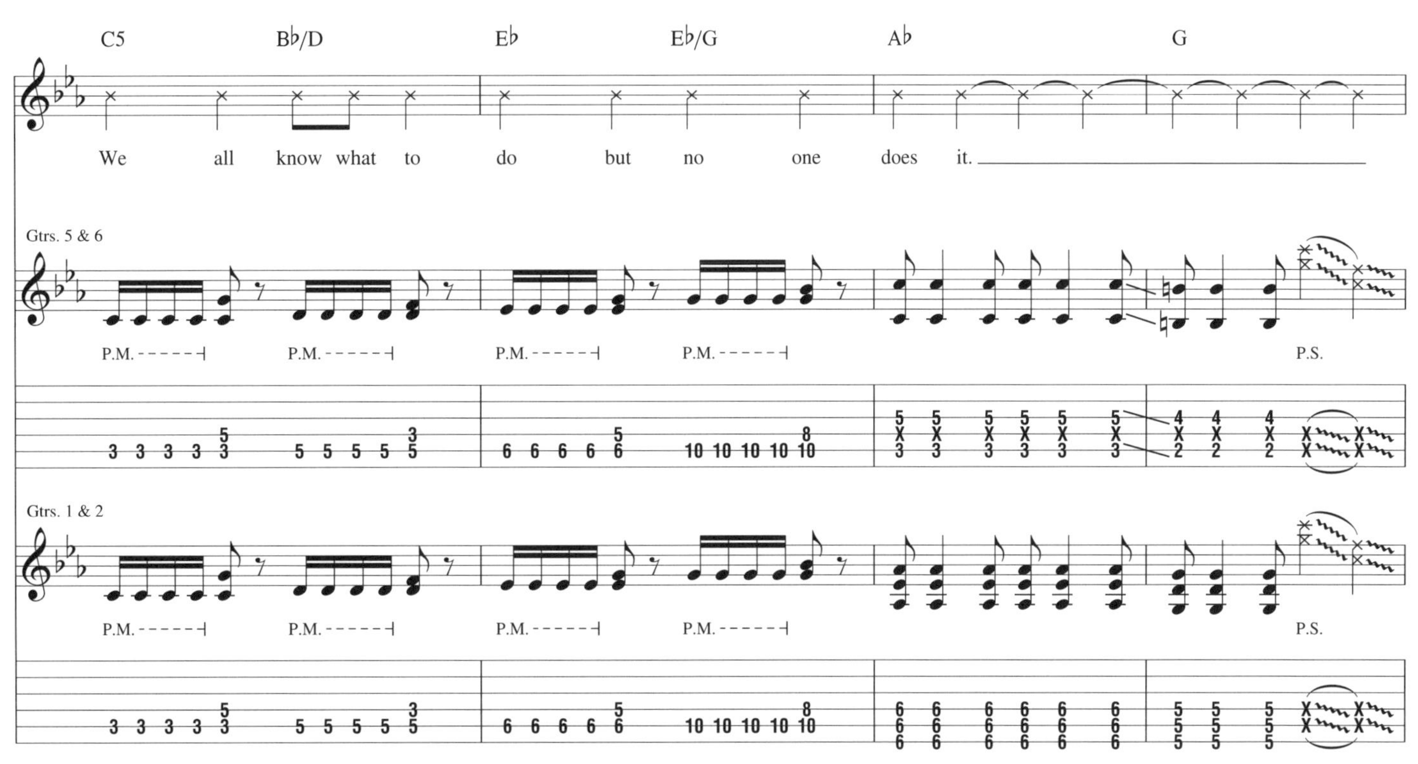
C5
B♭/D
E♭
E♭/G
A♭
G
We all know what to do but no one does it.
Gtrs. 5 & 6
P.M.
P.S.
Gtrs. 1 & 2
P.M.
P.S.

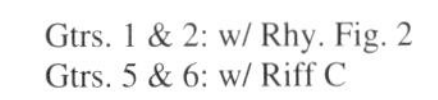

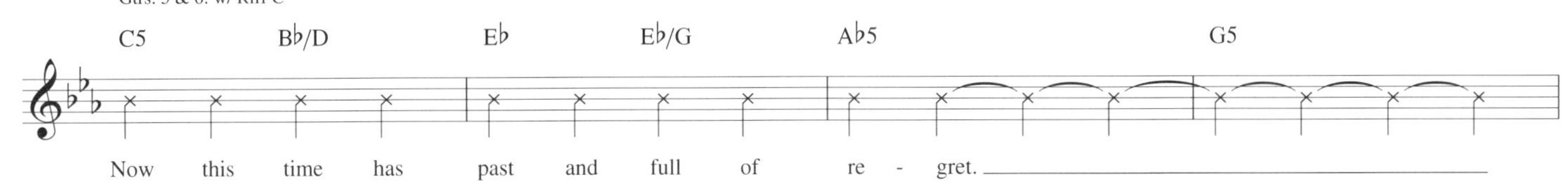

Bridge

End double-time feel Half-time feel

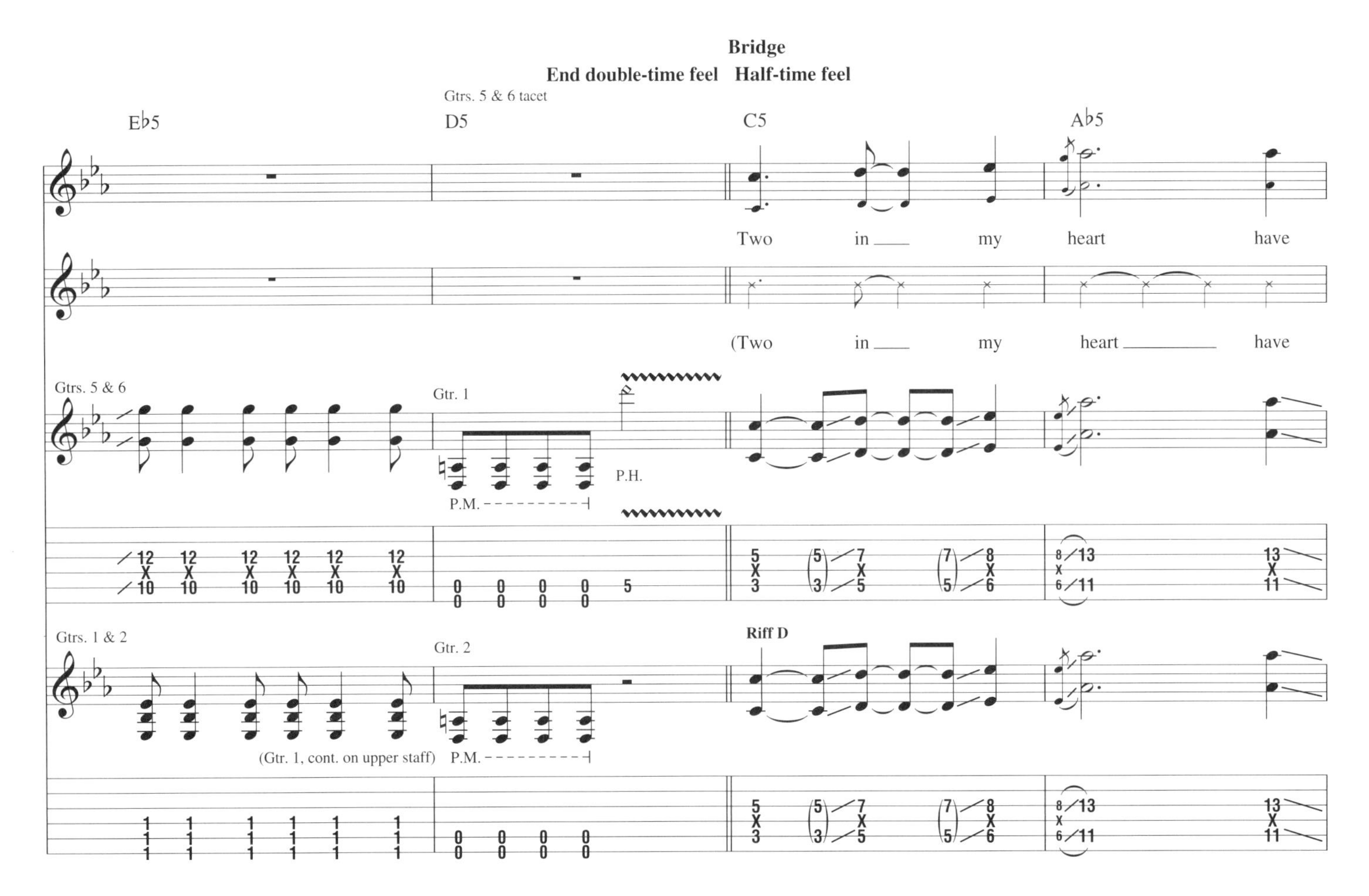

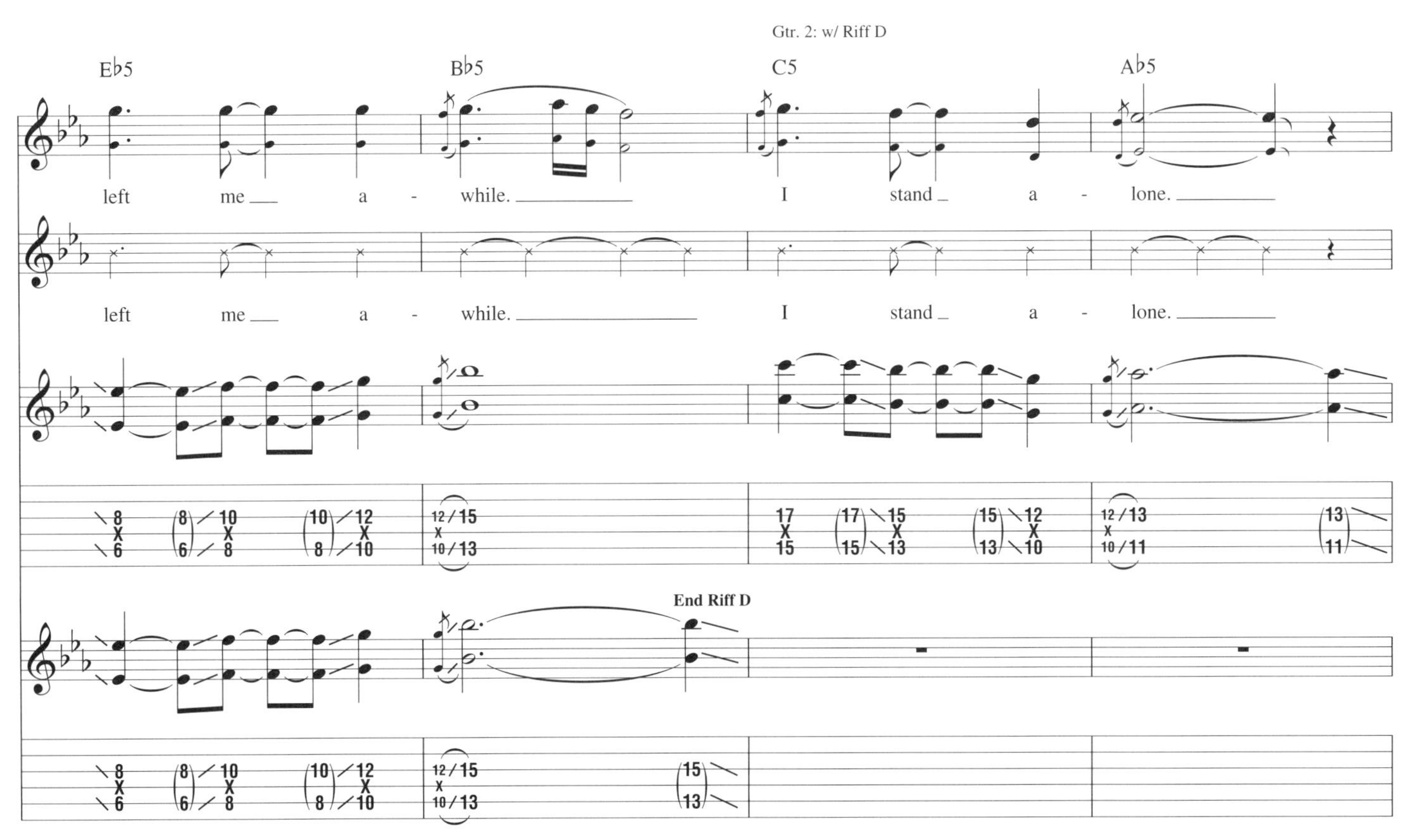

Interlude

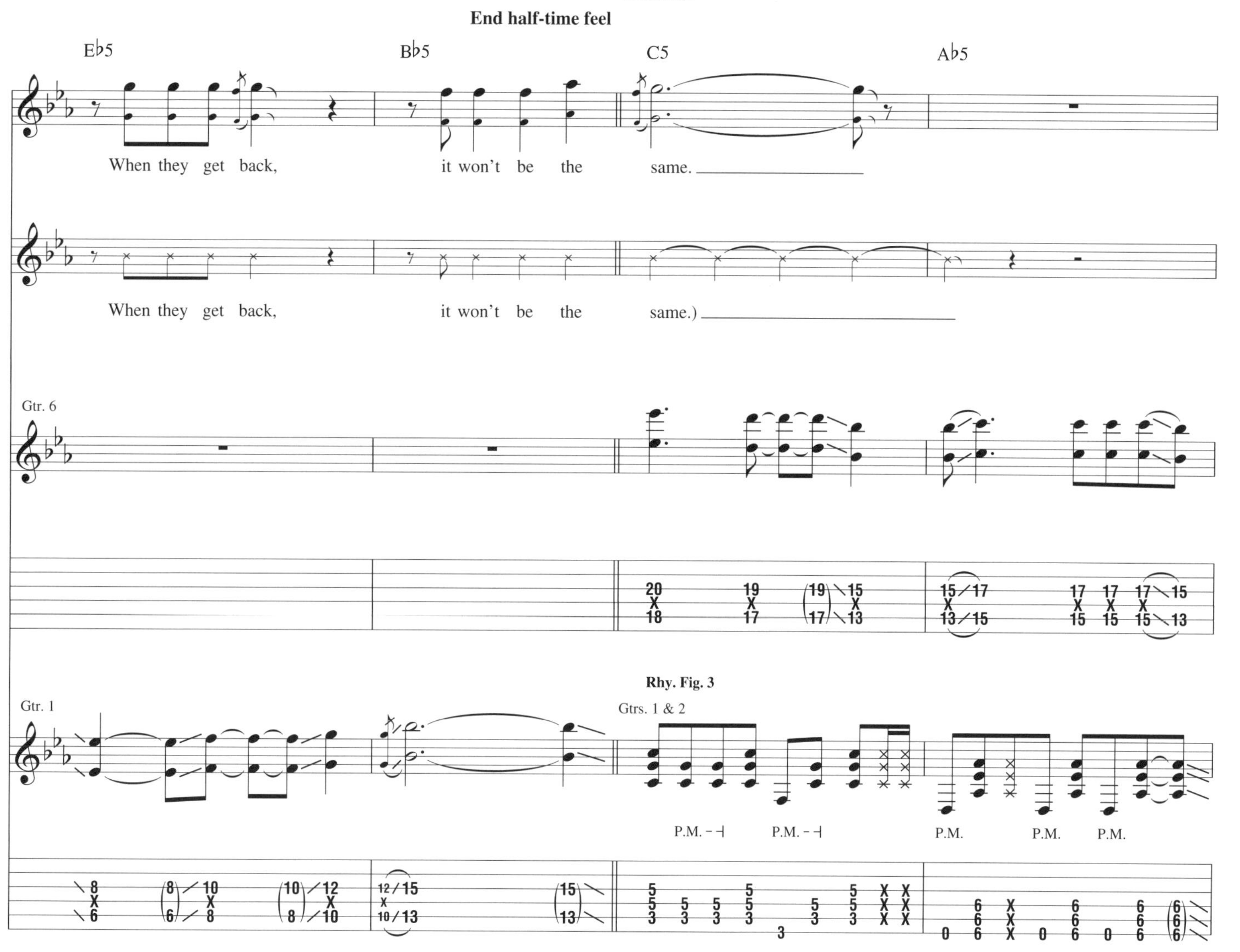
End half-time feel
Eb5
Bb5
C5
Ab5
When they get back, it won't be the same.
When they get back, it won't be the same.)
Gtr. 6
Gtr. 1
Rhy. Fig. 3
Gtrs. 1 & 2
P.M.
P.M.
P.M.
P.M.
P.M.

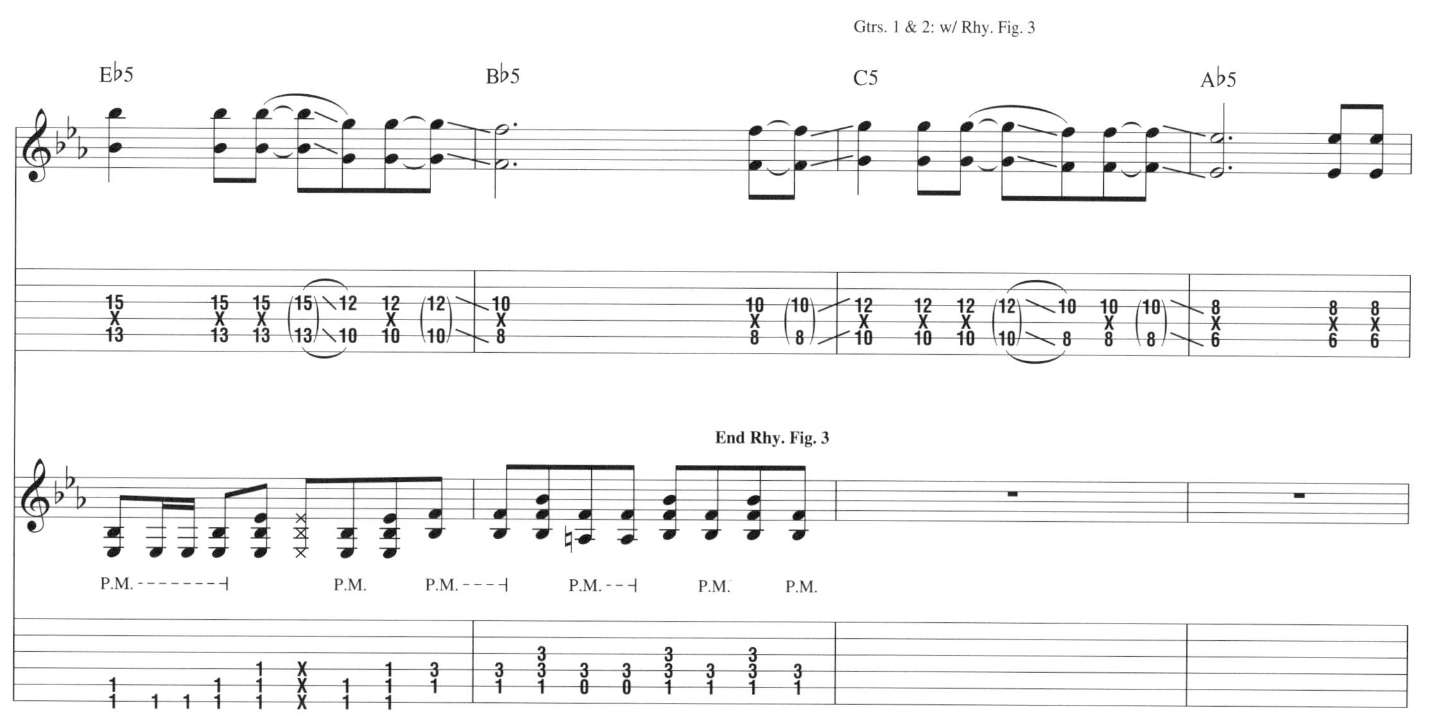
Gtrs. 1 & 2: w/ Rhy. Fig. 3
Eb5
Bb5
C5
Ab5
End Rhy. Fig. 3
P.M.
P.M.
P.M.
P.M.
P.M.
P.M.

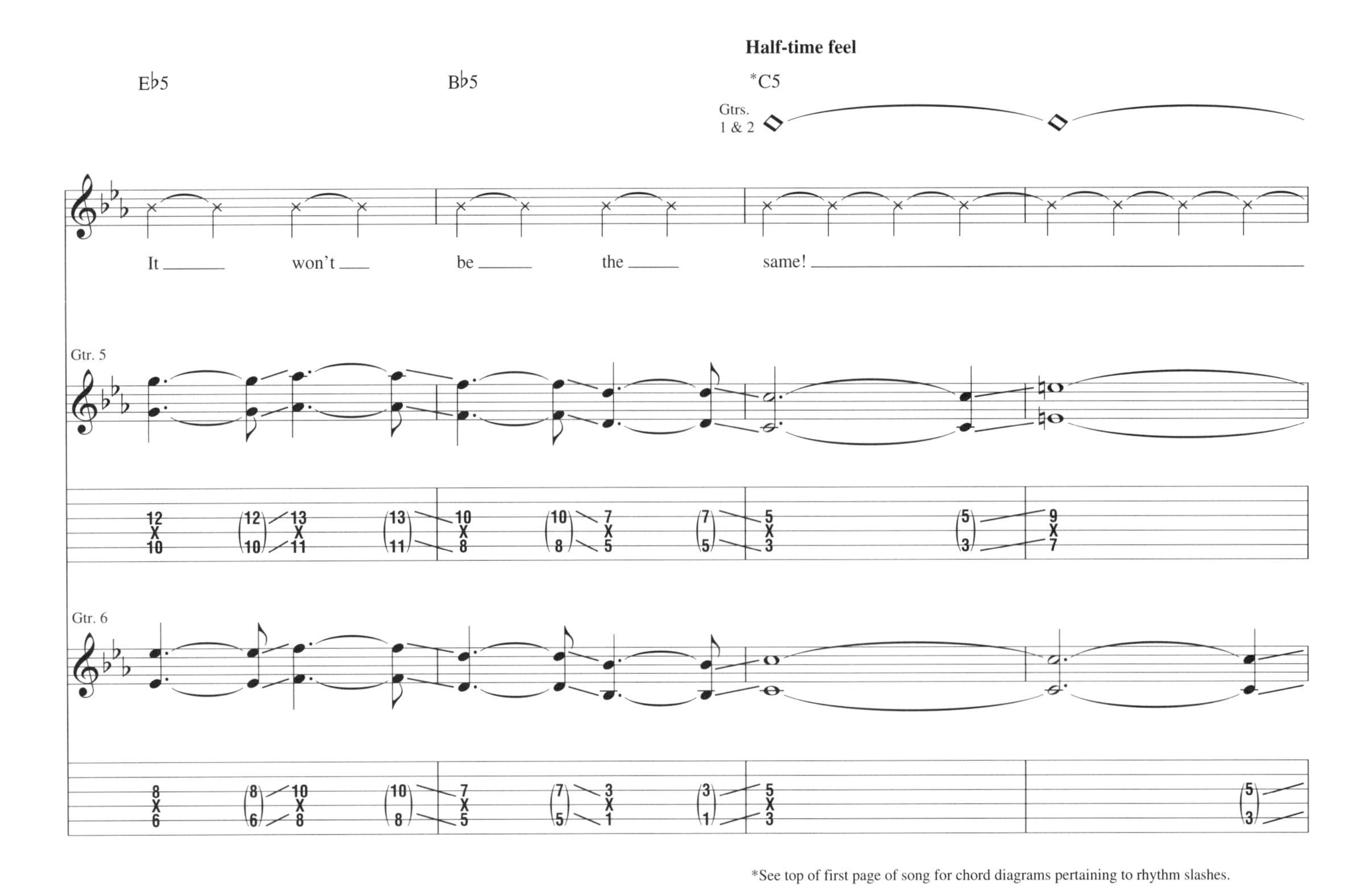

*See top of first page of song for chord diagrams pertaining to rhythm slashes.

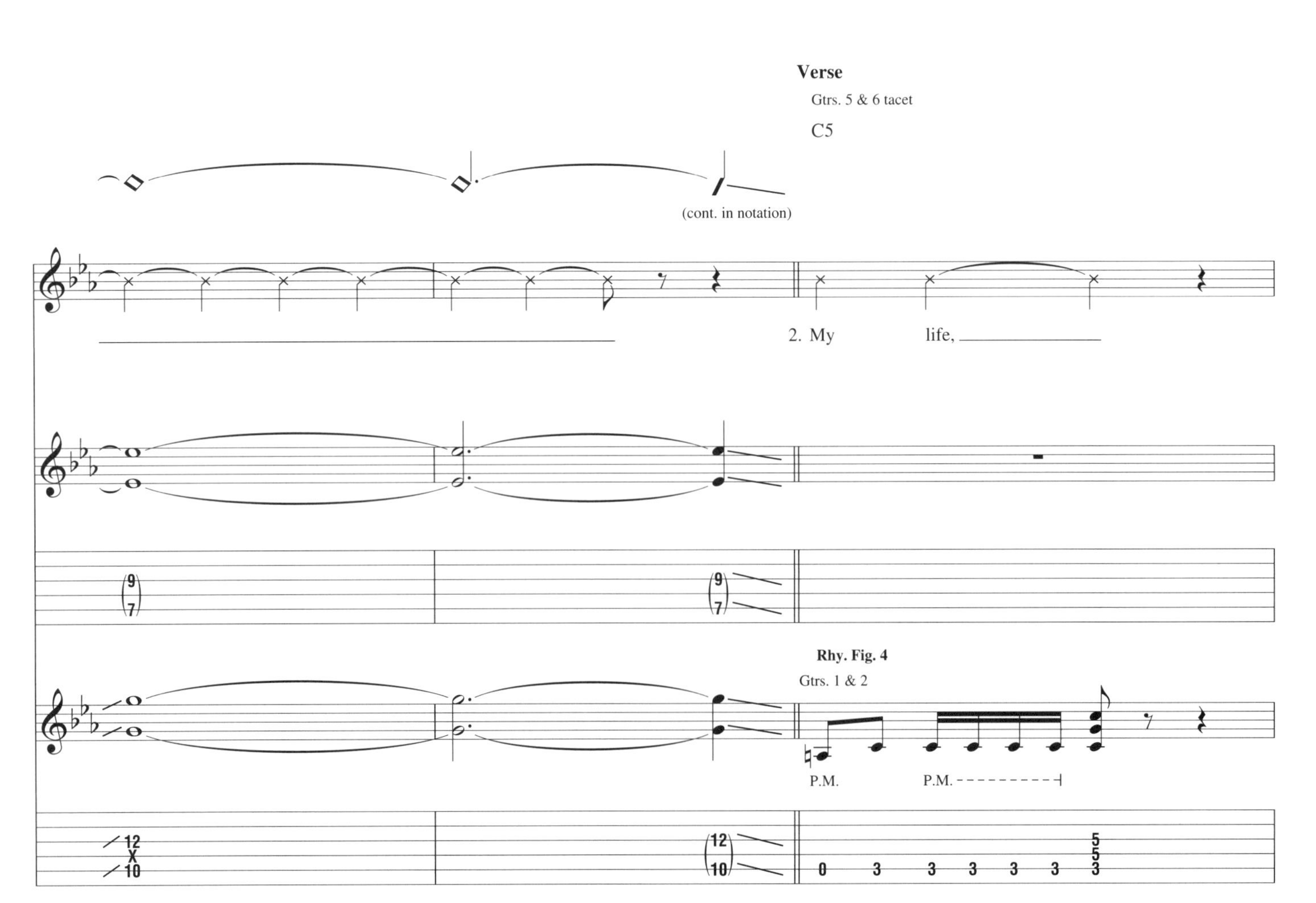

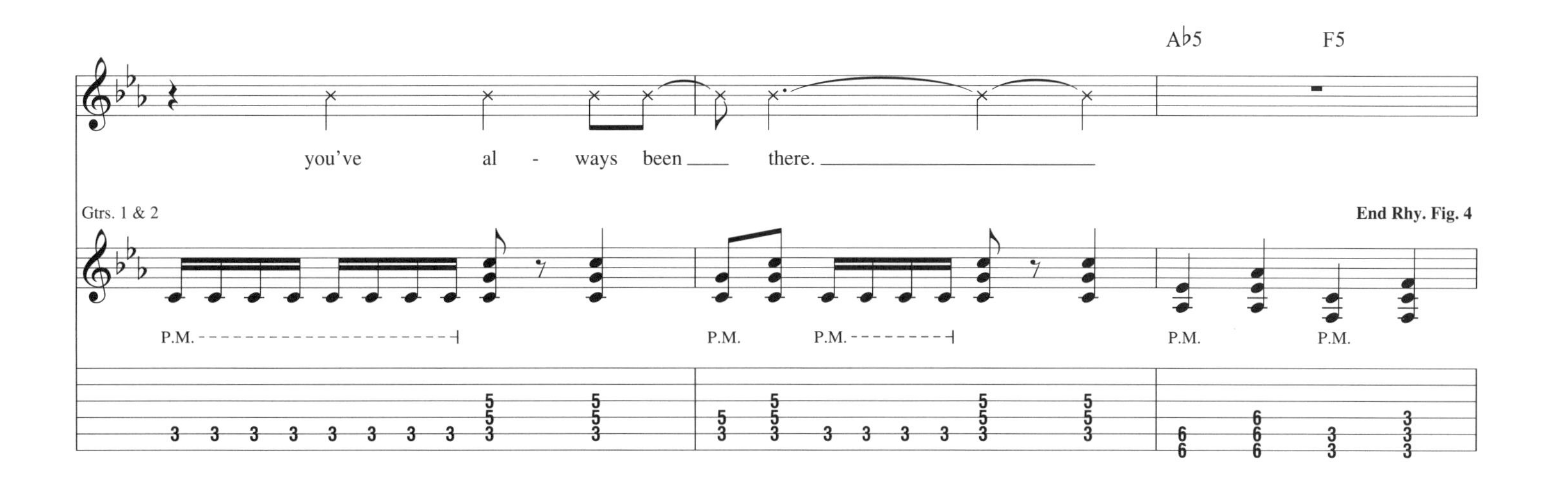
Ab5
F5
you've al - ways been there.
Gtrs. 1 & 2
End Rhy. Fig. 4
P.M.
P.M.
P.M.
P.M.
P.M.

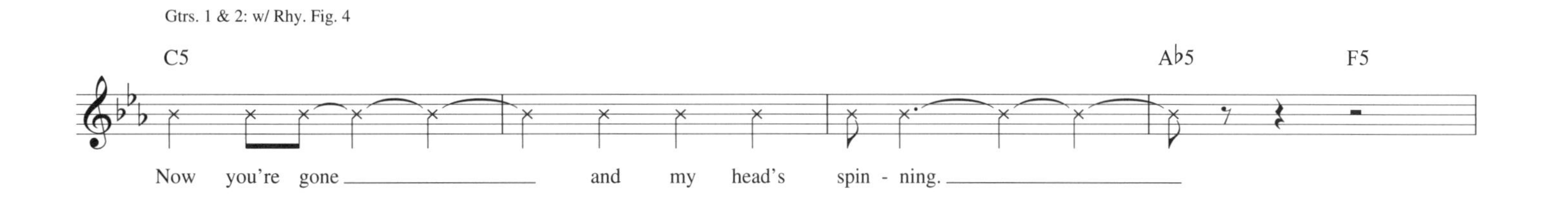
Gtrs. 1 & 2: w/ Rhy. Fig. 4
C5
Ab5
F5
Now you're gone and my head's spin - ning.

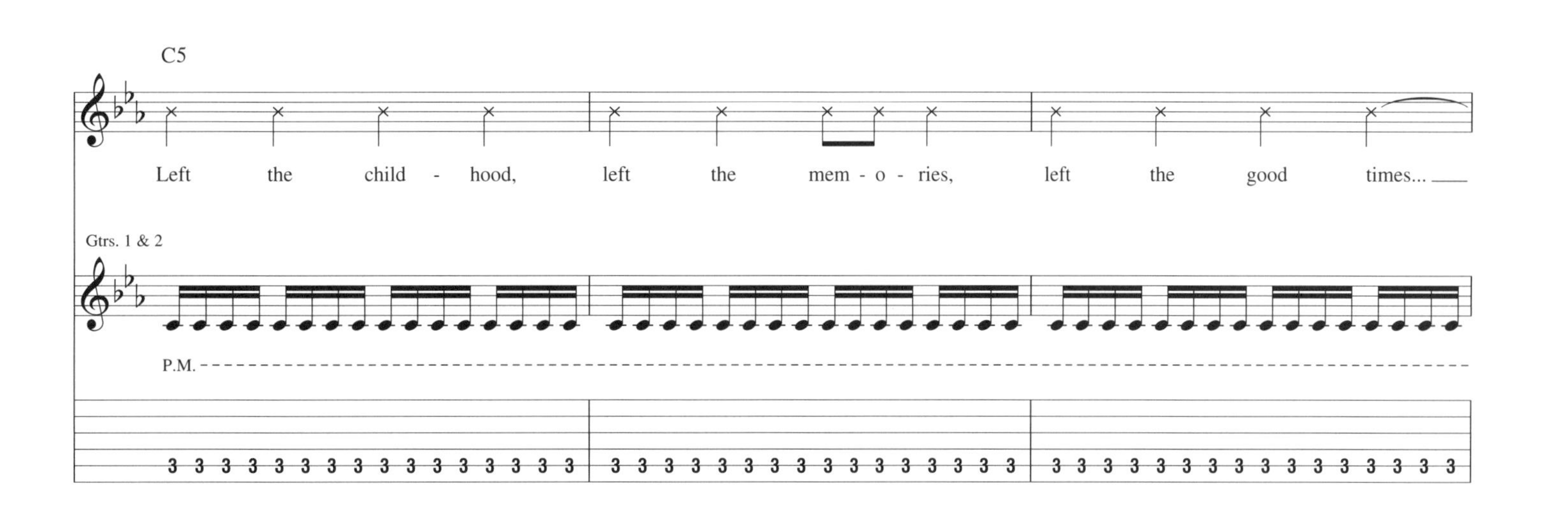
C5
Left the child - hood, left the mem - o - ries, left the good times...
Gtrs. 1 & 2
P.M.

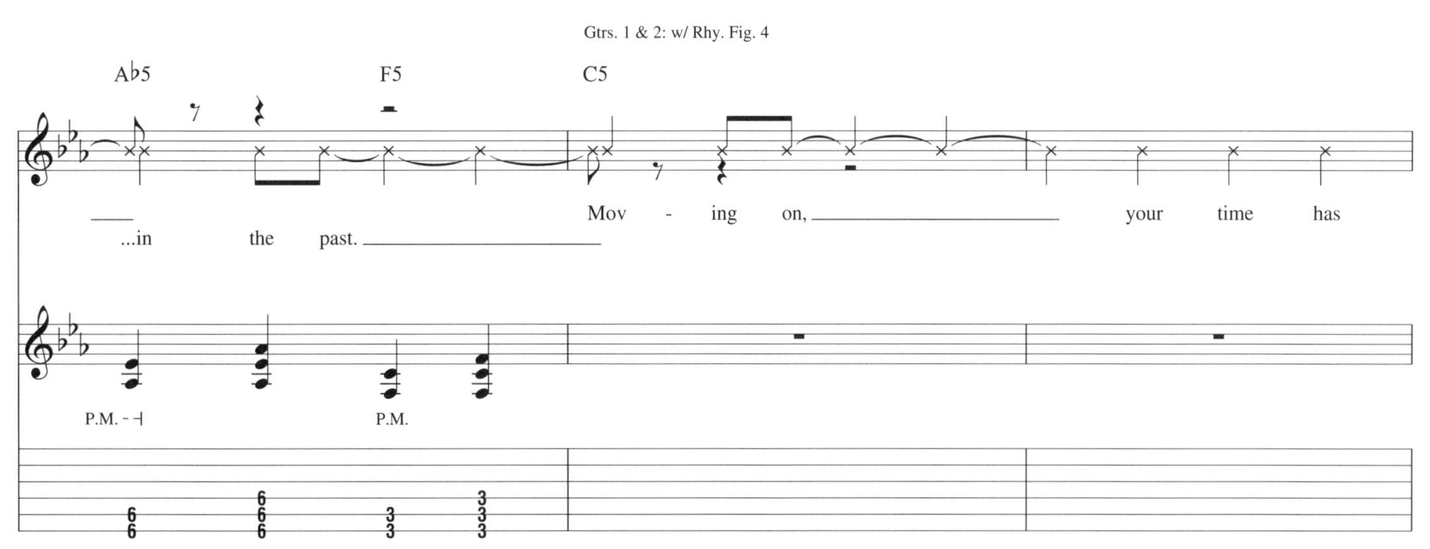
Gtrs. 1 & 2: w/ Rhy. Fig. 4
Ab5
F5
C5
Mov - ing on, your time has
...in the past.
P.M.
P.M.

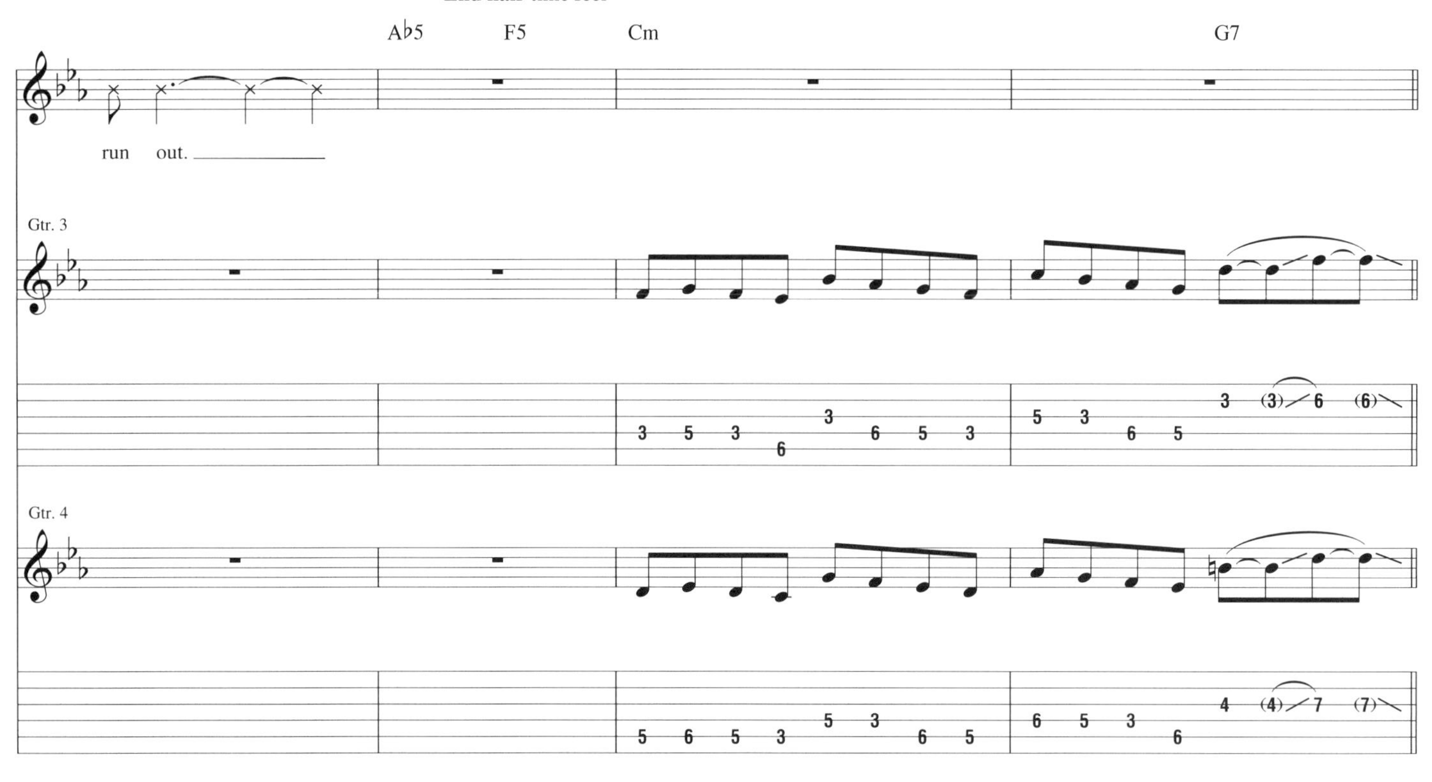
End half-time feel
A♭5
F5
Cm
G7
run out.
Gtr. 3
Gtr. 4

Bridge

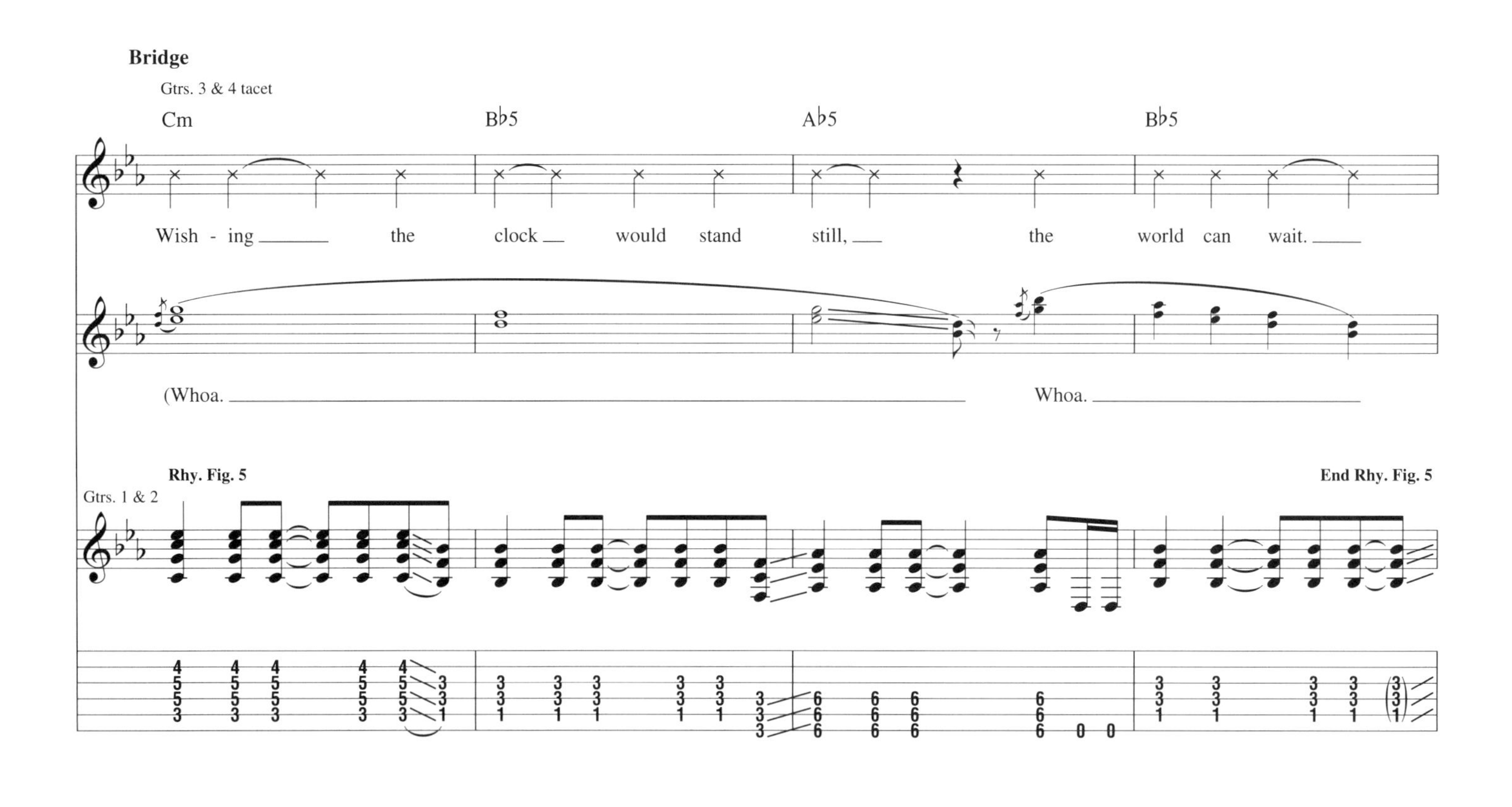
Gtrs. 3 & 4 tacet
Cm
B♭5
A♭5
B♭5
Wish - ing the clock would stand still, the world can wait.
(Whoa. Whoa.
Rhy. Fig. 5
End Rhy. Fig. 5
Gtrs. 1 & 2

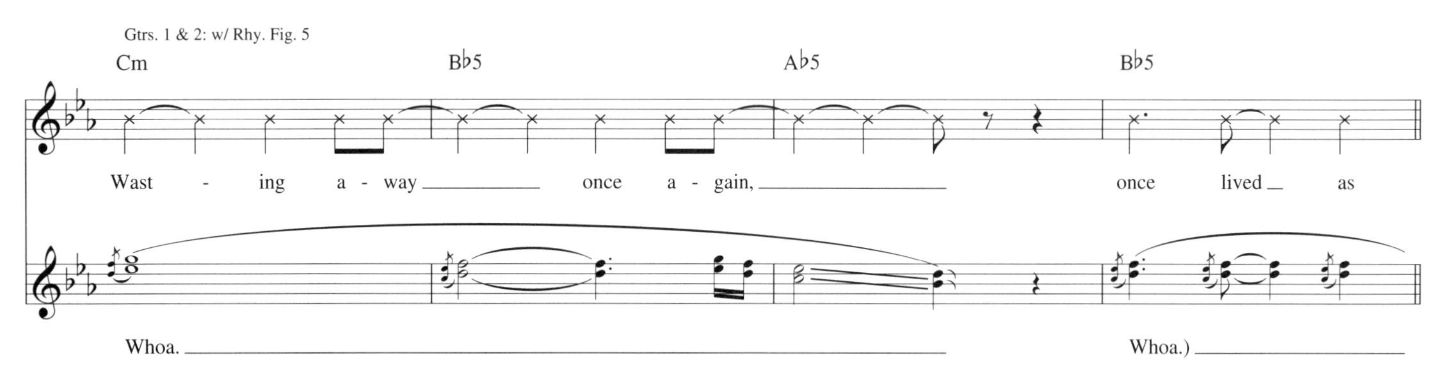
Gtrs. 1 & 2: w/ Rhy. Fig. 5
Cm
B♭5
A♭5
B♭5
Wast - ing a - way once a - gain, once lived as
Whoa. Whoa.)

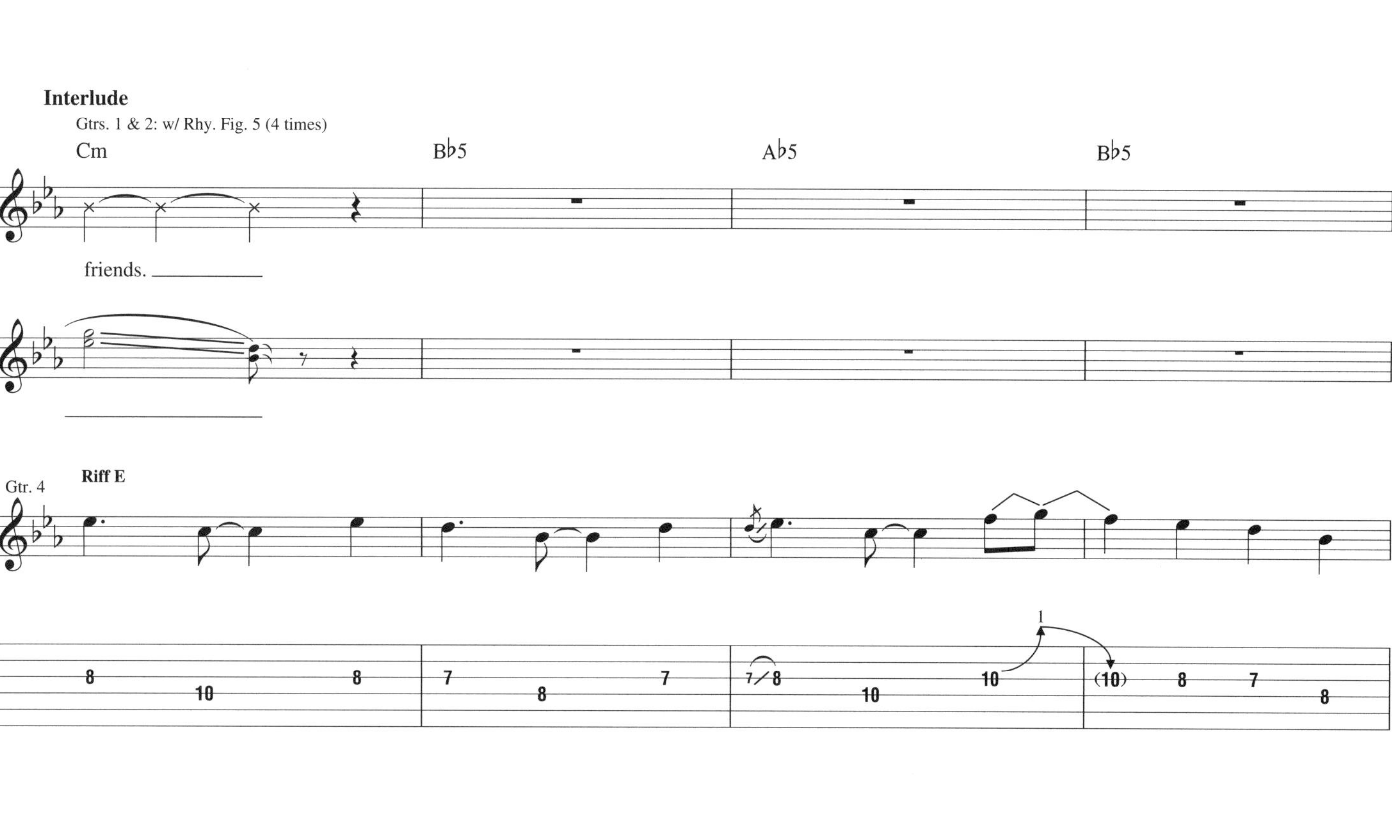
Interlude
Gtrs. 1 & 2: w/ Rhy. Fig. 5 (4 times)
Cm
B♭5
A♭5
B♭5
friends.
Riff E
Gtr. 4

Cm
B♭5
A♭5
B♭5
End Riff E
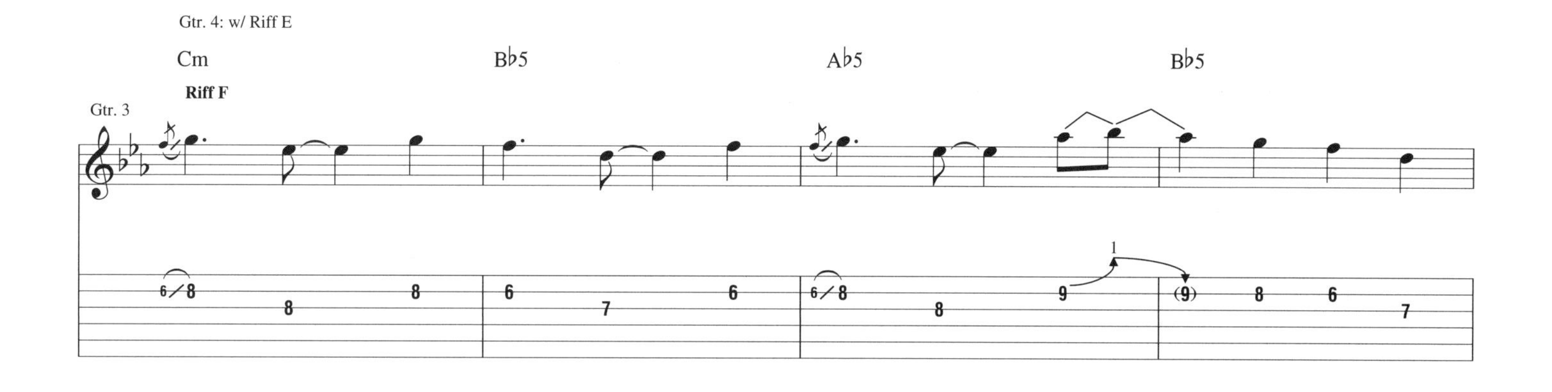
Gtr. 4: w/ Riff E
Cm
B♭5
A♭5
B♭5
Riff F
Gtr. 3

Cm
B♭5
A♭5
B♭5
As
End Riff F

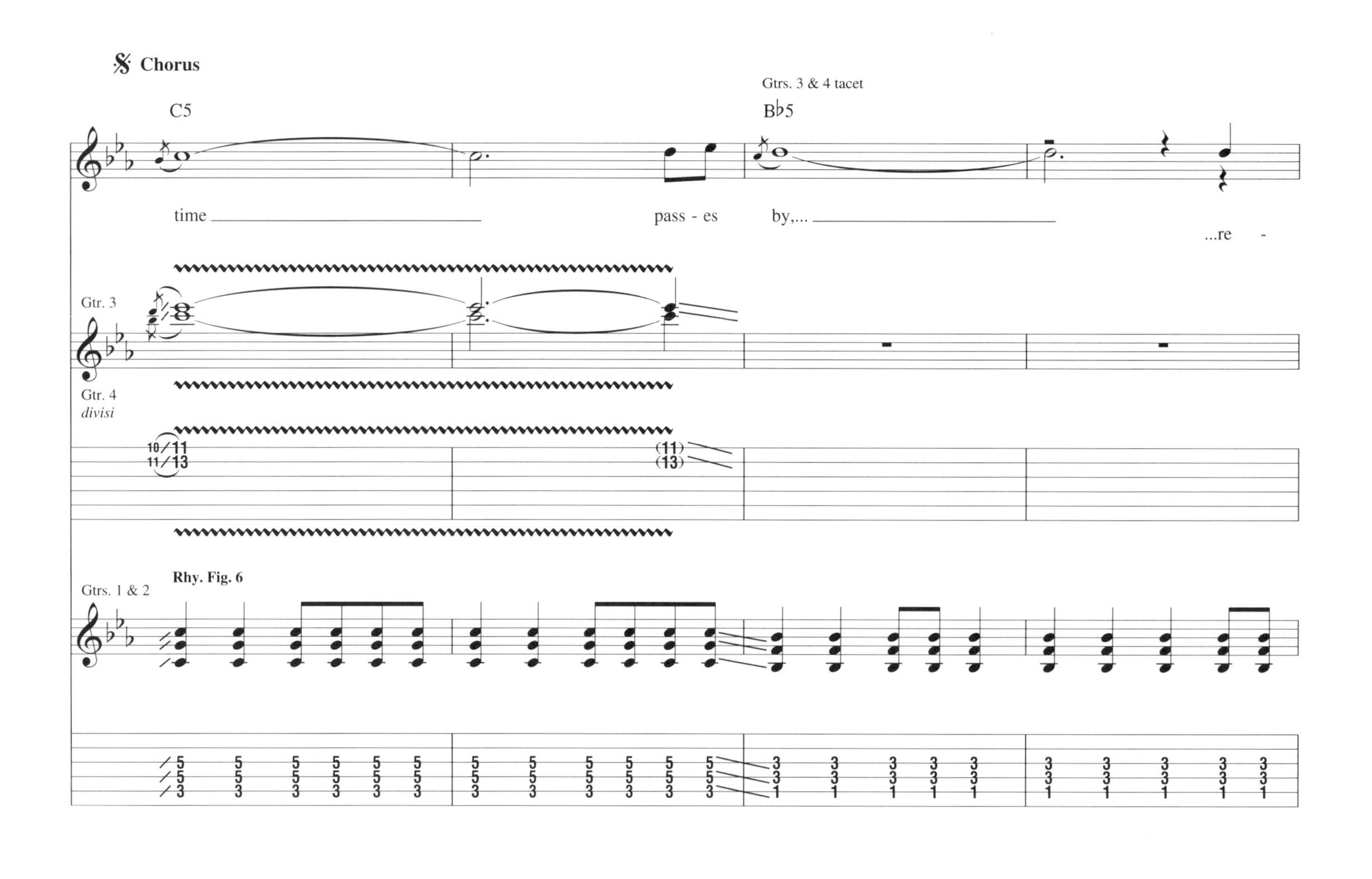
Chorus
Gtrs. 3 & 4 tacet
C5
B♭5
time
pass - es
by,...
...re -
Gtr. 3
Gtr. 4
divisi
Rhy. Fig. 6
Gtrs. 1 & 2

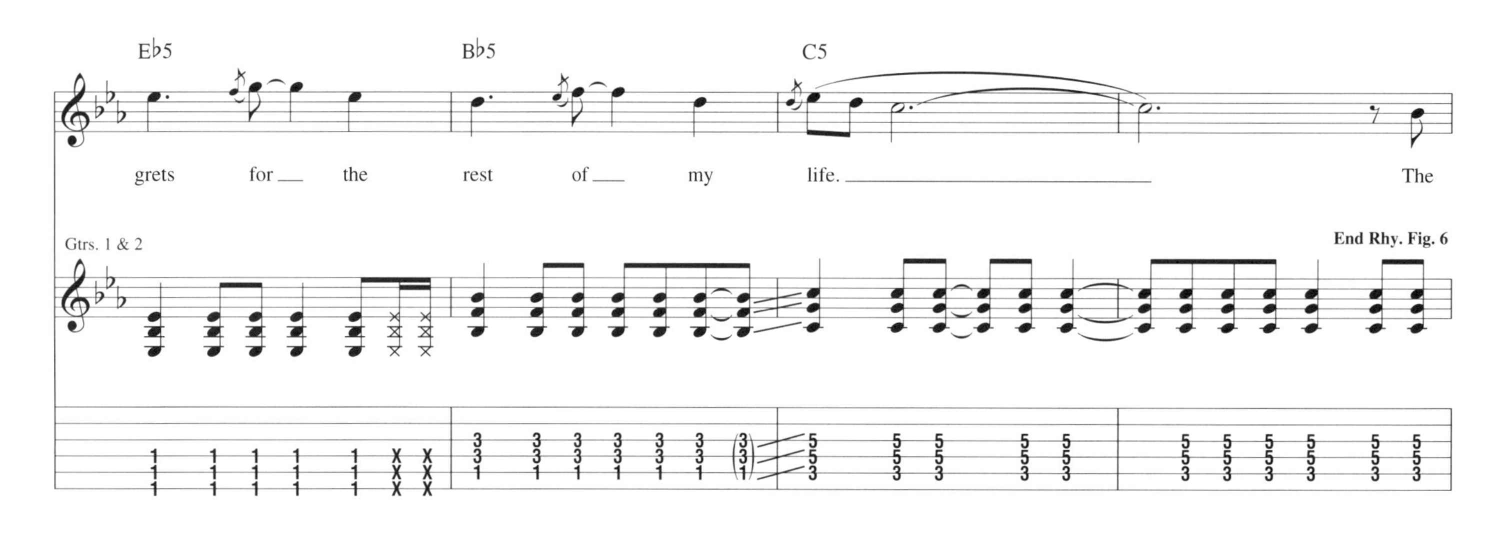
E♭5
B♭5
C5
grets
for
the
rest
of
my
life.
The
Gtrs. 1 & 2
End Rhy. Fig. 6

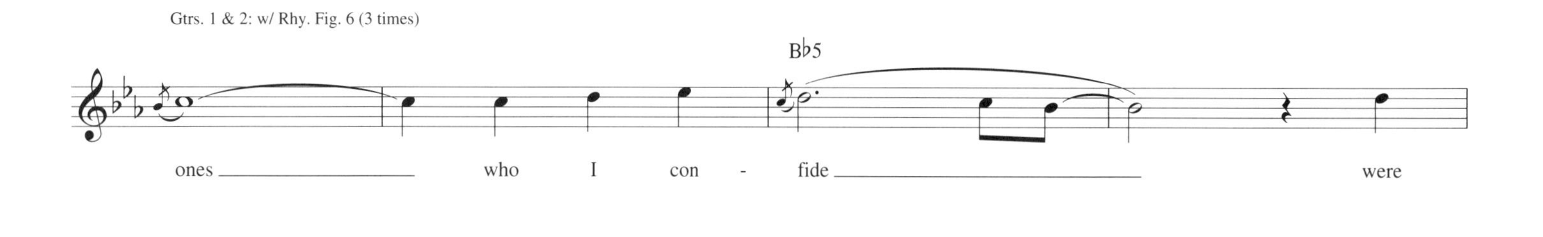
Gtrs. 1 & 2: w/ Rhy. Fig. 6 (3 times)
B♭5
ones
who
I
con -
fide
were

E♭5
B♭5
C5
gone
in
the
black
of
the
night.

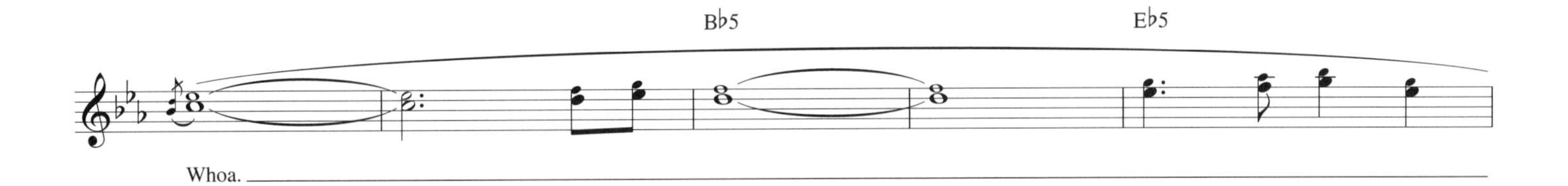
B♭5
E♭5
Whoa.

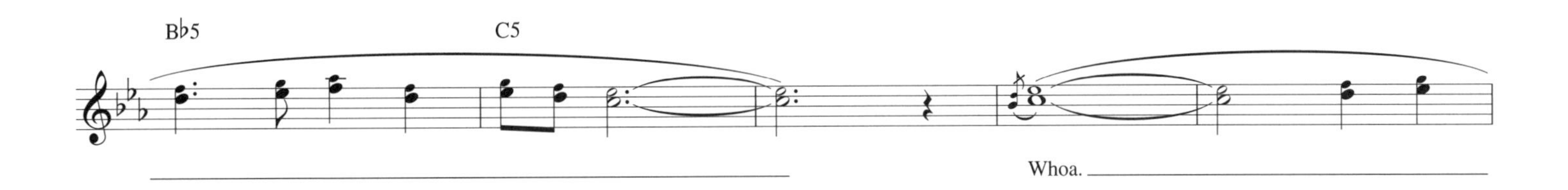
B♭5
C5
Whoa.

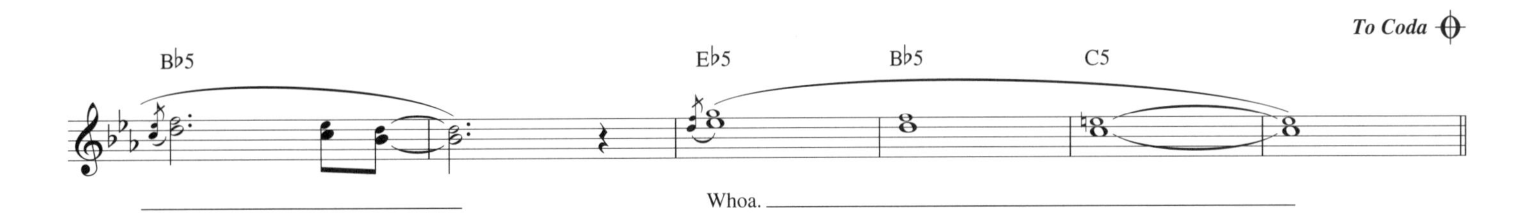
To Coda
B♭5
E♭5
B♭5
C5
Whoa.

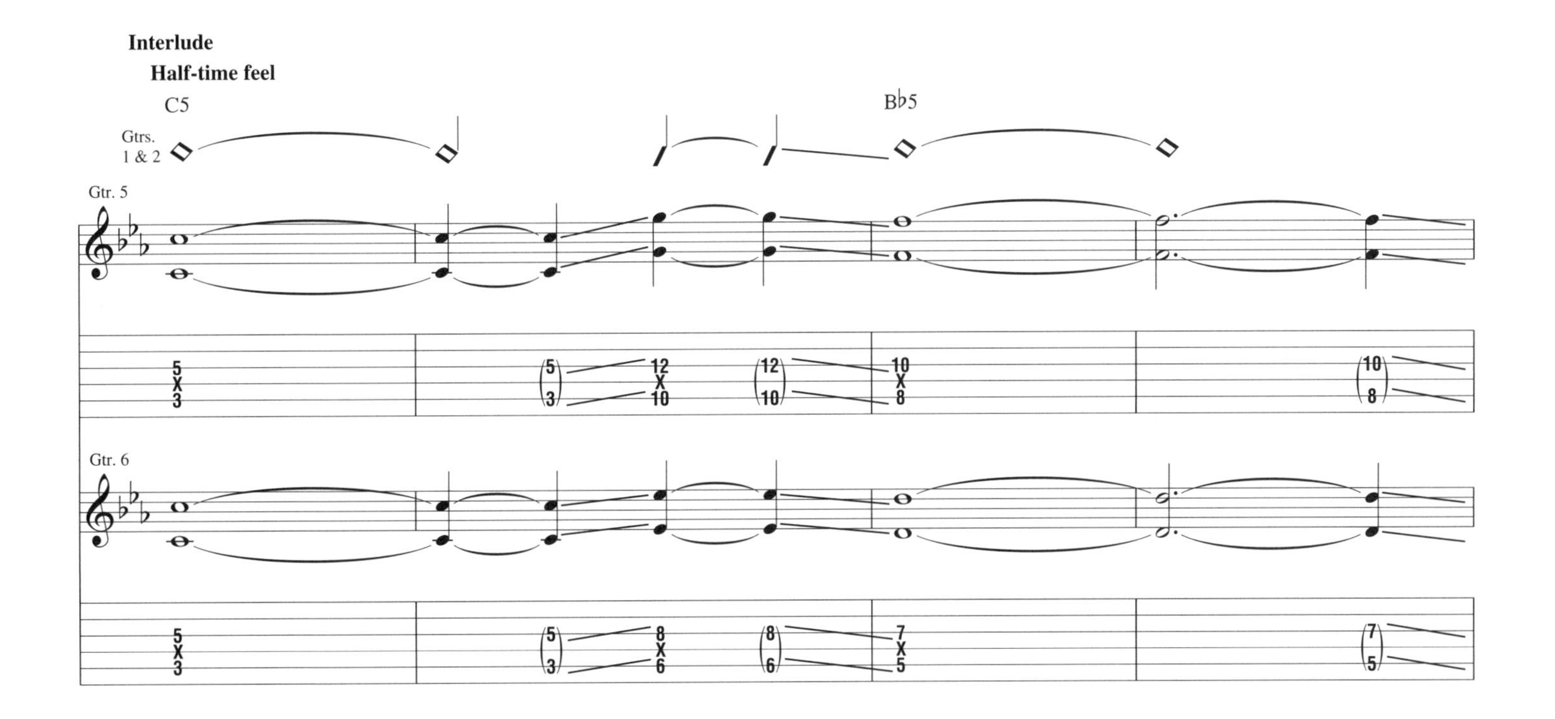
Interlude
Half-time feel
C5
B♭5
Gtrs. 1 & 2
Gtr. 5
Gtr. 6

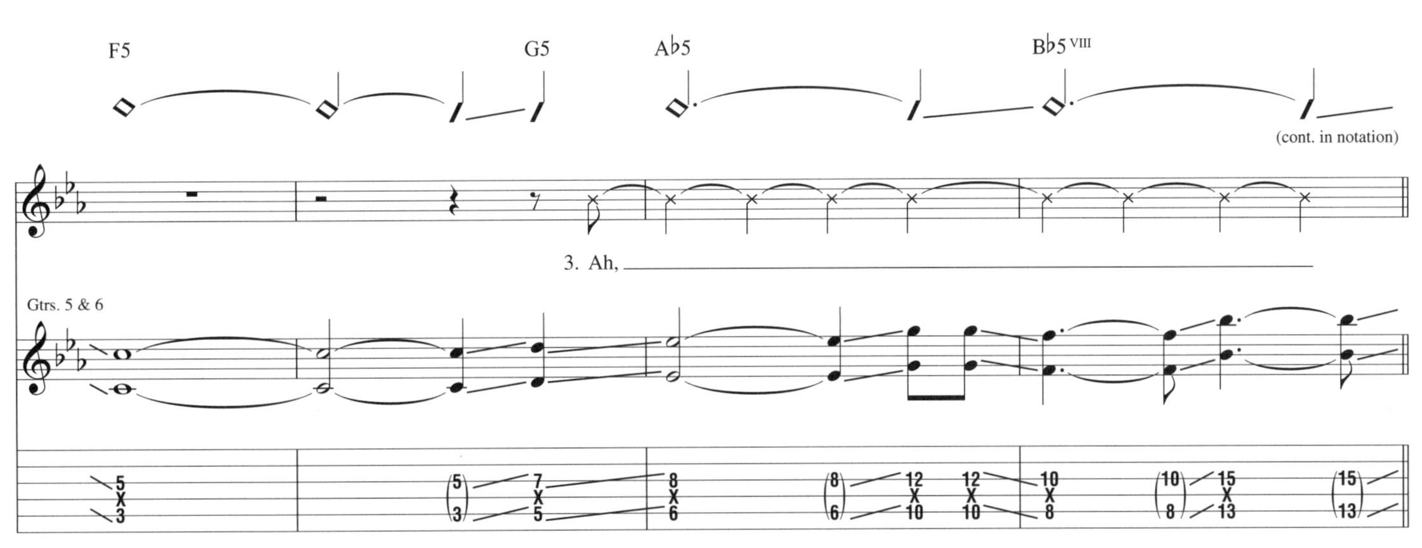
F5
G5
A♭5
B♭5 VIII
(cont. in notation)
3. Ah,
Gtrs. 5 & 6

Verse
Gtrs. 5 & 6 tacet
C5 D5 E♭5 D5 E♭5 F5 G5 B♭5 G/B
nev - er will I for - get you and all the mem - o - ries past.
So
Gtrs. 5 & 6
Rhy. Fig. 7
End Rhy. Fig. 7
Gtrs. 1 & 2
Gtrs. 1 & 2: w/ Rhy. Fig. 7 (3 times)
C5 D5 E♭5 D5 E♭5 F5 G5
rare - ly I get to see your face.
B♭5 G/B C5 D5 E♭5 D5 E♭5 F5
Grow - ing, I looked to you in
G5 B♭5 G/B C5 D5
guid - ance.
We knew that time would kill us...
...but you're

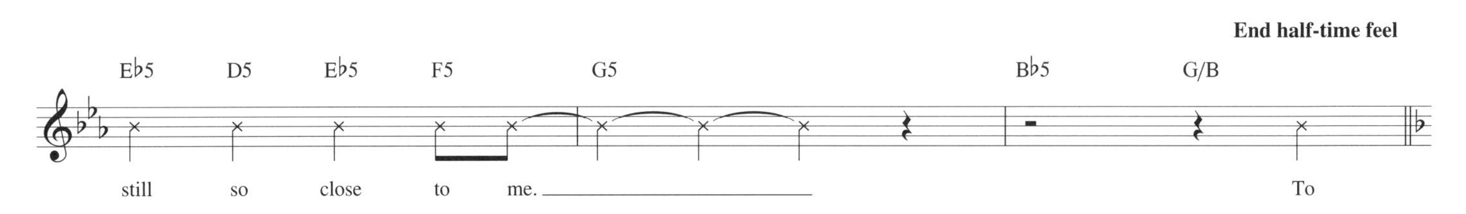
End half-time feel
E♭5 D5 E♭5 F5 G5 B♭5 G/B
still so close to me.
To

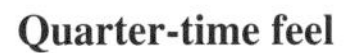
Quarter-time feel

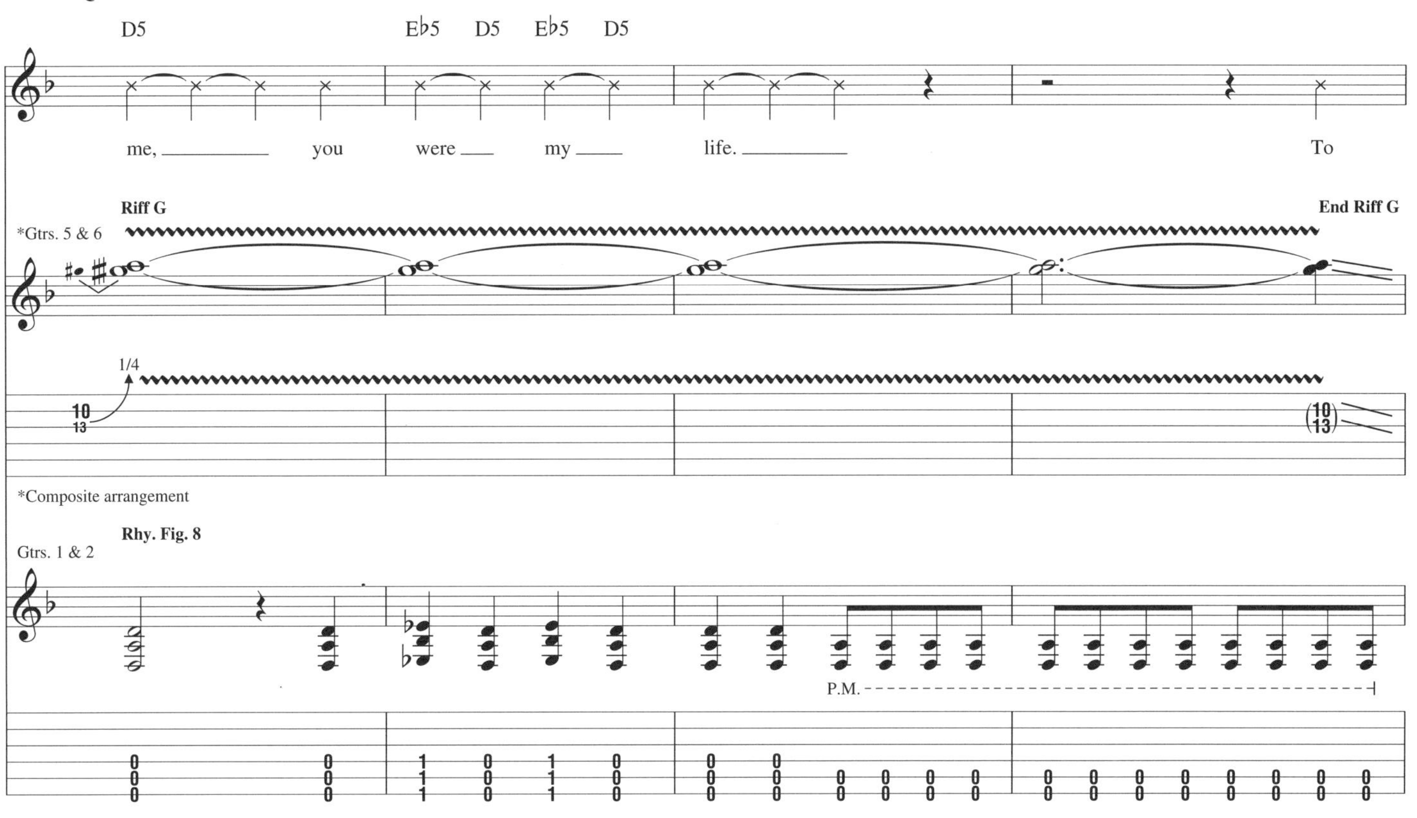
D5
E♭5 D5 E♭5 D5
me, you were my life. To
Riff G
End Riff G
*Gtrs. 5 & 6
1/4
*Composite arrangement
Rhy. Fig. 8
Gtrs. 1 & 2
P.M.

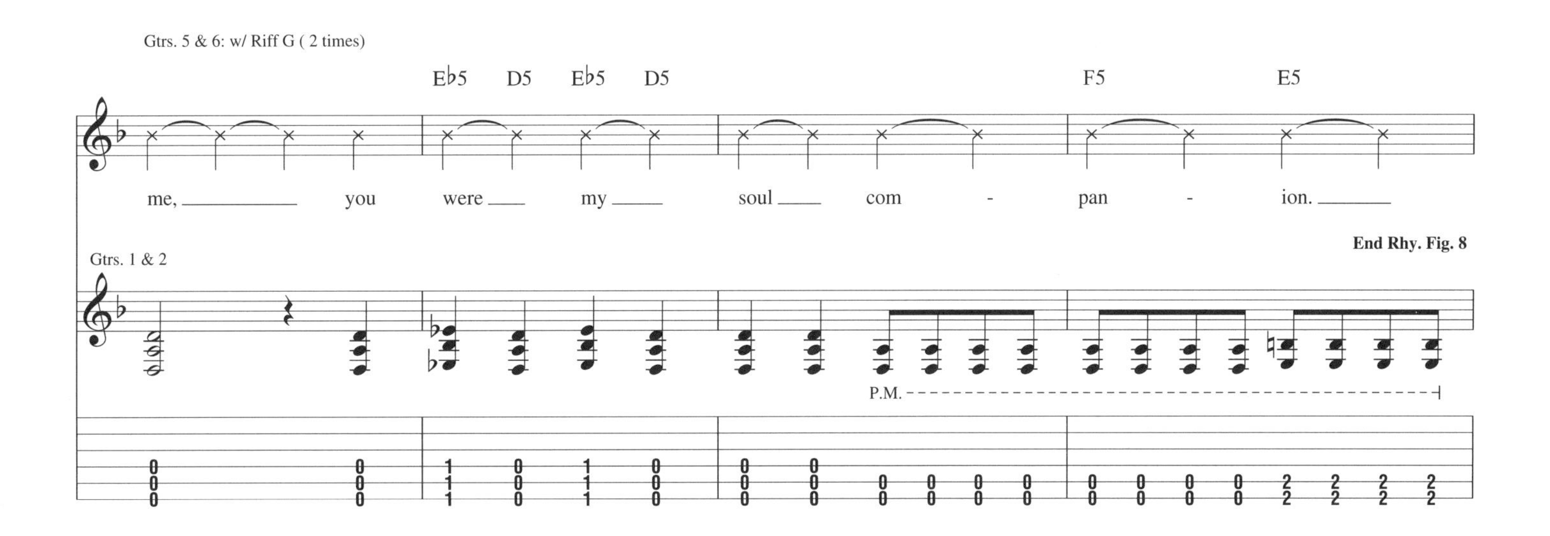
Gtrs. 5 & 6: w/ Riff G (2 times)
E♭5 D5 E♭5 D5
F5 E5
me, you were my soul com - pan - ion.
Gtrs. 1 & 2
End Rhy. Fig. 8
P.M.

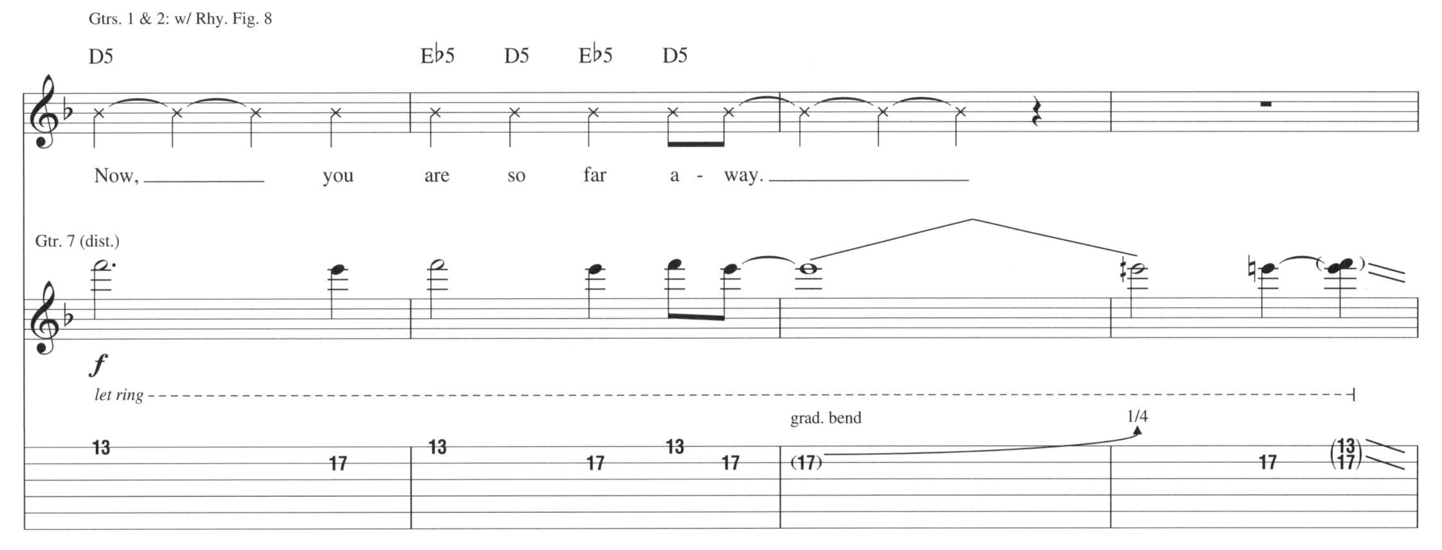
Gtrs. 1 & 2: w/ Rhy. Fig. 8
D5
E♭5 D5 E♭5 D5
Now, you are so far a - way.
Gtr. 7 (dist.)
f
let ring
grad. bend
1/4

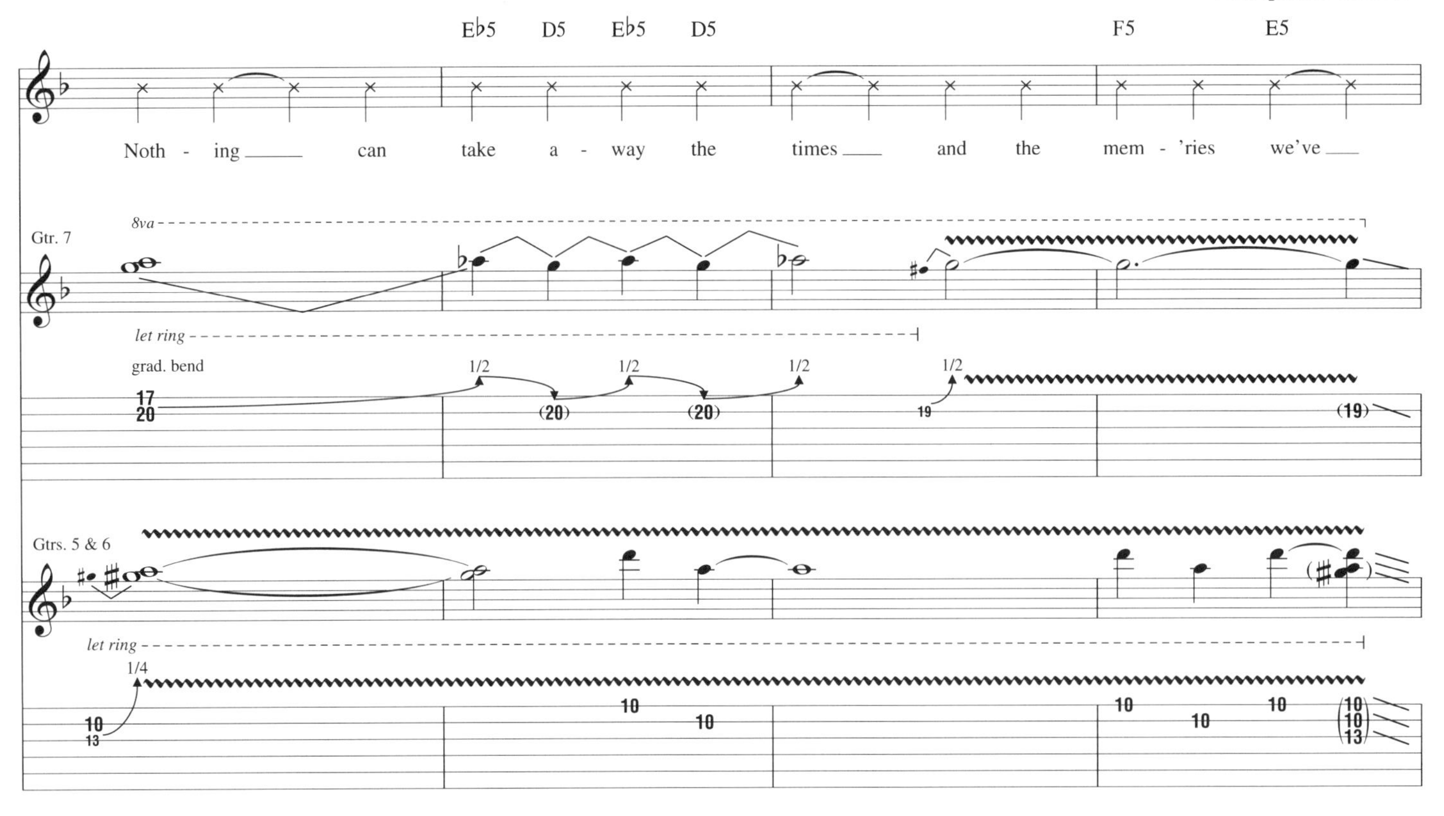
End quarter-time feel
E♭5
D5
E♭5
D5
F5
E5
Noth - ing can take a - way the times and the mem - 'ries we've
Gtr. 7
8va
let ring
grad. bend
1/2
1/2
1/2
1/2
Gtrs. 5 & 6
let ring
1/4

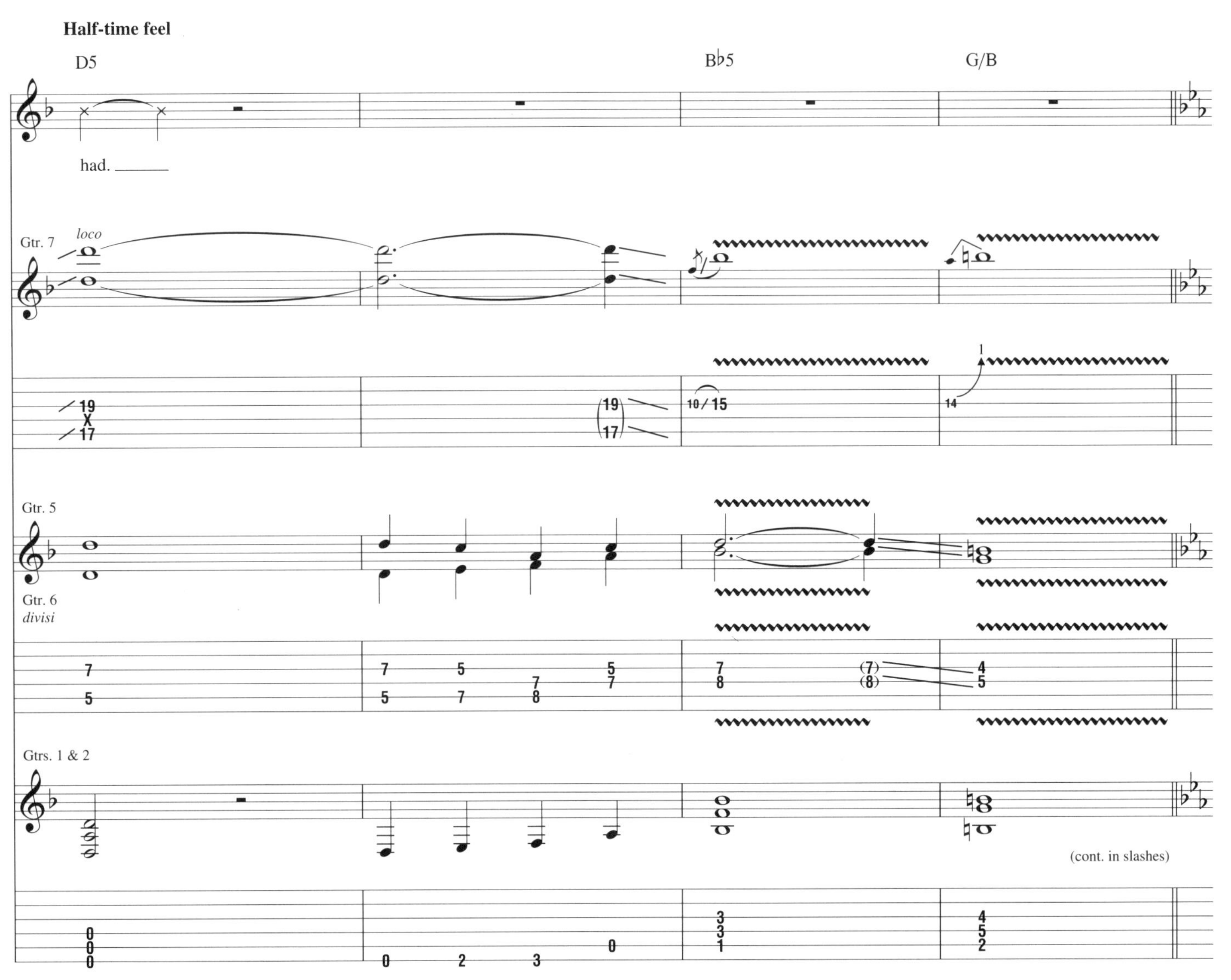
Half-time feel
D5
B♭5
G/B
had.
Gtr. 7
loco
1
Gtr. 5
Gtr. 6
divisi
Gtrs. 1 & 2
(cont. in slashes)

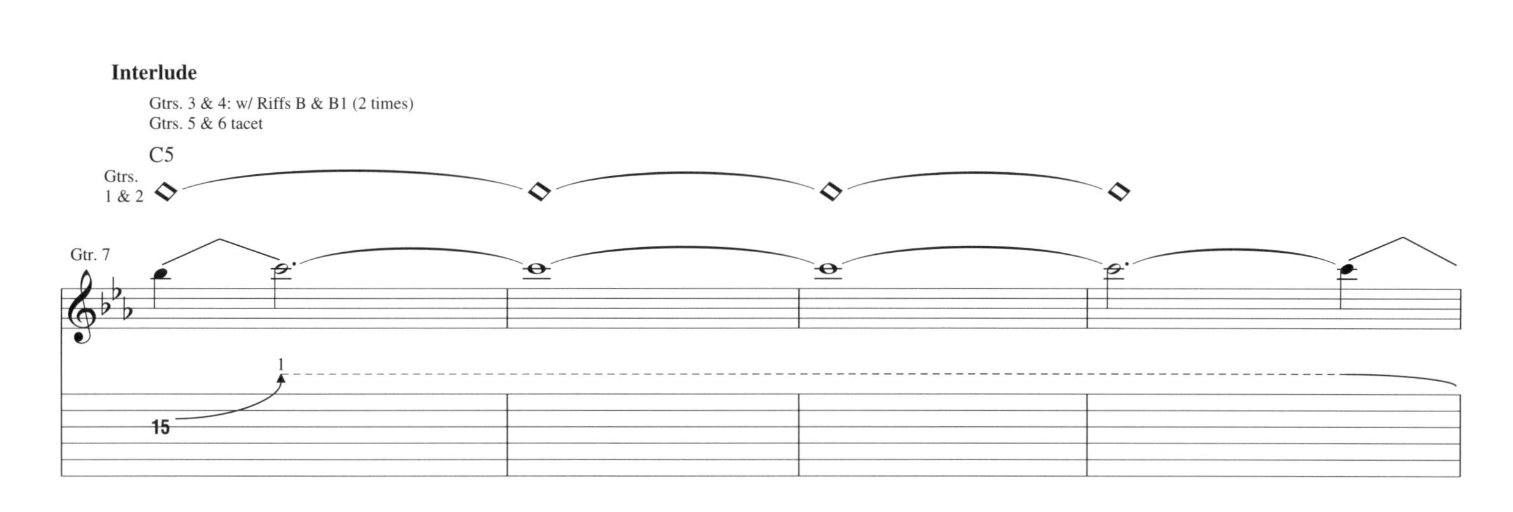
Interlude
Gtrs. 3 & 4: w/ Riffs B & B1 (2 times)
Gtrs. 5 & 6 tacet
C5
Gtrs. 1 & 2
Gtr. 7
1
15

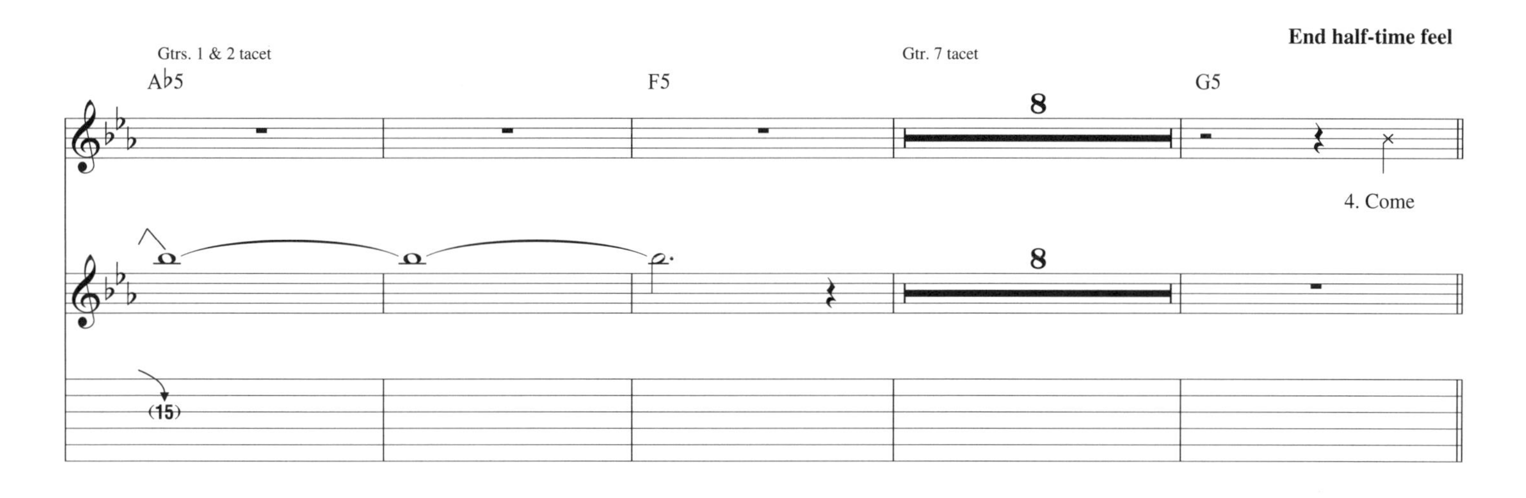
Gtrs. 1 & 2 tacet
Gtr. 7 tacet
End half-time feel
A♭5
F5
G5
8
4. Come
8
(15)

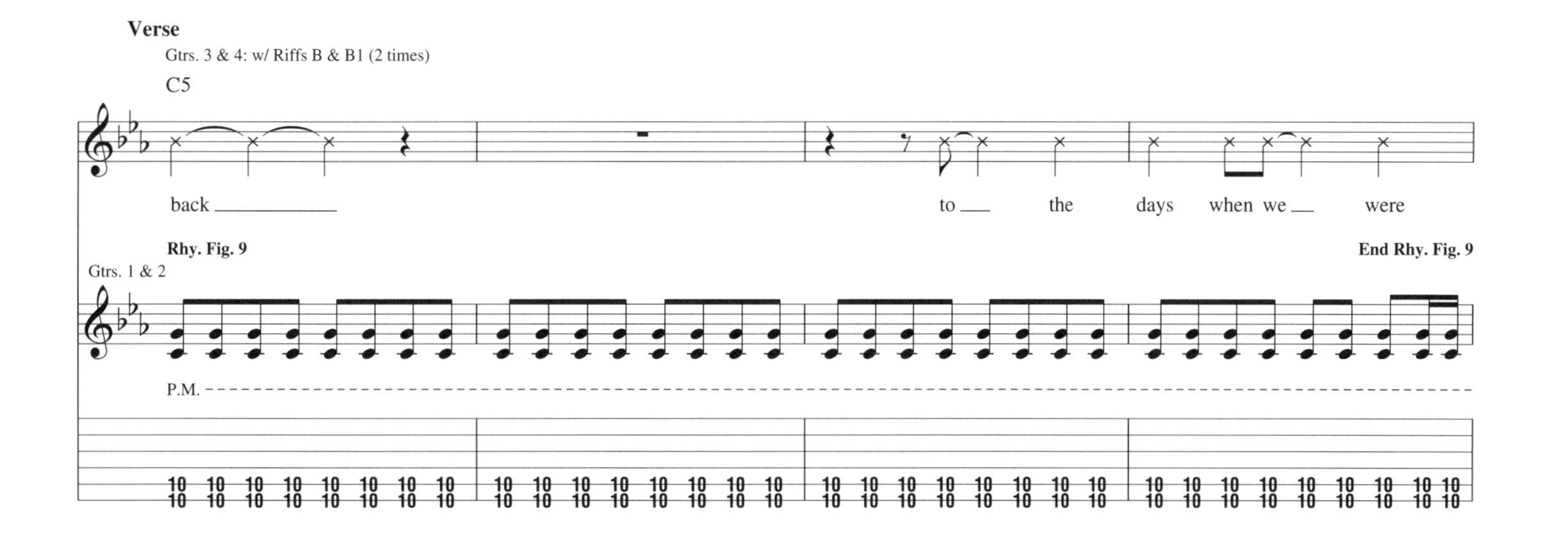
Verse
Gtrs. 3 & 4: w/ Riffs B & B1 (2 times)
C5
back
to the days when we were
Rhy. Fig. 9
End Rhy. Fig. 9
Gtrs. 1 & 2
P.M.

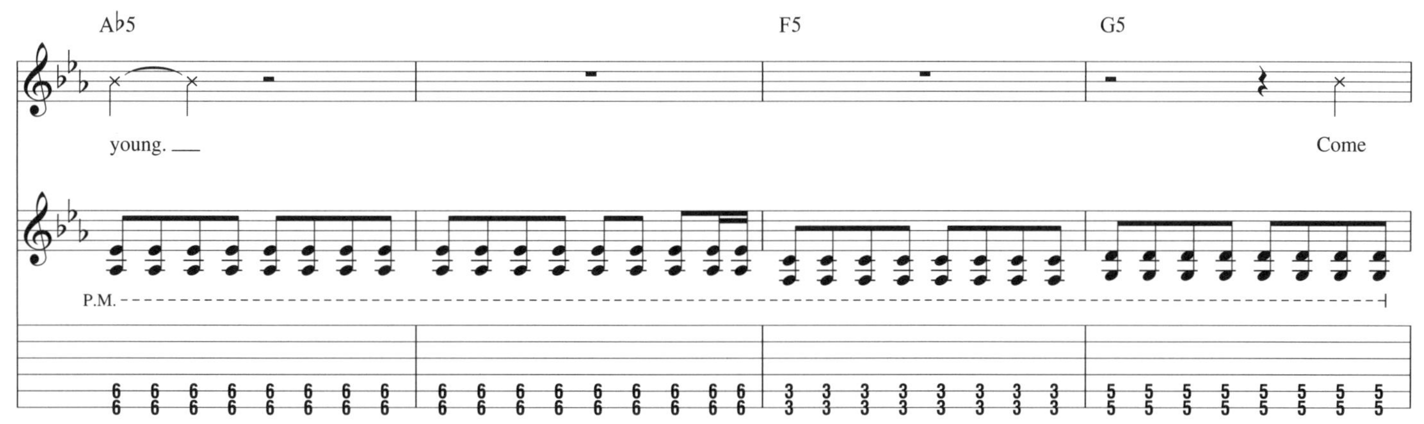
A♭5
F5
G5
young.
Come
P.M.

Gtrs. 1 & 2: w/ Rhy. Fig. 9

C5
back
to the days when noth - ing

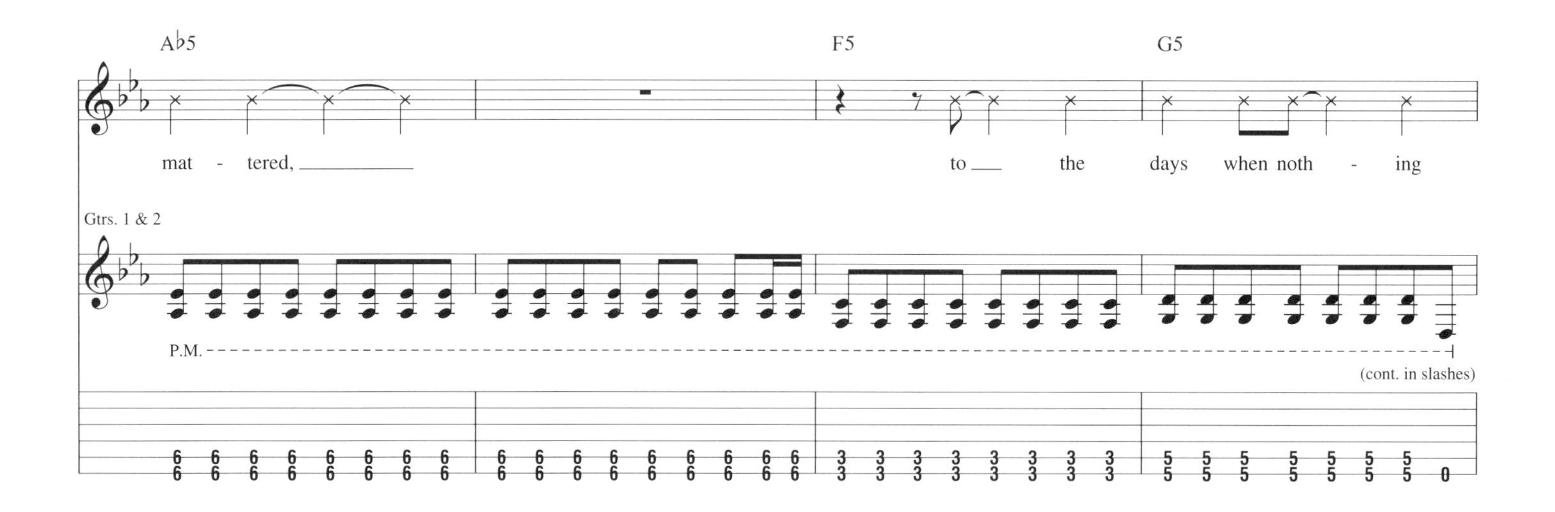
A♭5
F5
G5
mat - tered,
to the days when noth - ing
Gtrs. 1 & 2
P.M.
(cont. in slashes)

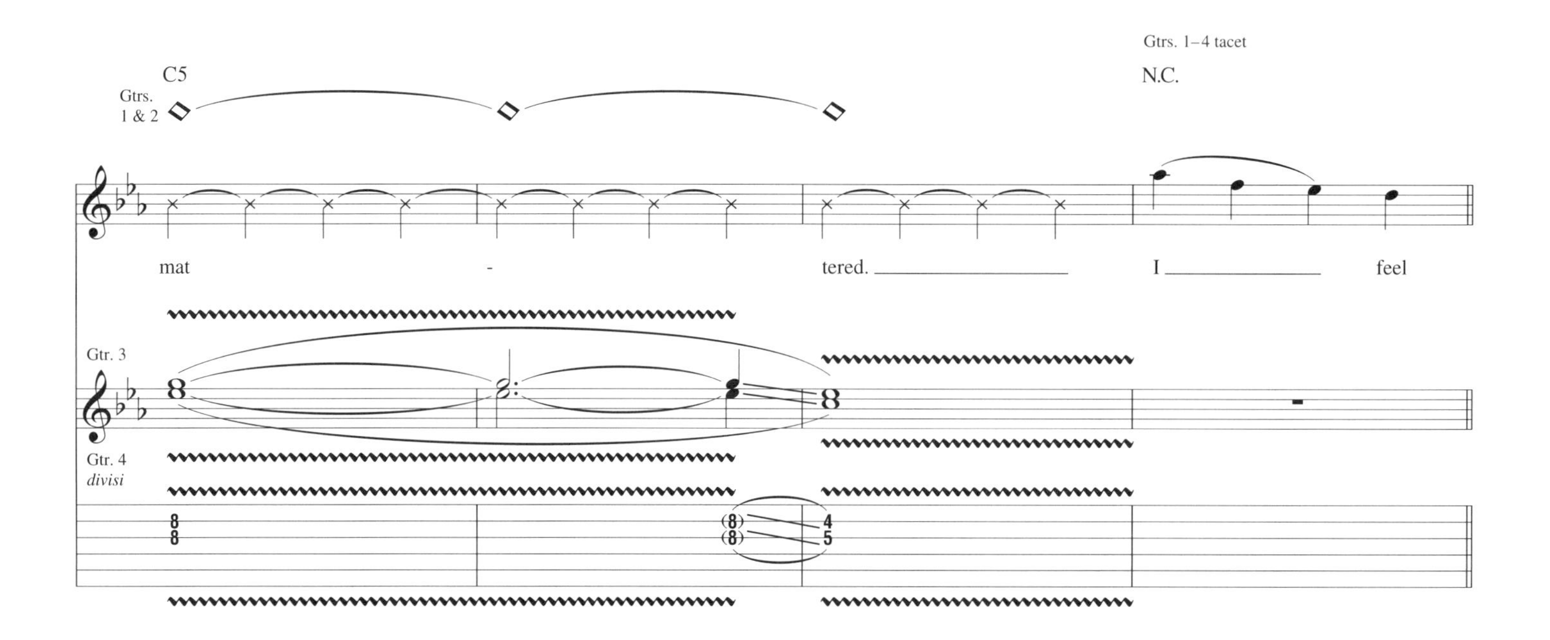
Gtrs. 1–4 tacet
C5
N.C.
Gtrs. 1 & 2
mat - tered.
I feel
Gtr. 3
Gtr. 4
divisi

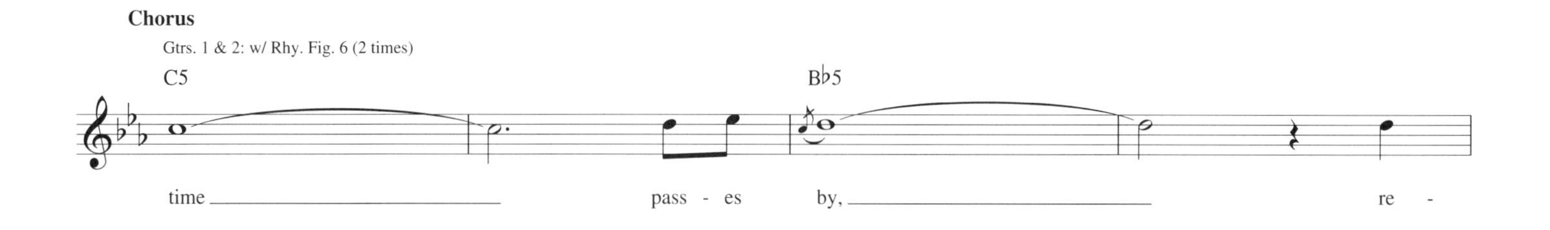
Chorus
Gtrs. 1 & 2: w/ Rhy. Fig. 6 (2 times)
C5
B♭5
time
pass - es
by,
re -

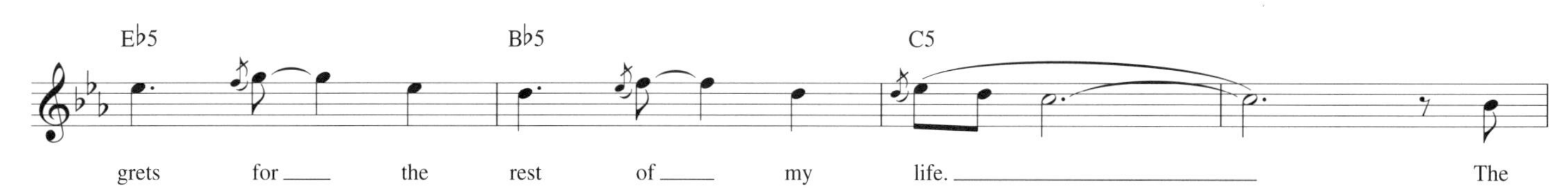
E♭5
B♭5
C5
grets for the rest of my life.
The

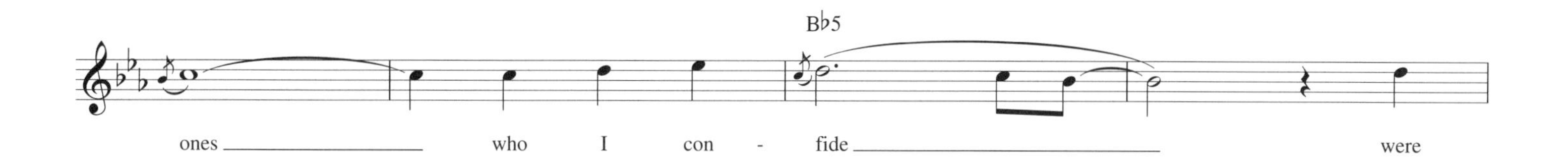
B♭5
ones who I con - fide were

E♭5
B♭5
C5
gone in the black of the night.

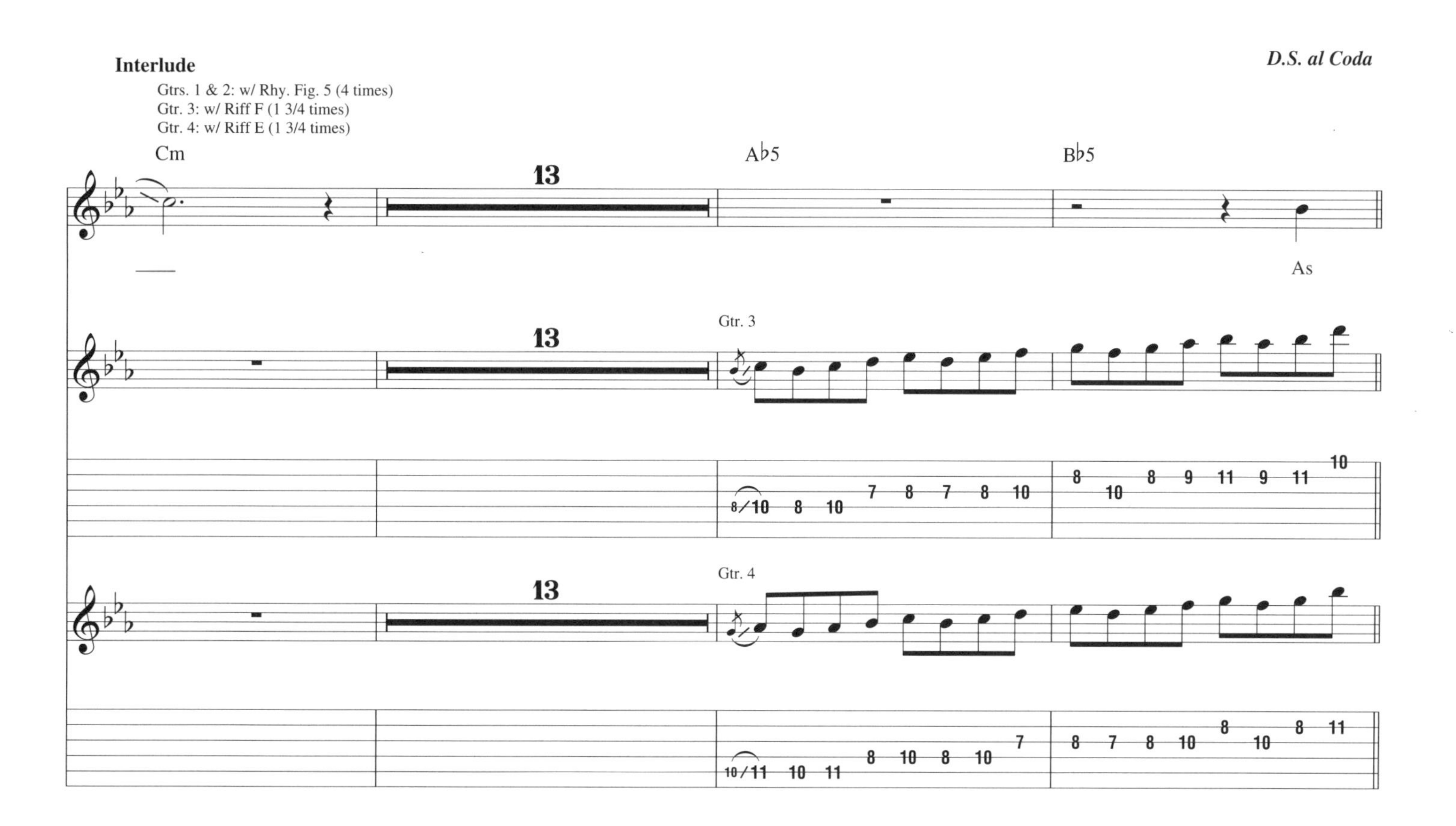
Interlude
D.S. al Coda
Gtrs. 1 & 2: w/ Rhy. Fig. 5 (4 times)
Gtr. 3: w/ Riff F (1 3/4 times)
Gtr. 4: w/ Riff E (1 3/4 times)
Cm
A♭5
B♭5
As
Gtr. 3
Gtr. 4

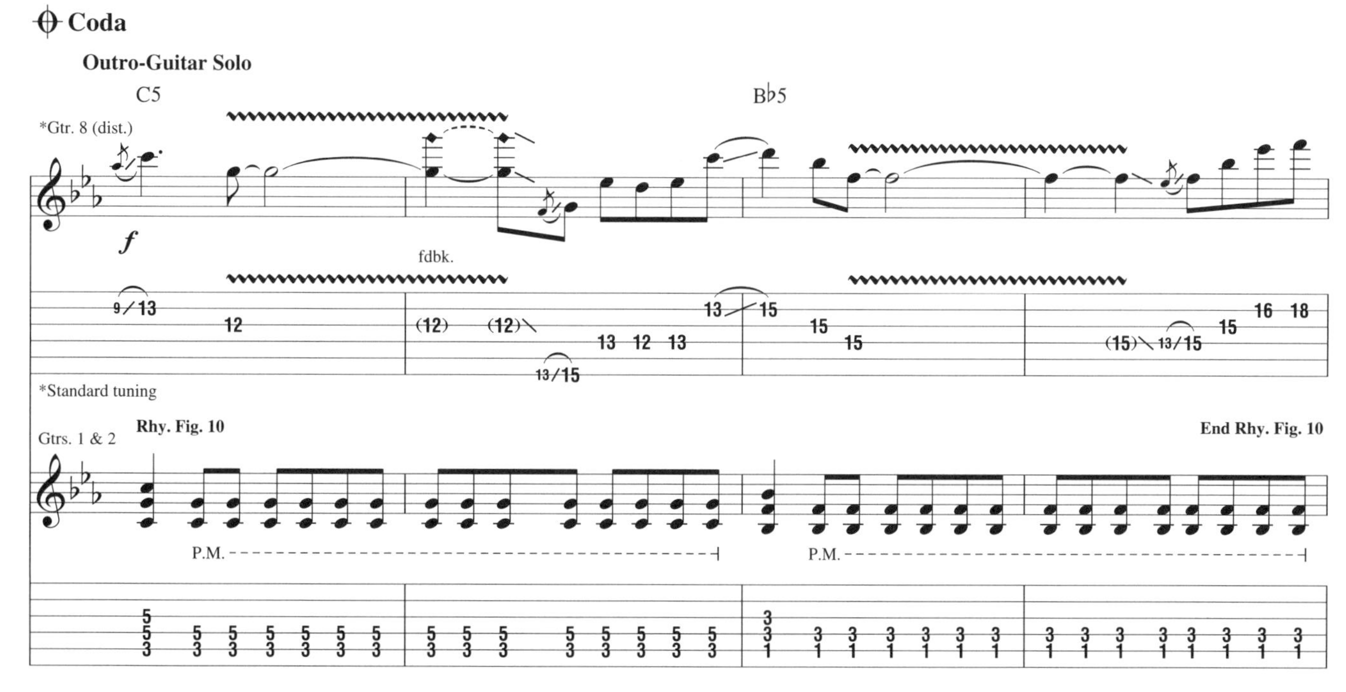
Coda
Outro-Guitar Solo
C5
B♭5
*Gtr. 8 (dist.)
fdbk.
*Standard tuning
Gtrs. 1 & 2
Rhy. Fig. 10
End Rhy. Fig. 10
P.M.

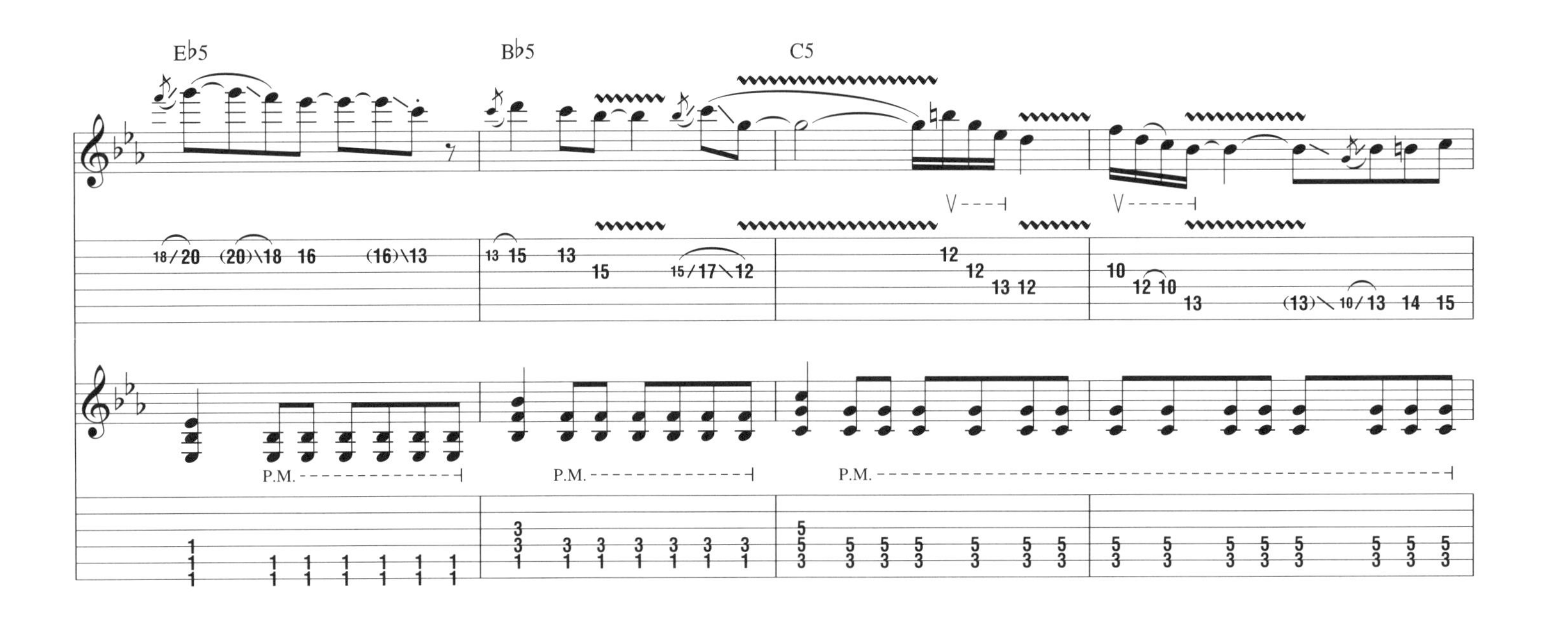
E♭5
B♭5
C5
P.M.
P.M.
P.M.

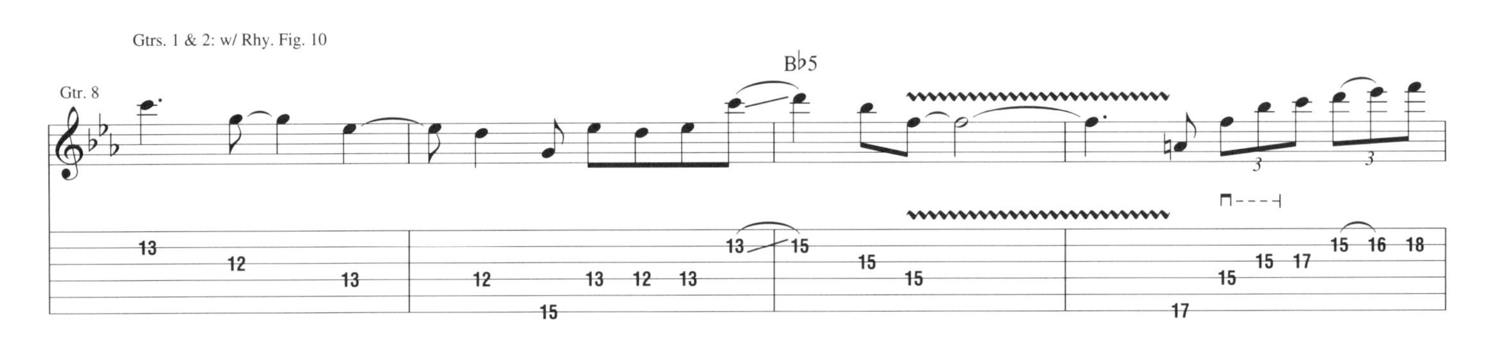
Gtrs. 1 & 2: w/ Rhy. Fig. 10
Gtr. 8
B♭5

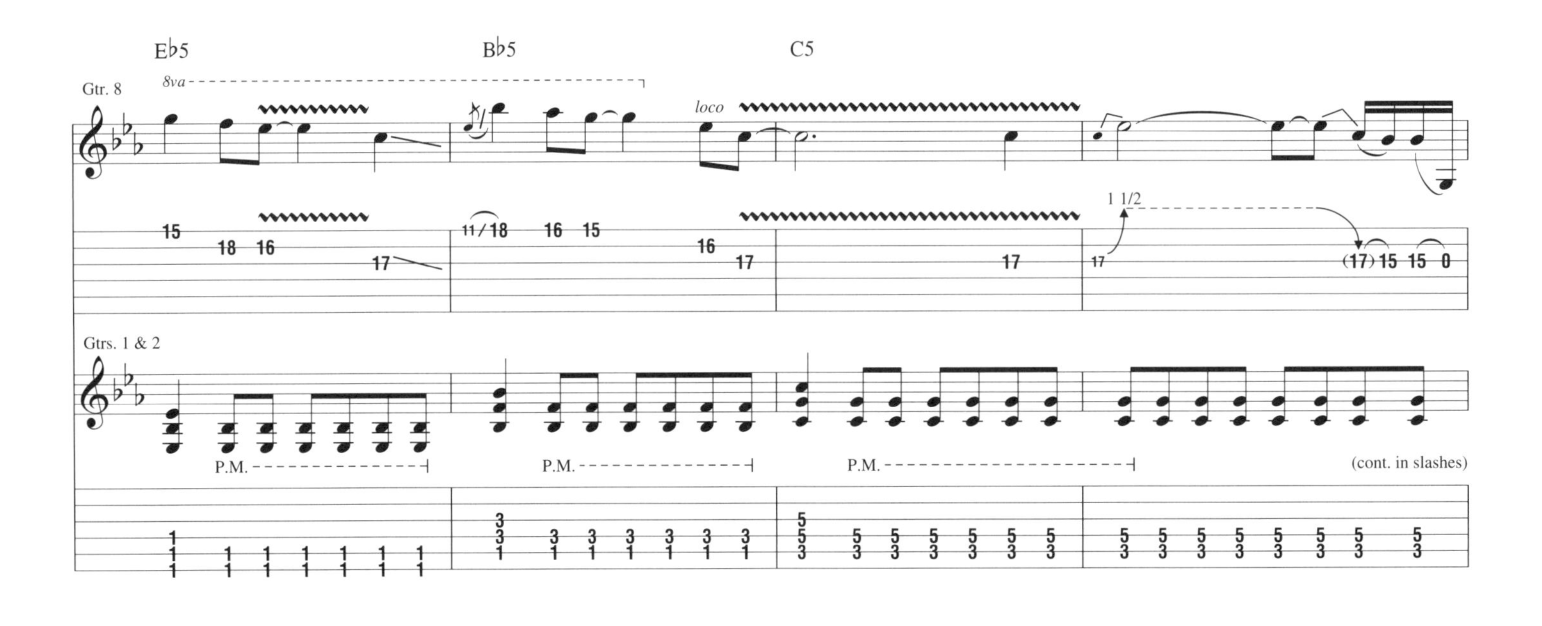
E♭5
B♭5
C5
Gtr. 8
8va
loco
1 1/2
Gtrs. 1 & 2
P.M.
P.M.
P.M.
(cont. in slashes)

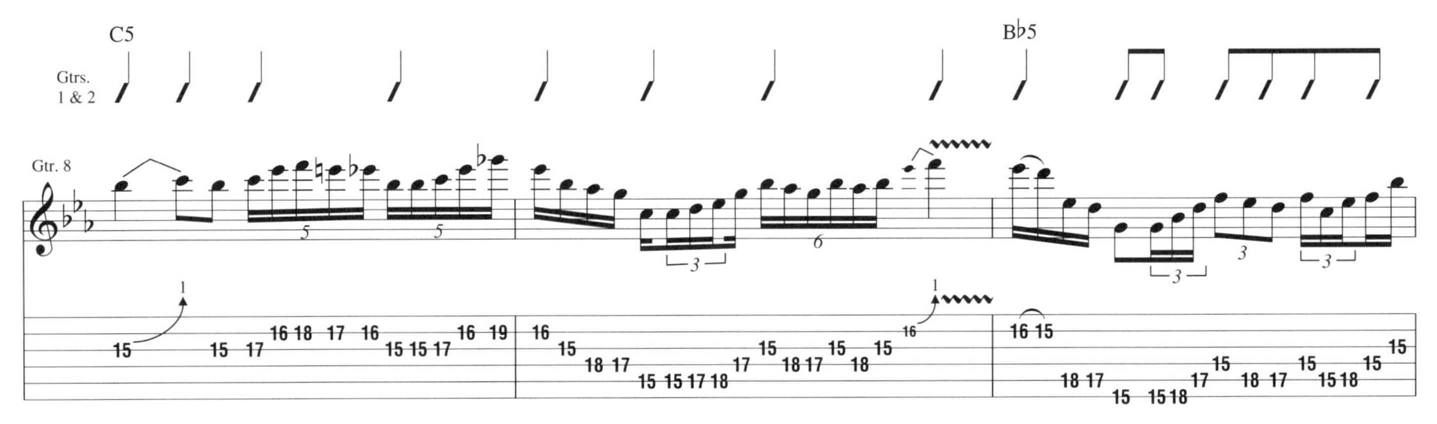
C5
B♭5
Gtrs. 1 & 2
Gtr. 8

E♭5
B♭5
8va
loco
C5
1/2
8va
B♭5
E♭5
(cont. in notation)
8va
1/2
loco
B♭5
C5
8va
Gtr. 8
Gtrs. 1 & 2
fdbk.
Pitch: G

Radiant Eclipse

Words and Music by Matthew Sanders, James Sullivan, Brian Haner, Jr. and Zachary Baker

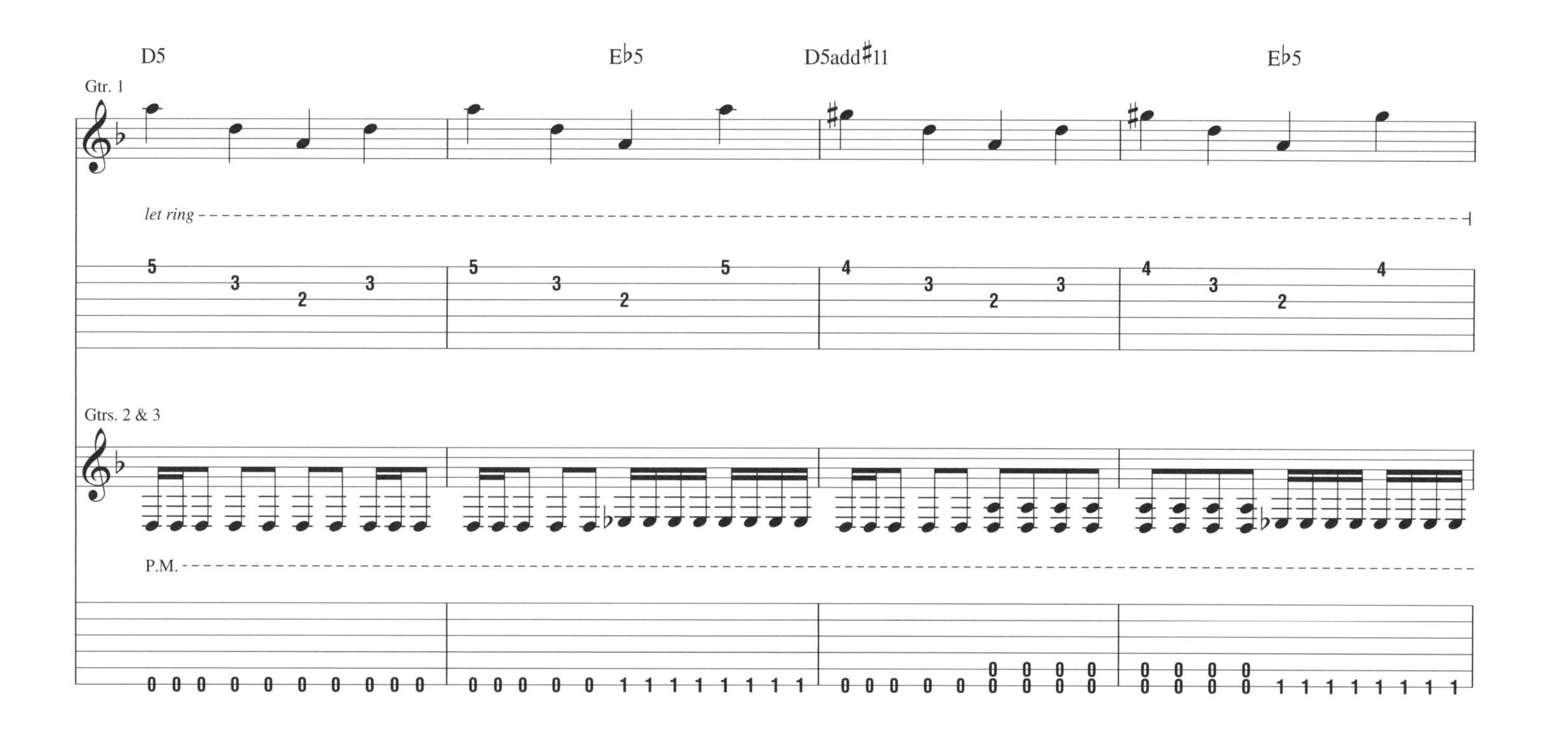
D5
E♭5
D5add♯11
E♭5
Gtr. 1
let ring
Gtrs. 2 & 3
P.M.

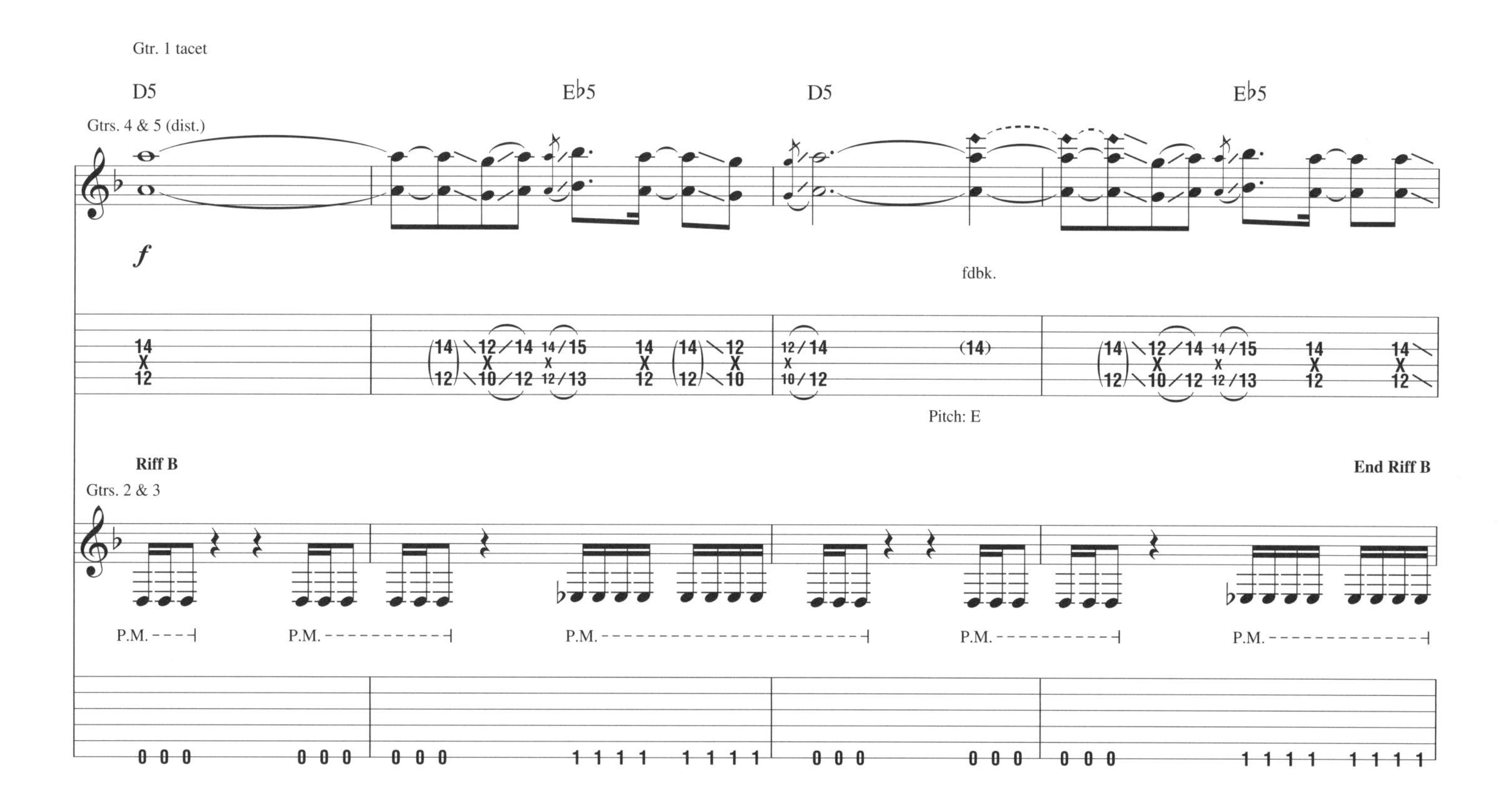
Gtr. 1 tacet
D5
E♭5
D5
E♭5
Gtrs. 4 & 5 (dist.)
fdbk.
Pitch: E
Riff B
End Riff B
Gtrs. 2 & 3
P.M.

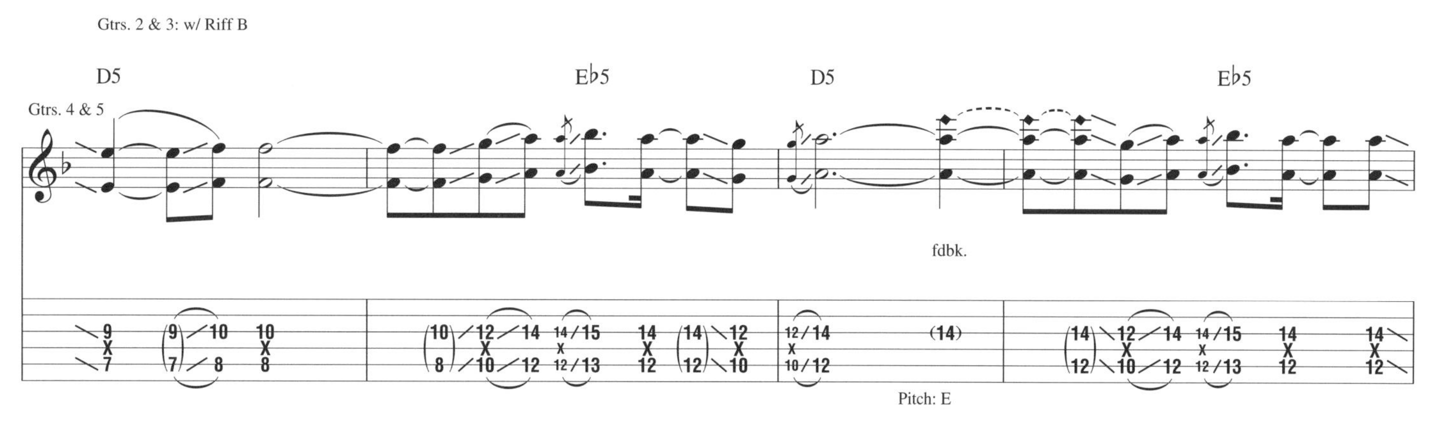
Gtrs. 2 & 3: w/ Riff B
D5
E♭5
D5
E♭5
Gtrs. 4 & 5
fdbk.
Pitch: E

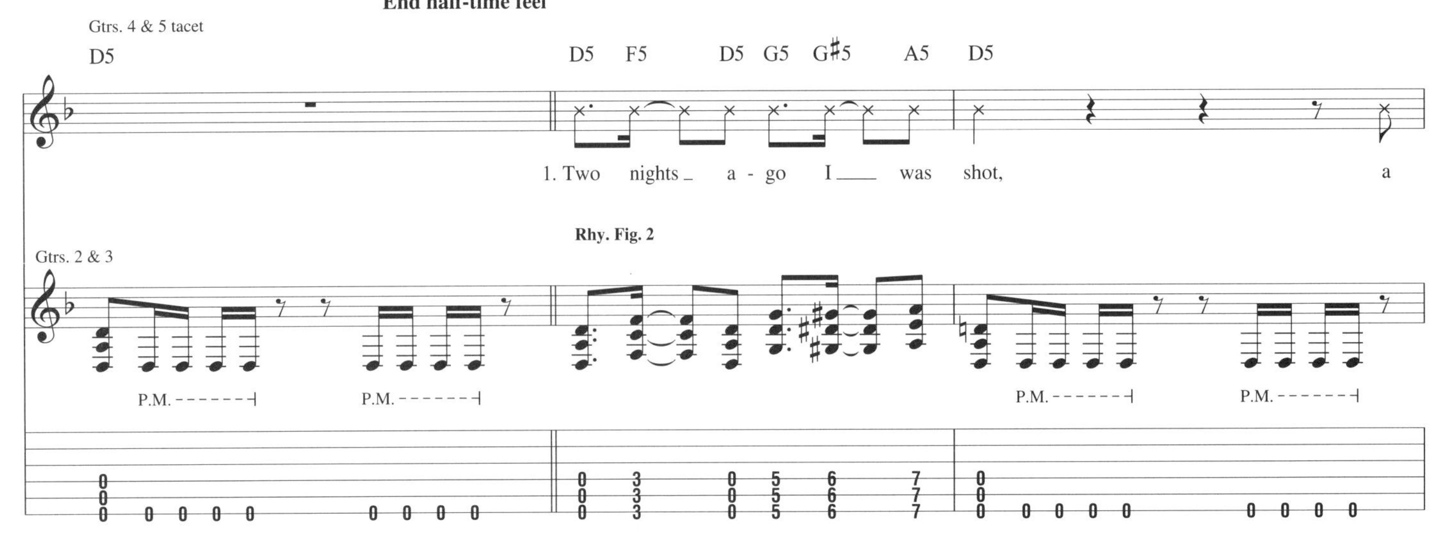
Verse
End half-time feel
Gtrs. 4 & 5 tacet
D5 D5 F5 D5 G5 G♯5 A5 D5
1. Two nights a - go I was shot, a
Gtrs. 2 & 3
Rhy. Fig. 2
P.M.

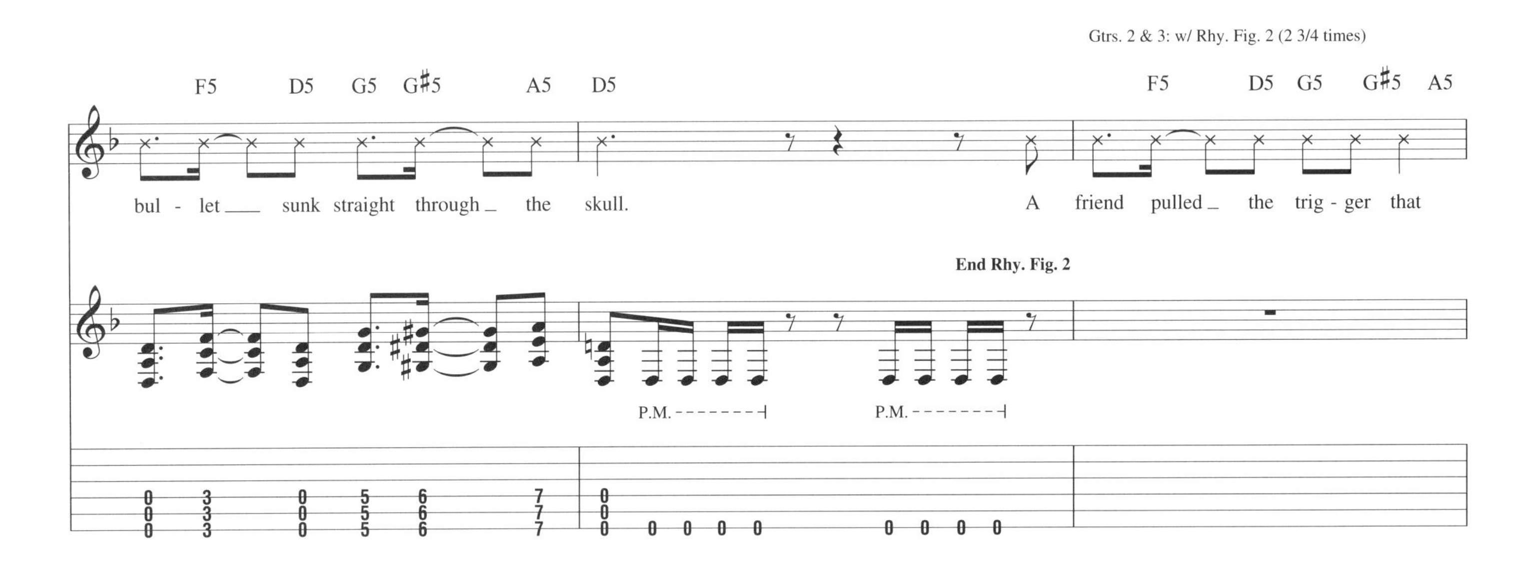
Gtrs. 2 & 3: w/ Rhy. Fig. 2 (2 3/4 times)
F5 D5 G5 G♯5 A5 D5 F5 D5 G5 G♯5 A5
bul - let sunk straight through the skull. A friend pulled the trig - ger that
End Rhy. Fig. 2
P.M.

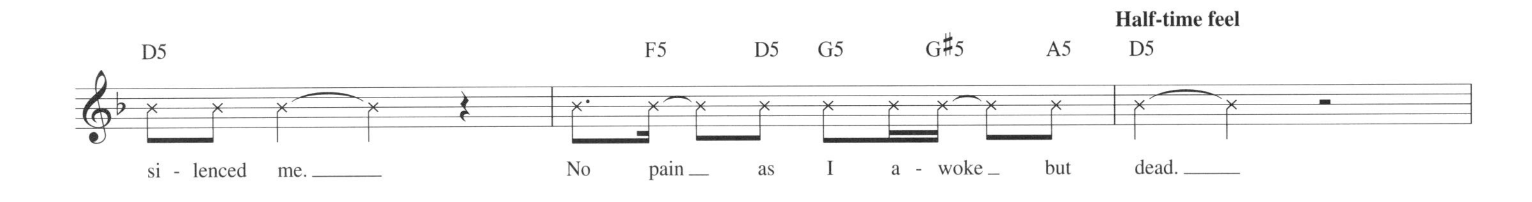
Half-time feel
D5 F5 D5 G5 G♯5 A5 D5
si - lenced me. No pain as I a - woke but dead.

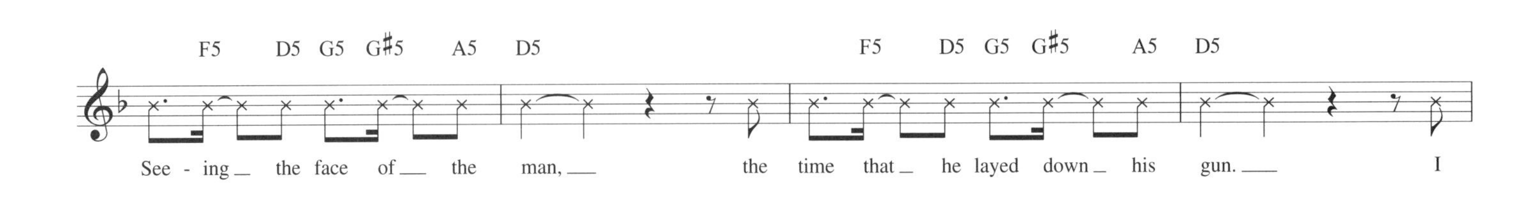
F5 D5 G5 G♯5 A5 D5 F5 D5 G5 G♯5 A5 D5
See - ing the face of the man, the time that he layed down his gun. I

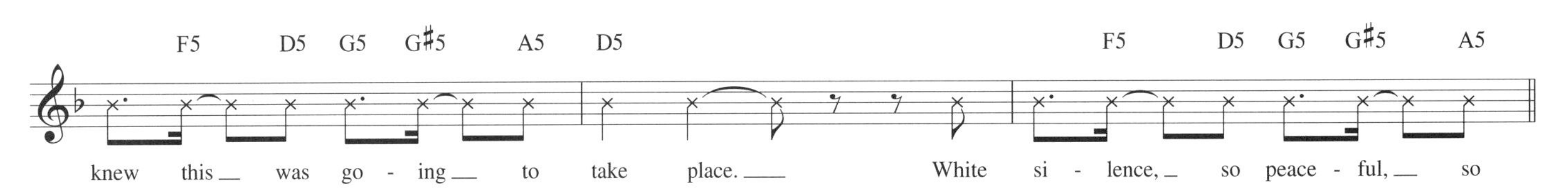
F5 D5 G5 G♯5 A5 D5 F5 D5 G5 G♯5 A5
knew this was go - ing to take place. White si - lence, so peace - ful, so

Pre-Chorus

*Bass plays E.

**Bass plays C♮.

End half-time feel

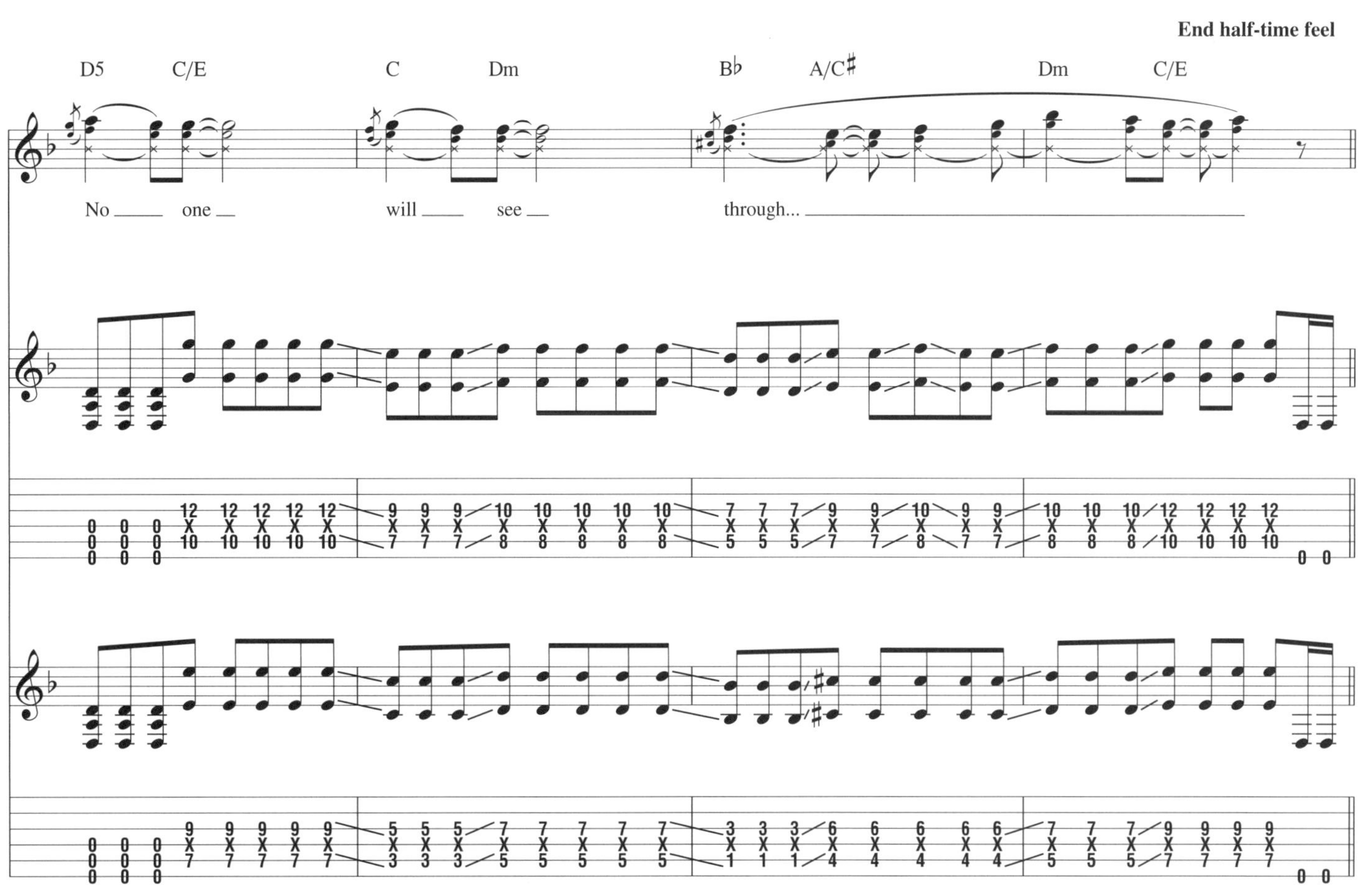

Verse
Double-time feel
F5 D5 N.C. D5 F5 G5 A♭5
2., 4. You're all gone to me.
(Gone to me.)
I've been pulled out to watch from
Rhy. Fig. 3
Gtrs. 2 & 3
End Rhy. Fig. 3
P.M.
Gtrs. 2 & 3: w/ Rhy. Fig. 3 (3 times)
my e-ter-nal sleep.
In-tu-i-tion and a warn-ing to be-lieve.
(Will be-lieve.)
End double-time feel
Some-thing went wrong and though I felt I had to stay,
mov-ing on seemed to be
som-ber bliss...
...with-out one good-bye.
Rhy. Fig. 4
To Coda 1
...I watch my moth-er shed tears.
End Rhy. Fig. 4
F5 D5 G5 G♯5 A5

Verse

Gtrs. 2 & 3: w/ Rhy. Fig. 2 (1 1/2 times)
D5
D5 F5 D5 G5 G♯5 A5 D5
No! 3. This gun has stopped time in its tracks, has
P.M.
P.M.

F5 D5 G5 G♯5 A5 D5
F5 D5 G5 G♯5 A5 D5
al - tered the course of my fate.
Des - ti - ny is shat - tered and time - less. Closed

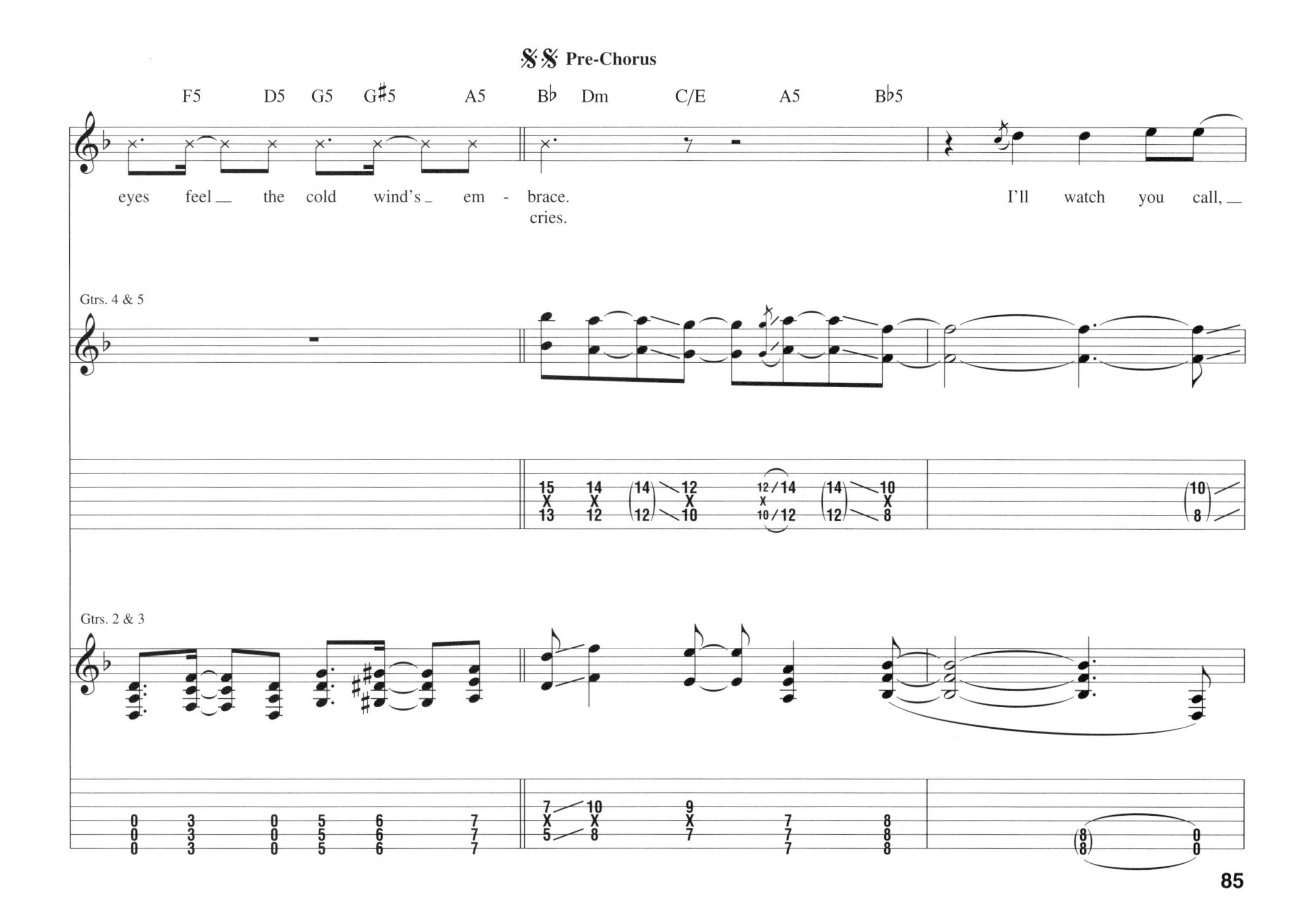
Pre-Chorus
F5 D5 G5 G♯5 A5 B♭ Dm C/E A5 B♭5
eyes feel the cold wind's em - brace.
cries.
I'll watch you call,
Gtrs. 4 & 5
Gtrs. 2 & 3

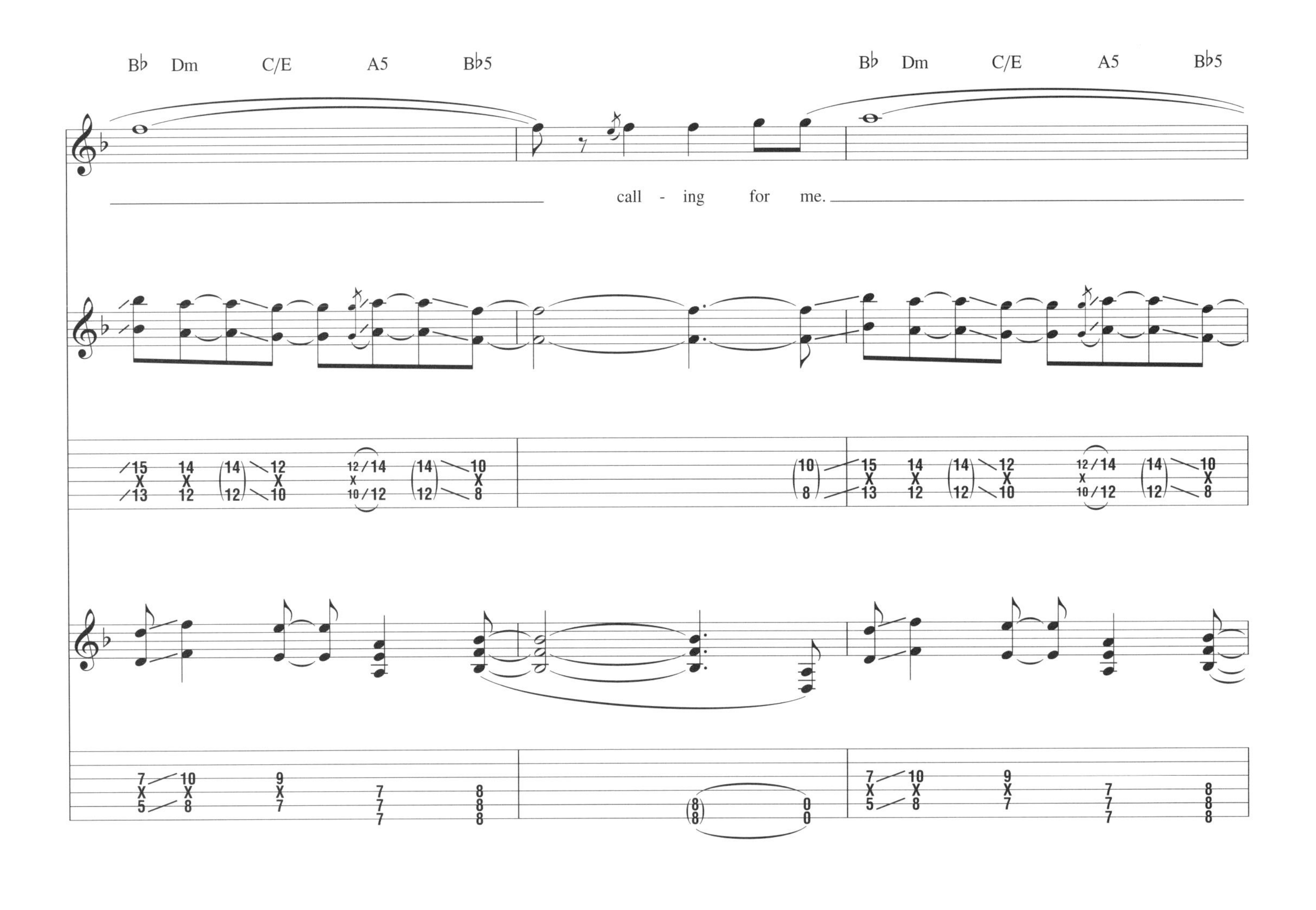
B♭ Dm C/E A5 B♭5
B♭ Dm C/E A5 B♭5
call - ing for me.

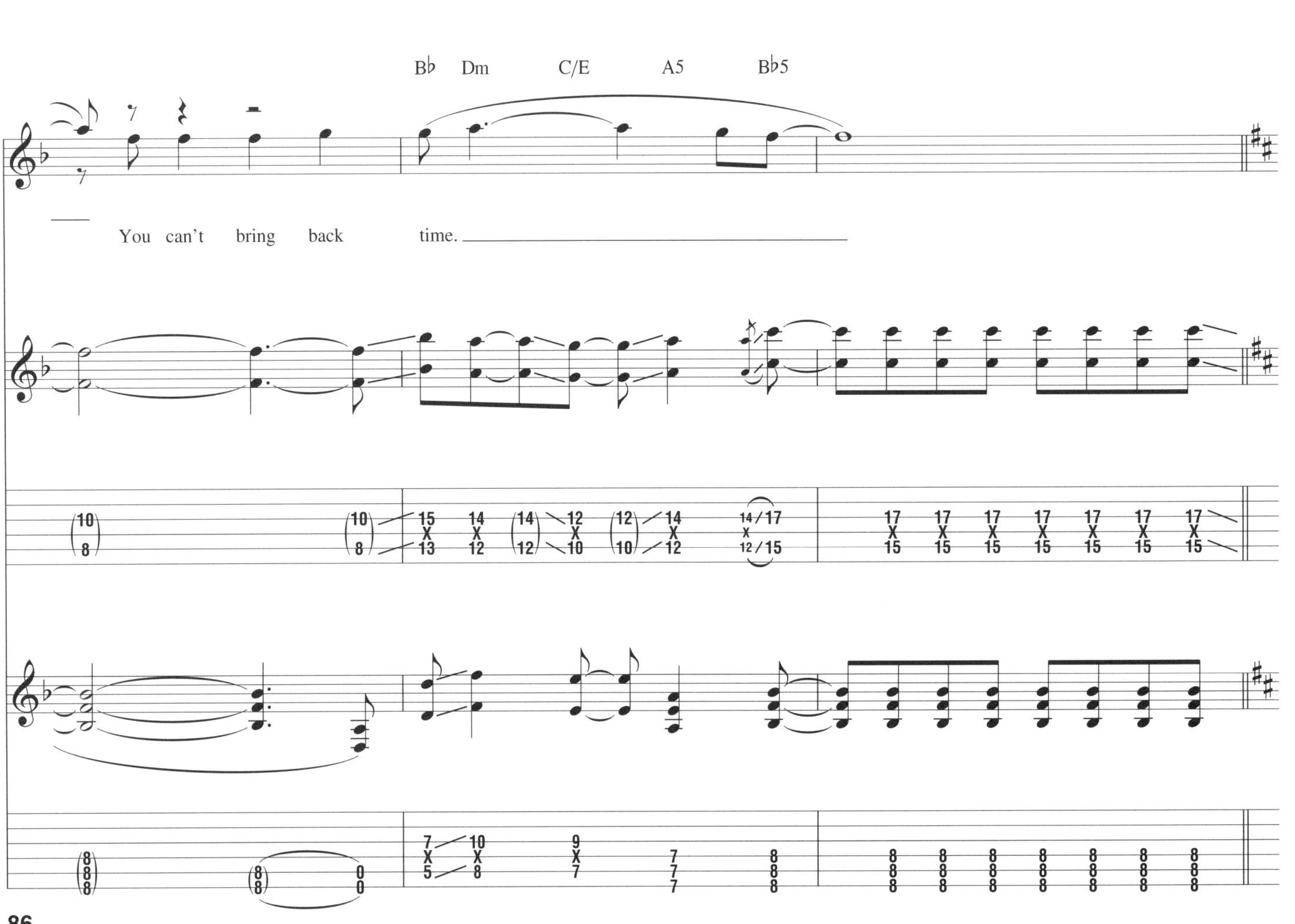
B♭ Dm C/E A5 B♭5
You can't bring back time.

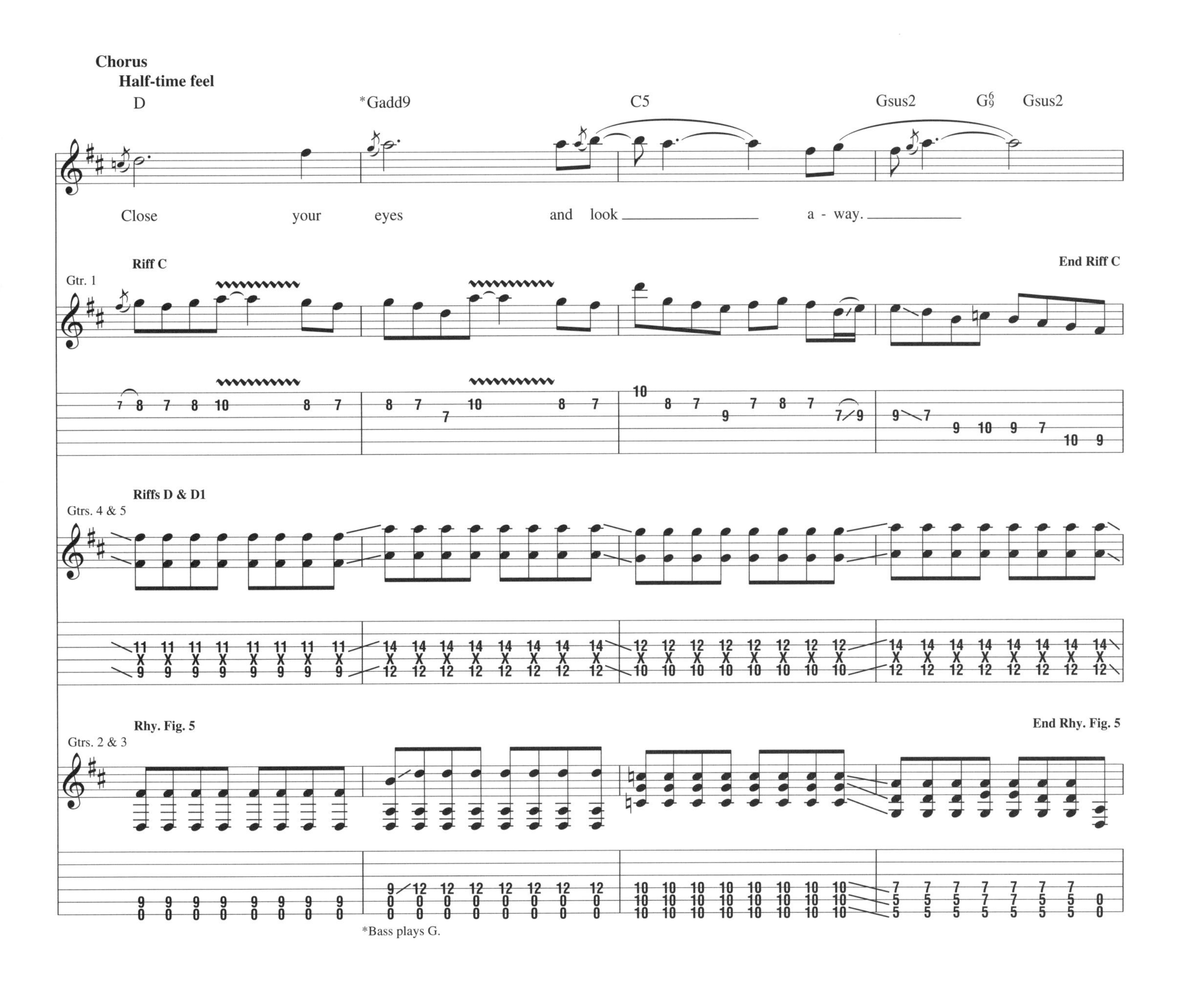
Chorus
Half-time feel
D
*Gadd9
C5
Gsus2
G6/9
Gsus2
Close your eyes and look a - way.
Riff C
Gtr. 1
End Riff C
Riffs D & D1
Gtrs. 4 & 5
Rhy. Fig. 5
Gtrs. 2 & 3
End Rhy. Fig. 5
*Bass plays G.

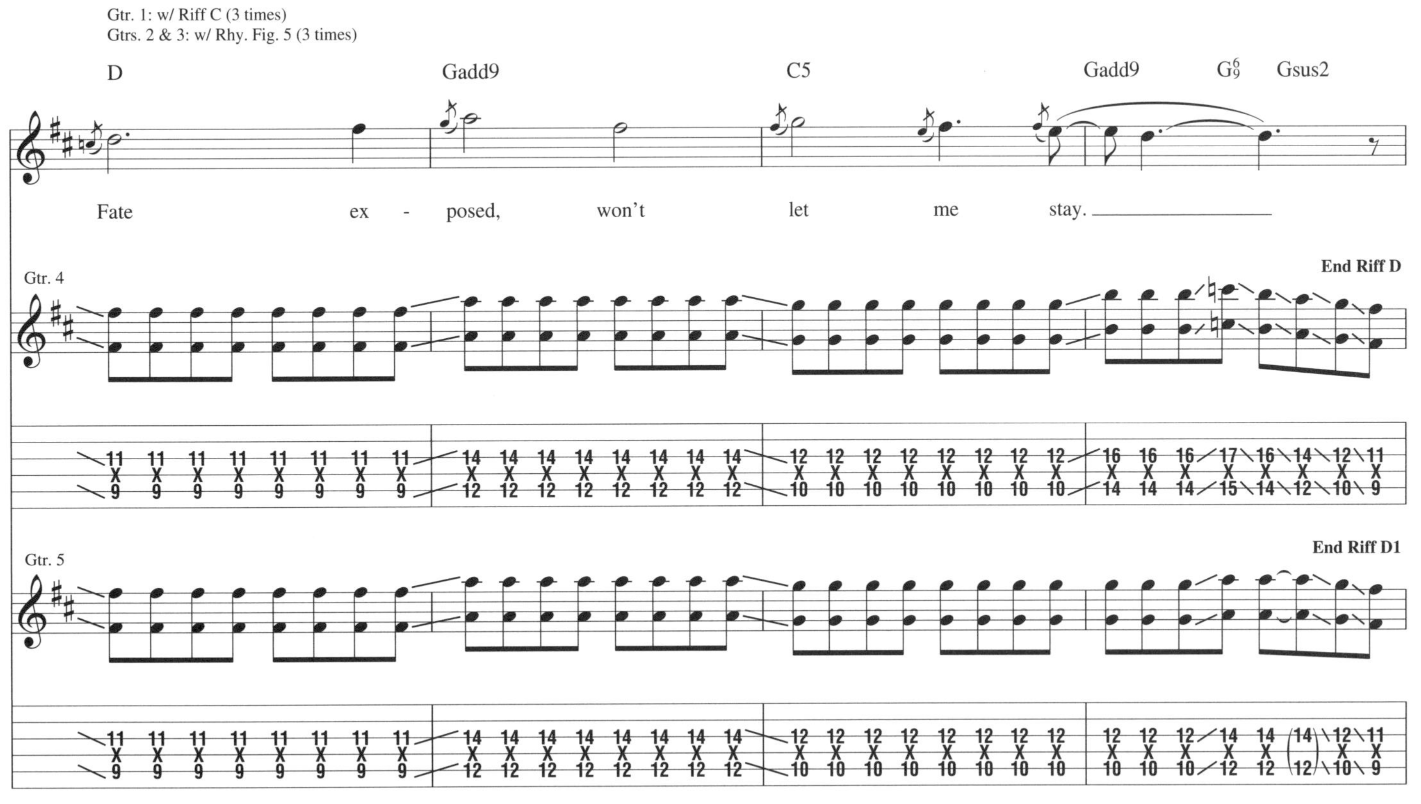
Gtr. 1: w/ Riff C (3 times)
Gtrs. 2 & 3: w/ Rhy. Fig. 5 (3 times)
D
Gadd9
C5
Gadd9
G6/9
Gsus2
Fate ex - posed, won't let me stay.
Gtr. 4
End Riff D
Gtr. 5
End Riff D1

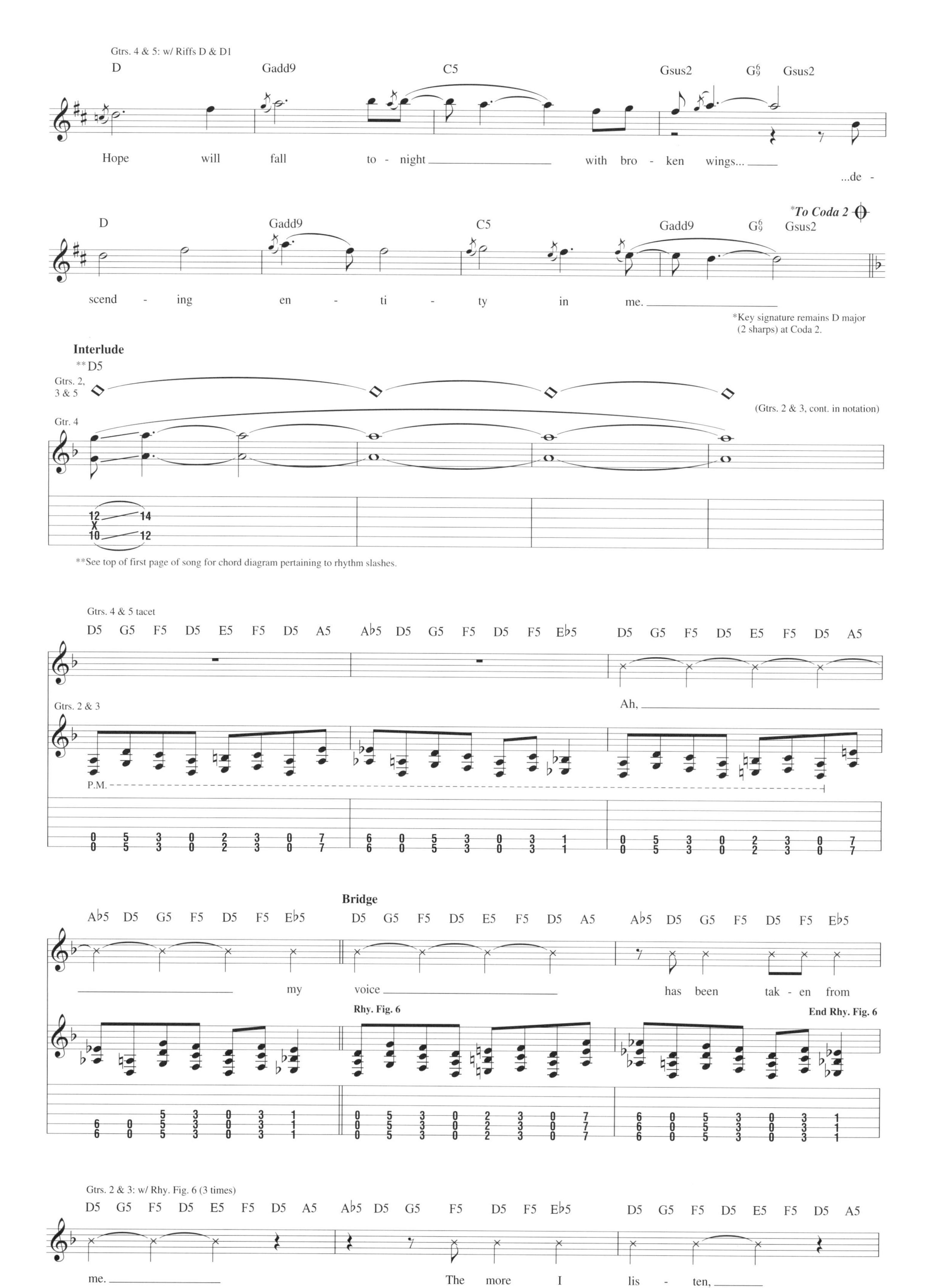

Gtrs. 4 & 5: w/ Riffs D & D1
D Gadd9 C5 Gsus2 G6/9 Gsus2
Hope will fall to - night with bro - ken wings... ...de -
D Gadd9 C5 Gadd9 G6/9 Gsus2
*To Coda 2
scend - ing en - ti - ty in me.
*Key signature remains D major (2 sharps) at Coda 2.
Interlude
**D5
Gtrs. 2, 3 & 5
Gtr. 4
(Gtrs. 2 & 3, cont. in notation)
**See top of first page of song for chord diagram pertaining to rhythm slashes.
Gtrs. 4 & 5 tacet
D5 G5 F5 D5 E5 F5 D5 A5 A♭5 D5 G5 F5 D5 F5 E♭5 D5 G5 F5 D5 E5 F5 D5 A5
Ah,
Gtrs. 2 & 3
P.M.
Bridge
A♭5 D5 G5 F5 D5 F5 E♭5 D5 G5 F5 D5 E5 F5 D5 A5 A♭5 D5 G5 F5 D5 F5 E♭5
my voice has been tak - en from
Rhy. Fig. 6
End Rhy. Fig. 6
Gtrs. 2 & 3: w/ Rhy. Fig. 6 (3 times)
D5 G5 F5 D5 E5 F5 D5 A5 A♭5 D5 G5 F5 D5 F5 E♭5 D5 G5 F5 D5 E5 F5 D5 A5
me. The more I lis - ten,

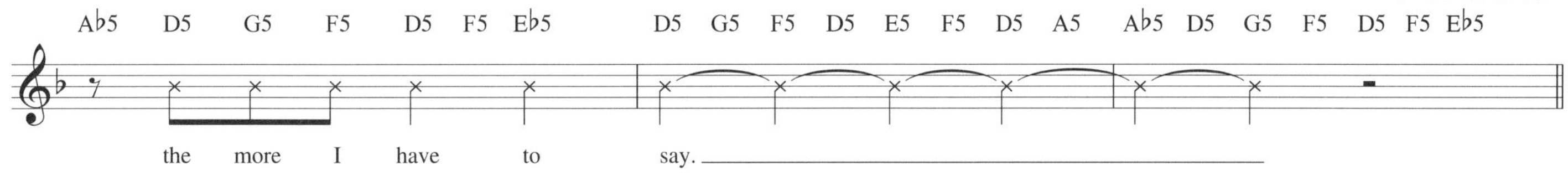
D.S. al Coda 1
End half-time feel
Ab5 D5 G5 F5 D5 F5 Eb5 D5 G5 F5 D5 E5 F5 D5 A5 Ab5 D5 G5 F5 D5 F5 Eb5
the more I have to say.

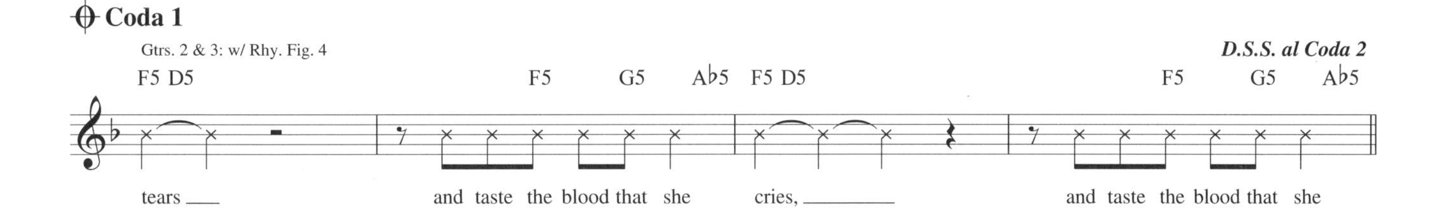
Coda 1
Gtrs. 2 & 3: w/ Rhy. Fig. 4
D.S.S. al Coda 2
F5 D5 F5 G5 Ab5 F5 D5 F5 G5 Ab5
tears and taste the blood that she cries, and taste the blood that she

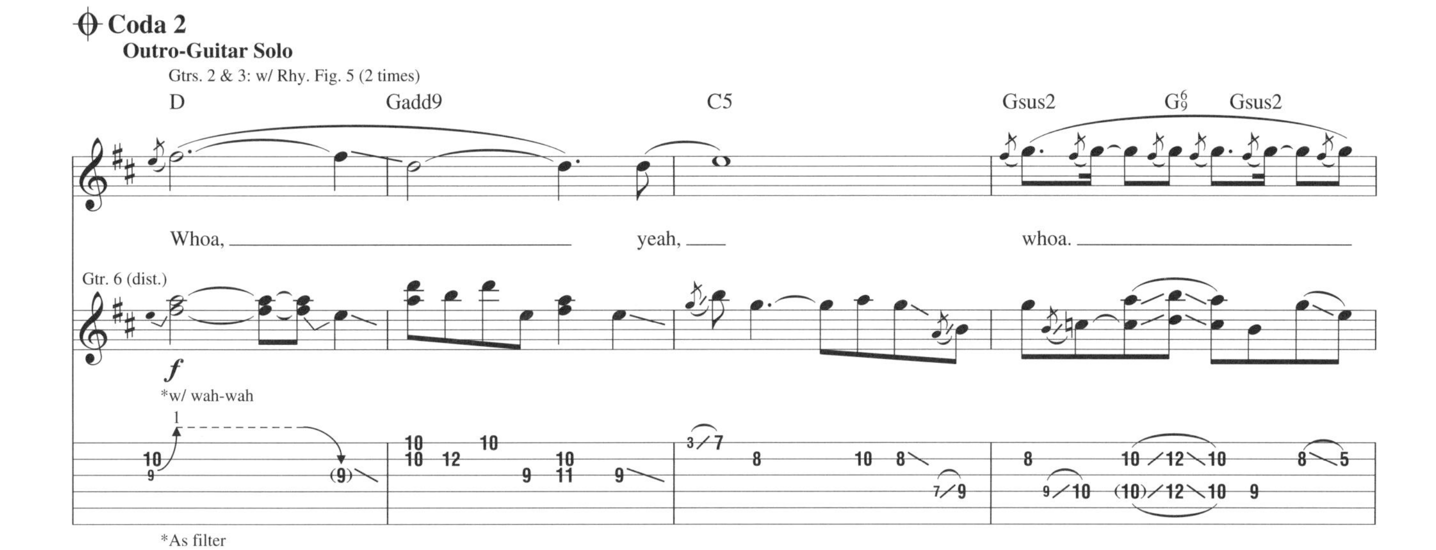
Coda 2
Outro-Guitar Solo
Gtrs. 2 & 3: w/ Rhy. Fig. 5 (2 times)
D Gadd9 C5 Gsus2 G6/9 Gsus2
Whoa, yeah, whoa.
Gtr. 6 (dist.)
f
*w/ wah-wah
*As filter

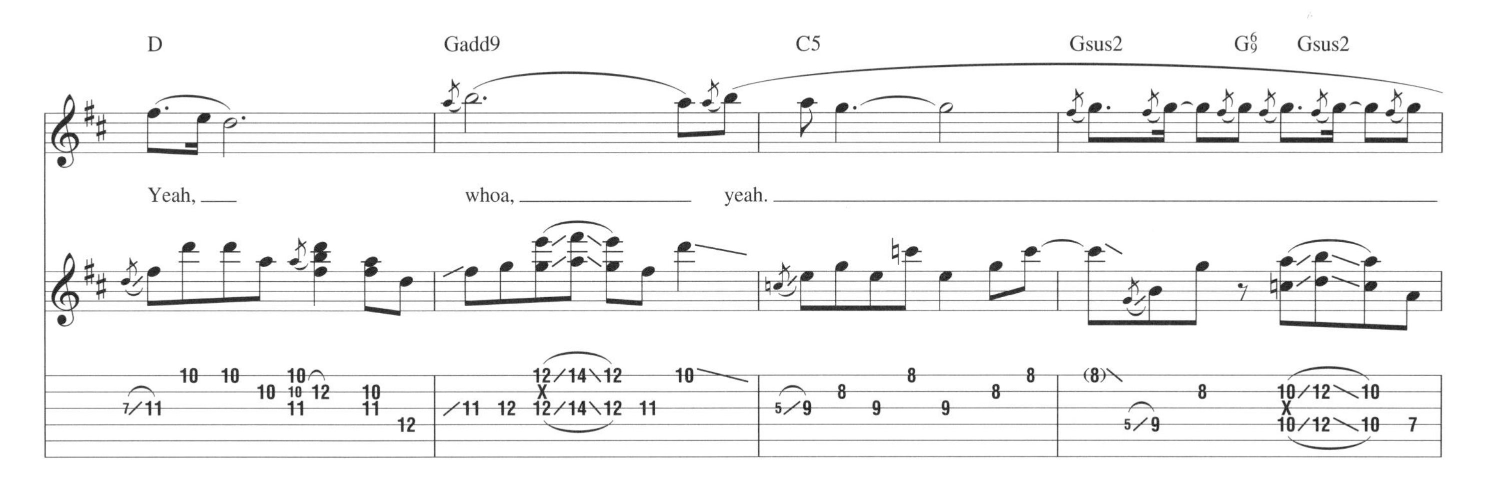
D Gadd9 C5 Gsus2 G6/9 Gsus2
Yeah, whoa, yeah.

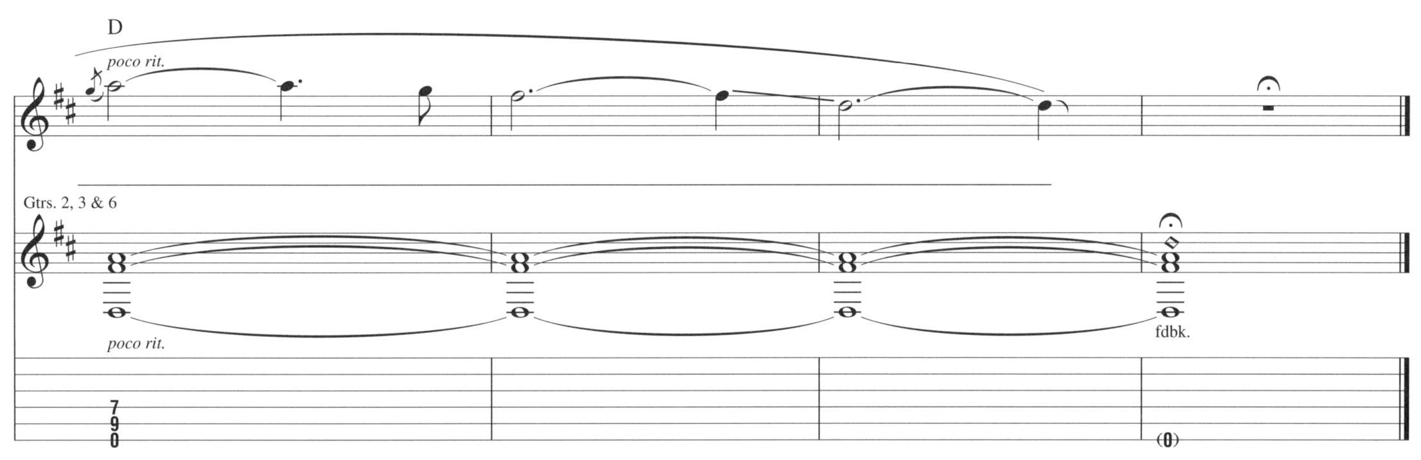
D
poco rit.
Gtrs. 2, 3 & 6
poco rit.
fdbk.

I Won't See You Tonight (Part I)

Words and Music by Matthew Sanders, James Sullivan, Brian Haner, Jr. and Zachary Baker

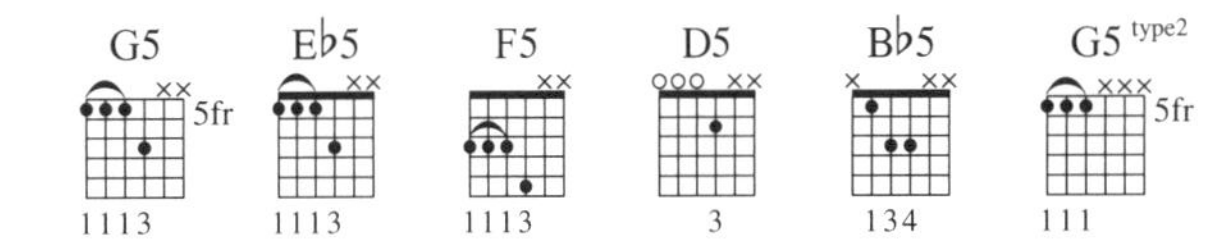

Drop D tuning:
(low to high) D-A-D-G-B-E

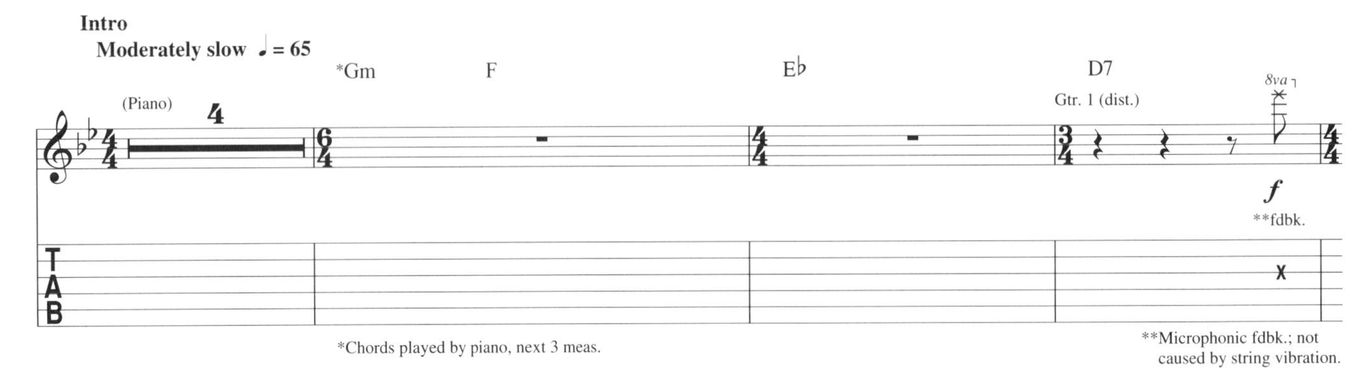

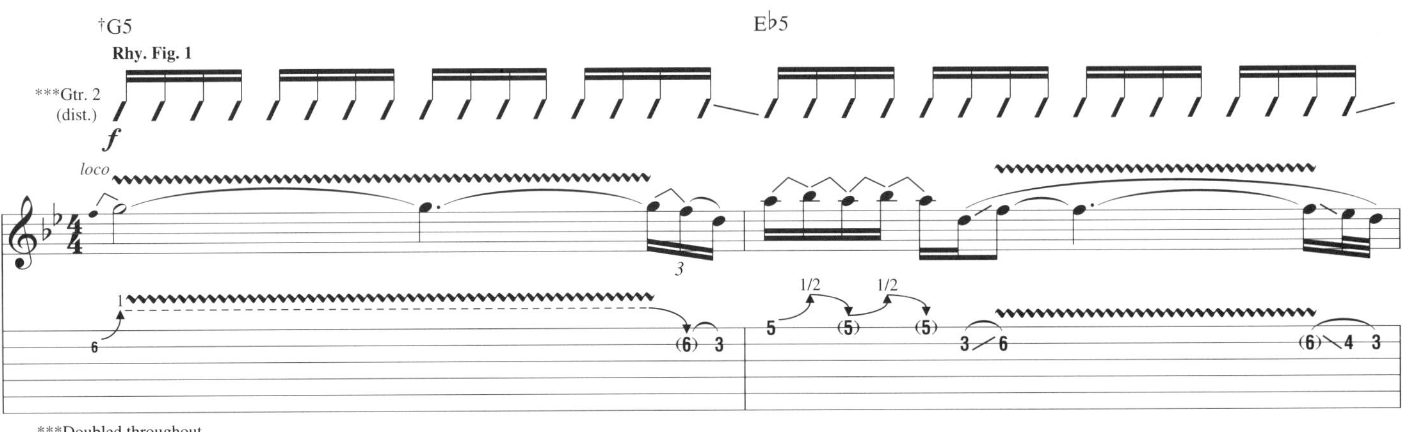

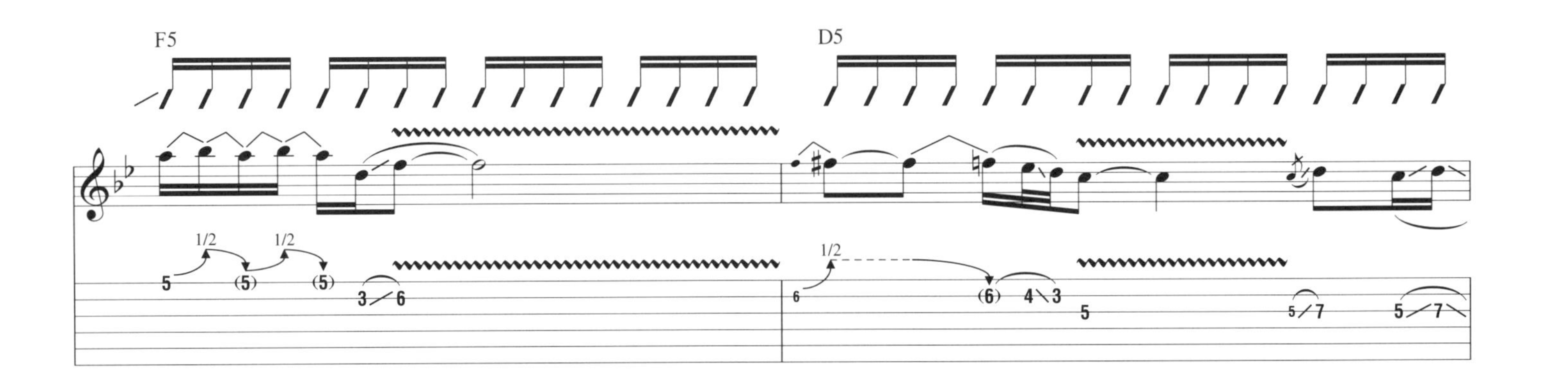

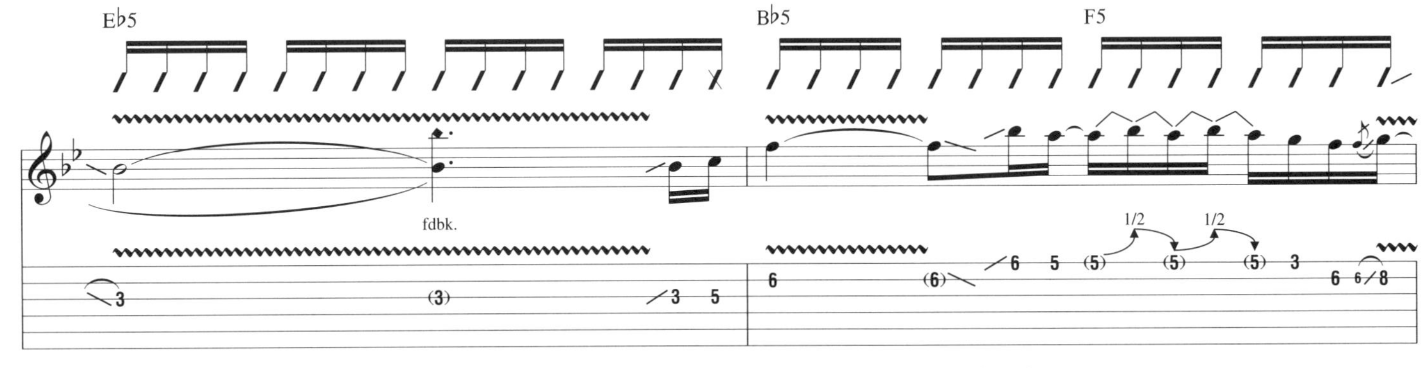

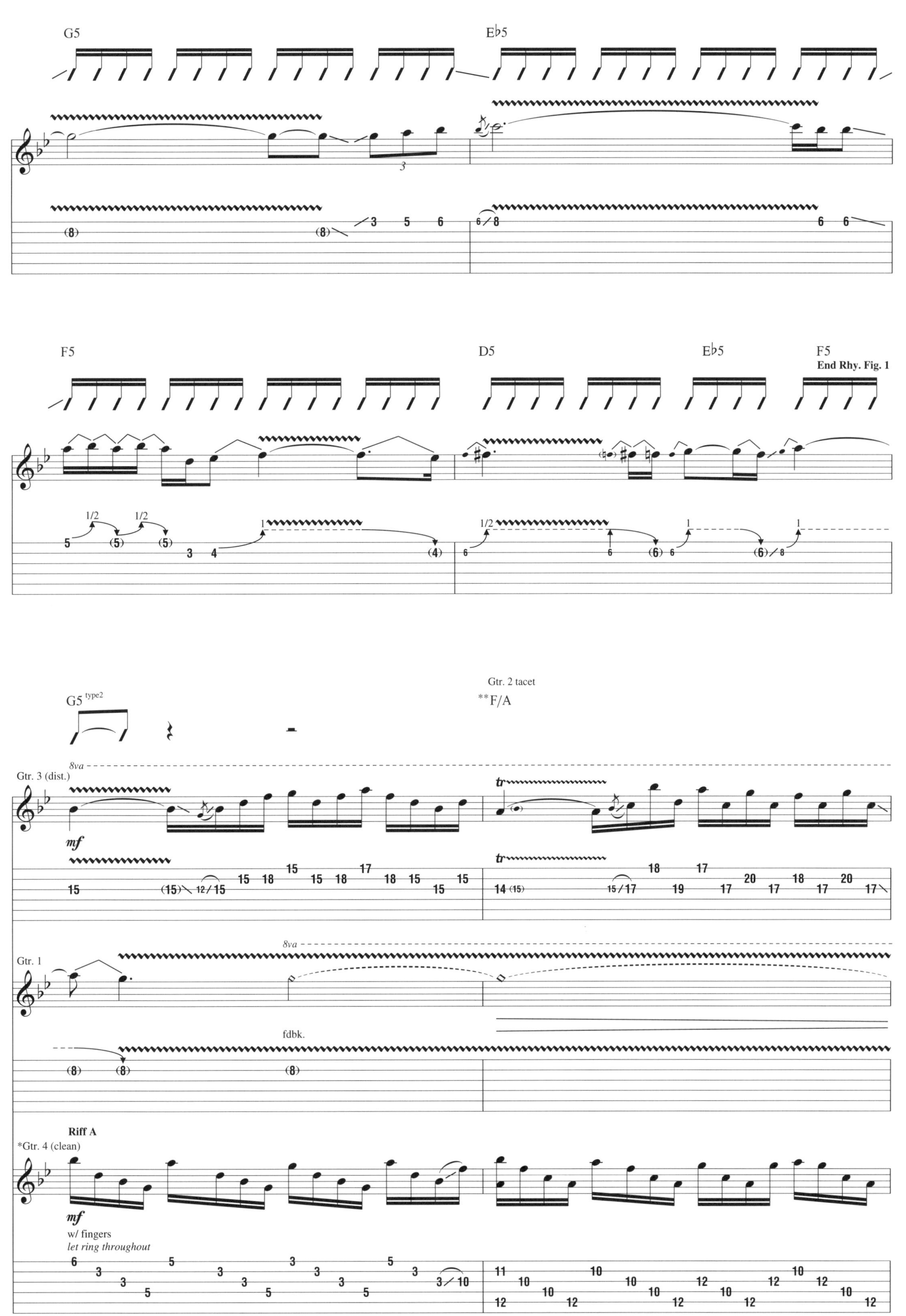

*Doubled throughout

**Chord symbols reflect implied harmony.

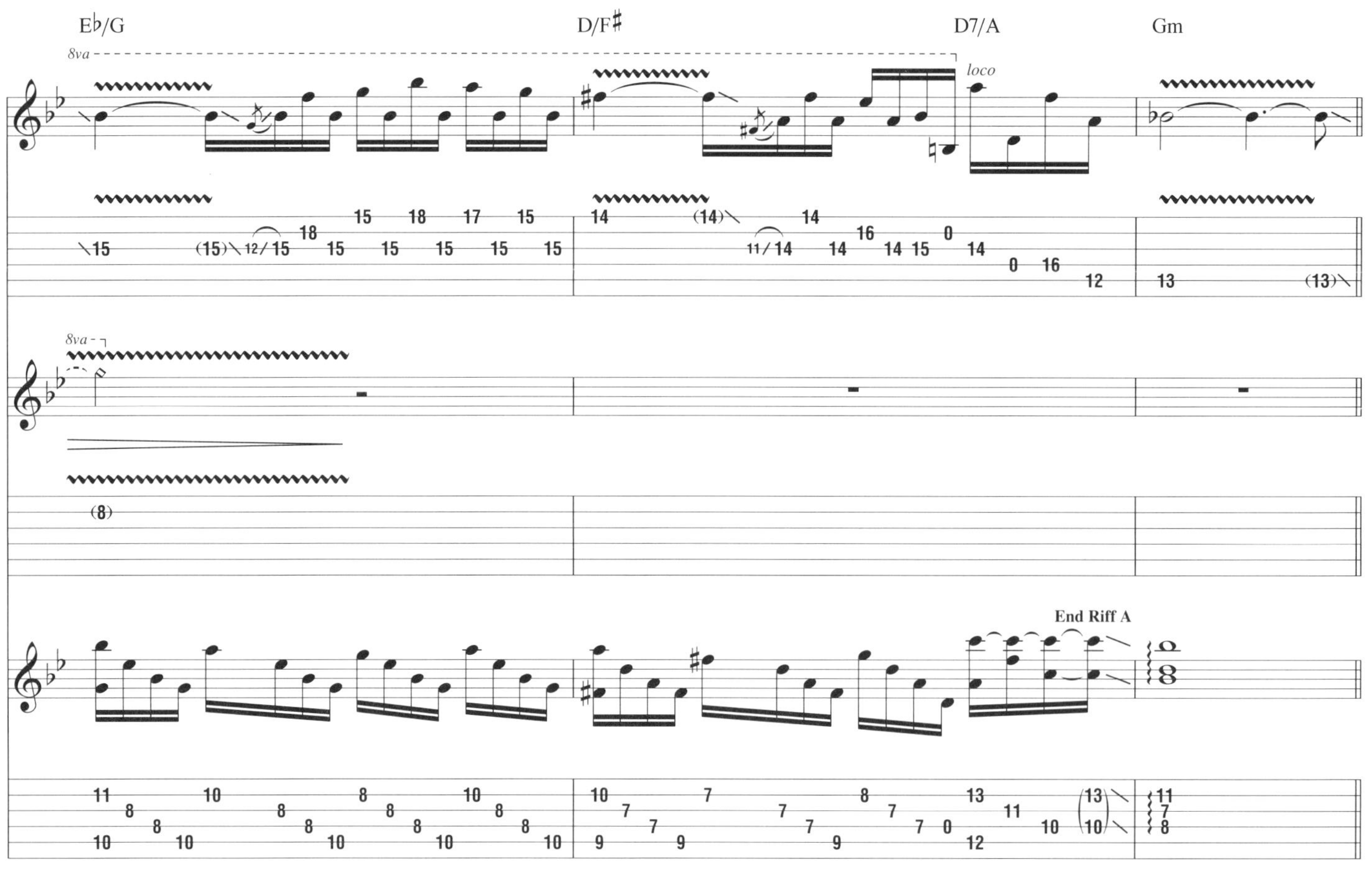
Gtr. 1 tacet
E♭/G
D/F♯
D7/A
Gm
8va
loco
End Riff A

Verse

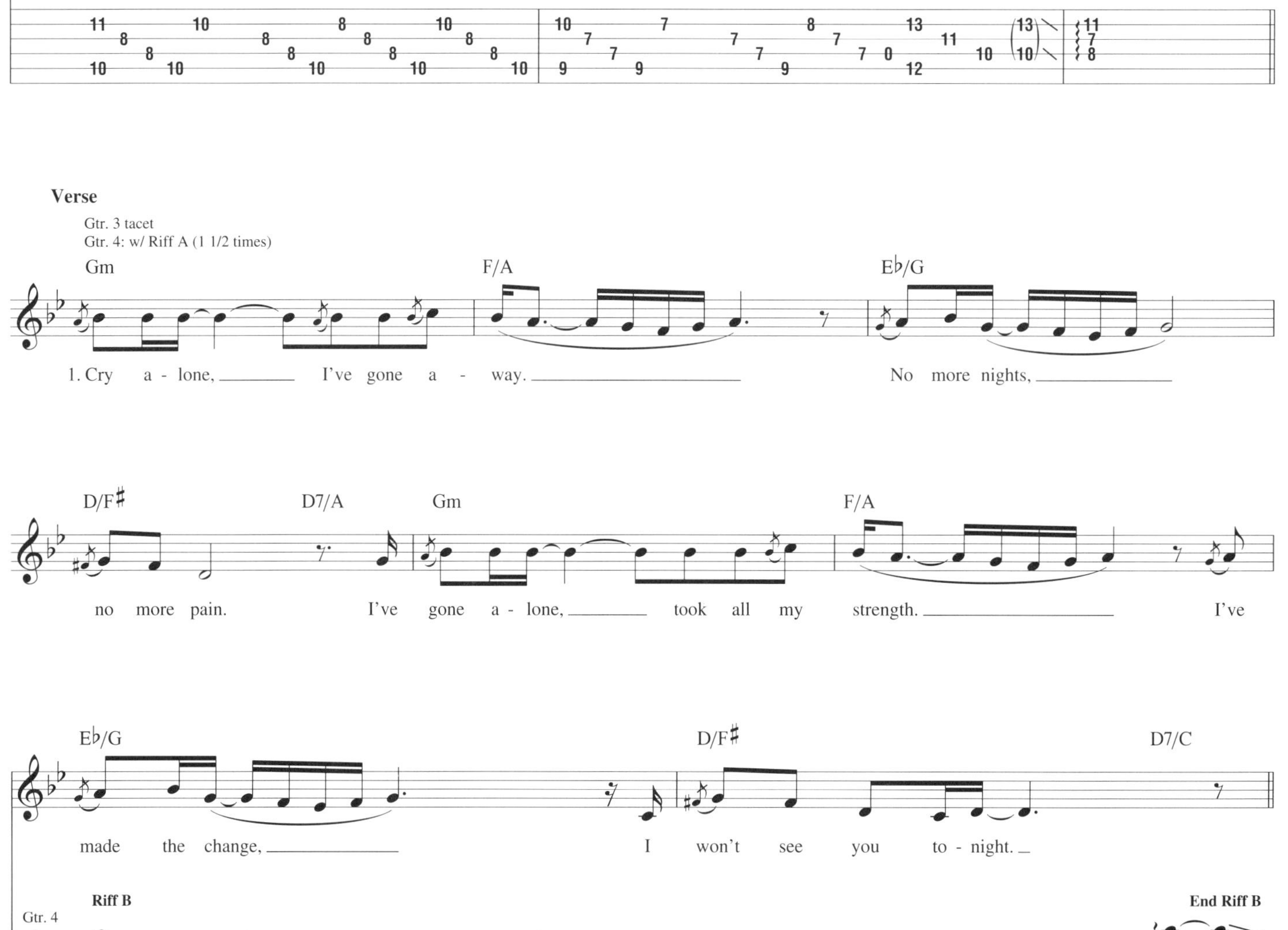
Gtr. 3 tacet
Gtr. 4: w/ Riff A (1 1/2 times)
Gm
F/A
E♭/G
1. Cry a - lone, I've gone a - way. No more nights,
D/F♯
D7/A
Gm
F/A
no more pain. I've gone a - lone, took all my strength. I've
E♭/G
D/F♯
D7/C
made the change, I won't see you to - night.
Gtr. 4
Riff B
End Riff B

Chorus
Gtr. 4 tacet
G5
Eb5
Sor - row sank deep in - side my blood.
Gtr. 2
Bb5
F5
Gb5
All the ones a - round me I cared for and loved.
2. It's
Verse
Gtr. 2 tacet
Gtr. 4: w/ Riff A (1 1/2 times)
Gm
F/A
build - ing up in - side of me, a
Eb/G
D/F#
D7/A
place of dark so cold I had to set me free. Don't
Gm
F/A
mourn for me, you're not the one to place the blame. As
Gtr. 4: w/ Riff B
Eb/G
D/F#
D7/C
bot - tles call my name, I won't see you to - night.

Chorus
G5
Eb5
Sor - row sank deep in - side my blood.
Rhy. Fig. 2
Gtr. 2
Bb5
F5
Gb5
All the ones a - round me I cared for and, most of all, I loved.
End Rhy. Fig. 2
Gtr. 2: w/ Rhy. Fig. 2
But I can't see my - self that way. Please don't for - get
me or cry while I'm a - way.
Guitar Solo
Gtr. 2: w/ Rhy. Fig. 1
8va
Gtr. 1
1
1 1/2

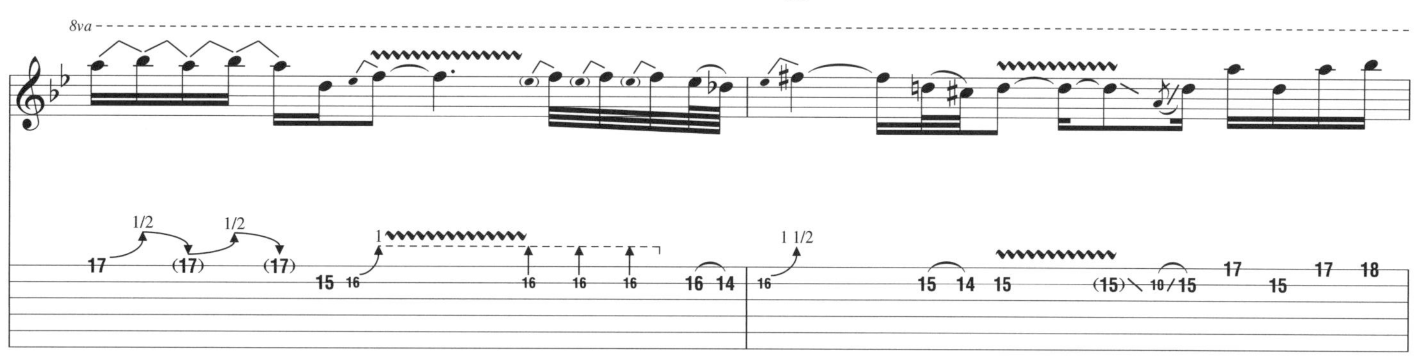
F5
D5
8va

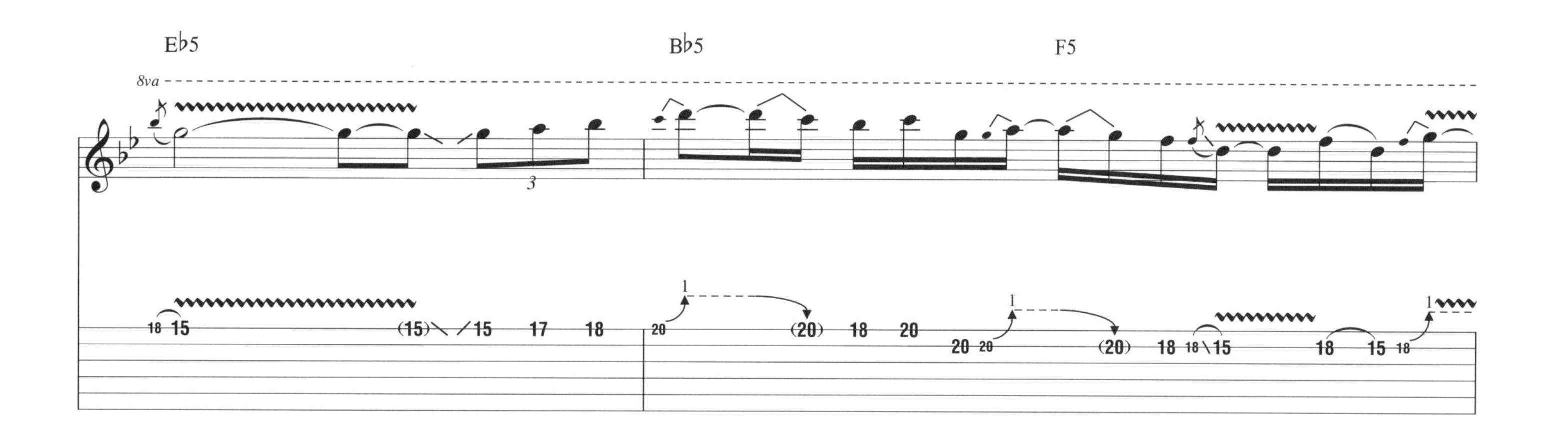
E♭5
B♭5
F5
8va

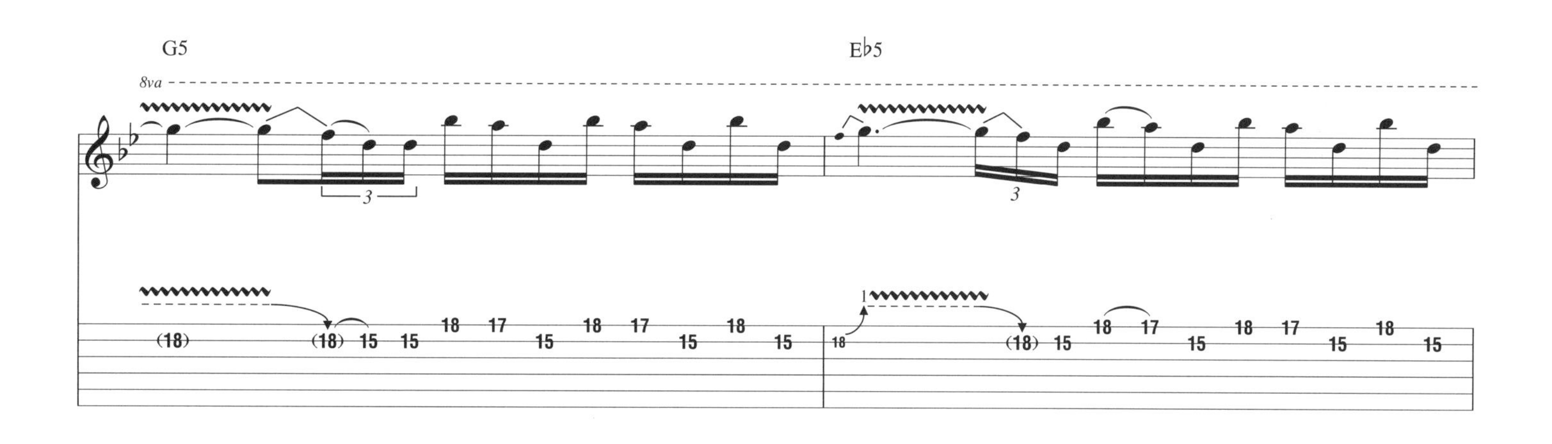
G5
E♭5
8va

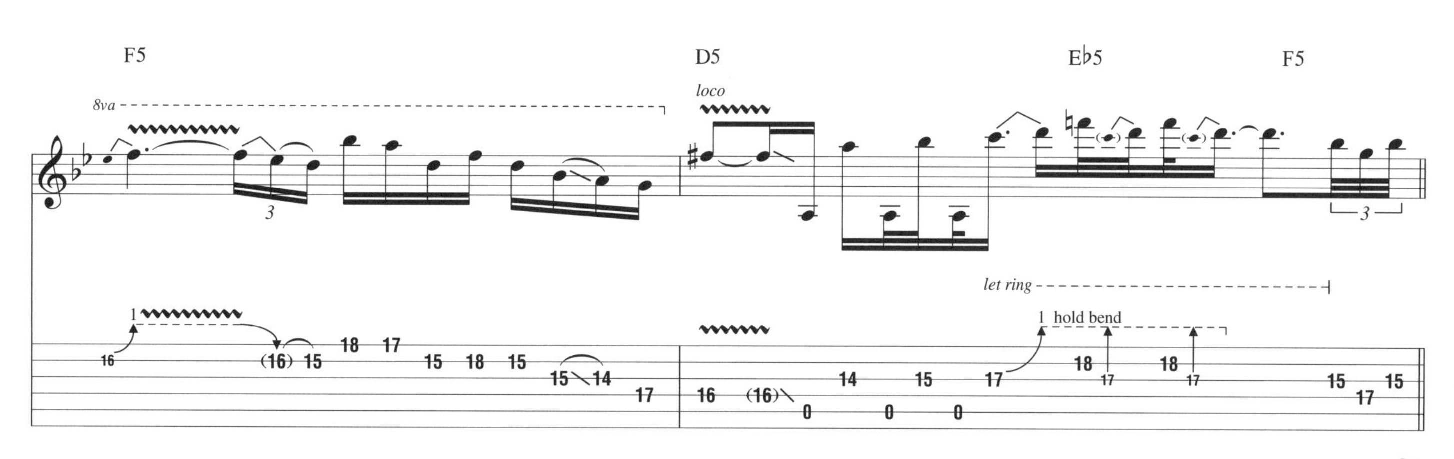
F5
D5
E♭5
F5
8va
loco
let ring
1 hold bend

Verse

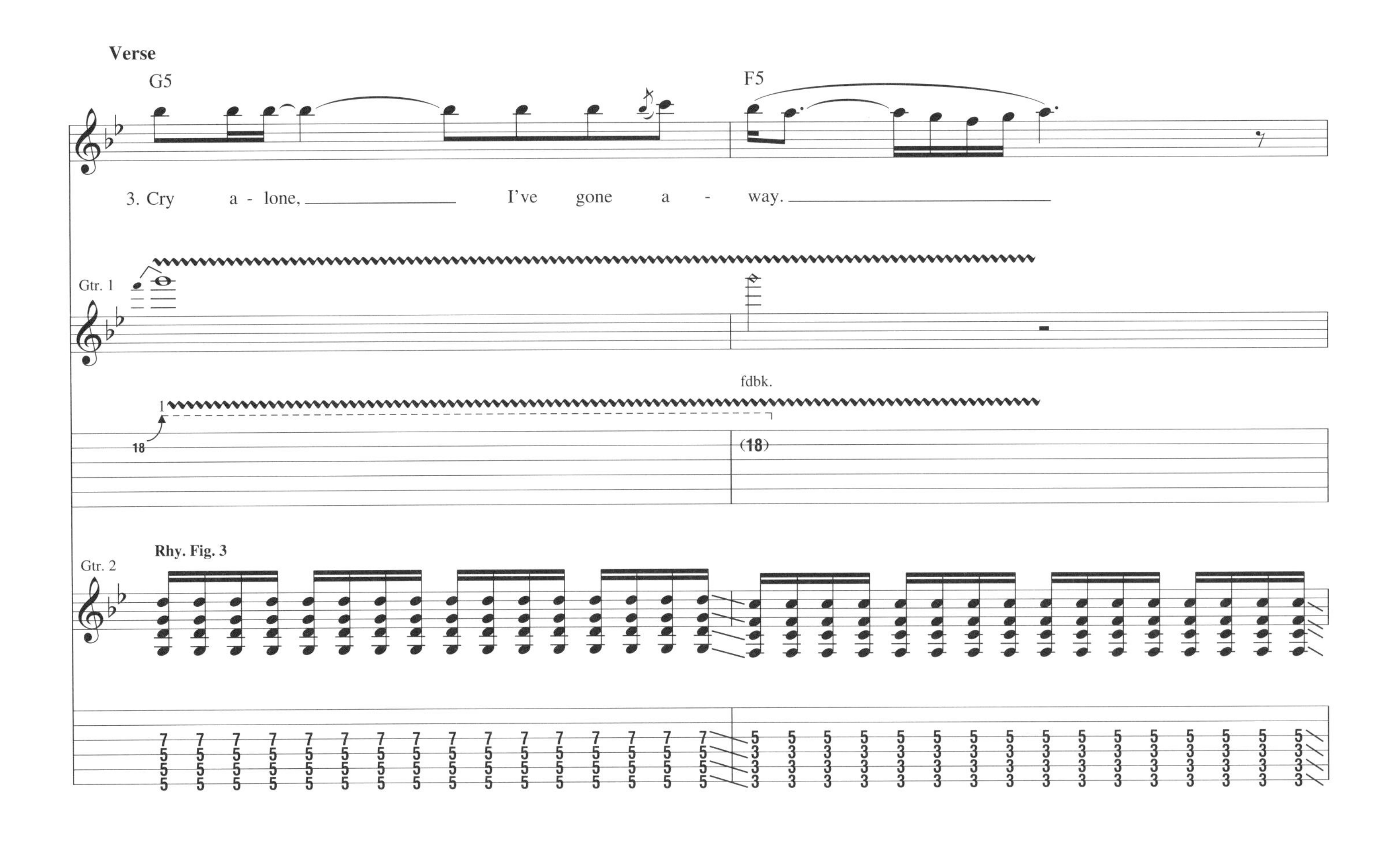

G5
F5
3. Cry a - lone, I've gone a - way.
Gtr. 1
fdbk.
Rhy. Fig. 3
Gtr. 2

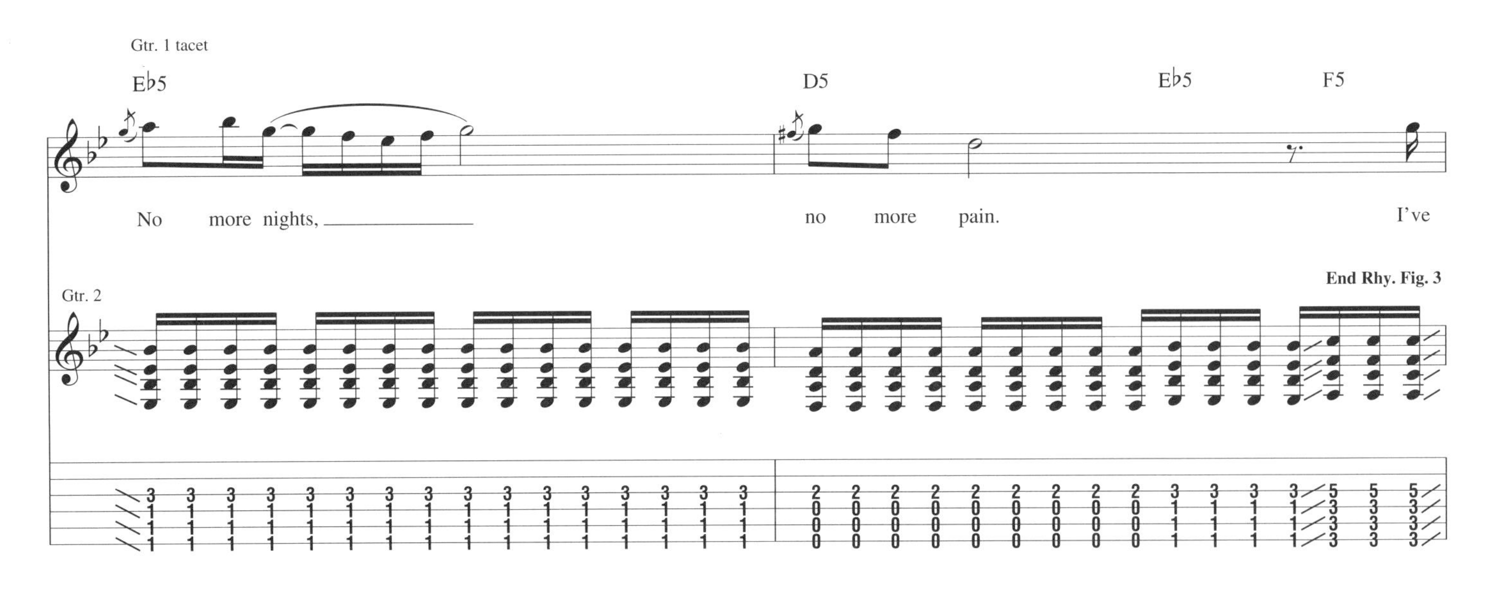

Gtr. 1 tacet
Eb5
D5
Eb5
F5
No more nights, no more pain. I've
Gtr. 2
End Rhy. Fig. 3

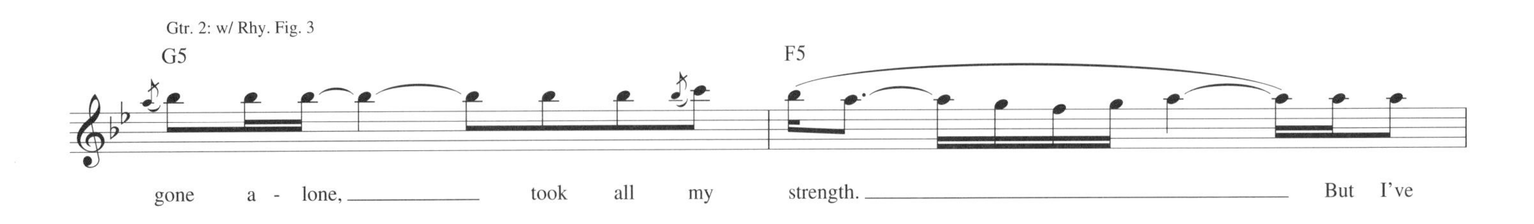

Gtr. 2: w/ Rhy. Fig. 3
G5
F5
gone a - lone, took all my strength. But I've

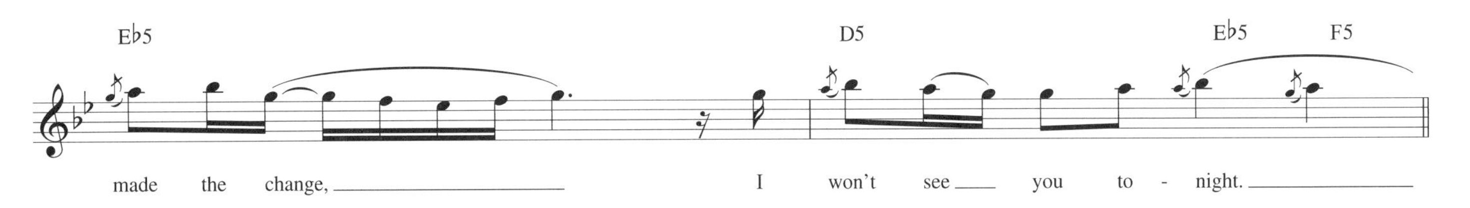

Eb5
D5
Eb5
F5
made the change, I won't see you to - night.

Bridge
Gtr. 2: w/ Rhy. Fig. 1
G5
E♭5
F5
(So far a - way, I'm
Gtr. 3
D5
E♭5
gone. Please don't
B♭5
F5
G5
E♭5
fol - low me to - night. And while I'm gone,
8va
F5
D5
E♭5
F5
ev - 'ry - thing will be al -
8va
loco

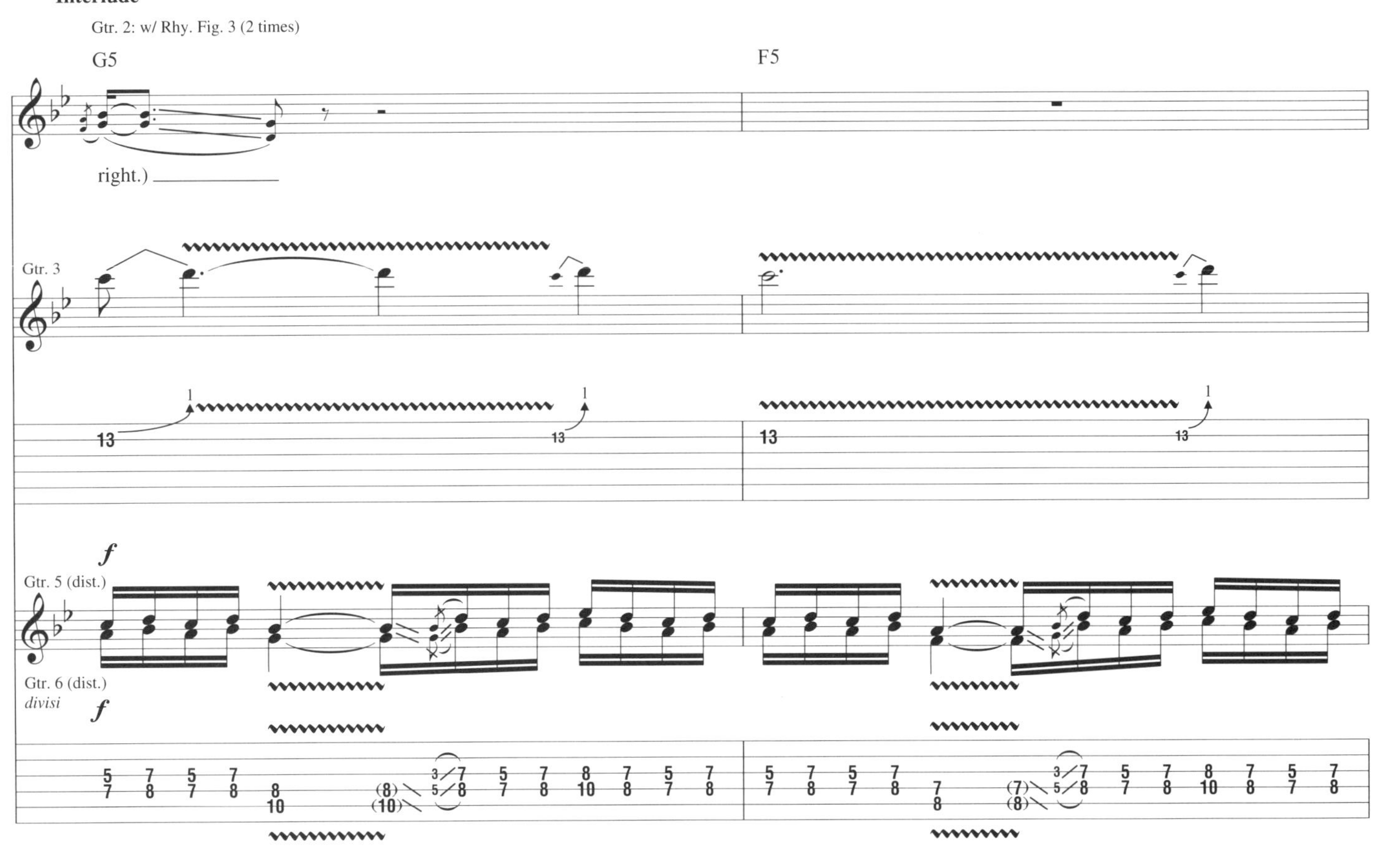
Gtr. 2: w/ Rhy. Fig. 3 (2 times)
G5
F5
right.)
Gtr. 3
Gtr. 5 (dist.)
Gtr. 6 (dist.)
divisi

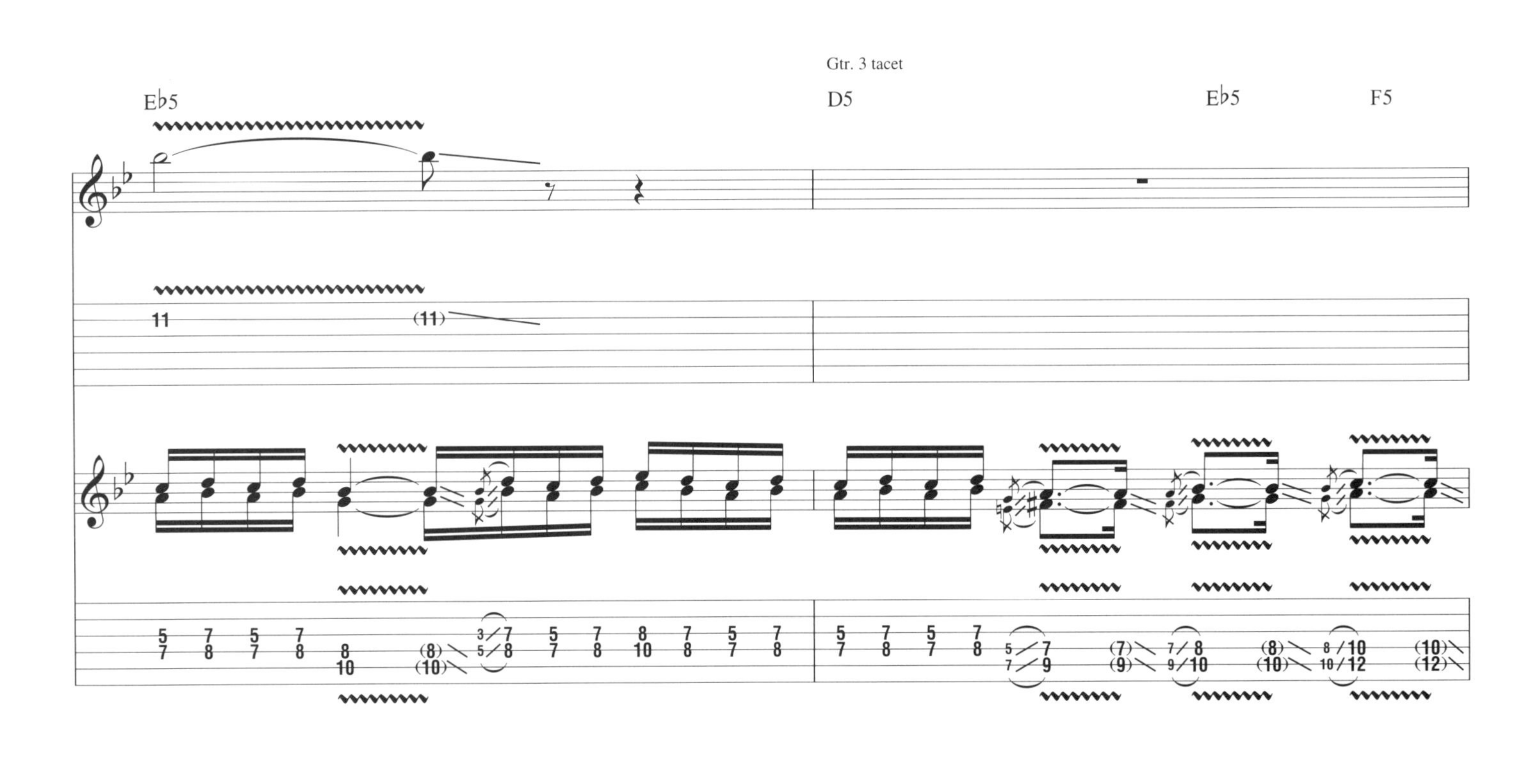
Gtr. 3 tacet
E♭5
D5
E♭5
F5

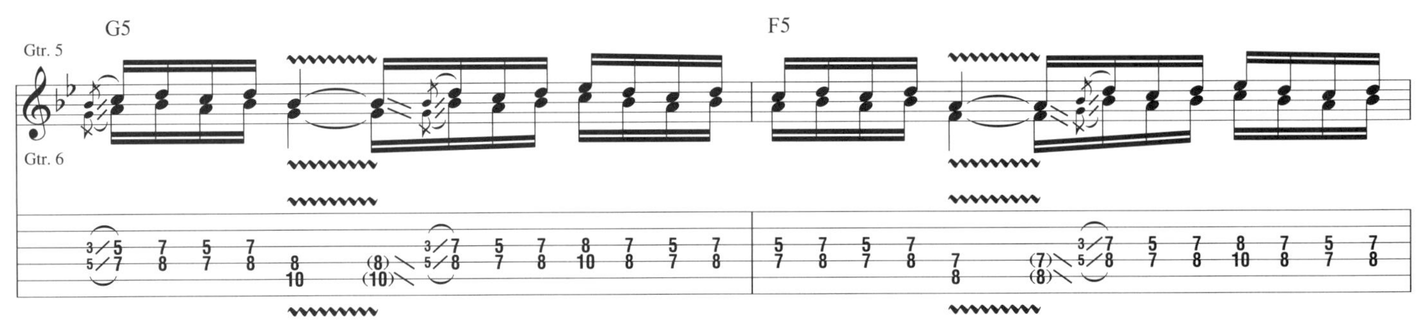
G5
F5
Gtr. 5
Gtr. 6

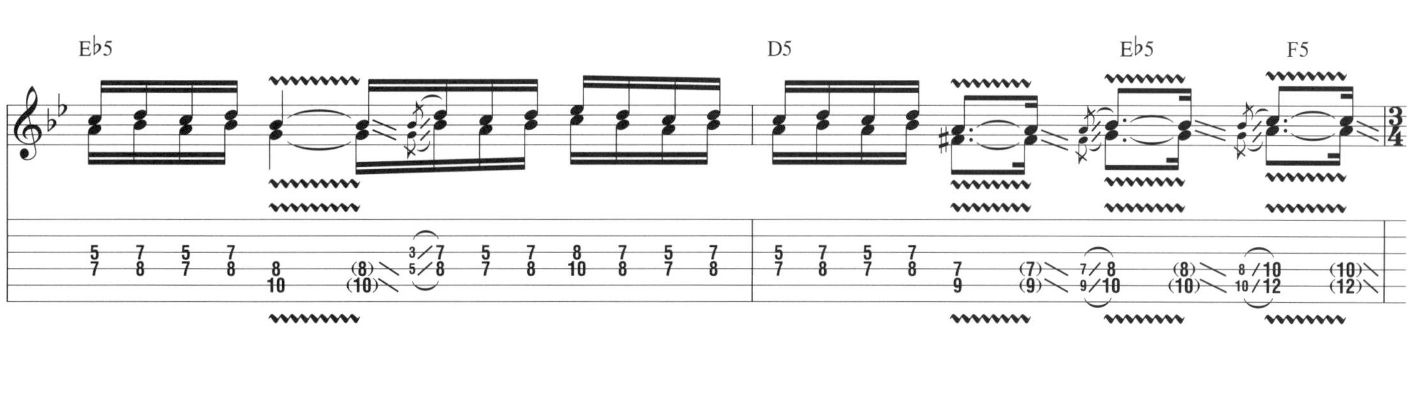
E♭5
D5
E♭5
F5

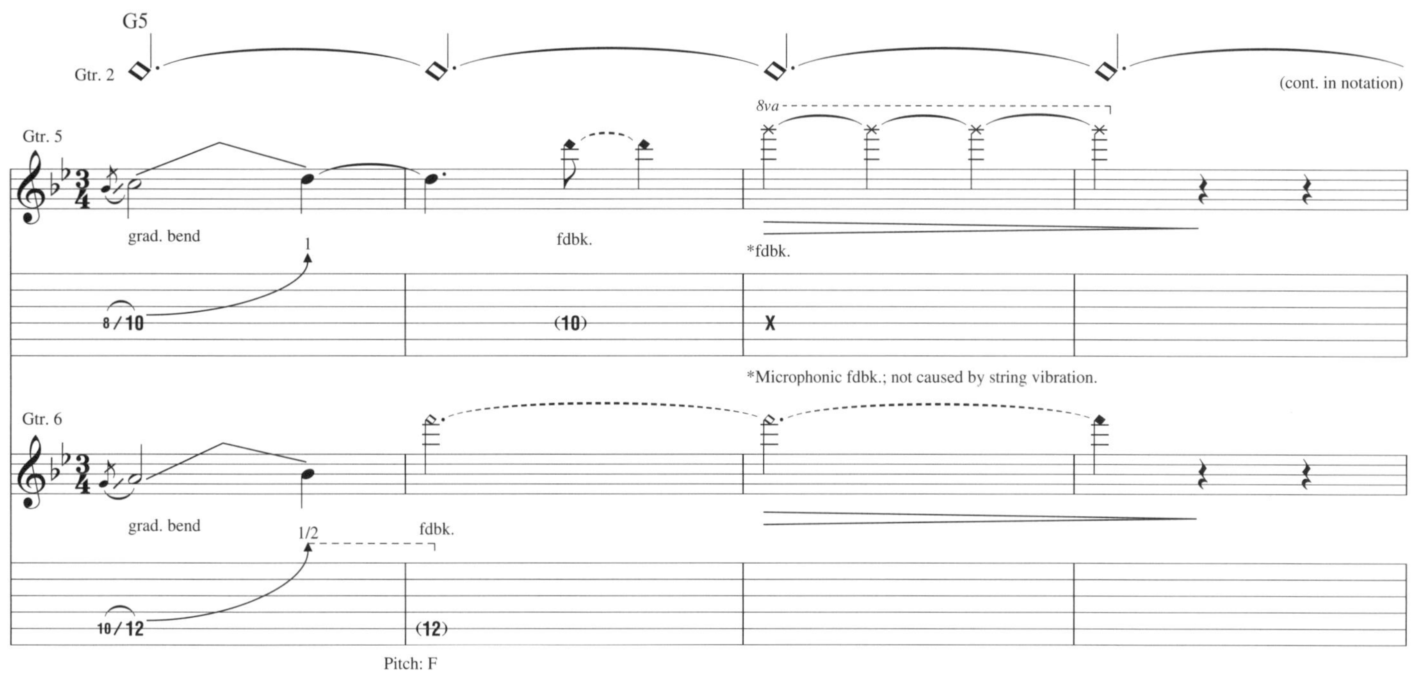
G5
Gtr. 2
(cont. in notation)
Gtr. 5
8va
grad. bend
1
fdbk.
*fdbk.
*Microphonic fdbk.; not caused by string vibration.
Gtr. 6
grad. bend
1/2
fdbk.
Pitch: F

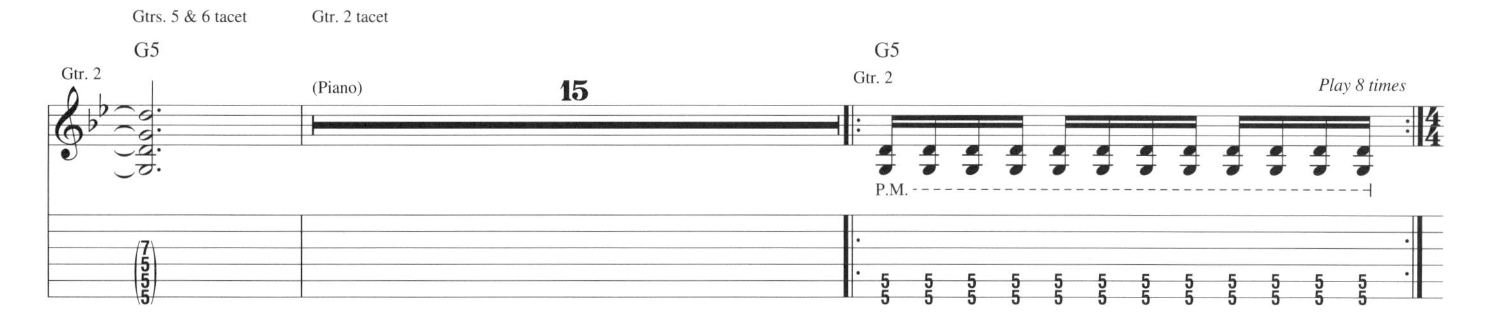
Gtrs. 5 & 6 tacet
Gtr. 2 tacet
G5
Gtr. 2
(Piano)
15
G5
Gtr. 2
Play 8 times
P.M.

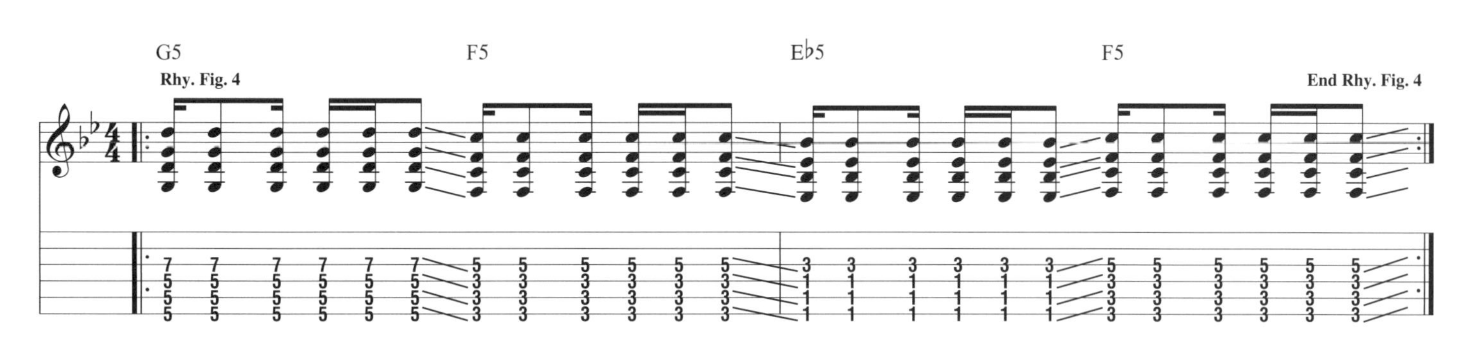
G5
F5
E♭5
F5
Rhy. Fig. 4
End Rhy. Fig. 4

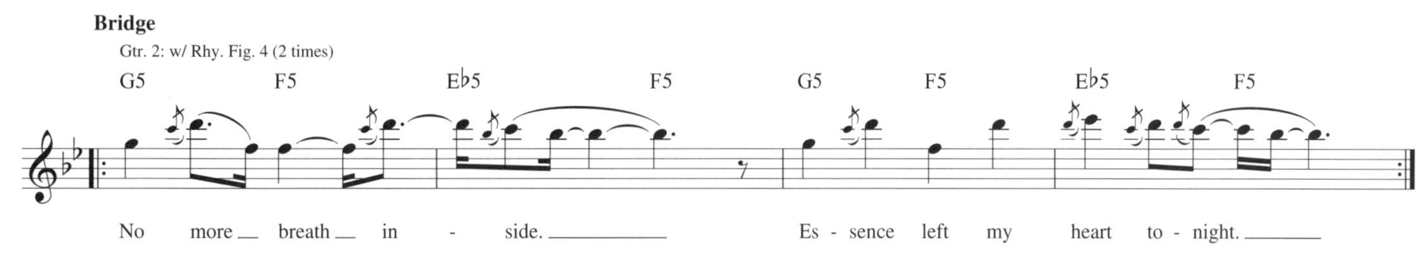
Bridge
Gtr. 2: w/ Rhy. Fig. 4 (2 times)
G5
F5
E♭5
F5
G5
F5
E♭5
F5
No more breath in - side.
Es - sence left my heart to - night.

Outro
G5
B♭5
F5
Whoa,
whoa,
yeah,
yeah.
Voc. Fig. 1
(Whoa,
whoa,
whoa,
whoa.)
Gtr. 2
Rhy. Fig. 5
E♭5
Bkgd. Voc.: w/ Voc. Fig. 1 (till fade)
Gtr. 2: w/ Rhy. Fig. 5 (till fade)
G5
B♭5
Whoa,
yeah.
End Voc. Fig. 1
End Rhy. Fig. 5
F5
E♭5
G5
B♭5
Yeah,
yeah,
yeah,
F5
E♭5
G5
whoa.
B♭5
F5
E♭5
Yeah,
yeah.
*Begin fade
Repeat and fade
G5
B♭5
F5
E♭5
Whoa,
whoa,
yeah,
whoa.
*Signal distortion increases as track fades out.

I Won't See You Tonight (Part II)

Words and Music by Matthew Sanders, James Sullivan, Brian Haner, Jr. and Zachary Baker

Drop D tuning:
(low to high) D-A-D-G-B-E

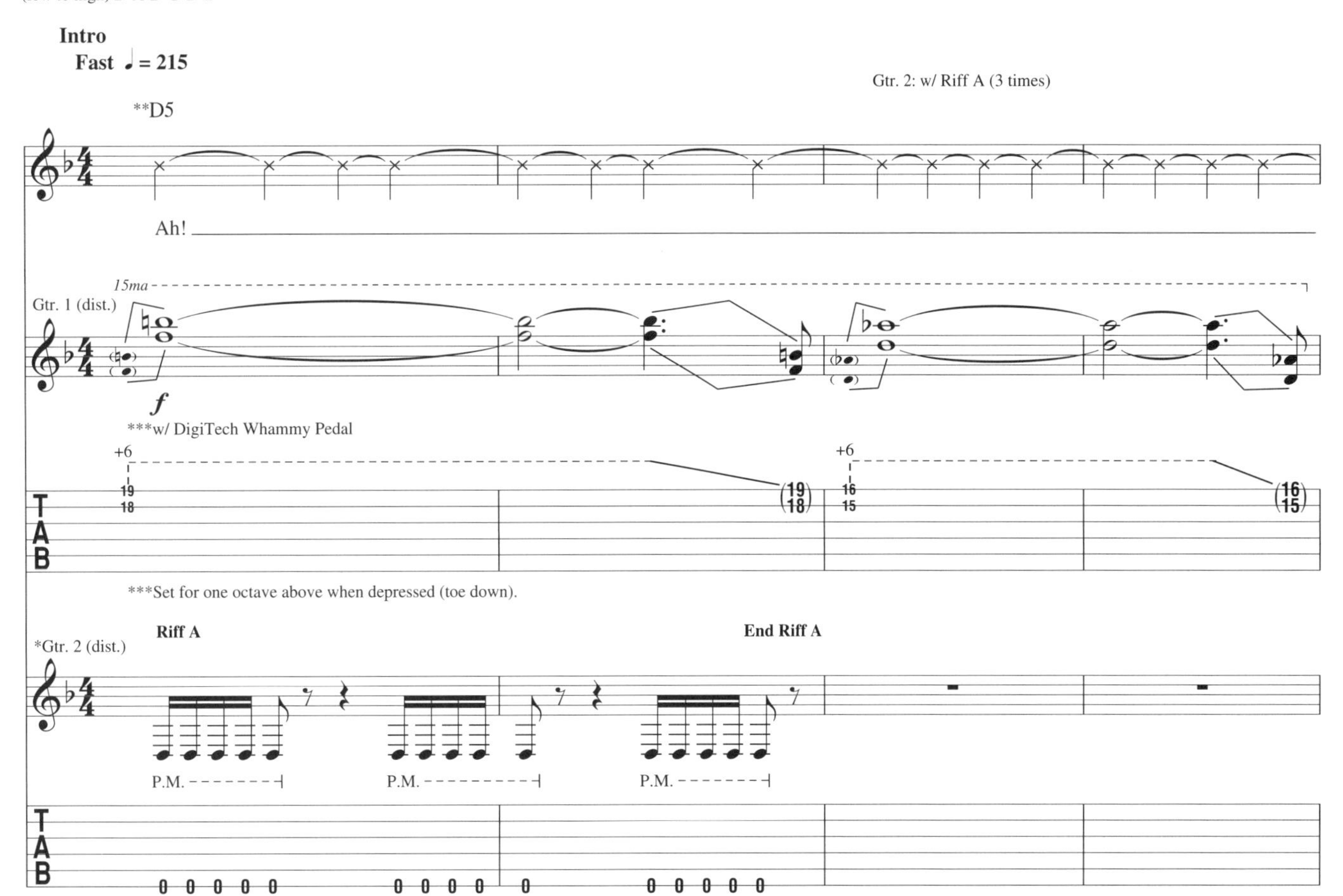

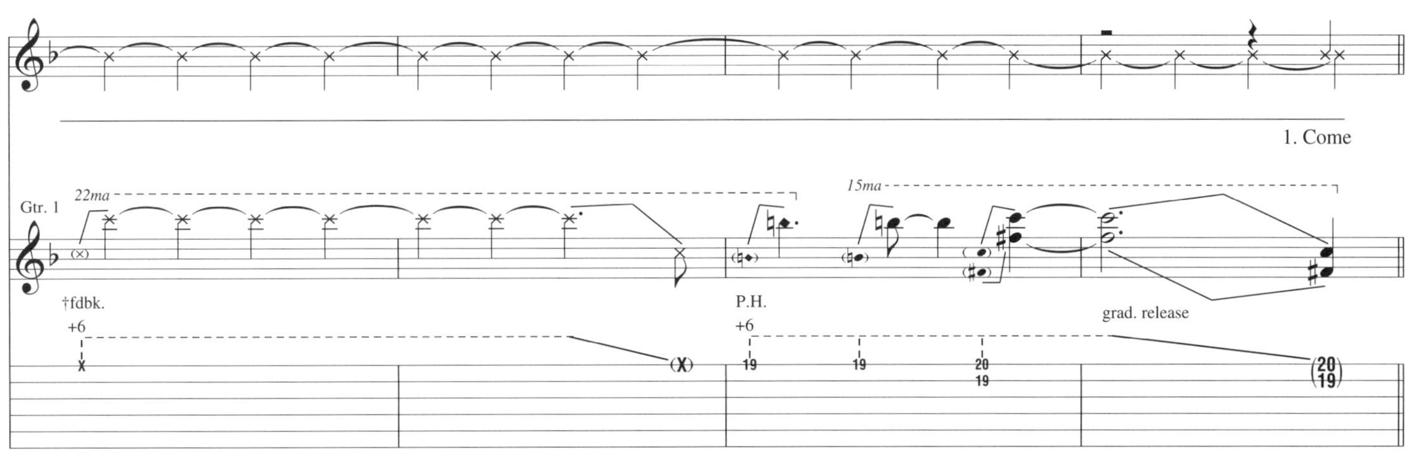

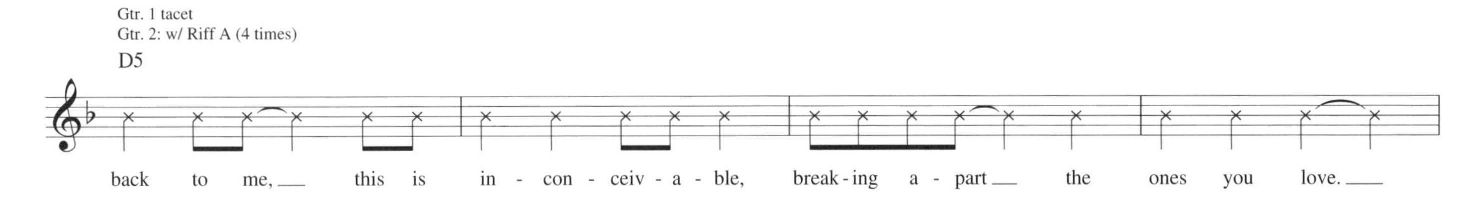

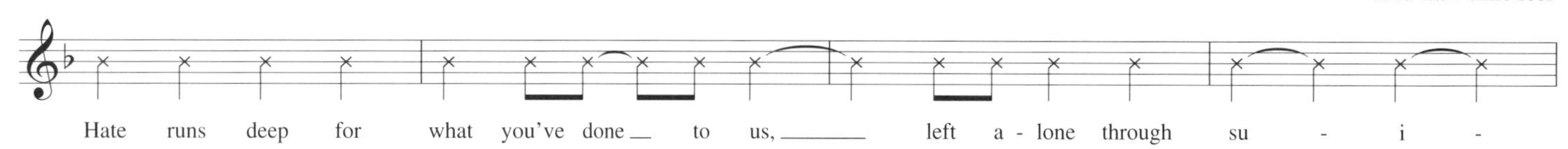
End half-time feel
Hate runs deep for what you've done to us, left a - lone through su - i -

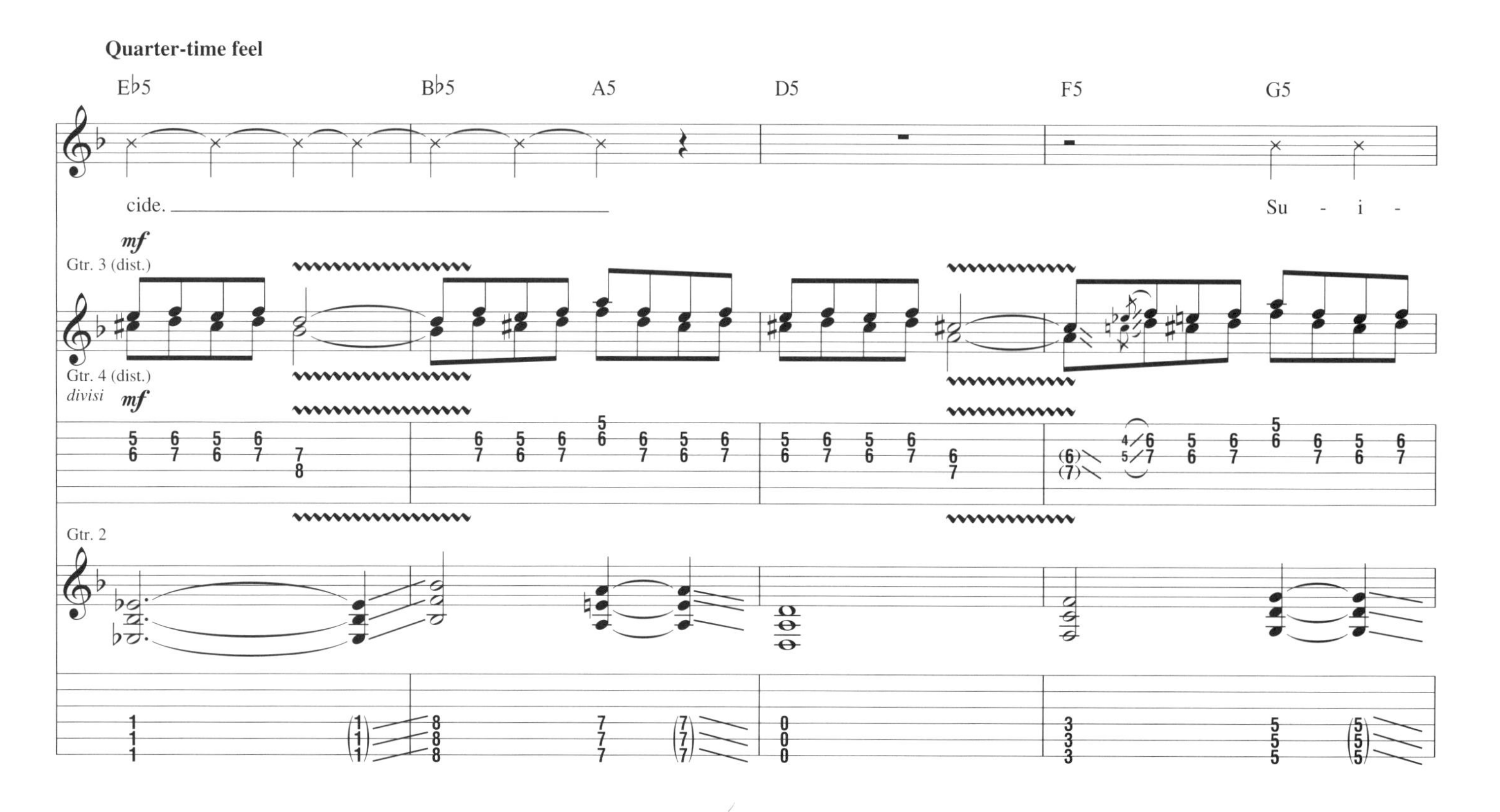
Quarter-time feel
E♭5
B♭5
A5
D5
F5
G5
cide.
Su - i -
mf
Gtr. 3 (dist.)
Gtr. 4 (dist.)
divisi
mf
Gtr. 2

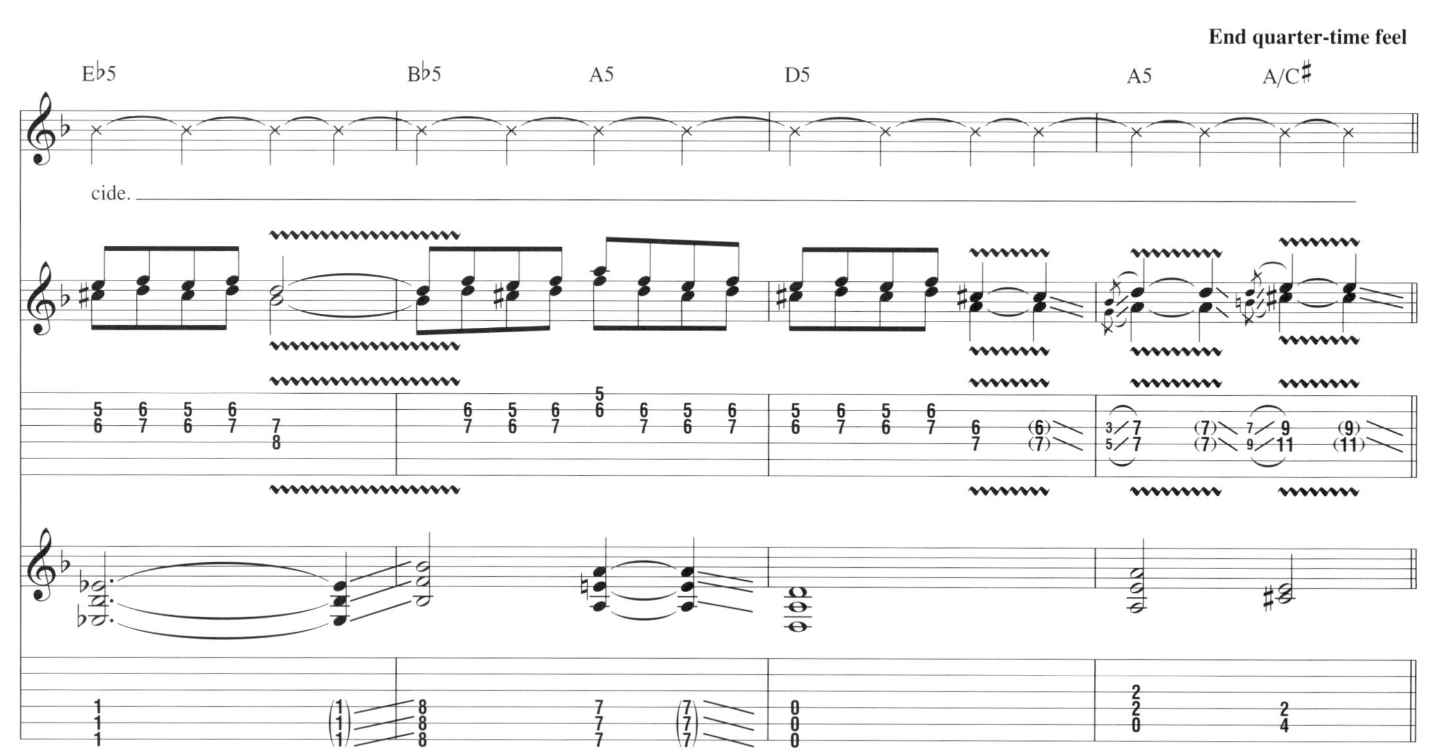
End quarter-time feel
E♭5
B♭5
A5
D5
A5
A/C♯
cide.

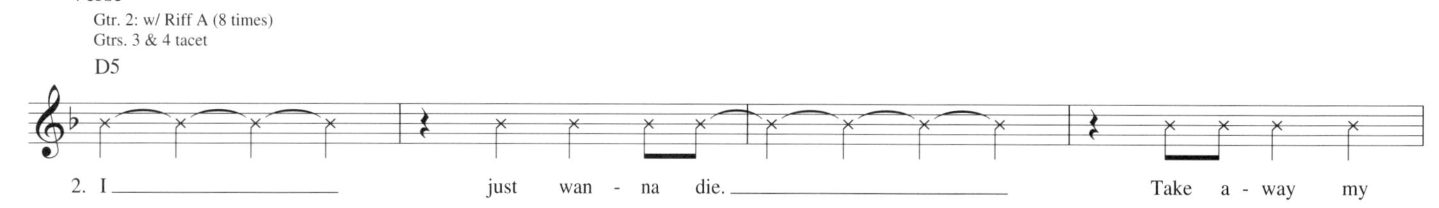
Verse
Gtr. 2: w/ Riff A (8 times)
Gtrs. 3 & 4 tacet
D5
2. I just wan - na die. Take a - way my

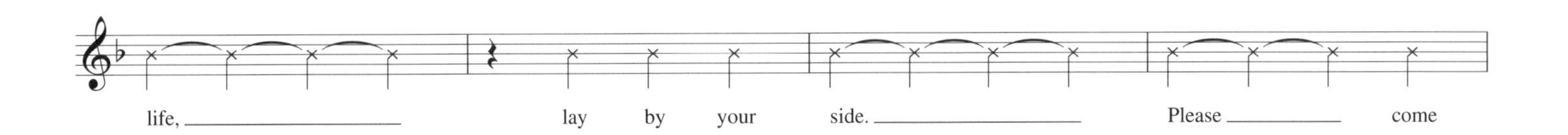
life,
lay by your side.
Please come

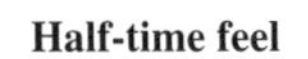
Half-time feel

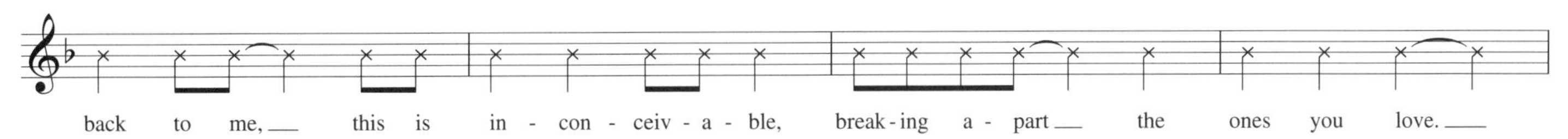
back to me, this is in - con - ceiv - a - ble, break-ing a - part the ones you love.

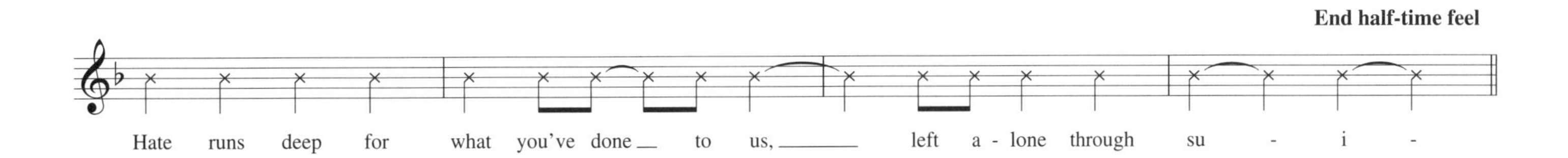
End half-time feel
Hate runs deep for what you've done to us, left a - lone through su - i -

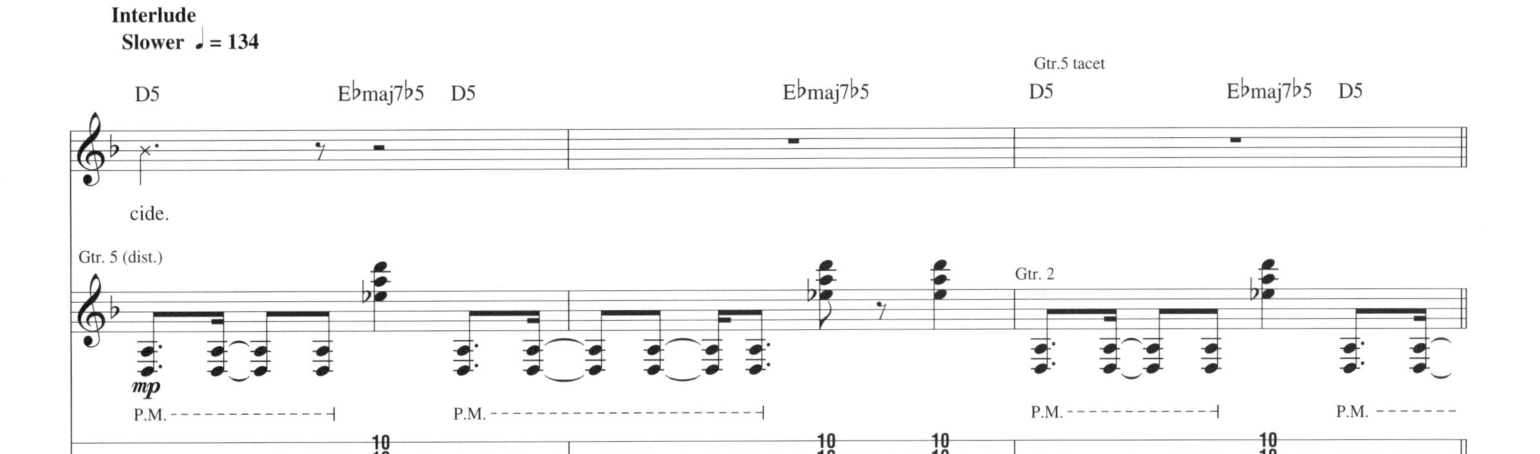
Interlude
Slower ♩ = 134
Gtr.5 tacet
D5
E♭maj7♭5
D5
cide.
Gtr. 5 (dist.)
Gtr. 2
mp
P.M.

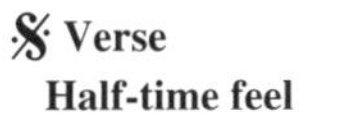
Verse
Half-time feel

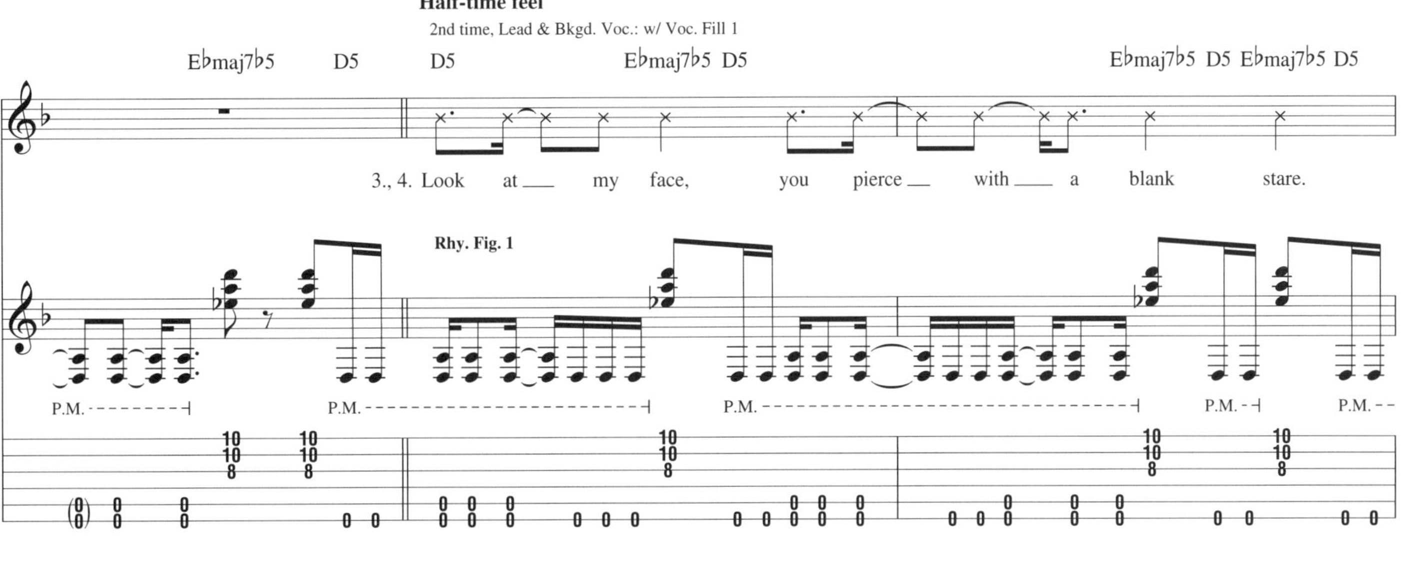
2nd time, Lead & Bkgd. Voc.: w/ Voc. Fill 1
E♭maj7♭5
D5
3., 4. Look at my face, you pierce with a blank stare.
Rhy. Fig. 1
P.M.

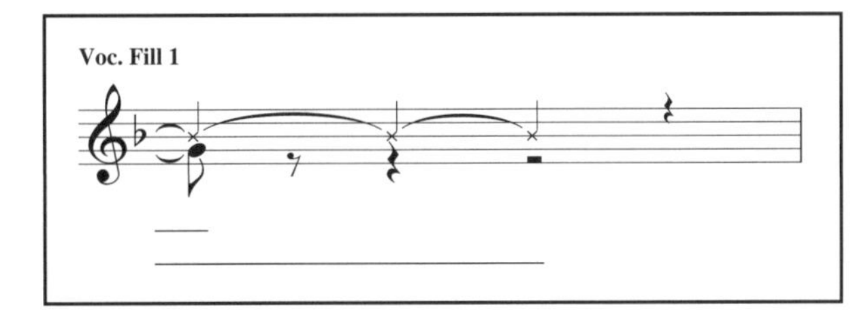
Voc. Fill 1

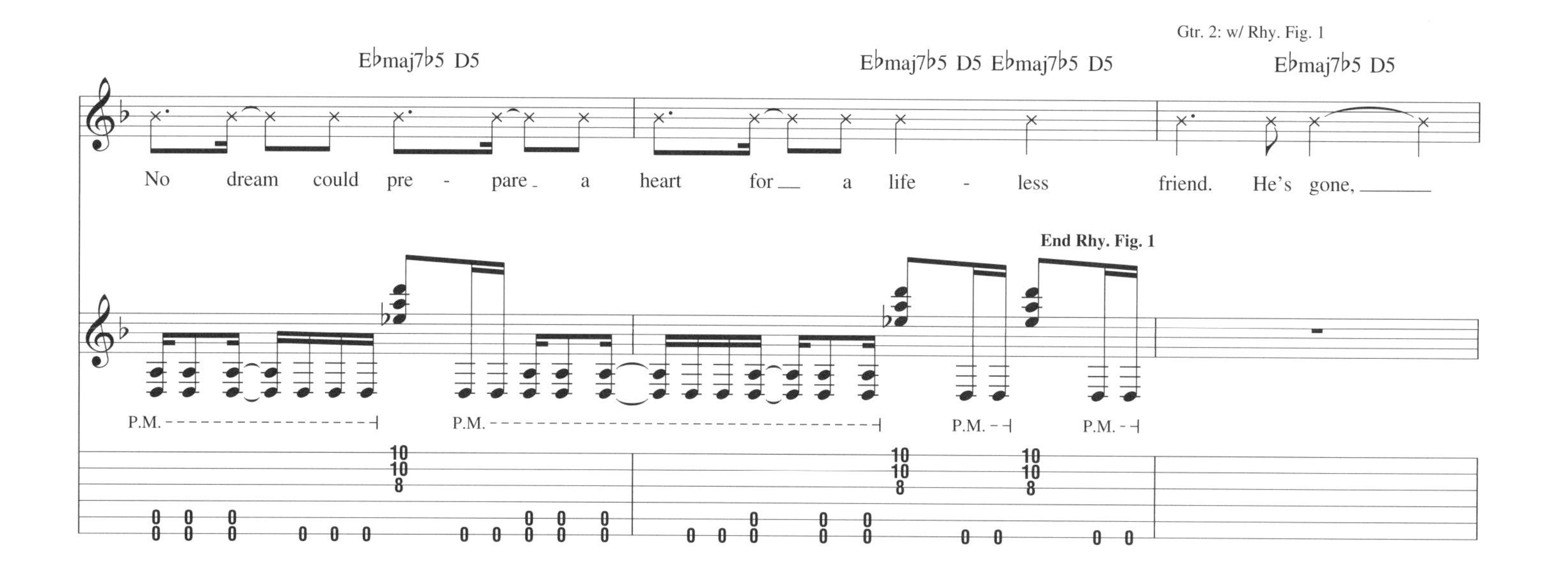
Gtr. 2: w/ Rhy. Fig. 1
E♭maj7♭5 D5
E♭maj7♭5 D5 E♭maj7♭5 D5
E♭maj7♭5 D5
No dream could pre - pare a heart for a life - less friend. He's gone,
End Rhy. Fig. 1
P.M.
P.M.
P.M.
P.M.

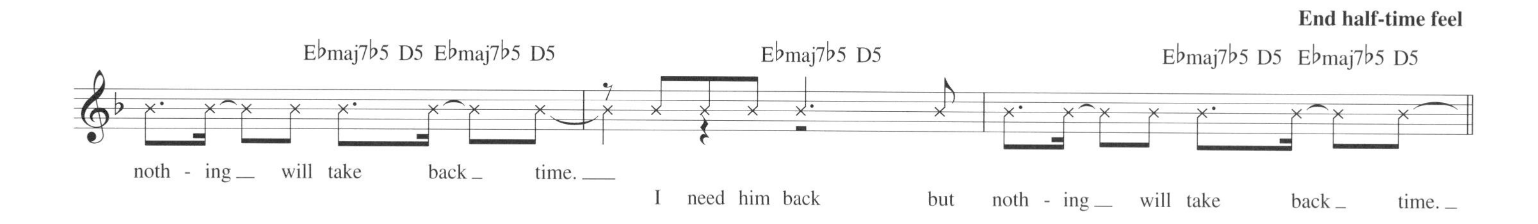
End half-time feel
E♭maj7♭5 D5 E♭maj7♭5 D5
E♭maj7♭5 D5
E♭maj7♭5 D5 E♭maj7♭5 D5
noth - ing will take back time.
I need him back but noth - ing will take back time.

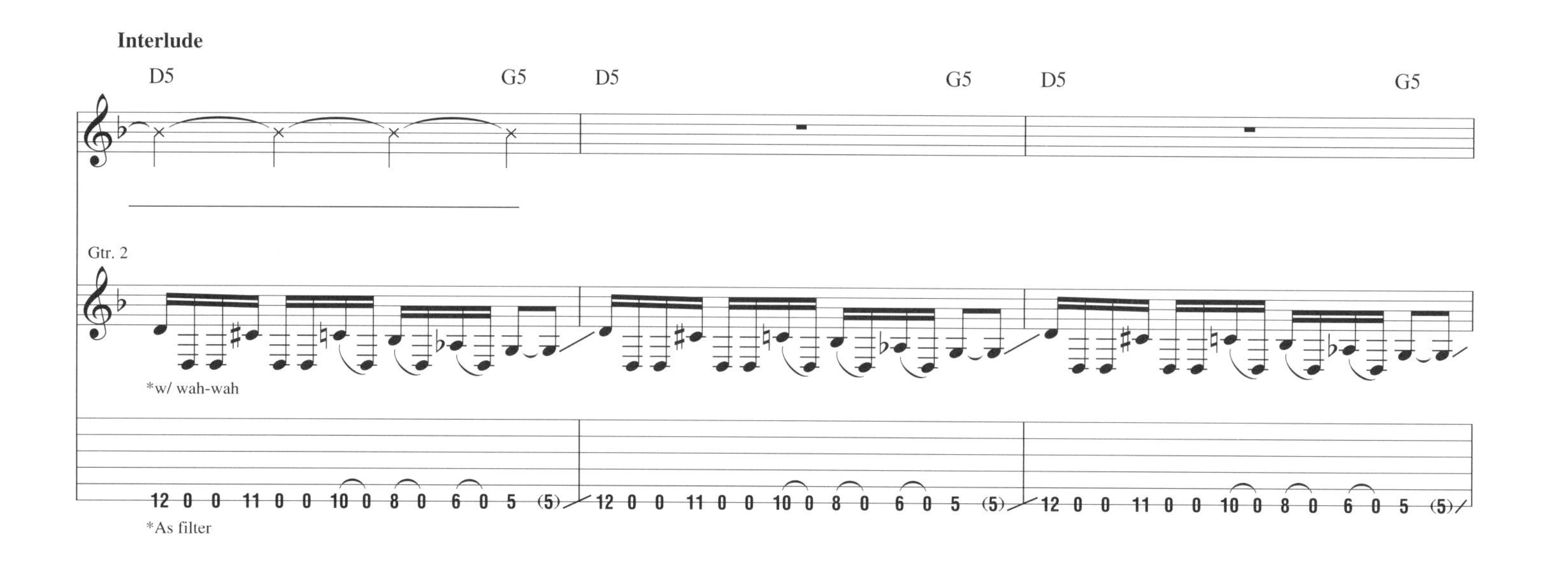
Interlude
D5
G5
D5
G5
D5
G5
Gtr. 2
*w/ wah-wah
*As filter

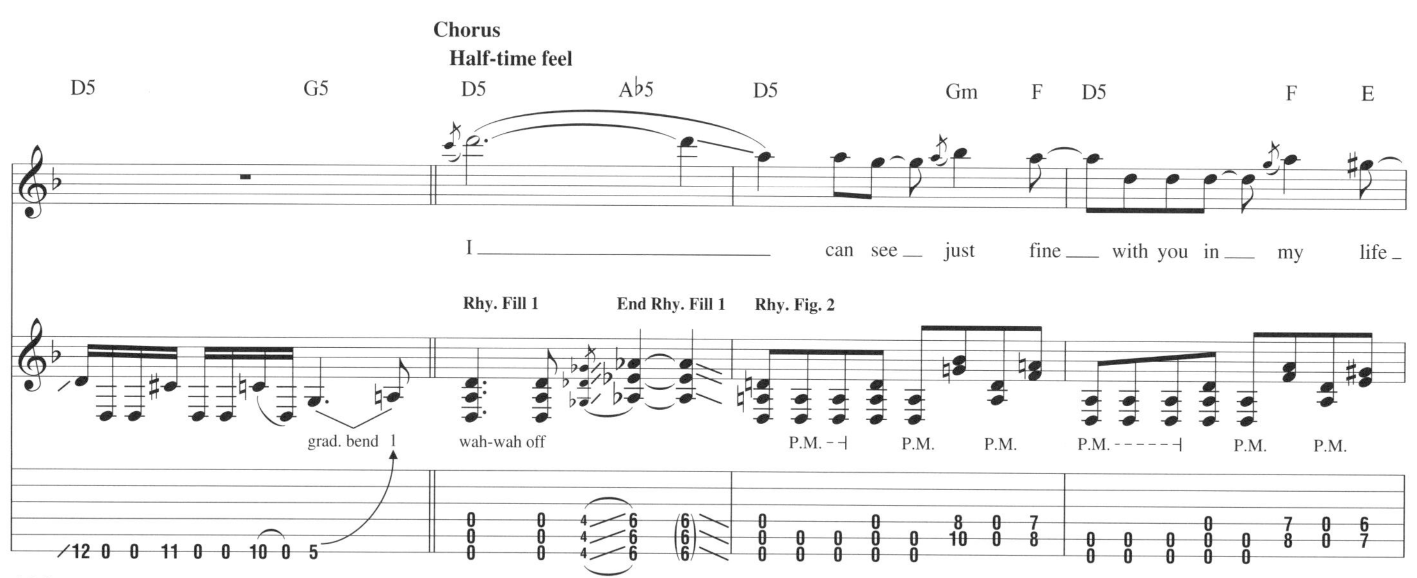
Chorus
Half-time feel
D5
G5
D5
A♭5
D5
Gm
F
D5
F
E
I can see just fine with you in my life
Rhy. Fill 1
End Rhy. Fill 1
Rhy. Fig. 2
grad. bend
wah-wah off
P.M.
P.M.
P.M.
P.M.
P.M.
P.M.

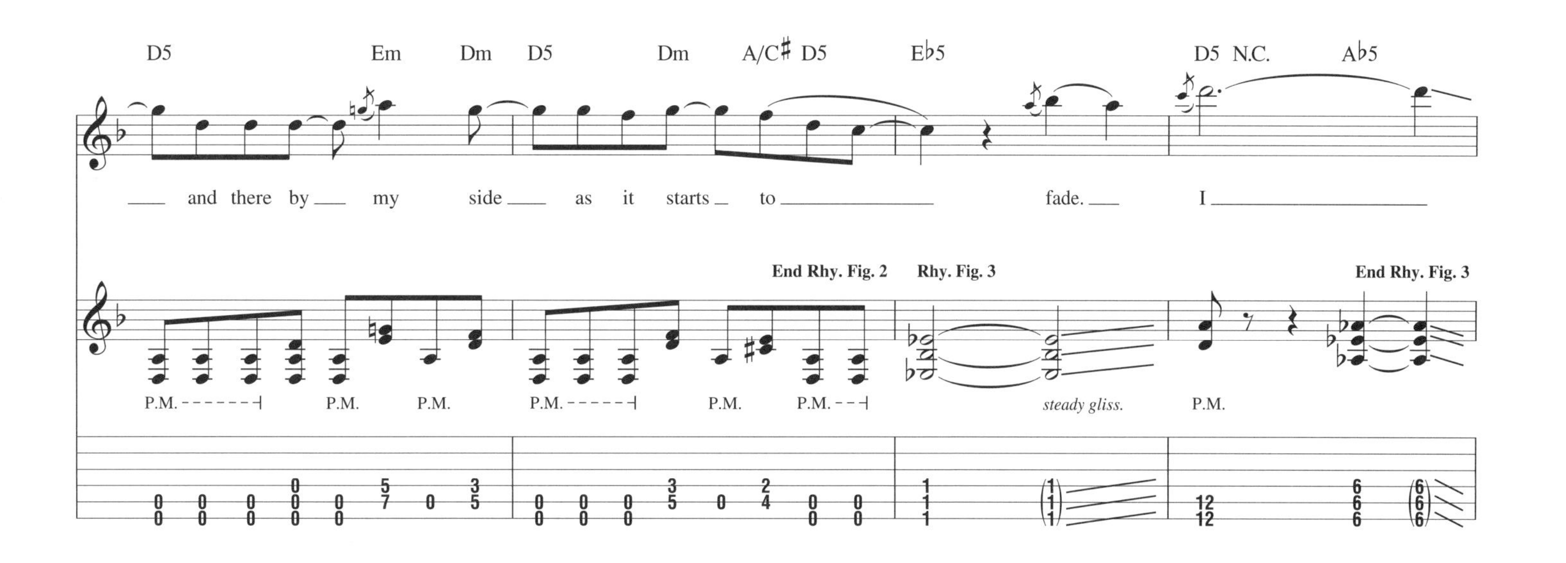
D5 Em Dm D5 Dm A/C♯ D5 E♭5 D5 N.C. A♭5
and there by my side as it starts to fade. I
End Rhy. Fig. 2
Rhy. Fig. 3
End Rhy. Fig. 3
P.M.
steady gliss.

Gtr. 2: w/ Rhy. Fig. 2
D5 Gm F D5 F E D5 Em Dm D5 Dm A/C♯ D5
know this can't be right, stuck in a dream, a night - mare full of sor - row.

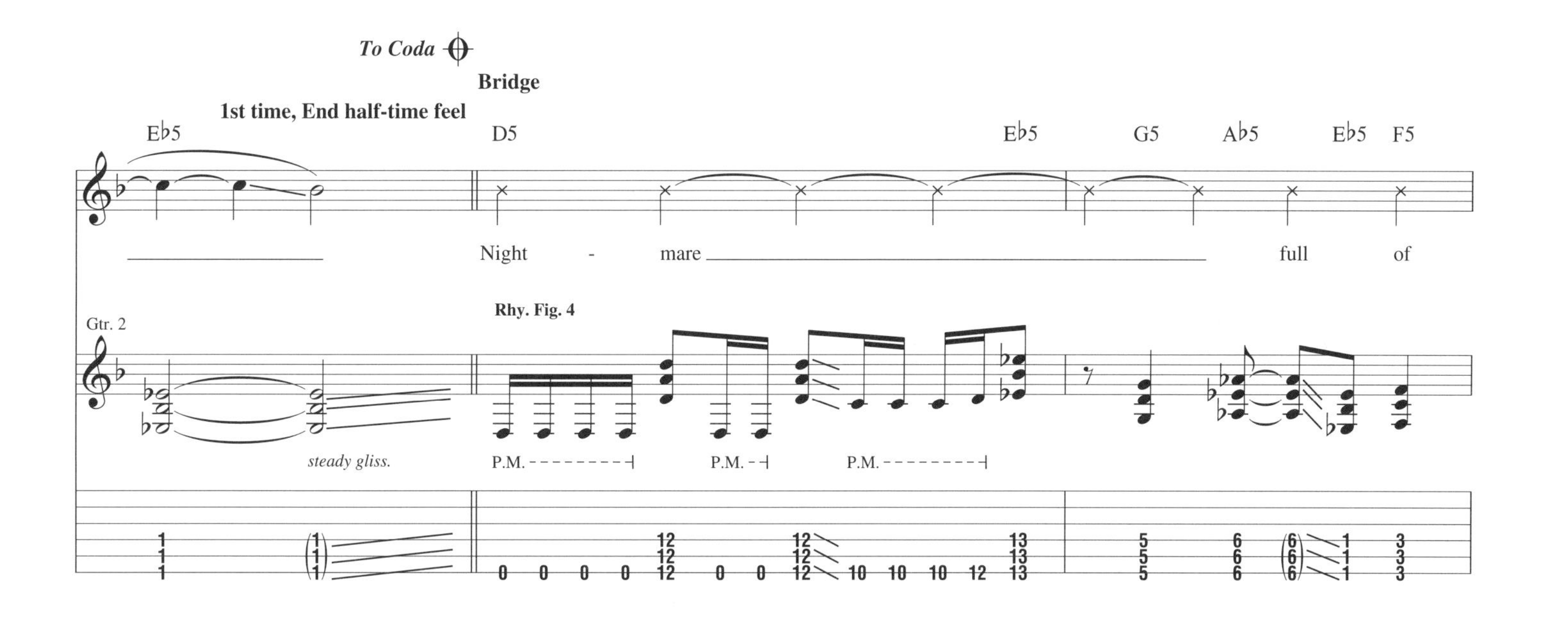
To Coda
Bridge
1st time, End half-time feel
E♭5 D5 E♭5 G5 A♭5 E♭5 F5
Night - mare full of
Gtr. 2
Rhy. Fig. 4
steady gliss.
P.M.

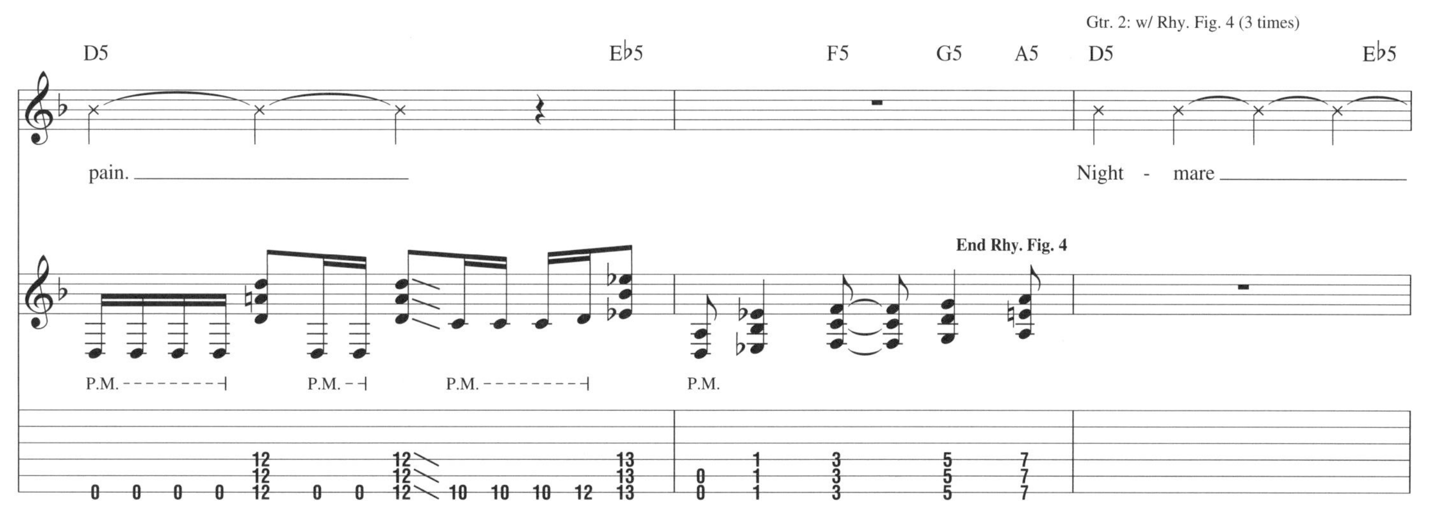
Gtr. 2: w/ Rhy. Fig. 4 (3 times)
D5 E♭5 F5 G5 A5 D5 E♭5
pain. Night - mare
End Rhy. Fig. 4
P.M.

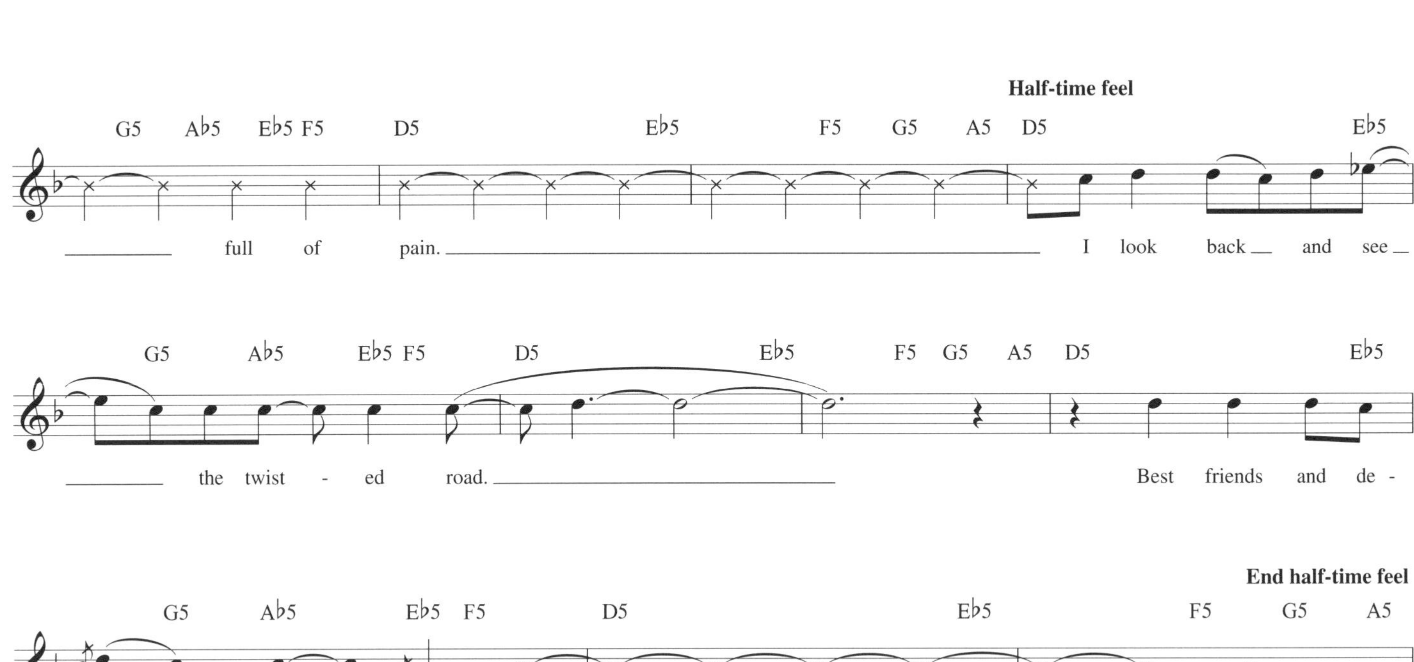
G5 A♭5 E♭5 F5 D5 E♭5 F5 G5 A5 D5 E♭5
full of pain. I look back and see
G5 A♭5 E♭5 F5 D5 E♭5 F5 G5 A5 D5 E♭5
the twist - ed road. Best friends and de -

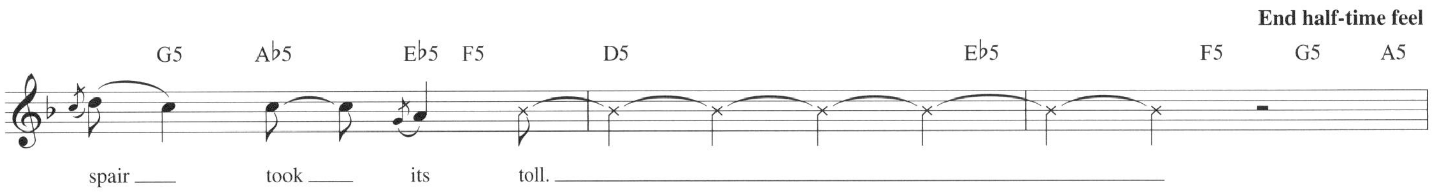
End half-time feel
G5 A♭5 E♭5 F5 D5 E♭5 F5 G5 A5
spair took its toll.

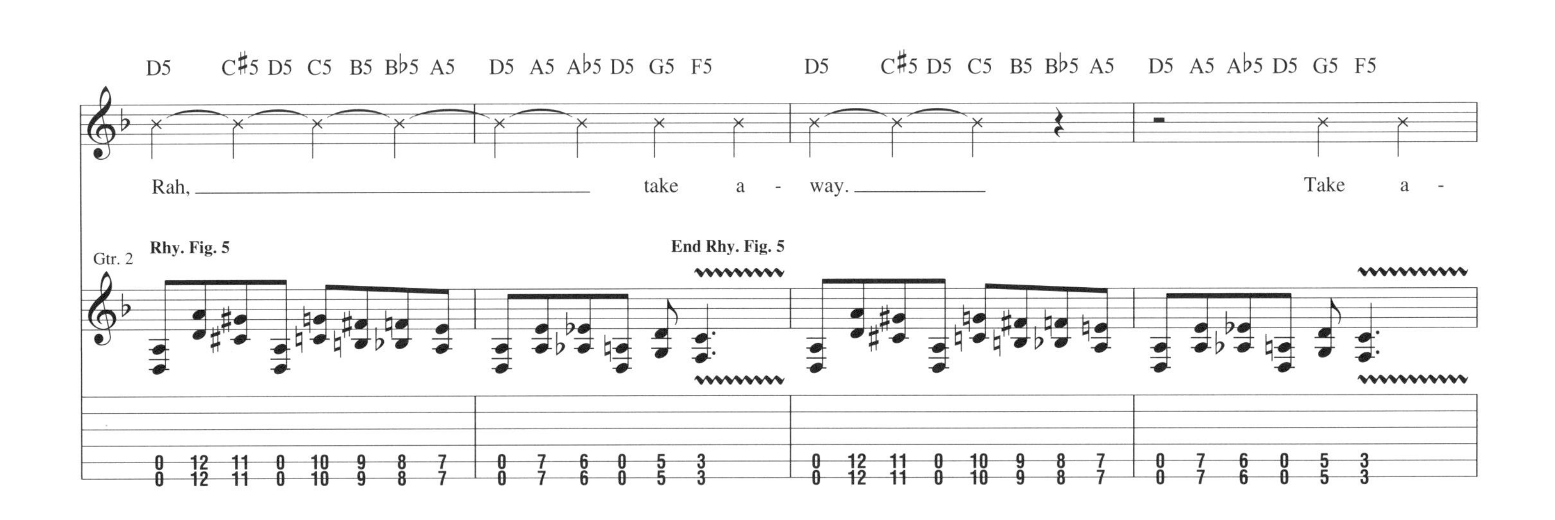
D5 C♯5 D5 C5 B5 B♭5 A5 D5 A5 A♭5 D5 G5 F5 D5 C♯5 D5 C5 B5 B♭5 A5 D5 A5 A♭5 D5 G5 F5
Rah, take a - way. Take a -
Gtr. 2
Rhy. Fig. 5
End Rhy. Fig. 5
0 12 11 0 10 9 8 7
0 12 11 0 10 9 8 7
0 7 6 0 5 3
0 7 6 0 5 3
0 12 11 0 10 9 8 7
0 12 11 0 10 9 8 7
0 7 6 0 5 3
0 7 6 0 5 3

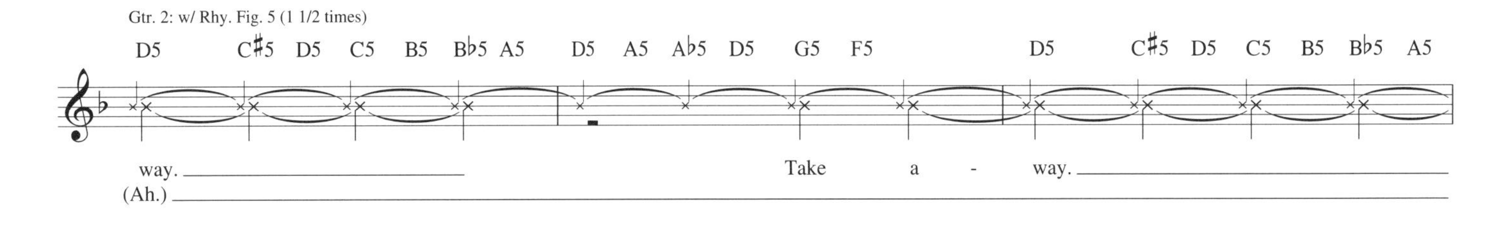
Gtr. 2: w/ Rhy. Fig. 5 (1 1/2 times)
D5 C♯5 D5 C5 B5 B♭5 A5 D5 A5 A♭5 D5 G5 F5 D5 C♯5 D5 C5 B5 B♭5 A5
way. Take a - way.
(Ah.)

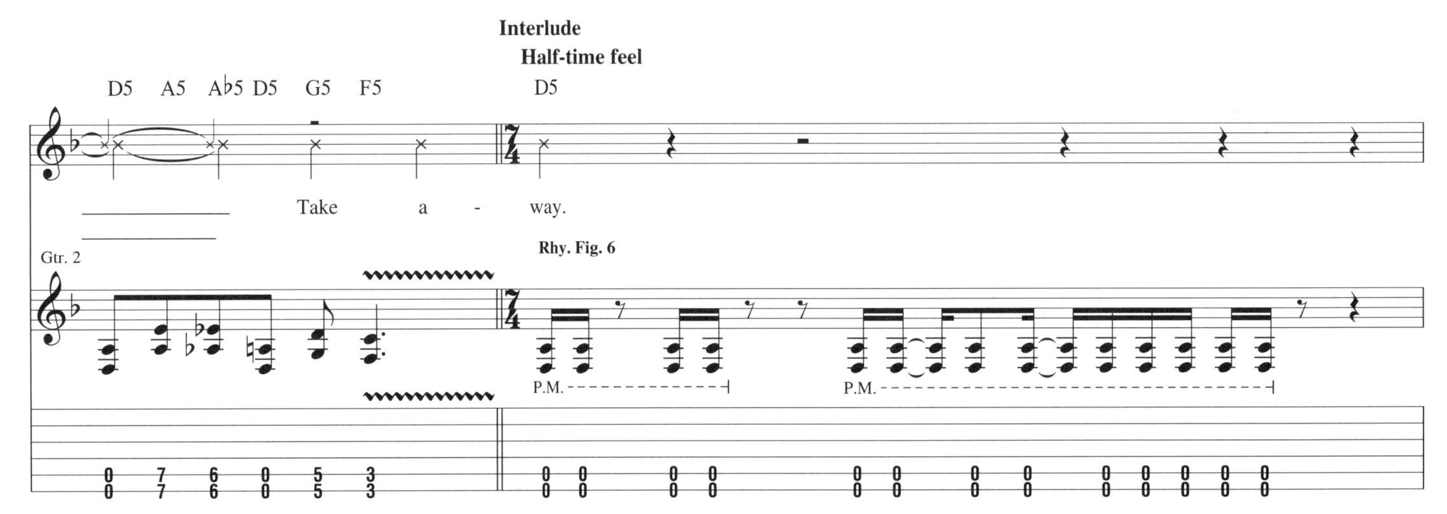
Interlude
Half-time feel
D5 A5 A♭5 D5 G5 F5 D5
Take a - way.
Gtr. 2
Rhy. Fig. 6
P.M.
P.M.
0 7 6 0 5 3
0 7 6 0 5 3
0 0 0 0 0 0 0 0 0 0 0 0 0 0
0 0 0 0 0 0 0 0 0 0 0 0 0 0

Gtr. 2: w/ Rhy. Fig. 6

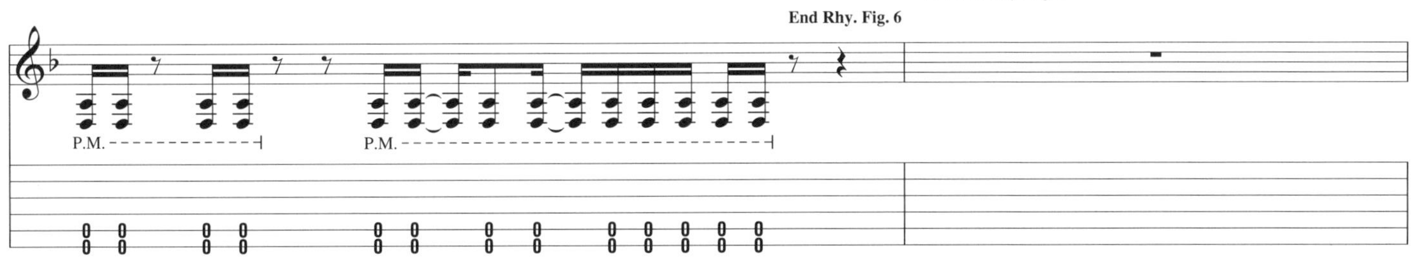
End Rhy. Fig. 6
P.M.
P.M.

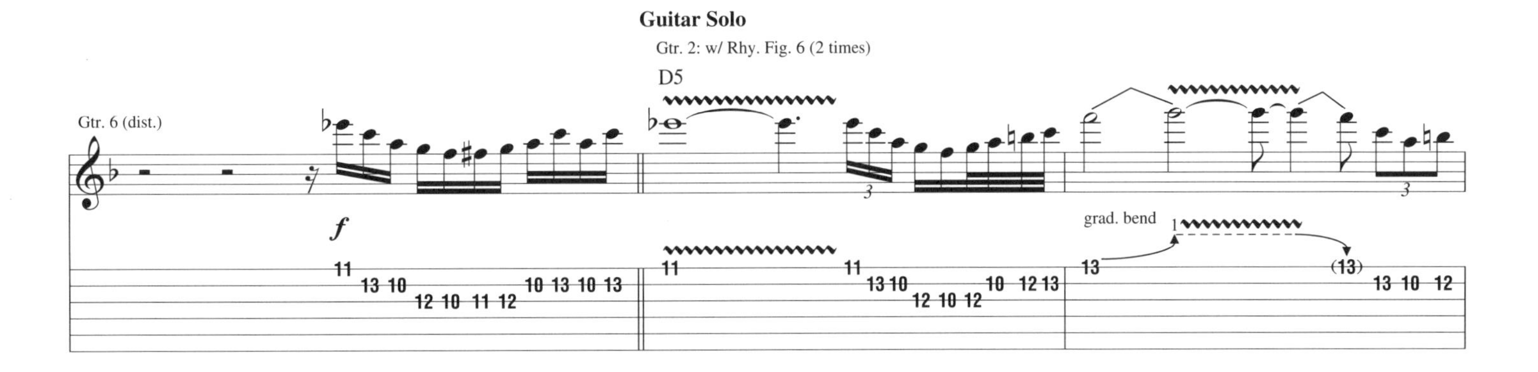
Guitar Solo
Gtr. 2: w/ Rhy. Fig. 6 (2 times)
D5
Gtr. 6 (dist.)
grad. bend

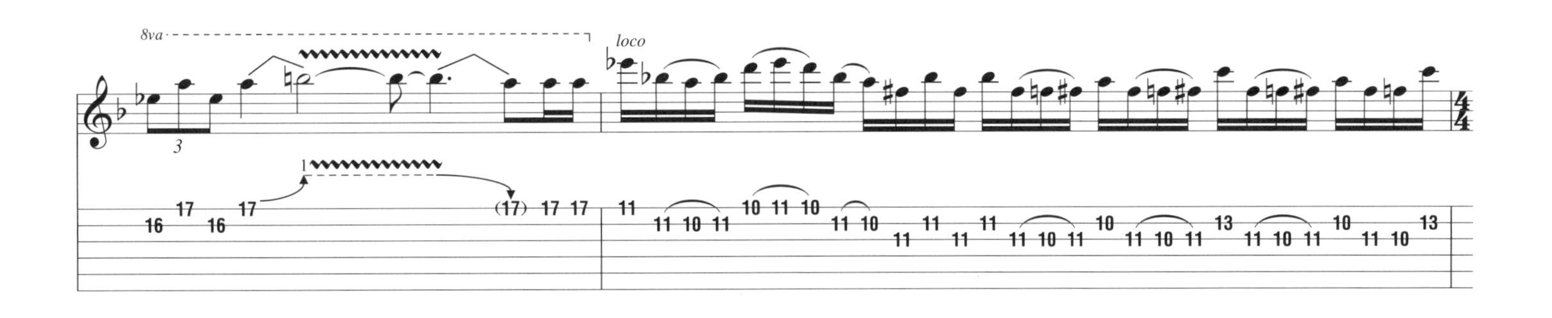
8va
loco

Double-time feel
Gtr. 6 tacet
A♭5
G5
F5 G5
D5
E♭5
F5
Gtr. 7 (dist.)
8va
loco
Gtr. 6
grad. bend
Gtr. 2
Rhy. Fig. 7
End Rhy. Fig. 7
P.M.

Gtr. 2: w/ Rhy. Fig. 7 (3 times)

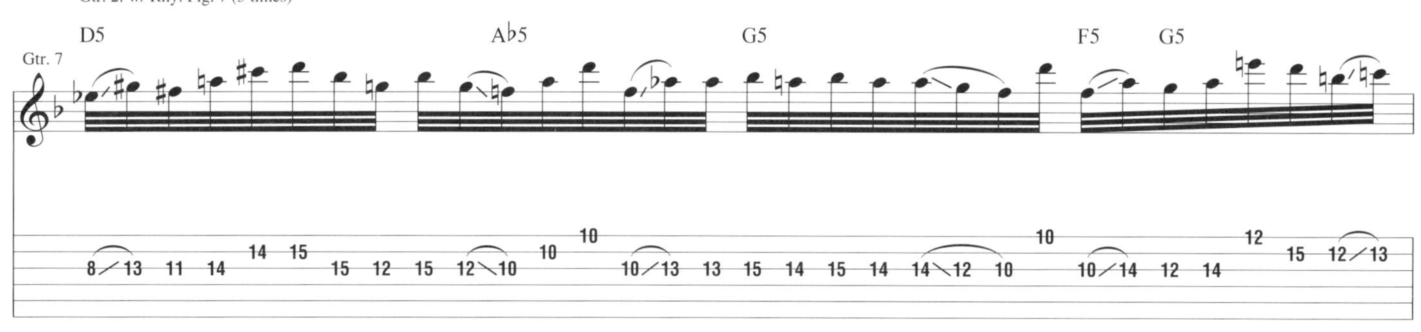

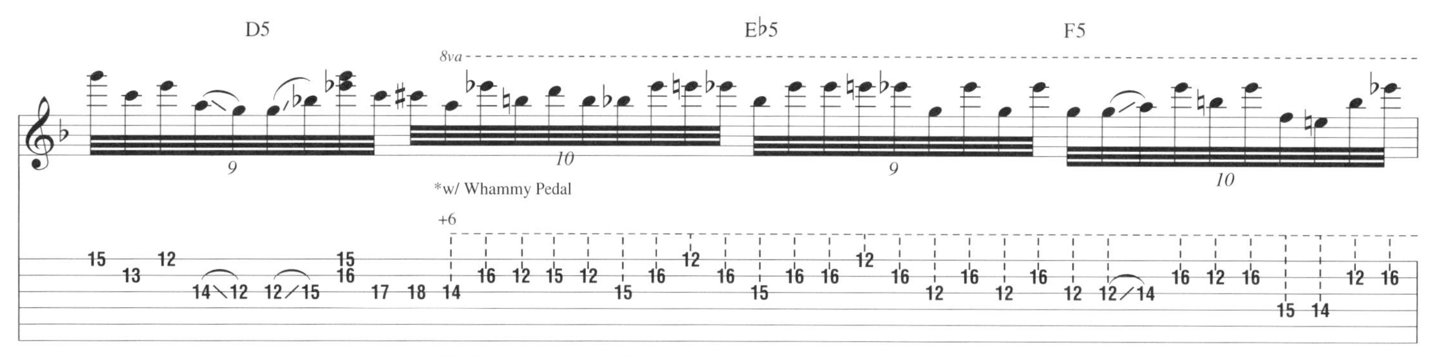

*Set for one octave above when depressed (toe down).

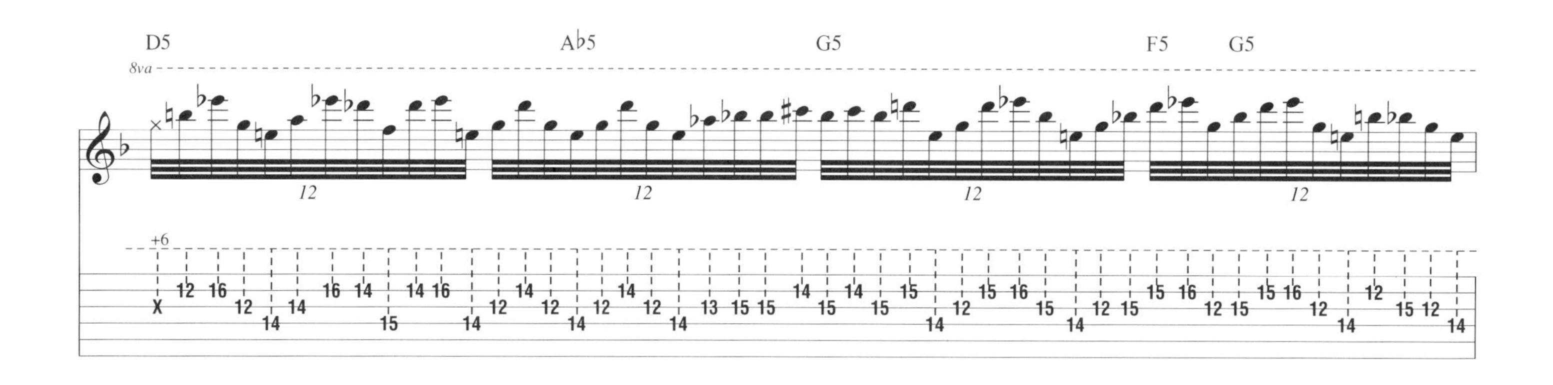

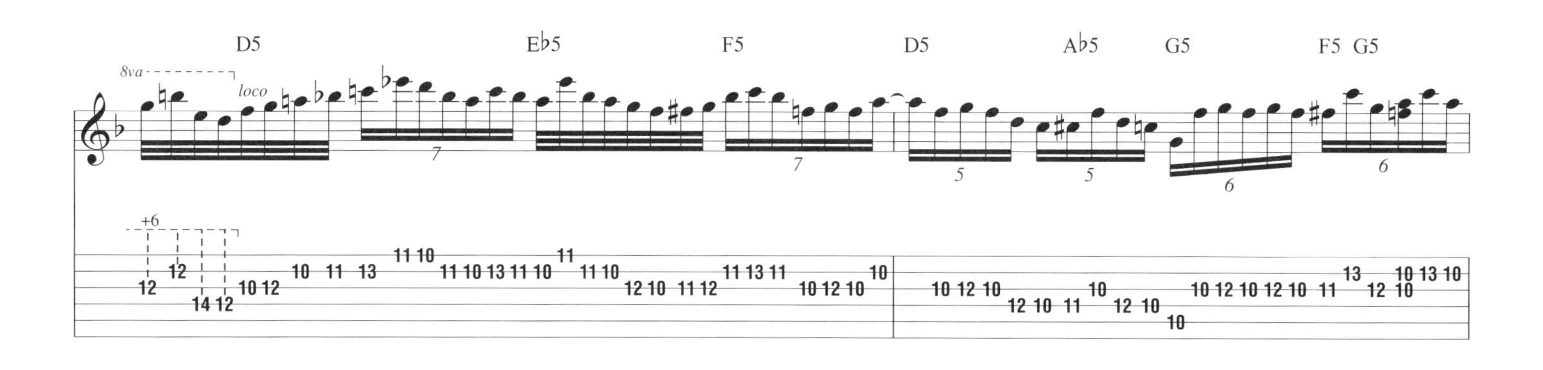

End double-time feel

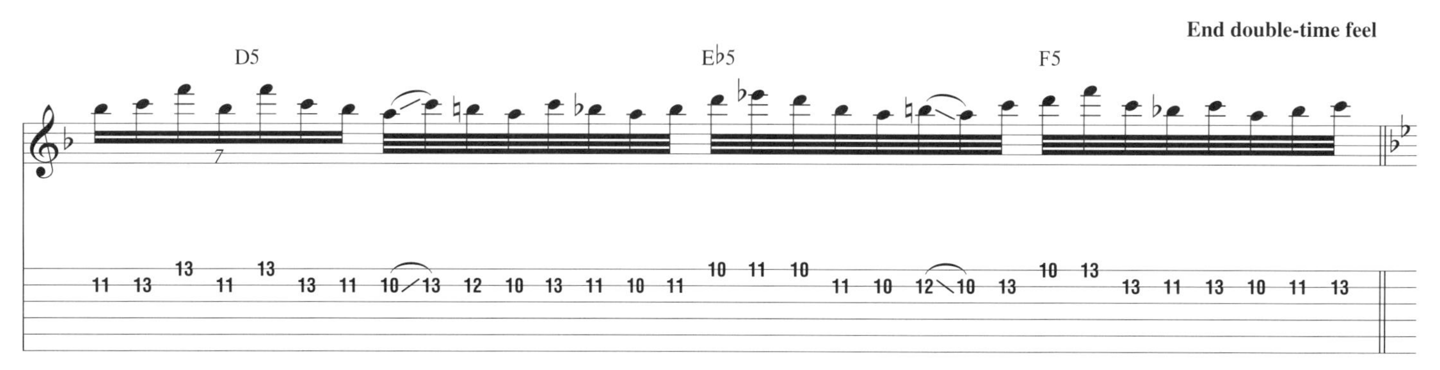

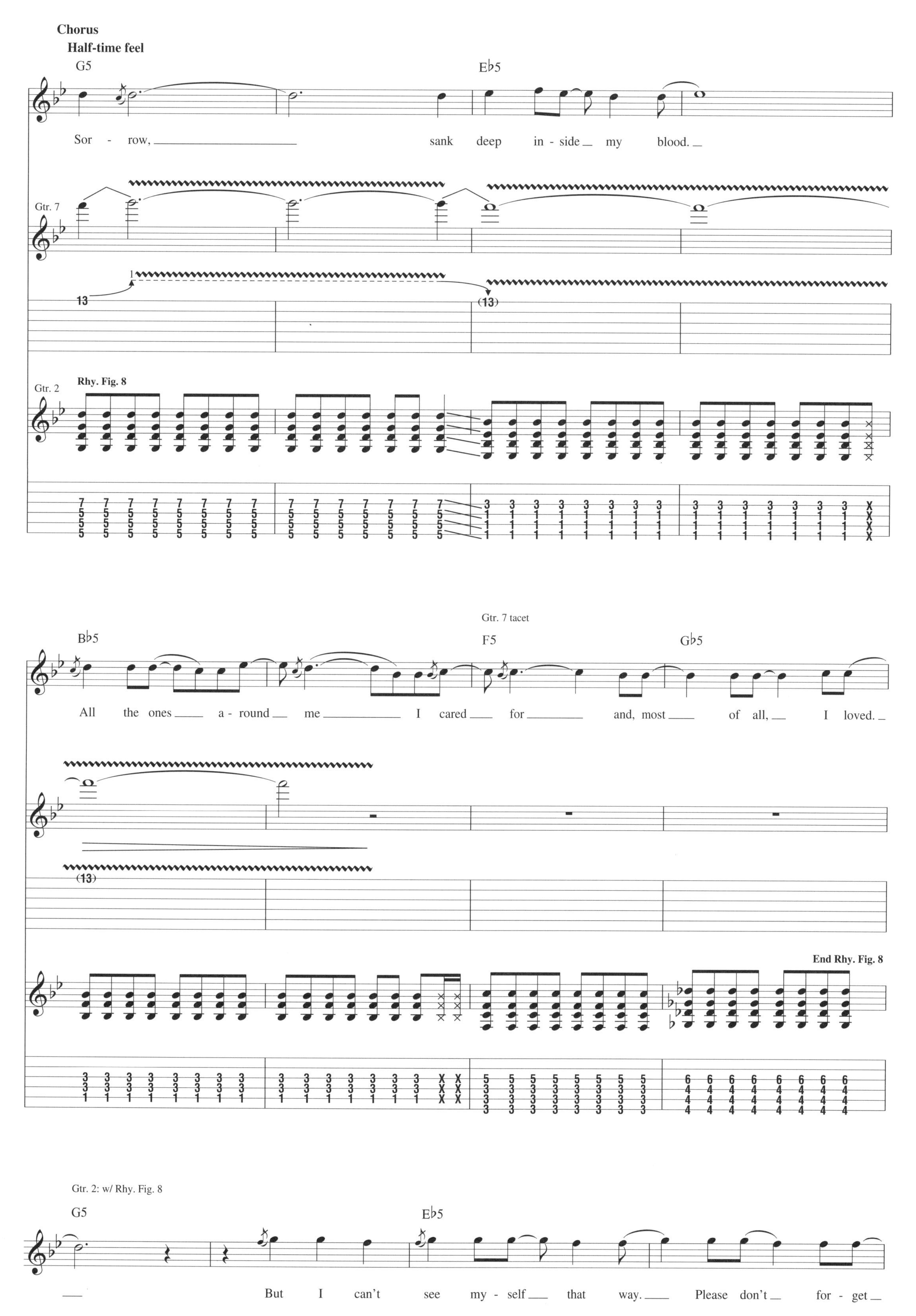
Chorus
Half-time feel
G5
Eb5
Sor - row,
sank deep in - side my blood.
Gtr. 7
Gtr. 2
Rhy. Fig. 8
Bb5
Gtr. 7 tacet
F5
Gb5
All the ones a - round me I cared for and, most of all, I loved.
End Rhy. Fig. 8
Gtr. 2: w/ Rhy. Fig. 8
G5
Eb5
But I can't see my - self that way. Please don't for - get

D.S. al Coda

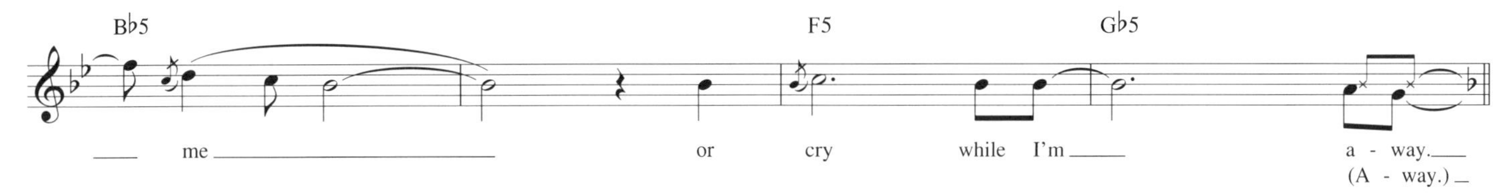
B♭5
F5
G♭5
me or cry while I'm a - way.
(A - way.)

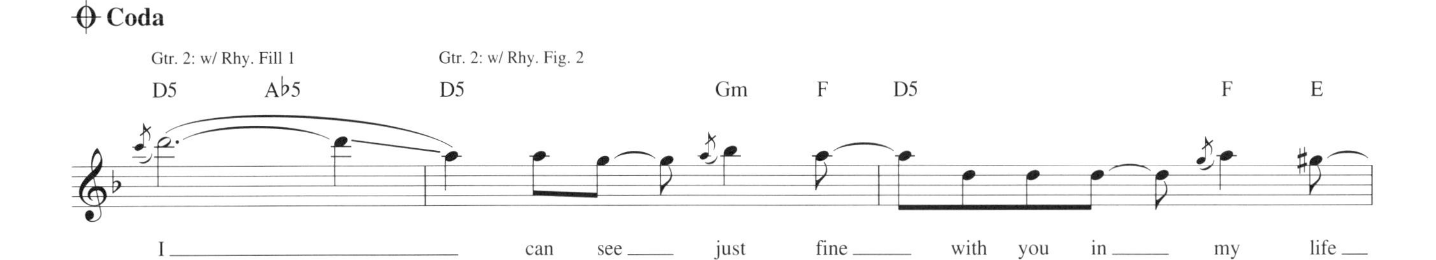
Coda
Gtr. 2: w/ Rhy. Fill 1
Gtr. 2: w/ Rhy. Fig. 2
D5 A♭5 D5 Gm F D5 F E
I can see just fine with you in my life

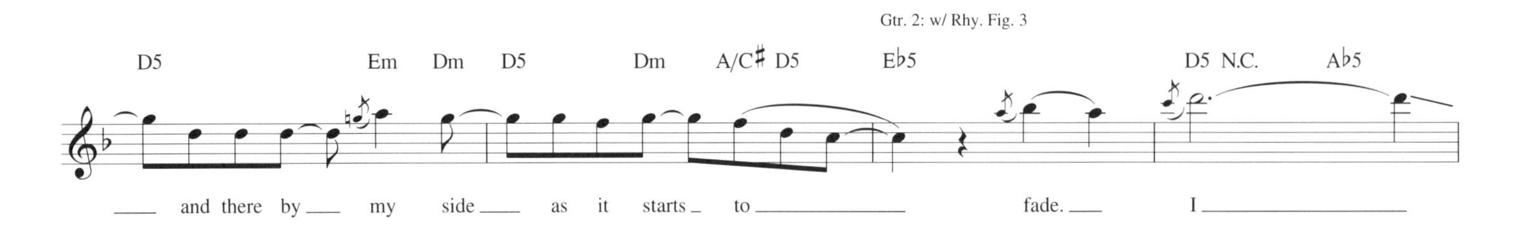
Gtr. 2: w/ Rhy. Fig. 3
D5 Em Dm D5 Dm A/C♯ D5 E♭5 D5 N.C. A♭5
and there by my side as it starts to fade. I

Gtr. 2: w/ Rhy. Fig. 2
End half-time feel
D5 Gm F D5 F E D5 Em Dm D5 Dm A/C♯ D5
know this can't be right, stuck in a dream, a night - mare full of sor - row.

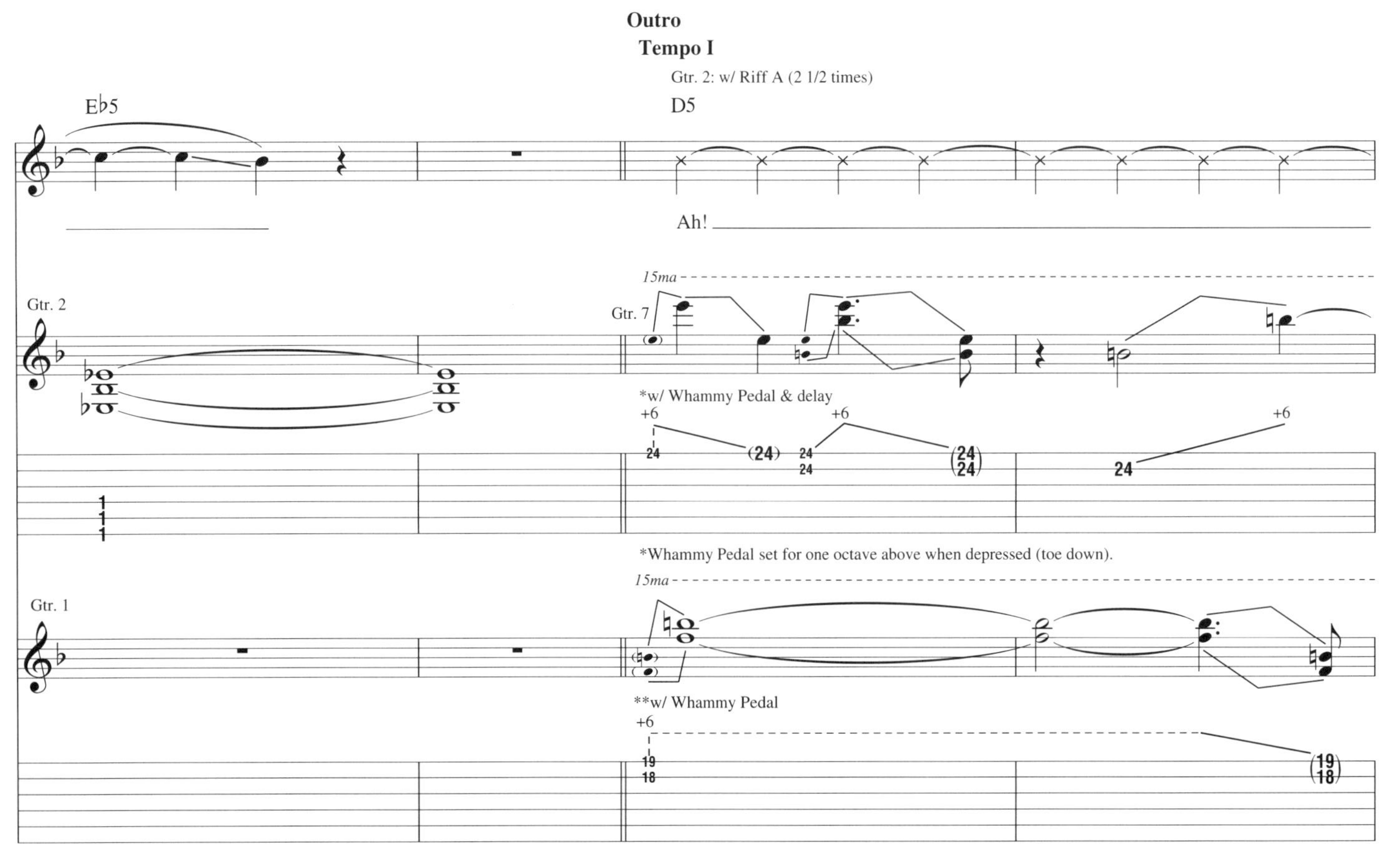
Outro
Tempo I
Gtr. 2: w/ Riff A (2 1/2 times)
E♭5
D5
Ah!
15ma
Gtr. 2
Gtr. 7
*w/ Whammy Pedal & delay
+6
*Whammy Pedal set for one octave above when depressed (toe down).
Gtr. 1
**w/ Whammy Pedal
**Set for one octave above when depressed (toe down).

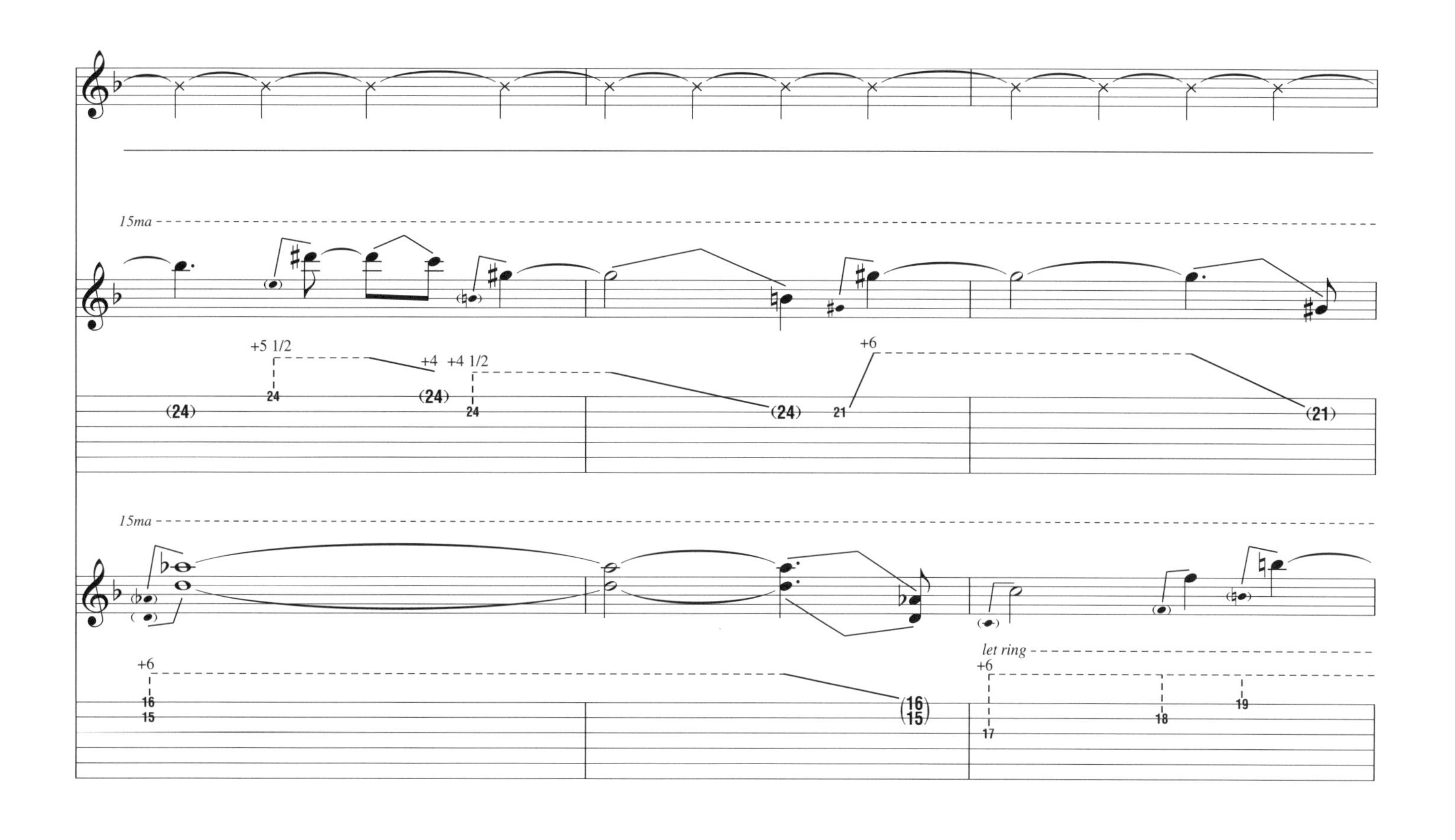
15ma
+5 1/2
+4
+4 1/2
24
(24)
21
+6
(21)
+6
16
15
let ring
17
18
19

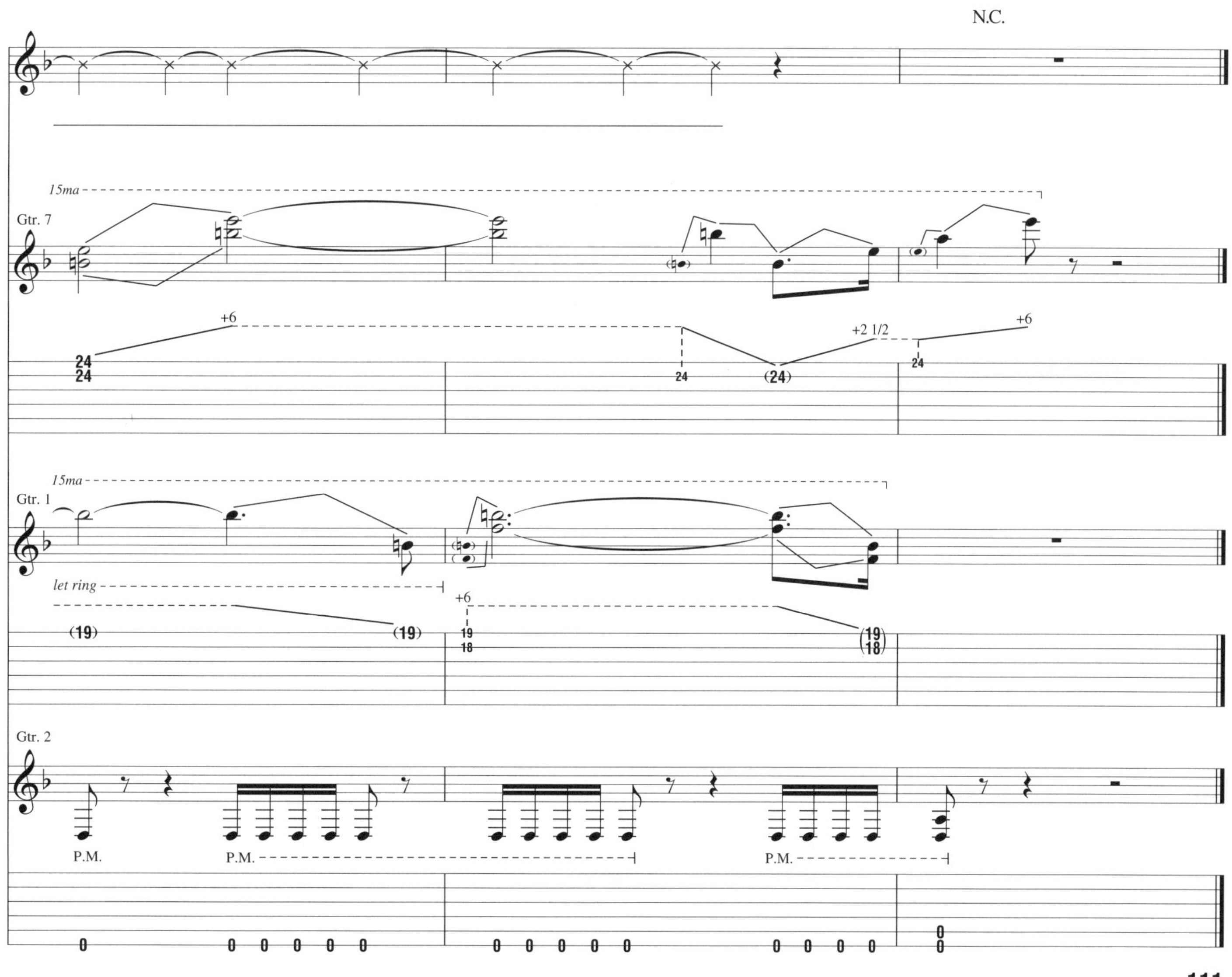
N.C.
15ma
Gtr. 7
+6
24
24
+2 1/2
(24)
Gtr. 1
let ring
(19)
+6
19
18
Gtr. 2
P.M.

Clairvoyant Disease

Words and Music by Matthew Sanders, James Sullivan, Brian Haner, Jr. and Zachary Baker

Gtrs. 1, 2 & 5–11: Drop D tuning:
(low to high) D-A-D-G-B-E

*Chord symbols reflect implied harmony.

***Standard tuning

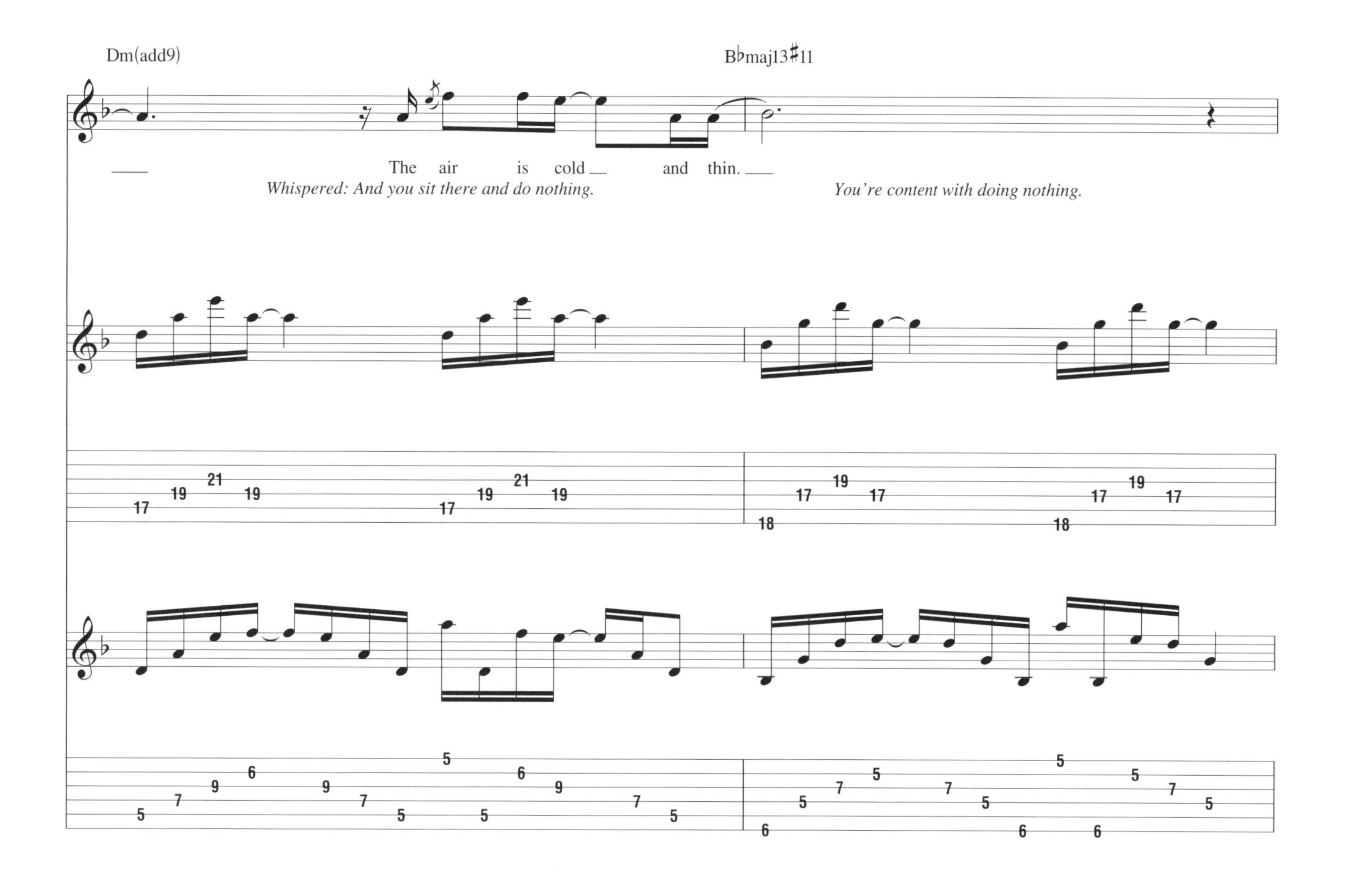
Dm(add9)
B♭maj13♯11
The air is cold and thin.
Whispered: And you sit there and do nothing.
You're content with doing nothing.

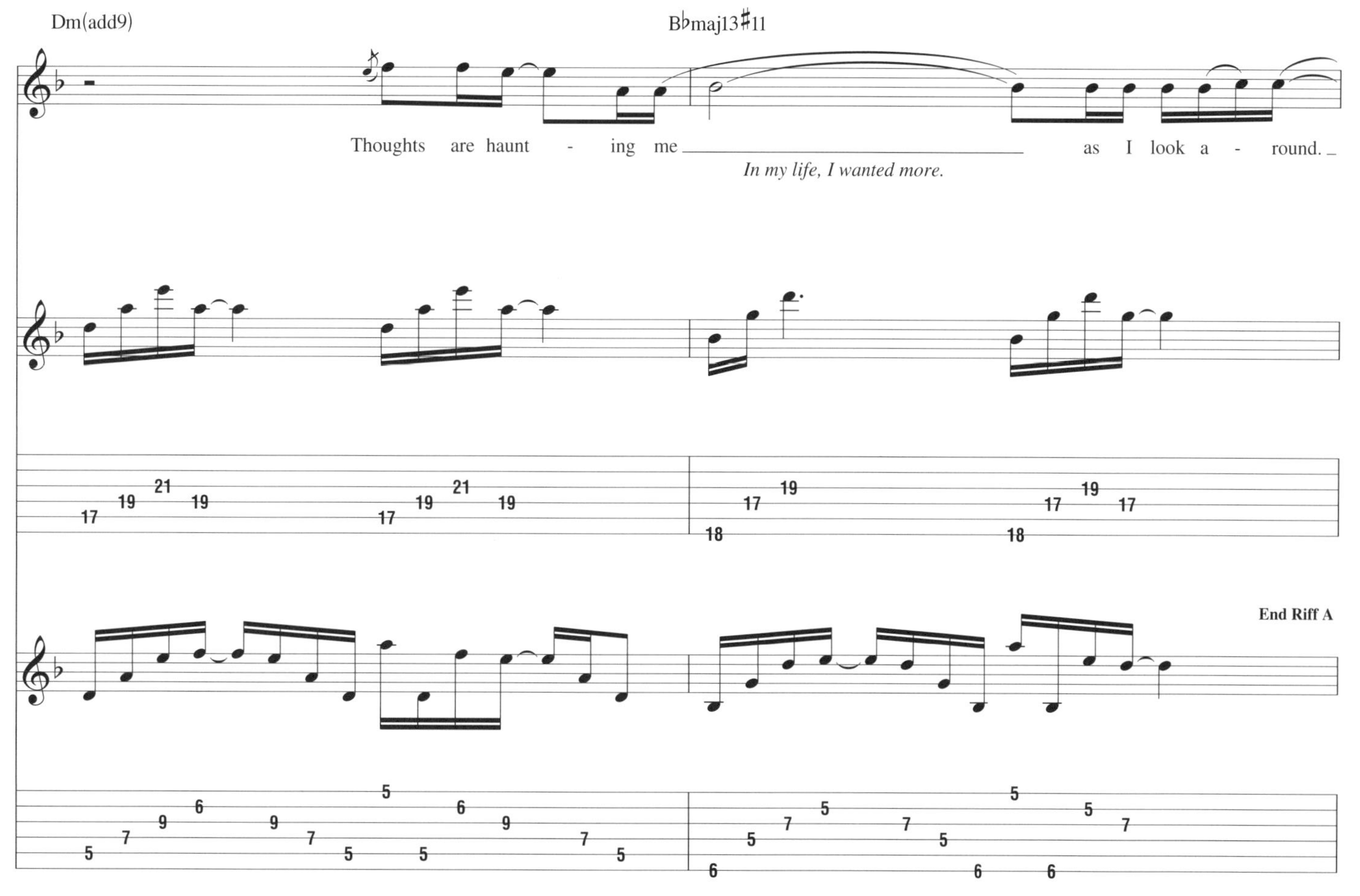
Dm(add9)
B♭maj13♯11
Thoughts are haunt - ing me as I look a - round.
In my life, I wanted more.
End Riff A

Dm(add9)
Bbmaj13#11
This will nev - er end when I bleed for - ev - er.
So I'll never end.
End Riff B
Chorus
Gtrs. 3 & 4 tacet
D5 Em/D D5 F/D Bb5/D Bb(#4)/D E/D A5/D
Don't ac - knowl - edge right, just dwell on wrong.
*Gtrs. 5 & 6 (dist.)
**w/ wah-wah
*Composite arrangement
**As filter
Rhy. Fig. 1
End Rhy. Fig. 1
Gtrs. 1 & 2
P.M.
Gtrs. 1 & 2: w/ Rhy. Fig. 1 (3 times)
D5 Em/D D5 F/D Bb5/D Bb(#4)/D E/D A5/D
This spot in hell's where I be - long.
Gtrs. 5 & 6

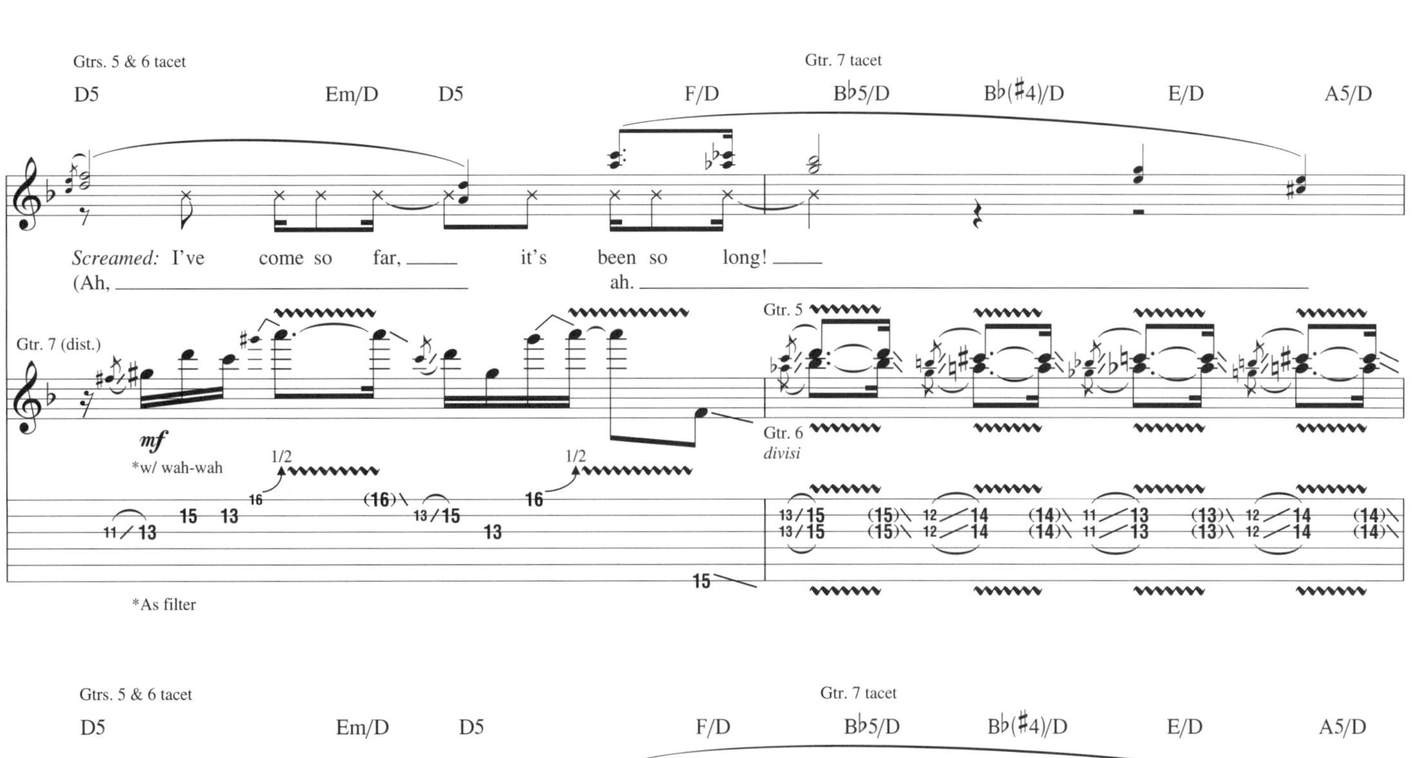
Gtrs. 5 & 6 tacet
Gtr. 7 tacet
D5 Em/D D5 F/D B♭5/D B♭(♯4)/D E/D A5/D
Screamed: I've come so far, it's been so long!
(Ah, ah.
Gtr. 7 (dist.)
Gtr. 5
Gtr. 6
divisi
mf
*w/ wah-wah
1/2
*As filter

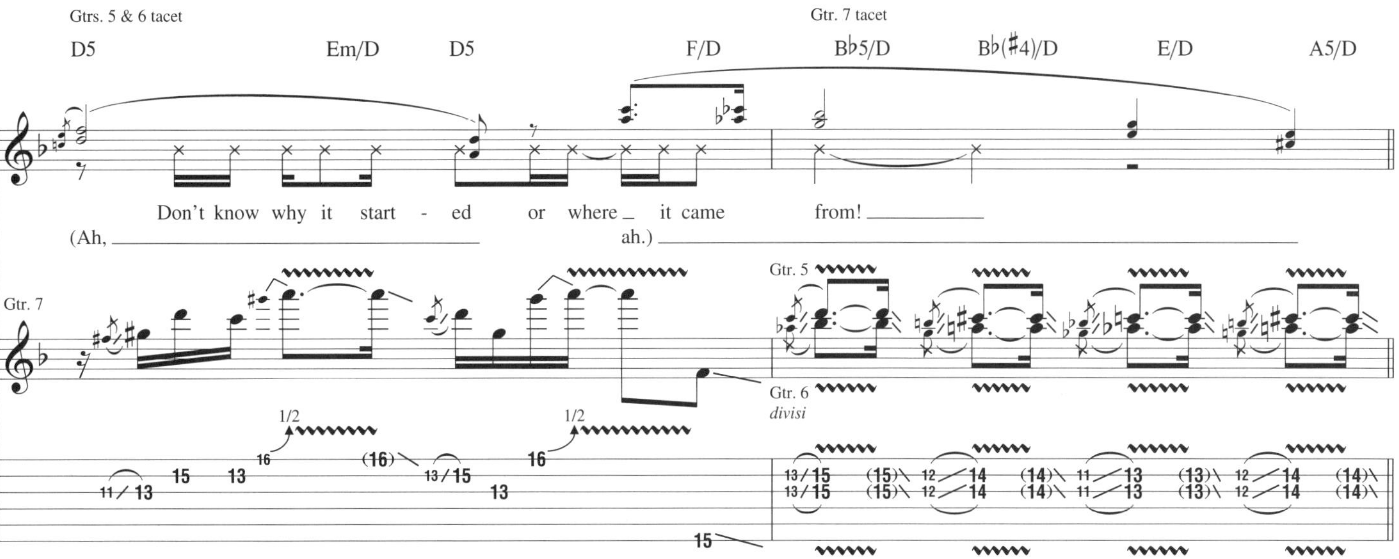
Gtrs. 5 & 6 tacet
Gtr. 7 tacet
D5 Em/D D5 F/D B♭5/D B♭(♯4)/D E/D A5/D
Don't know why it start - ed or where it came from!
(Ah, ah.)
Gtr. 7
Gtr. 5
Gtr. 6
divisi
1/2

Verse
Gtr. 4: w/ Riff B
Gtrs. 5 & 6 tacet
Dm(add9) B♭6
2. Out - side shell is strong, con - fi - dent
Whispered: There's nowhere to run and hide.
Riff C
Gtr. 8 (slight dist.)
End Riff C
mp
P.M.

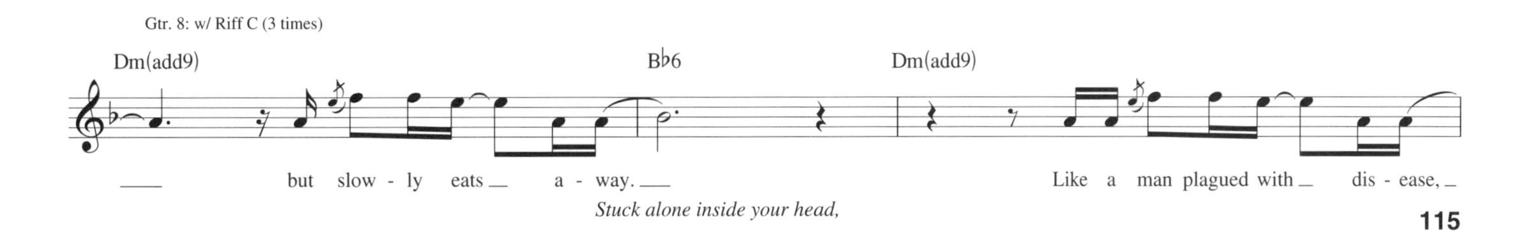
Gtr. 8: w/ Riff C (3 times)
Dm(add9) B♭6 Dm(add9)
but slow - ly eats a - way. Like a man plagued with dis - ease,
Stuck alone inside your head,

*Composite arrangement

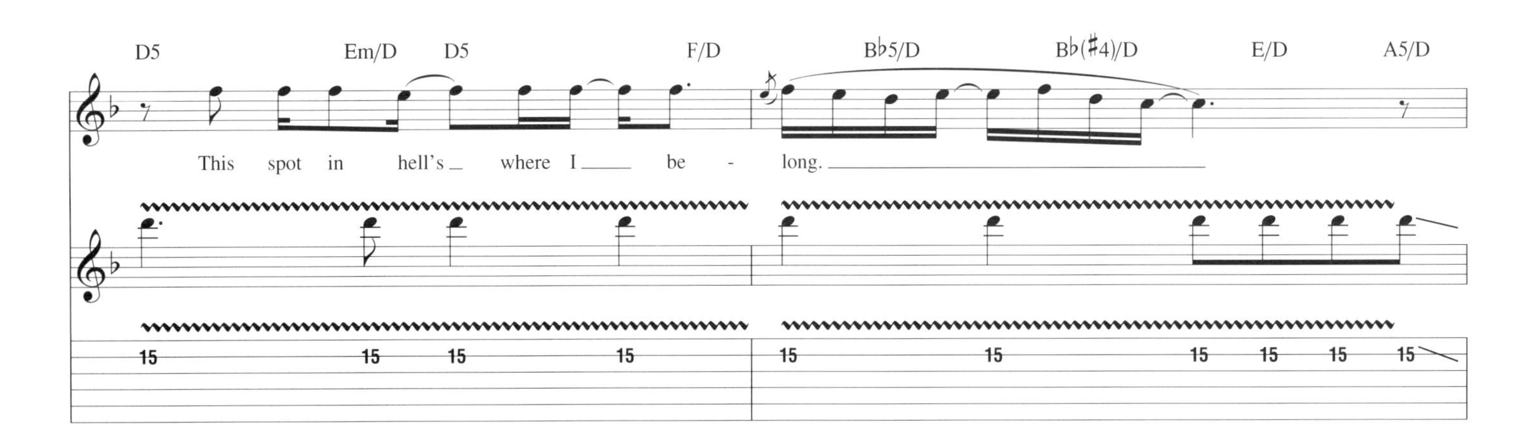

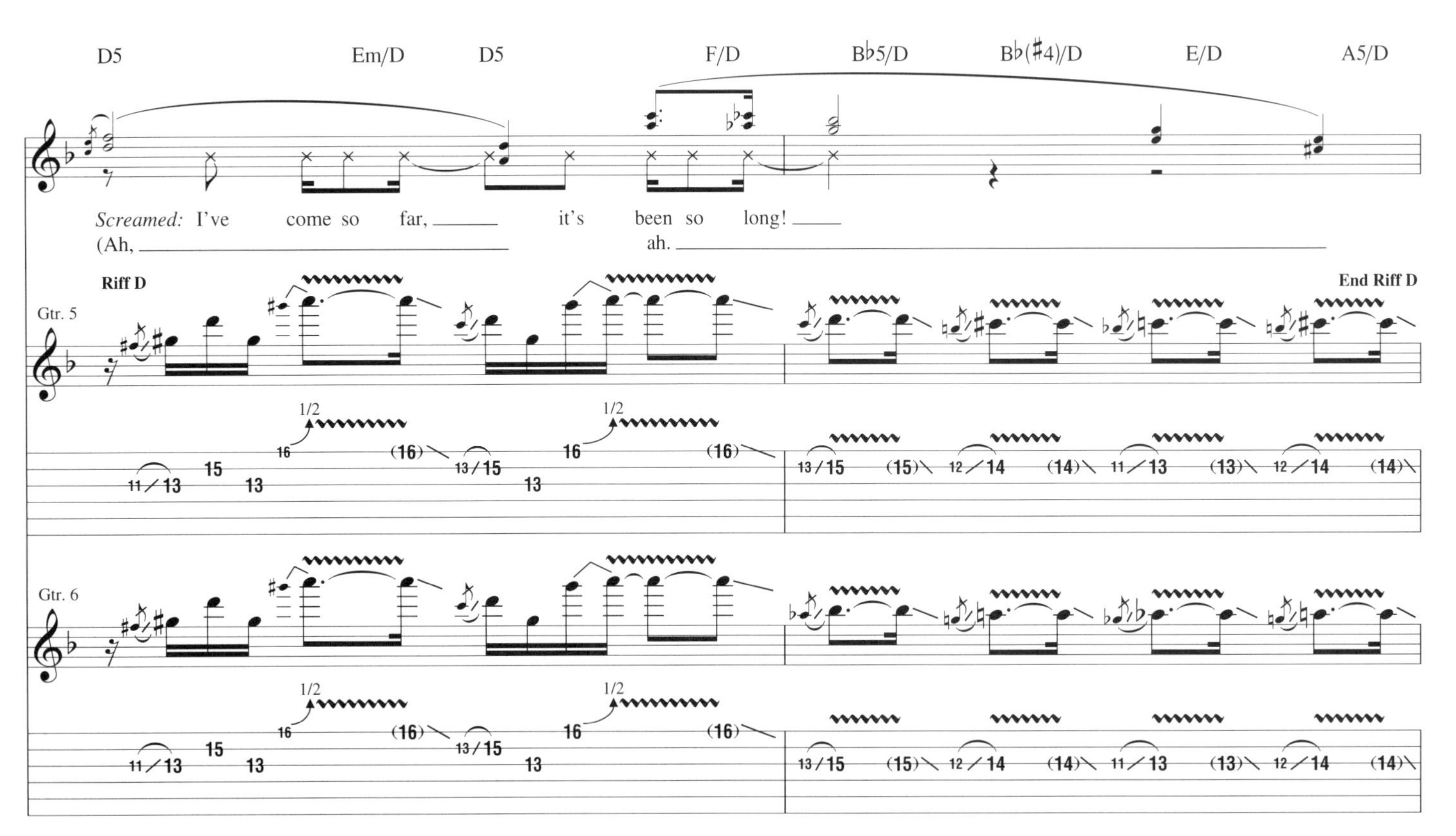

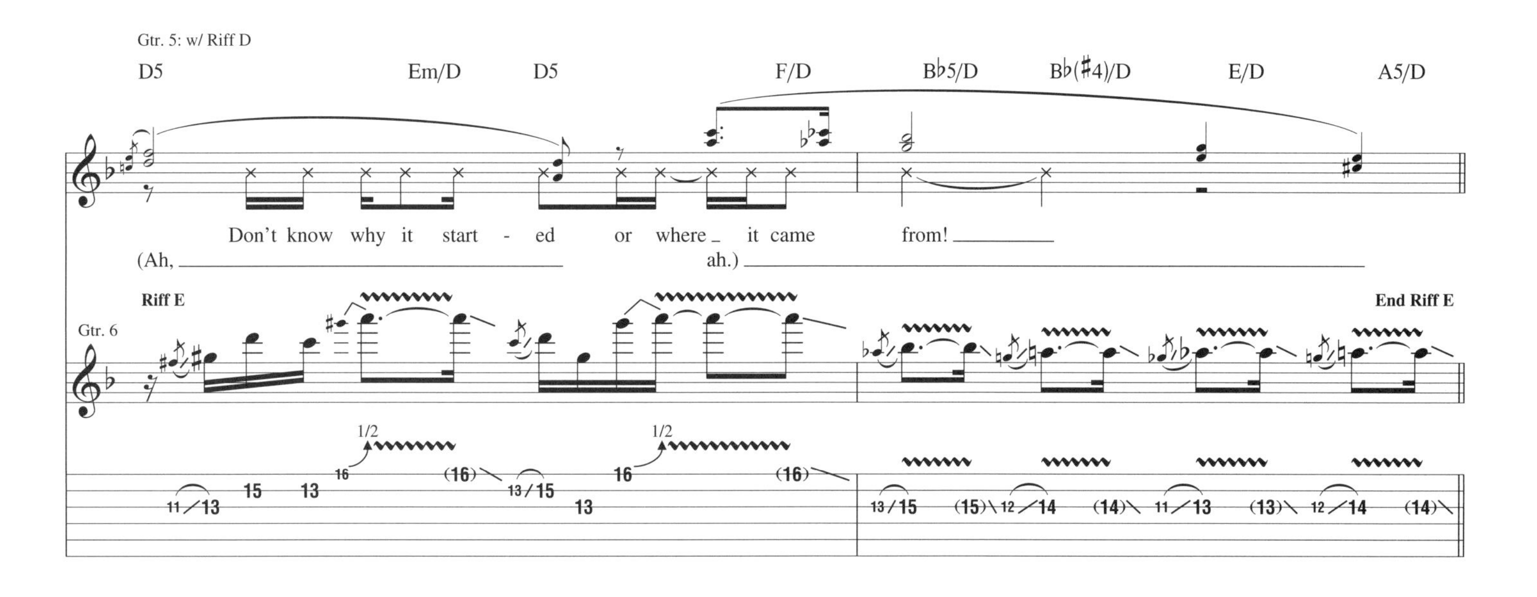
Gtr. 5: w/ Riff D
D5 Em/D D5 F/D B♭5/D B♭(♯4)/D E/D A5/D
Don't know why it start - ed or where it came from!
(Ah, ah.)
Riff E
End Riff E
Gtr. 6
1/2
1/2

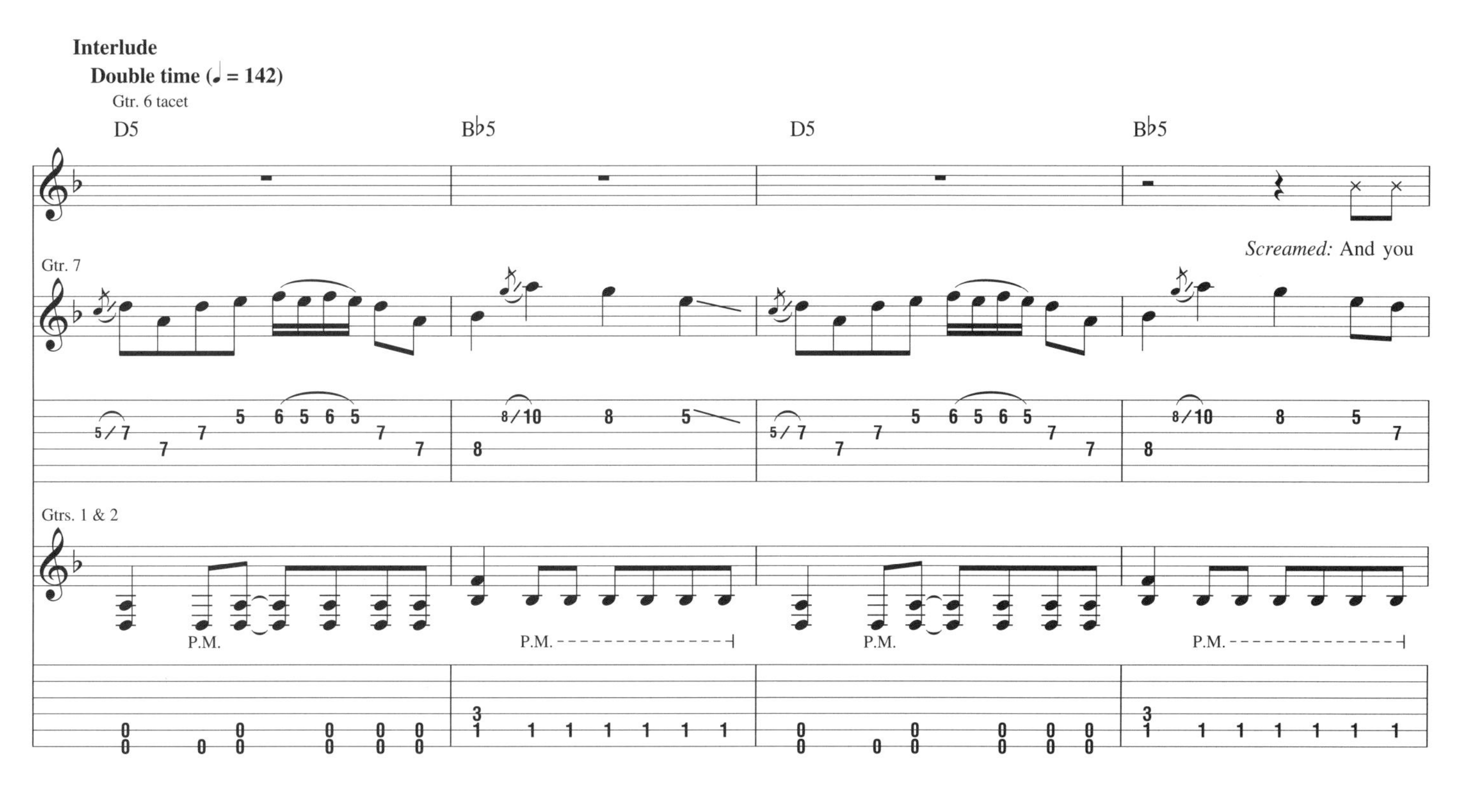
Interlude
Double time (♩ = 142)
Gtr. 6 tacet
D5 B♭5 D5 B♭5
Screamed: And you
Gtr. 7
Gtrs. 1 & 2
P.M.

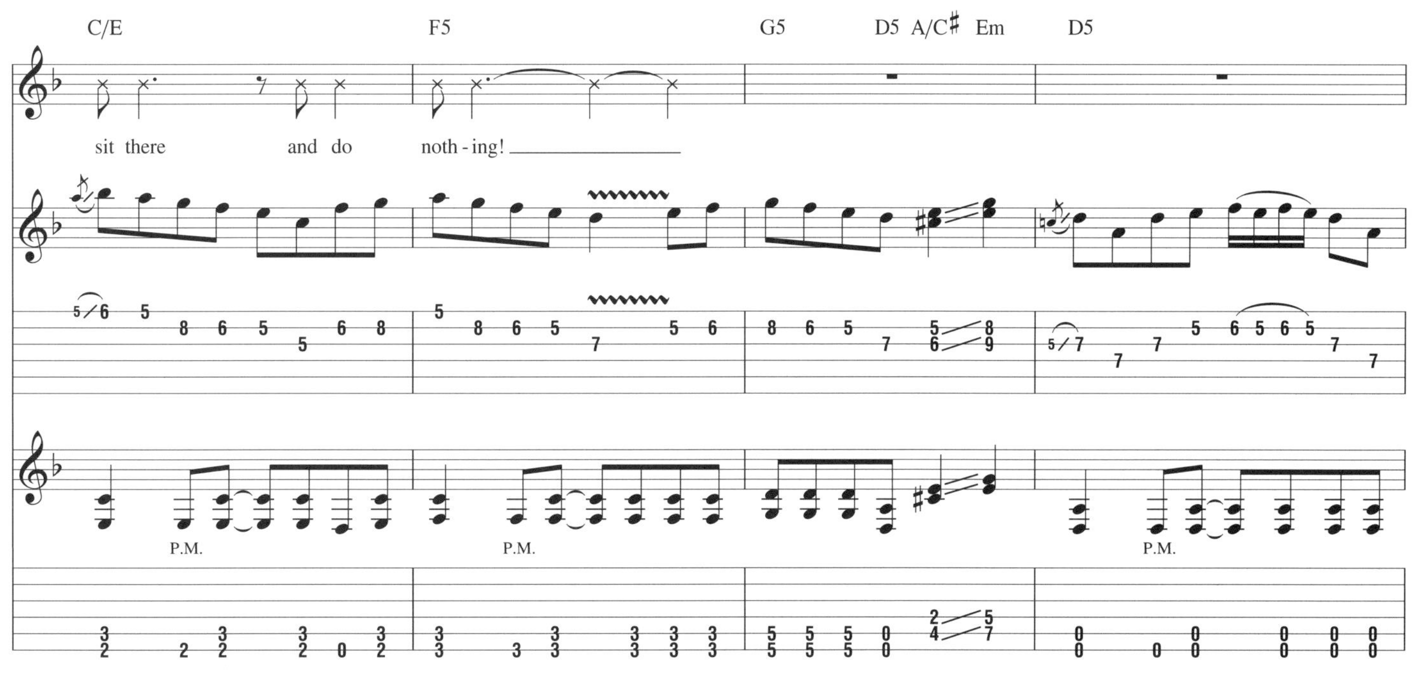
C/E F5 G5 D5 A/C♯ Em D5
sit there and do noth - ing!
P.M.

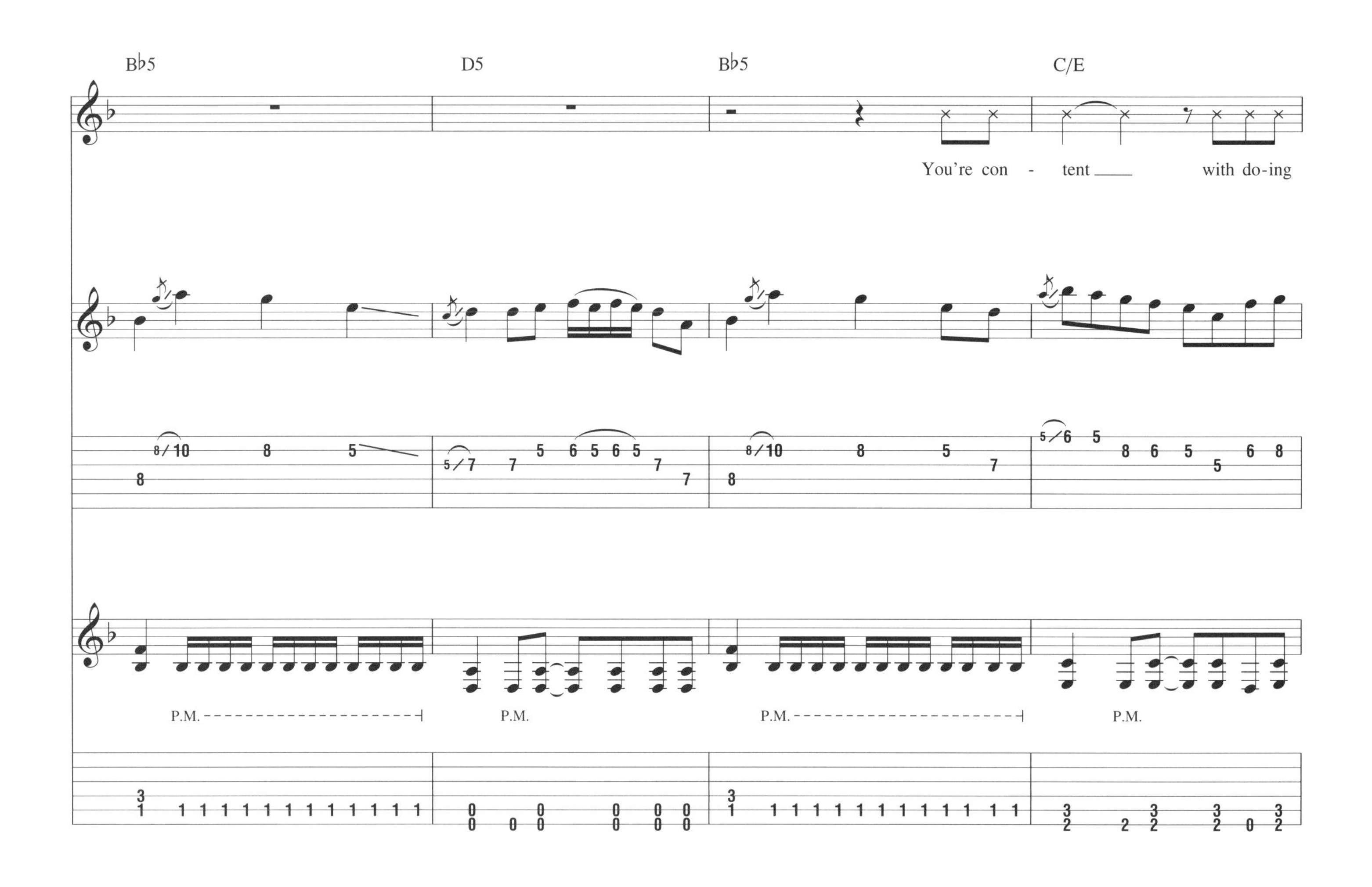
B♭5
D5
B♭5
C/E
You're con - tent with do-ing
P.M.
P.M.
P.M.
P.M.

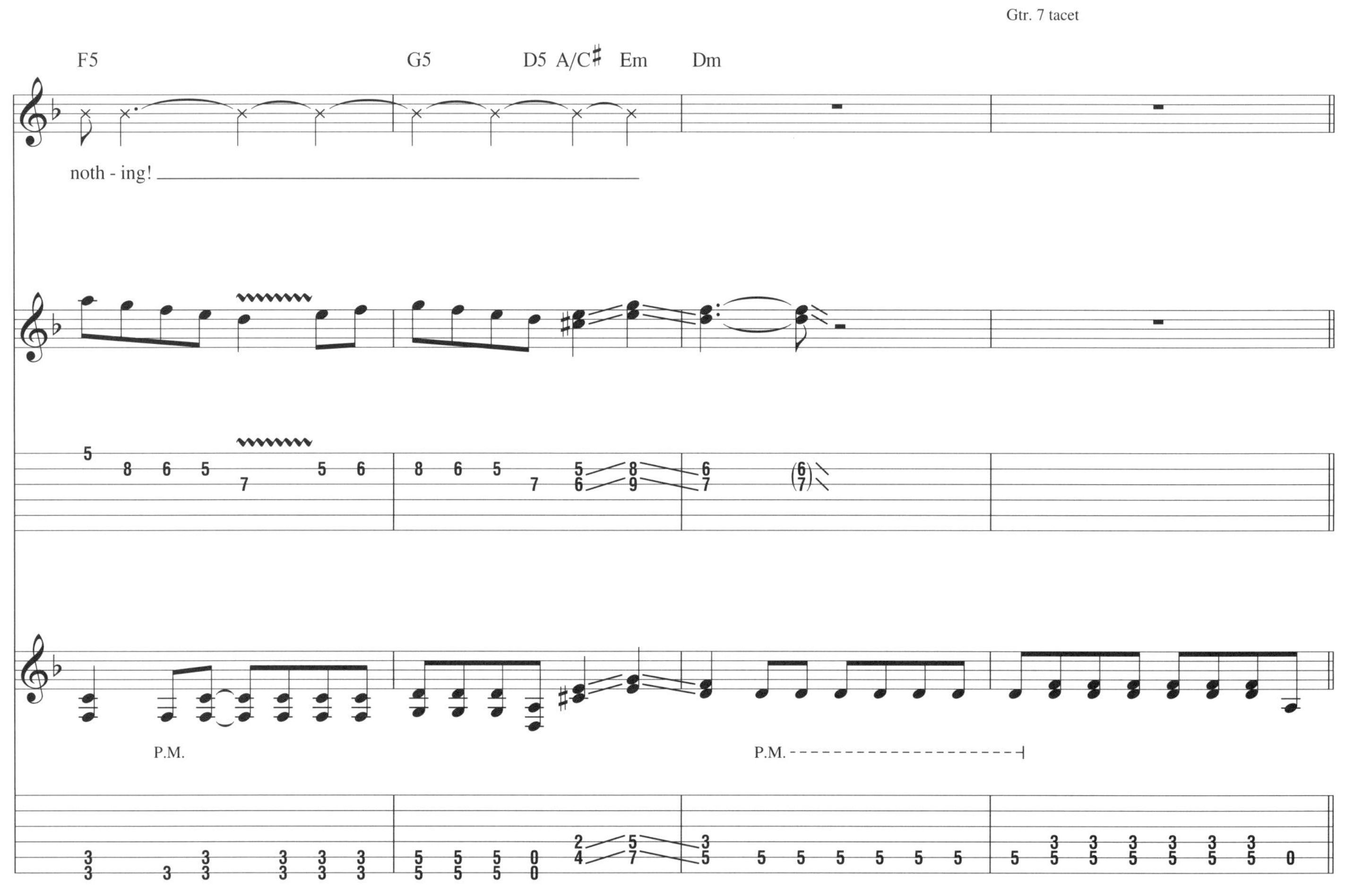
Gtr. 7 tacet
F5
G5
D5 A/C♯ Em
Dm
noth - ing!
P.M.
P.M.

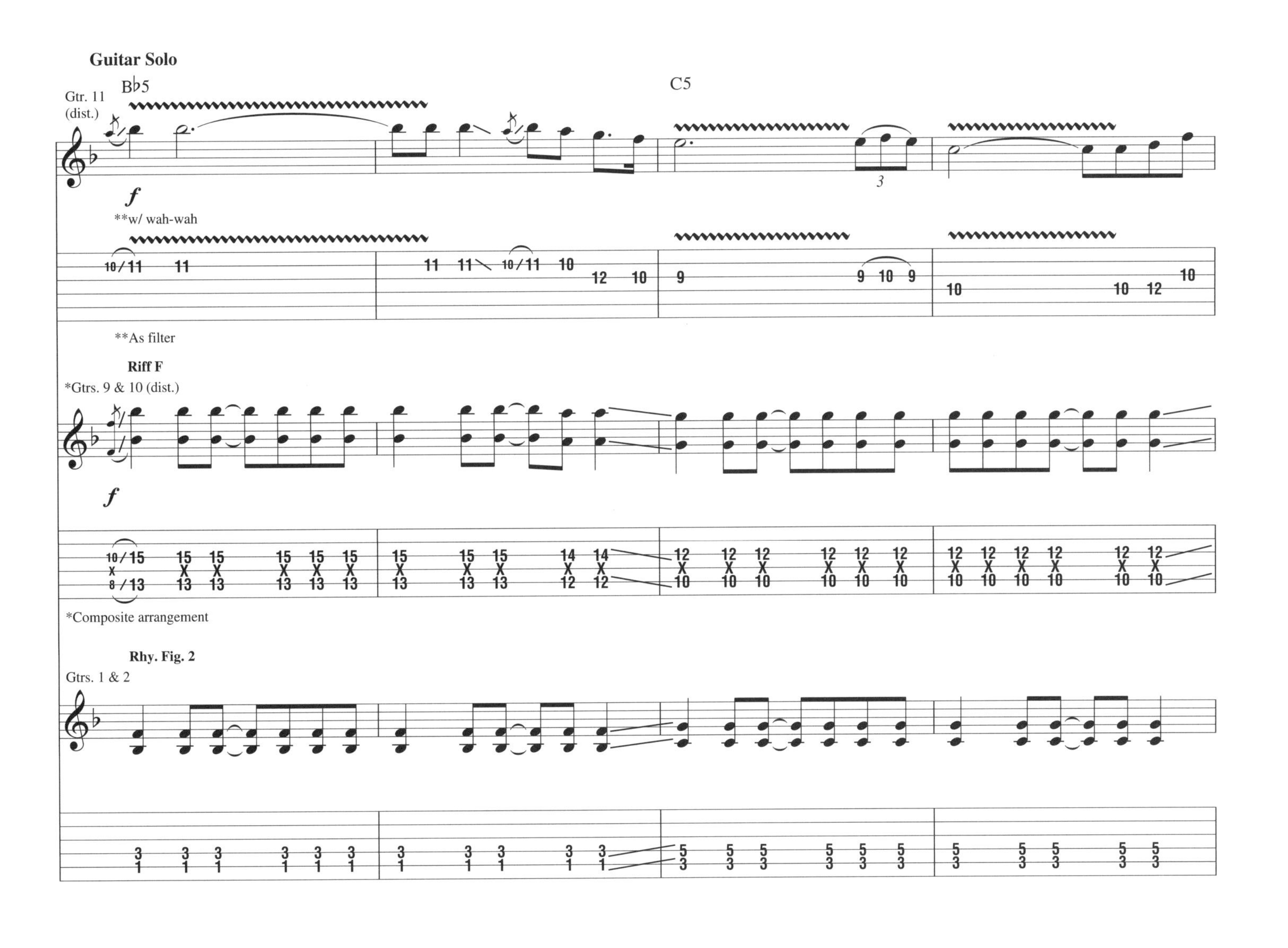
Guitar Solo
B♭5
C5
Gtr. 11
(dist.)
f
**w/ wah-wah
**As filter
Riff F
*Gtrs. 9 & 10 (dist.)
f
*Composite arrangement
Rhy. Fig. 2
Gtrs. 1 & 2

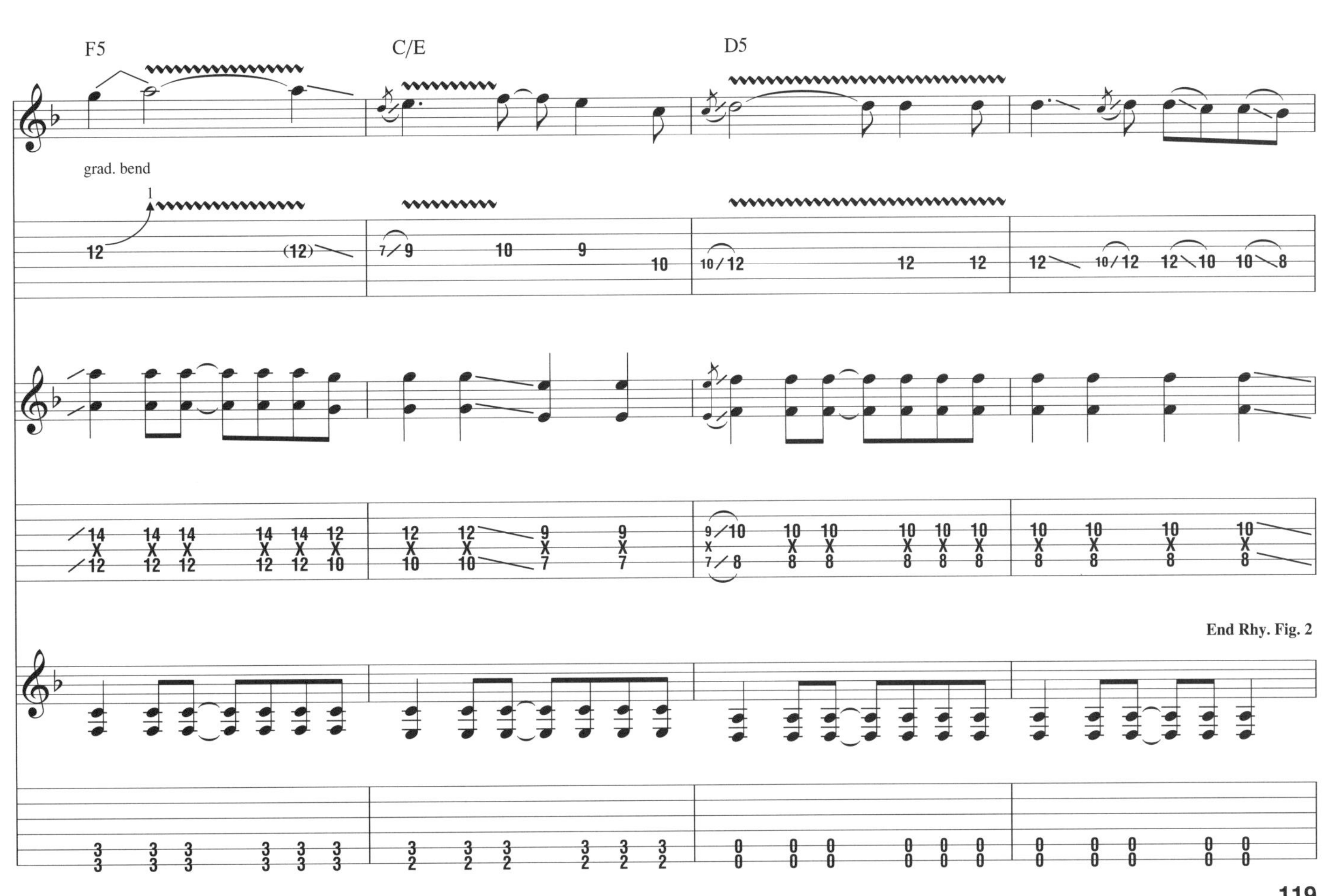
F5
C/E
D5
grad. bend
End Rhy. Fig. 2

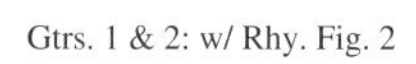
Gtrs. 1 & 2: w/ Rhy. Fig. 2

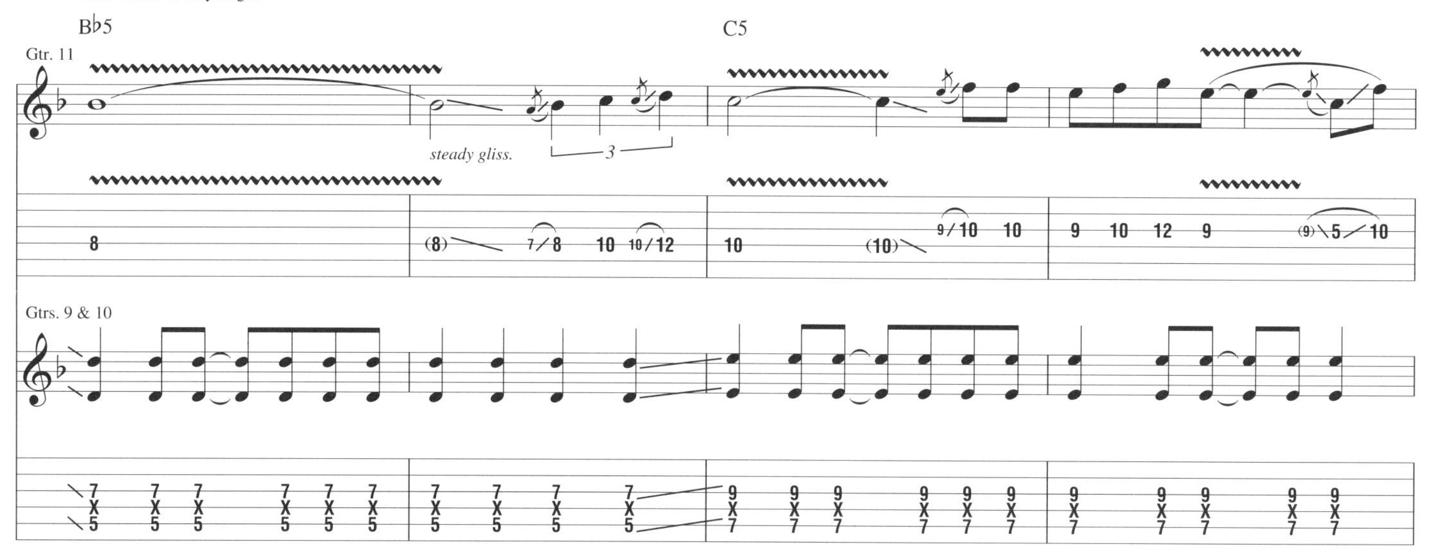
B♭5
C5
Gtr. 11
steady gliss.
3
Gtrs. 9 & 10

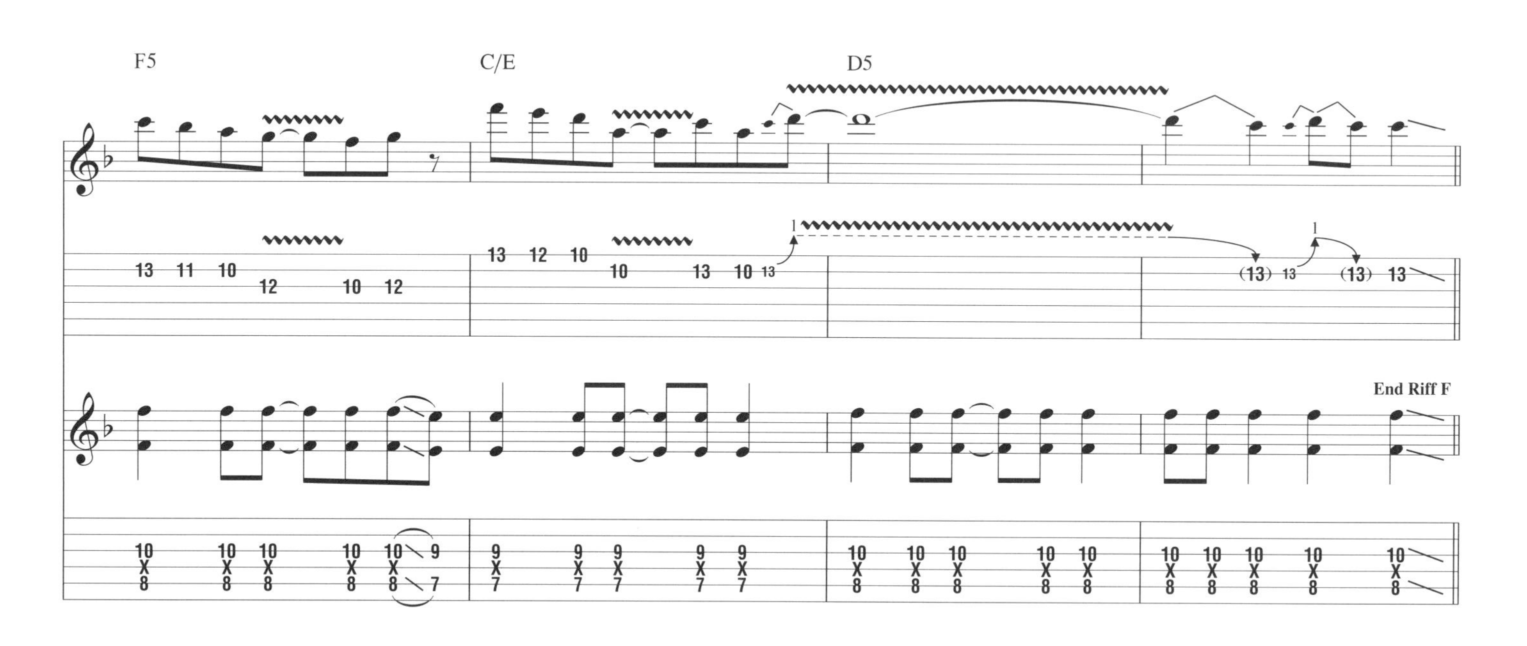
F5
C/E
D5
End Riff F

Bridge

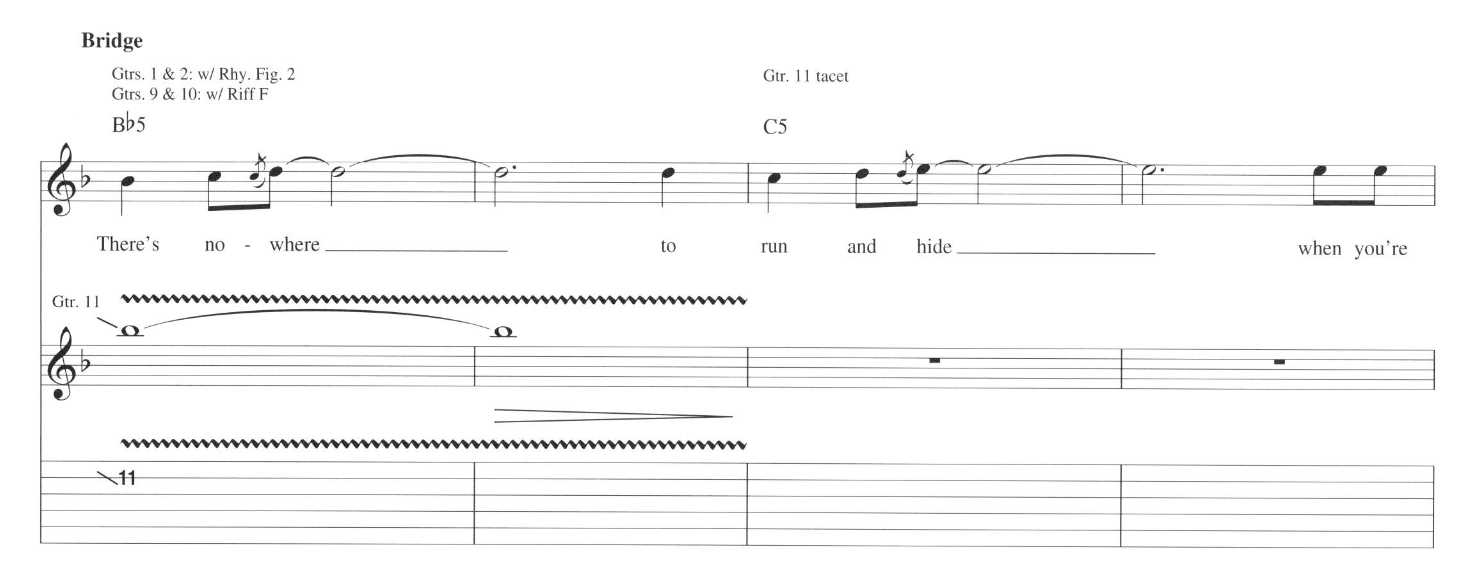
Gtrs. 1 & 2: w/ Rhy. Fig. 2
Gtrs. 9 & 10: w/ Riff F
Gtr. 11 tacet
B♭5
C5
There's no - where to run and hide when you're
Gtr. 11

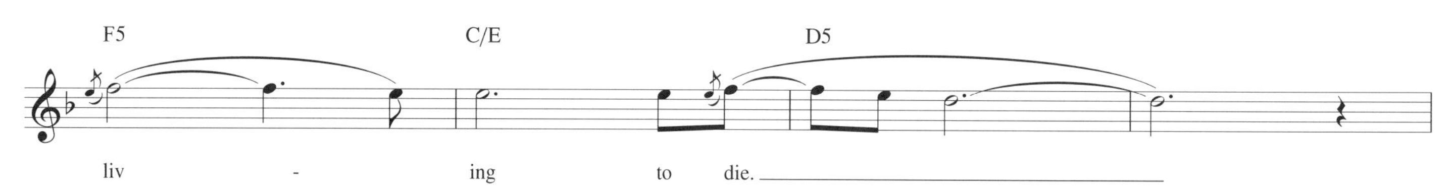
F5
C/E
D5
liv - ing to die.

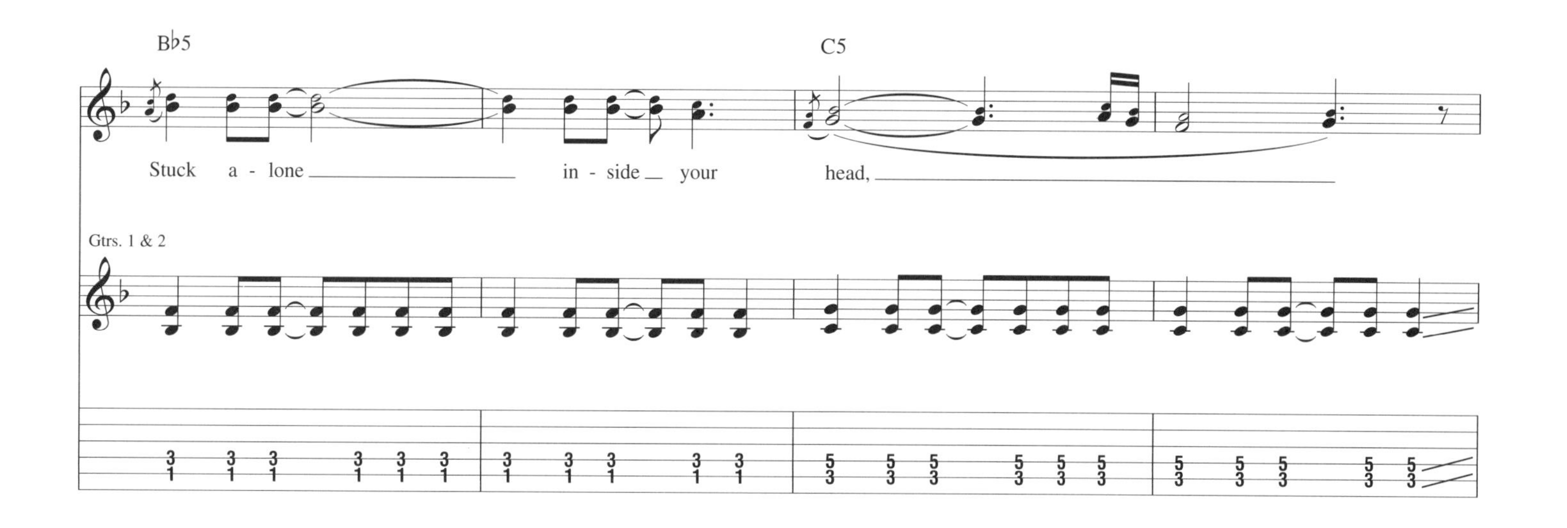
B♭5
C5
Stuck a - lone inside your head,
Gtrs. 1 & 2

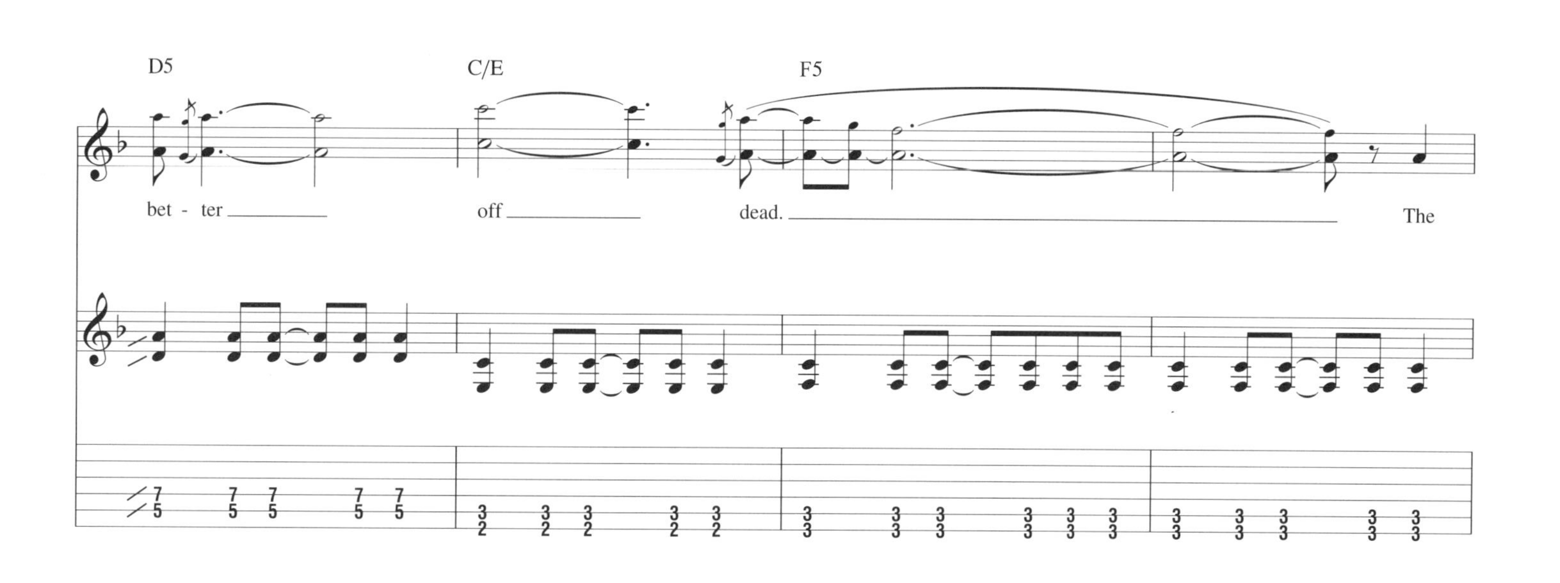
D5
C/E
F5
bet - ter off dead. The

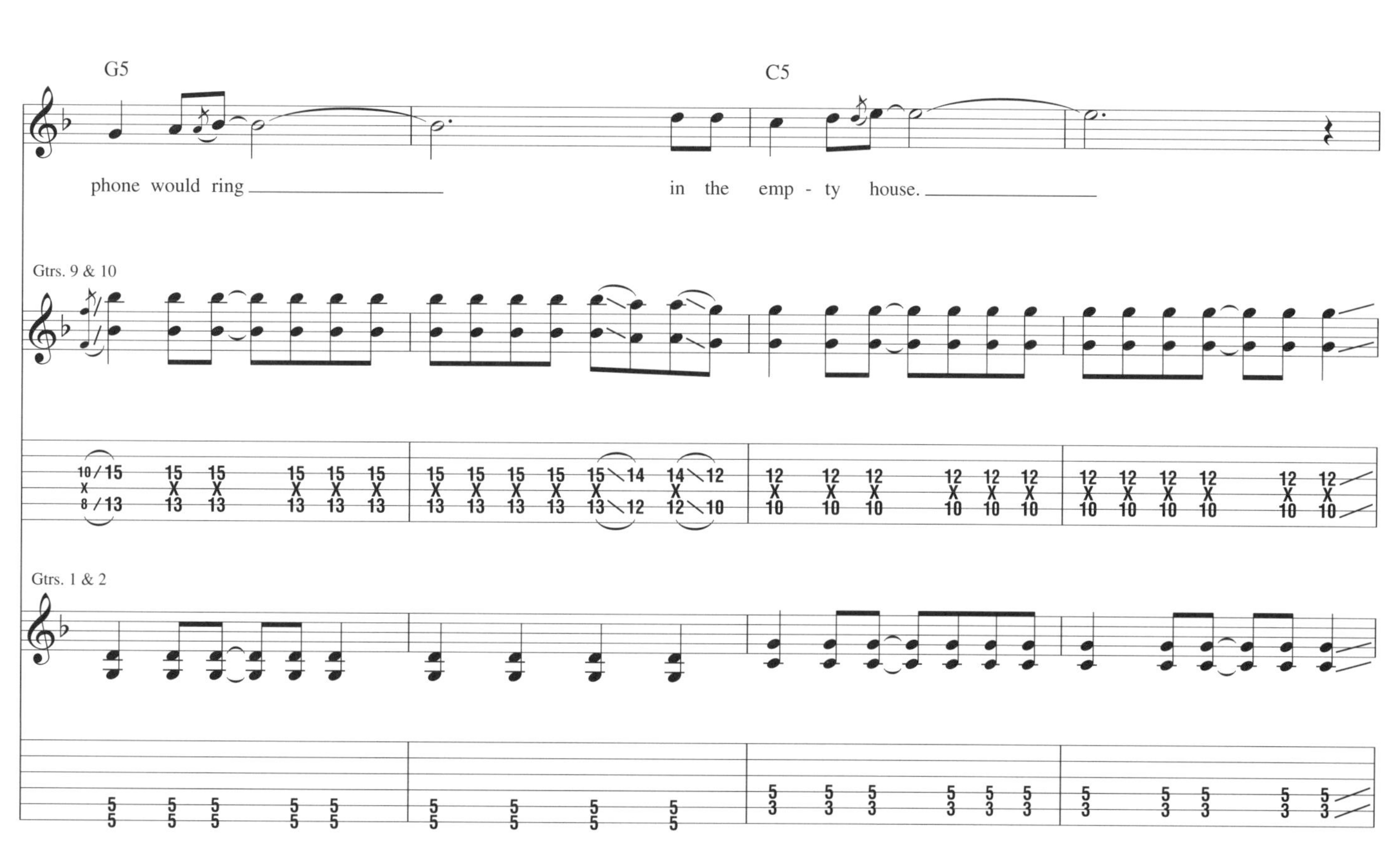
G5
C5
phone would ring in the emp - ty house.
Gtrs. 9 & 10
Gtrs. 1 & 2

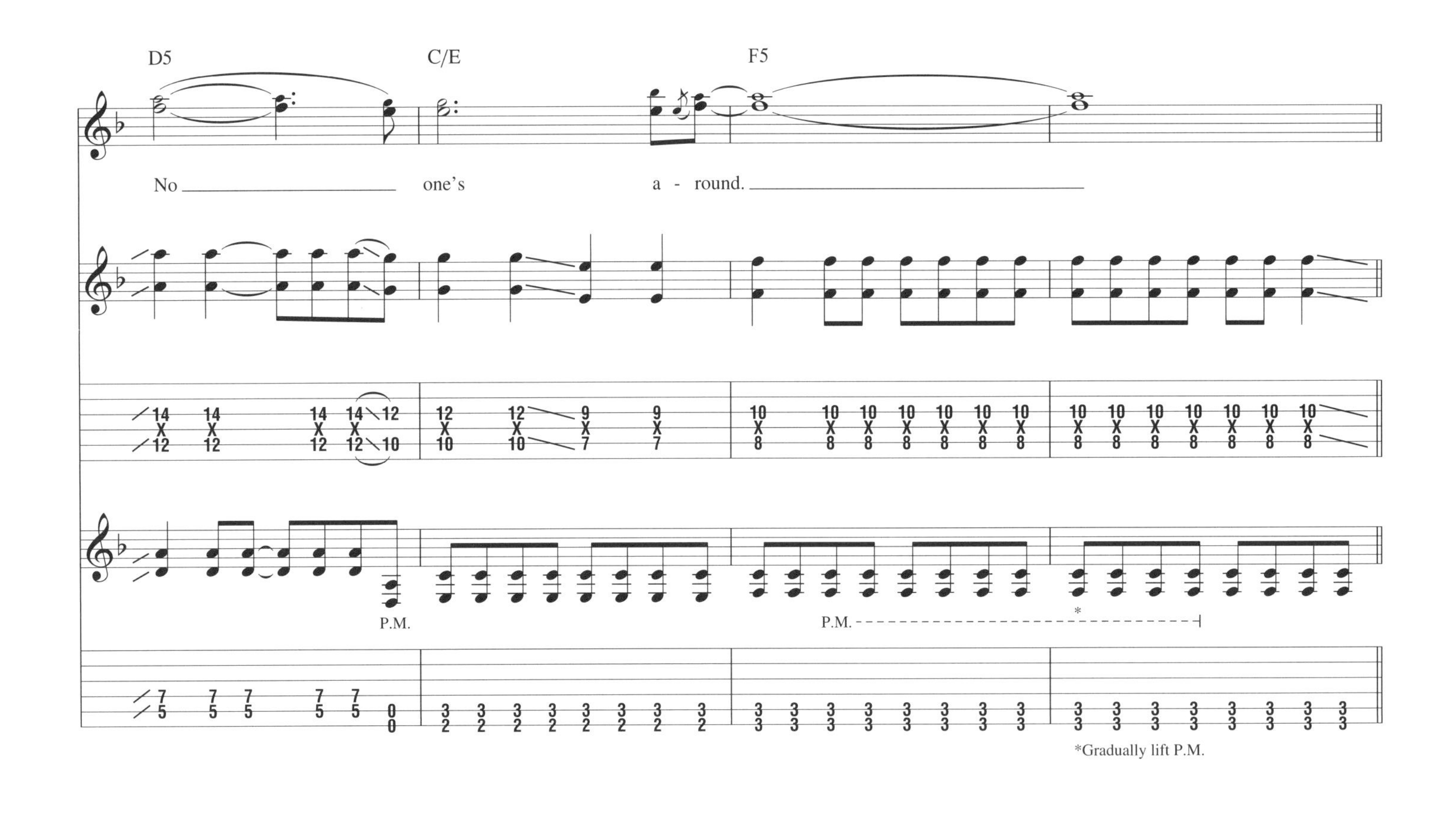

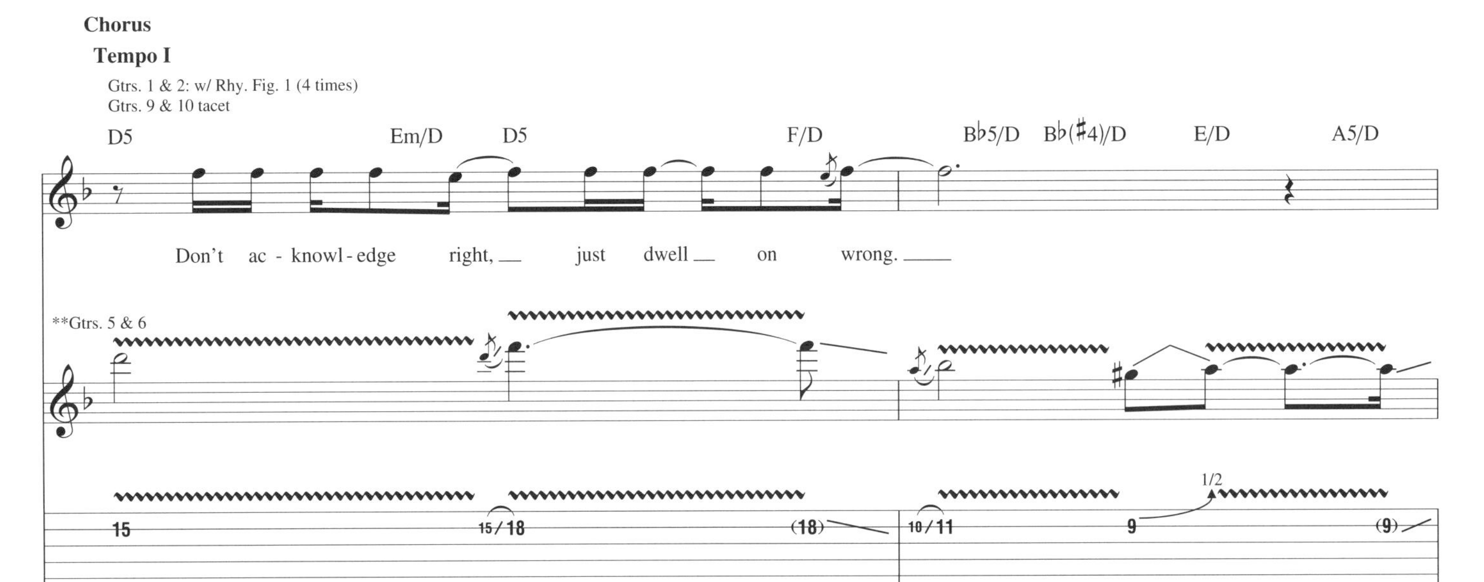

**Composite arrangement

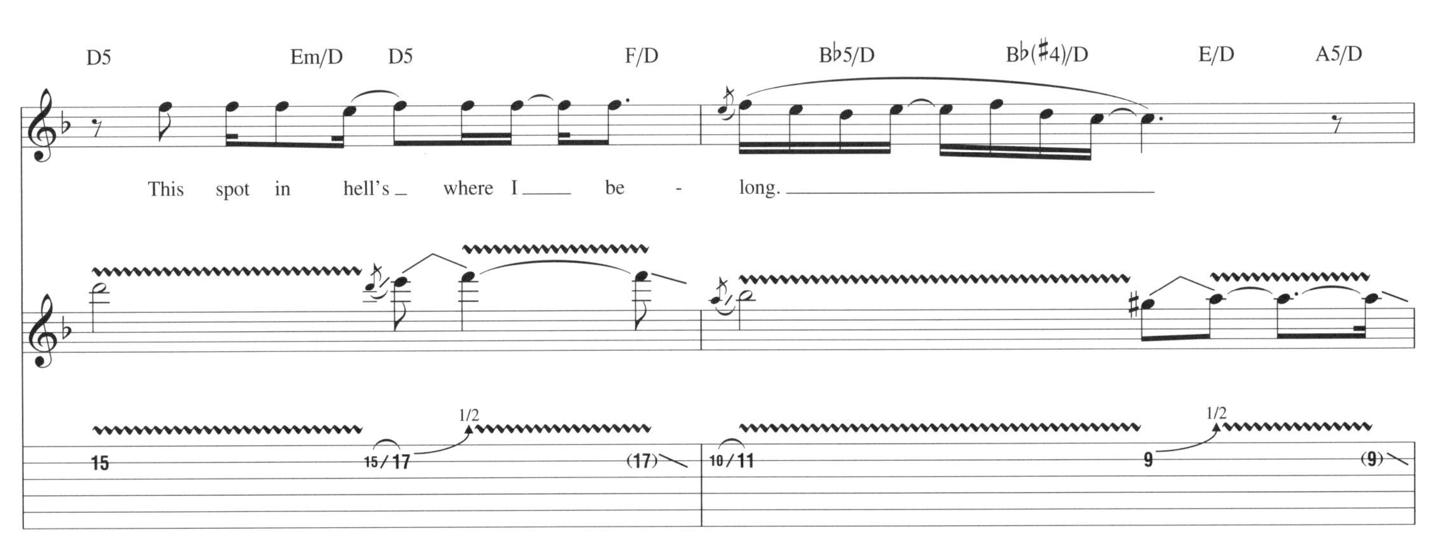

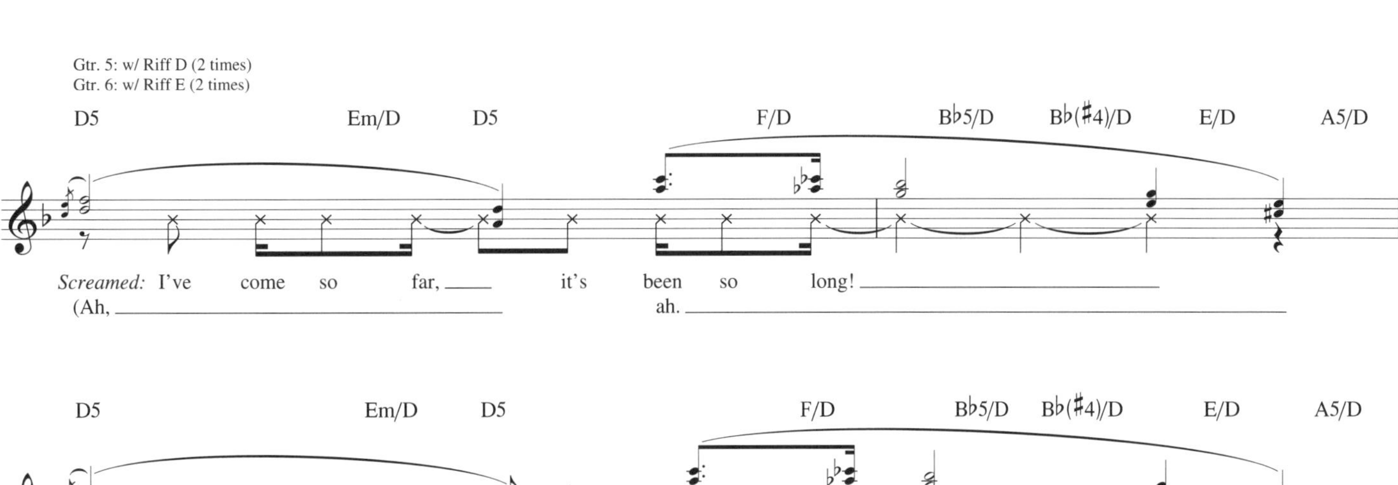
Gtr. 5: w/ Riff D (2 times)
Gtr. 6: w/ Riff E (2 times)
D5 Em/D D5 F/D B♭5/D B♭(♯4)/D E/D A5/D
Screamed: I've come so far, it's been so long!
(Ah, ah.

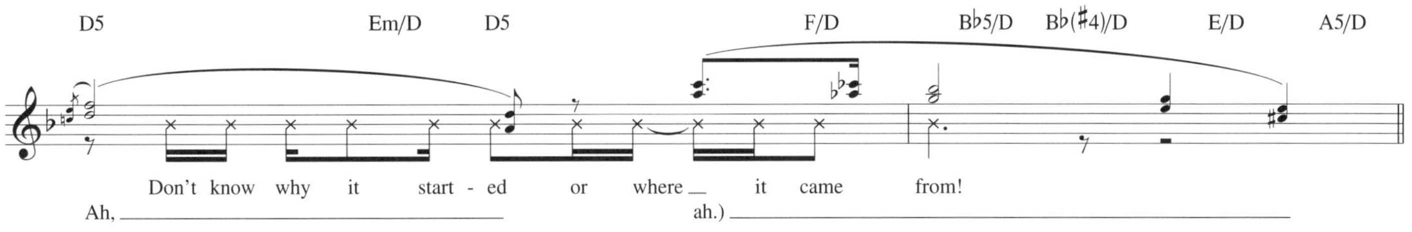
D5 Em/D D5 F/D B♭5/D B♭(♯4)/D E/D A5/D
Don't know why it start - ed or where it came from!
Ah, ah.)

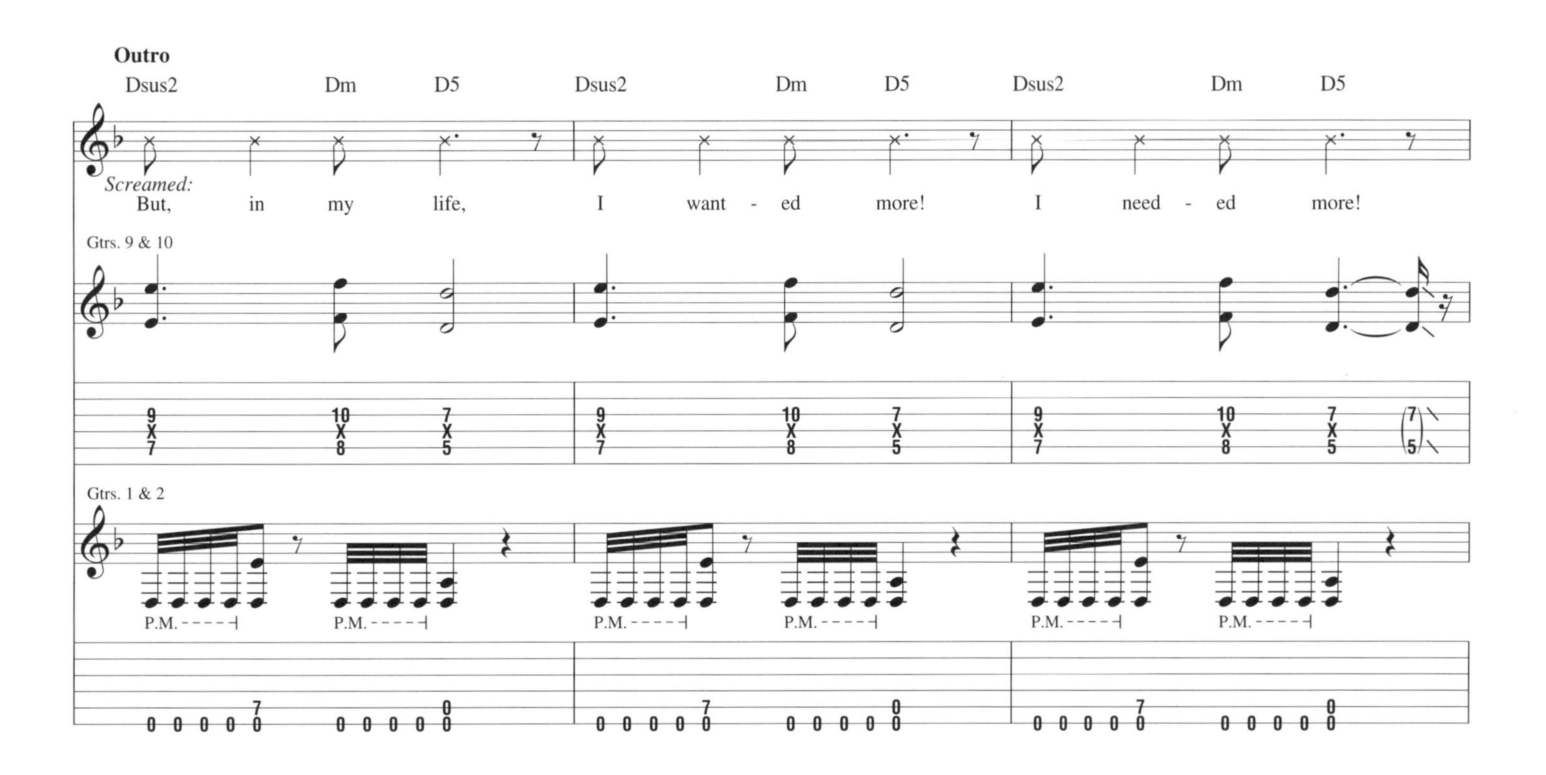
Outro
Dsus2 Dm D5 Dsus2 Dm D5 Dsus2 Dm D5
Screamed:
But, in my life, I want - ed more! I need - ed more!
Gtrs. 9 & 10
Gtrs. 1 & 2
P.M.

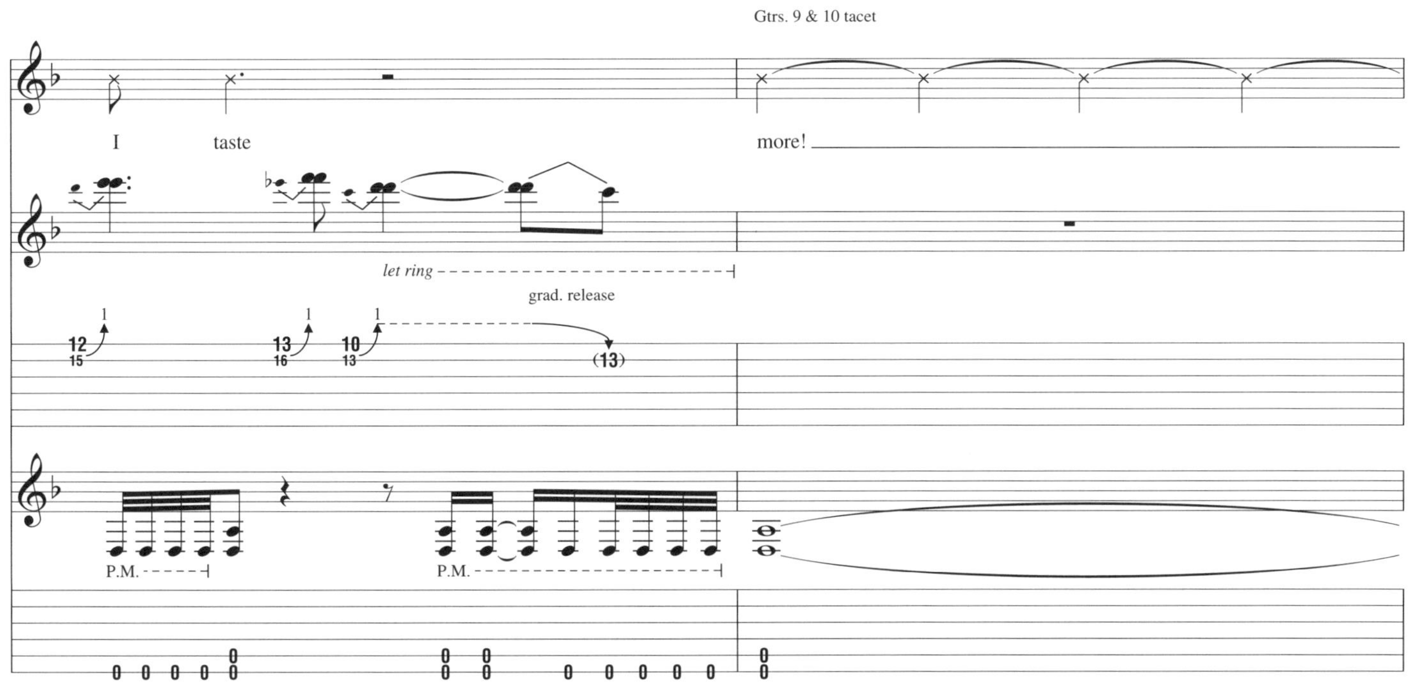
Gtrs. 9 & 10 tacet
I taste more!
let ring
grad. release
P.M.

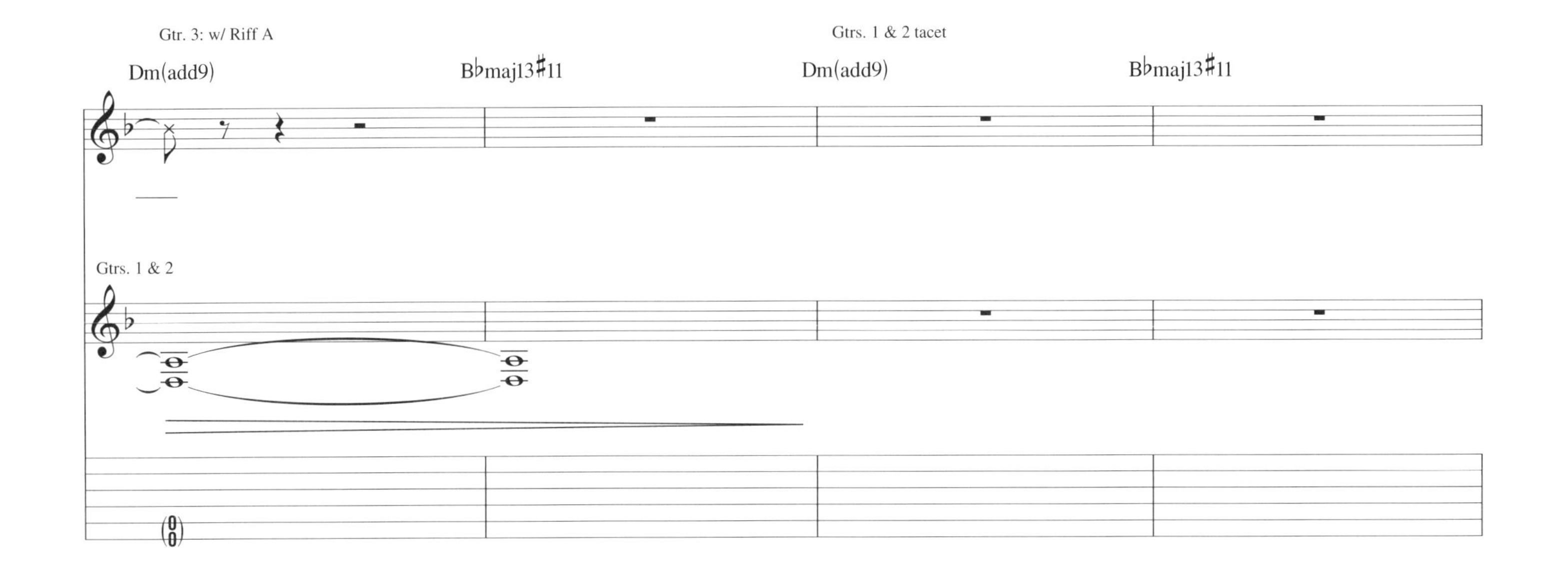

Gtr. 3: w/ Riff A
Gtrs. 1 & 2 tacet
Dm(add9)
B♭maj13♯11
Dm(add9)
B♭maj13♯11
Gtrs. 1 & 2

Gtr. 8: w/ Riff C
Dm(add9)
B♭maj13♯11
(Oo.

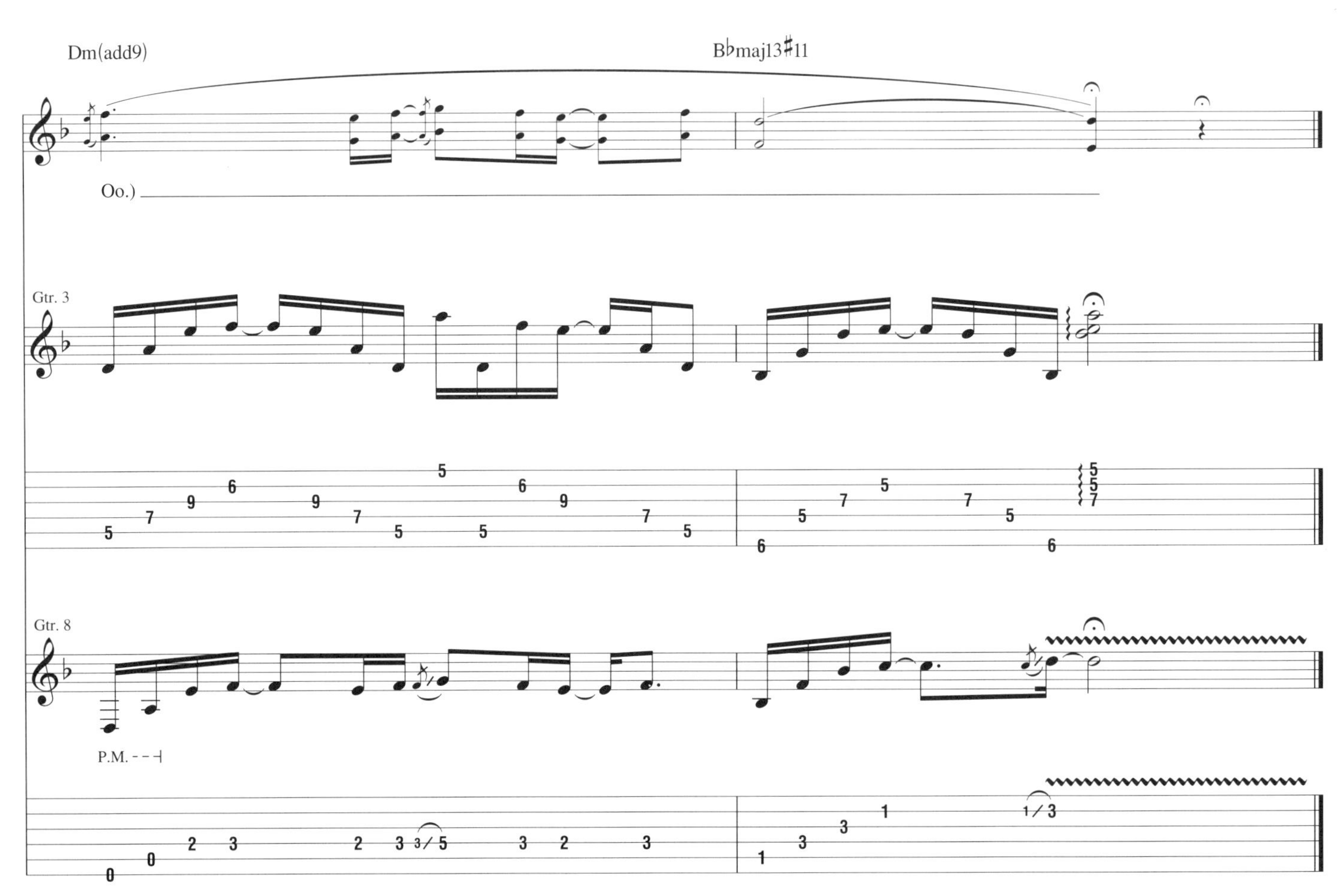

Dm(add9)
B♭maj13♯11
Oo.)
Gtr. 3
Gtr. 8
P.M.

And All Things Will End

Words and Music by Matthew Sanders, James Sullivan, Brian Haner, Jr. and Zachary Baker

Drop D tuning:
(low to high) D-A-D-G-B-E

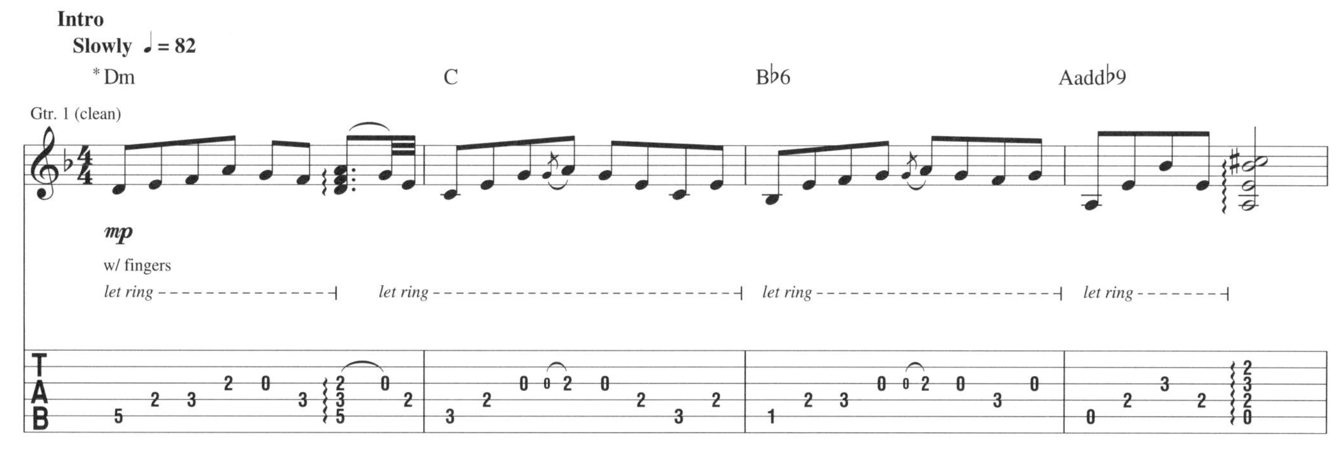

*Chord symbols reflect implied harmony.

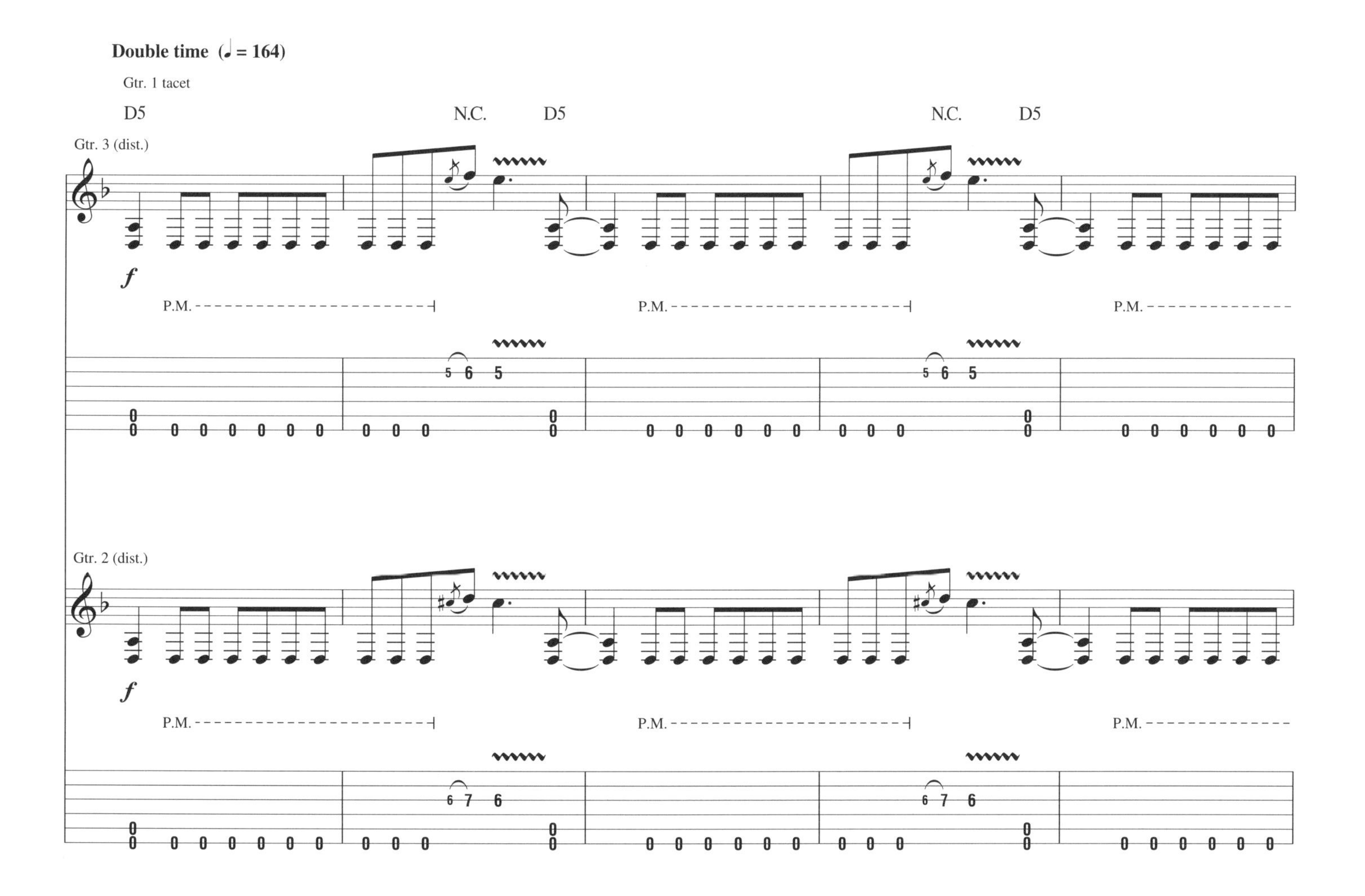

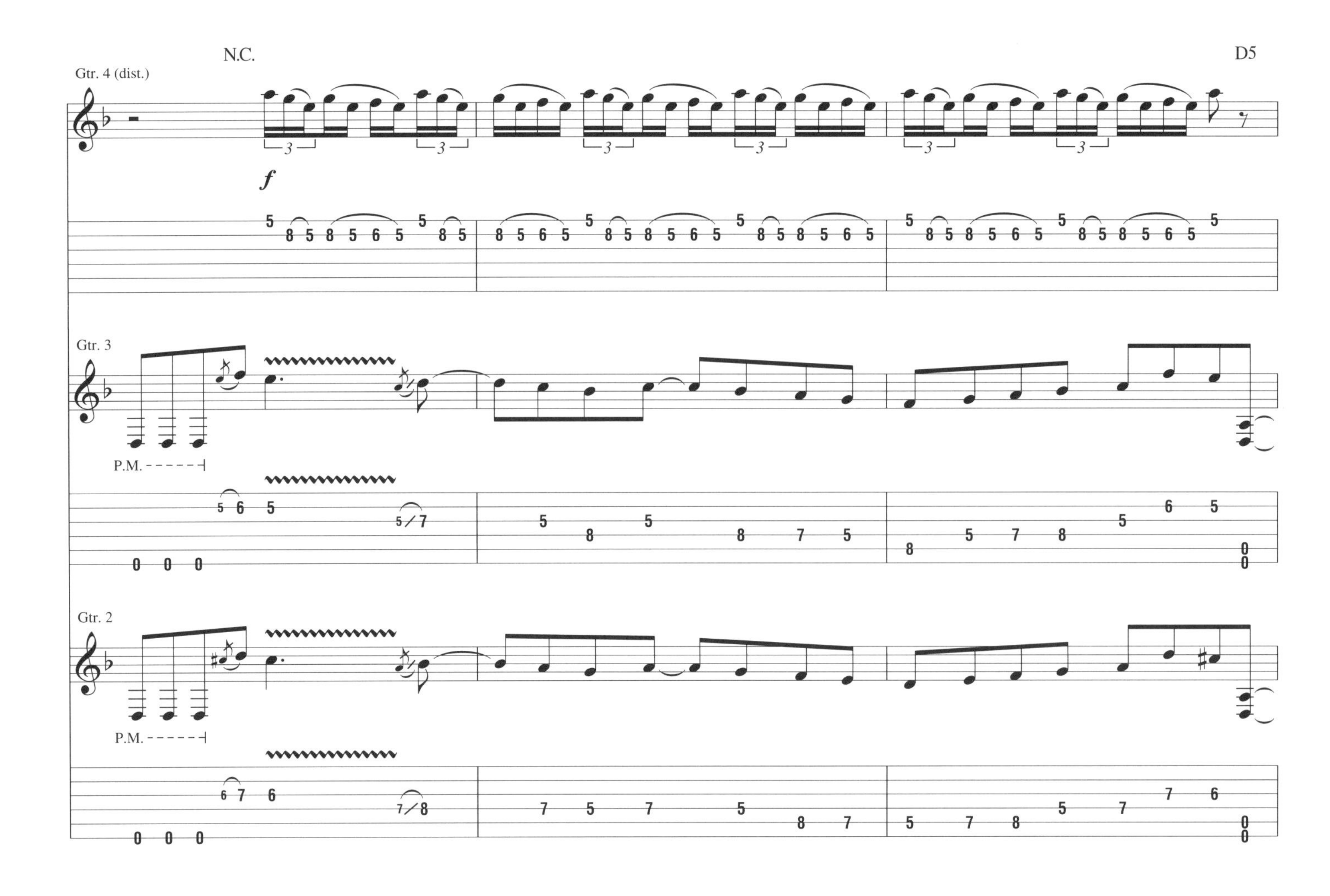
N.C.
D5
Gtr. 4 (dist.)
Gtr. 3
P.M.
Gtr. 2
P.M.

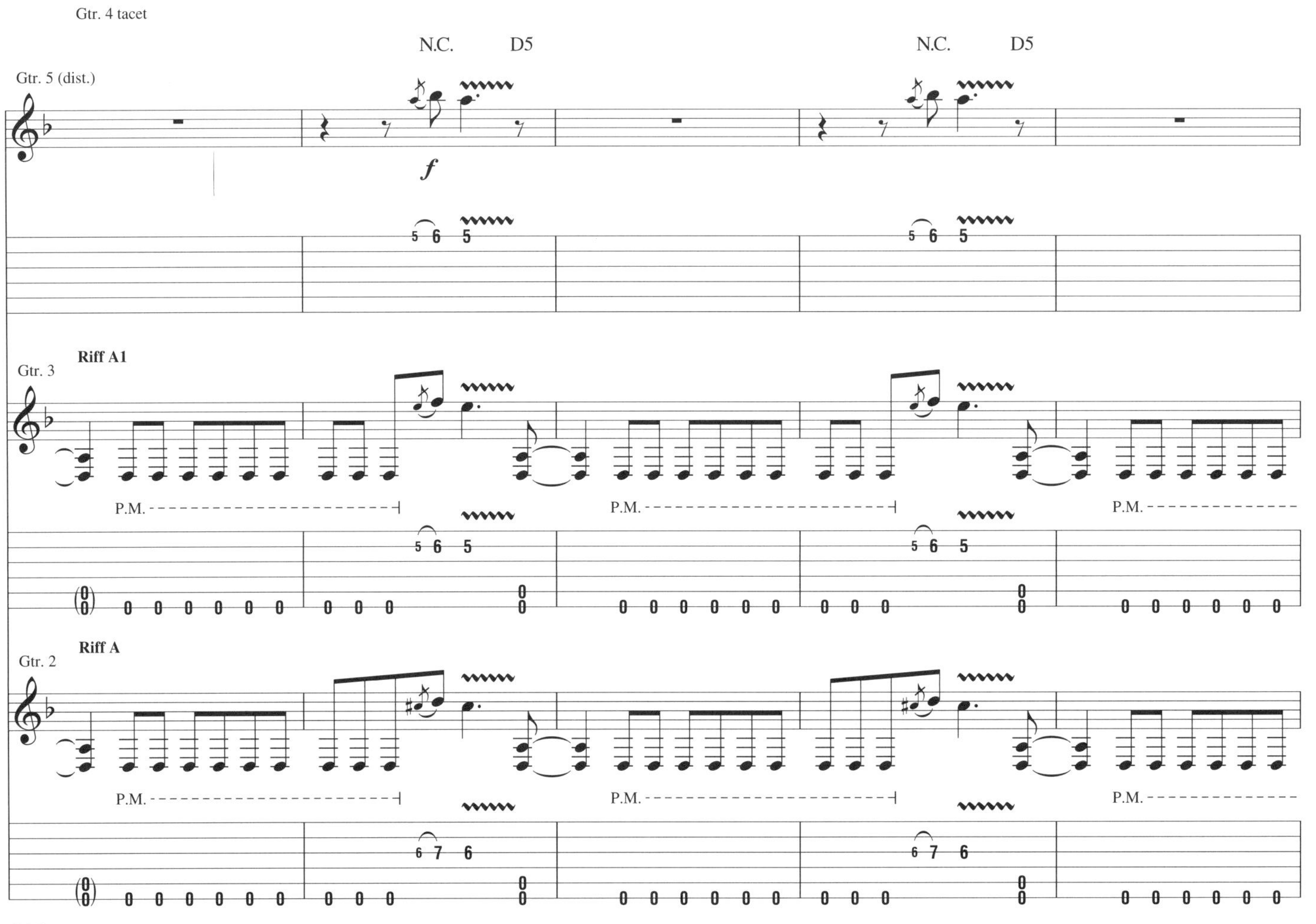
Gtr. 4 tacet
N.C.
D5
N.C.
D5
Gtr. 5 (dist.)
Riff A1
Gtr. 3
P.M.
P.M.
P.M.
Riff A
Gtr. 2
P.M.
P.M.
P.M.

Gtr. 5 tacet

Gtr. 4
N.C.
D5
N.C.
grad. bend
Riff B
Gtr. 5
End Riff B
Gtr. 3
P.M.
End Riff A1
Gtr. 2
P.M.
End Riff A

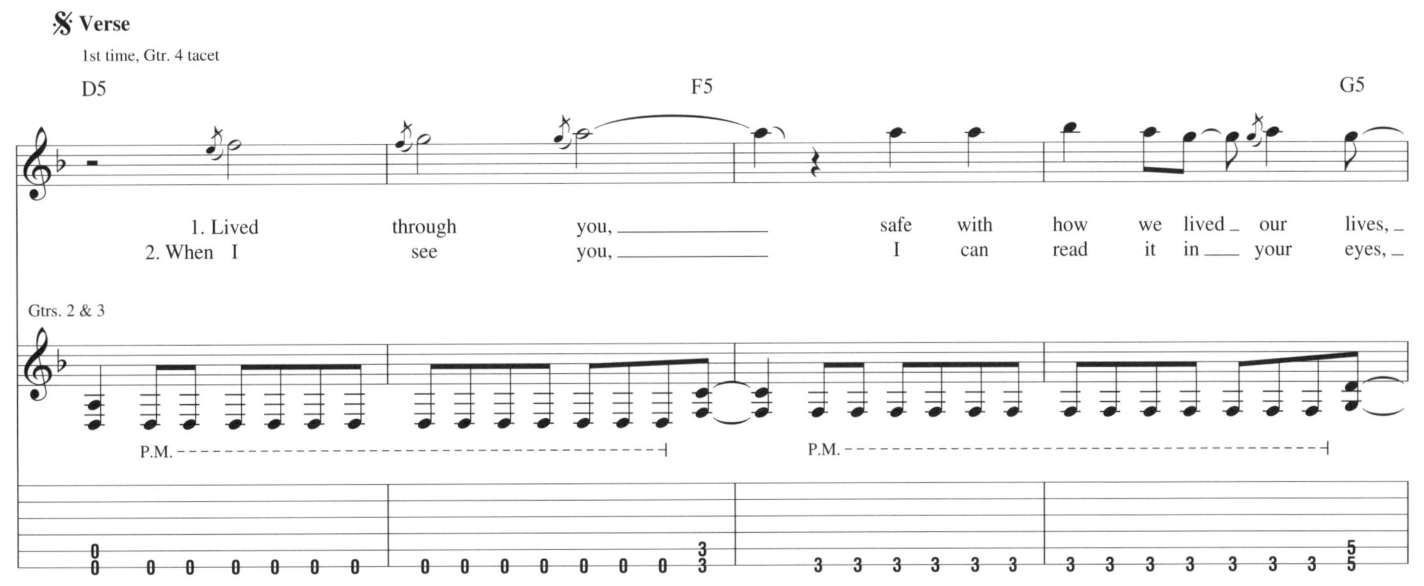
Verse
1st time, Gtr. 4 tacet
D5
F5
G5
1. Lived through you, safe with how we lived our lives,
2. When I see you, I can read it in your eyes,
Gtrs. 2 & 3
P.M.
P.M.

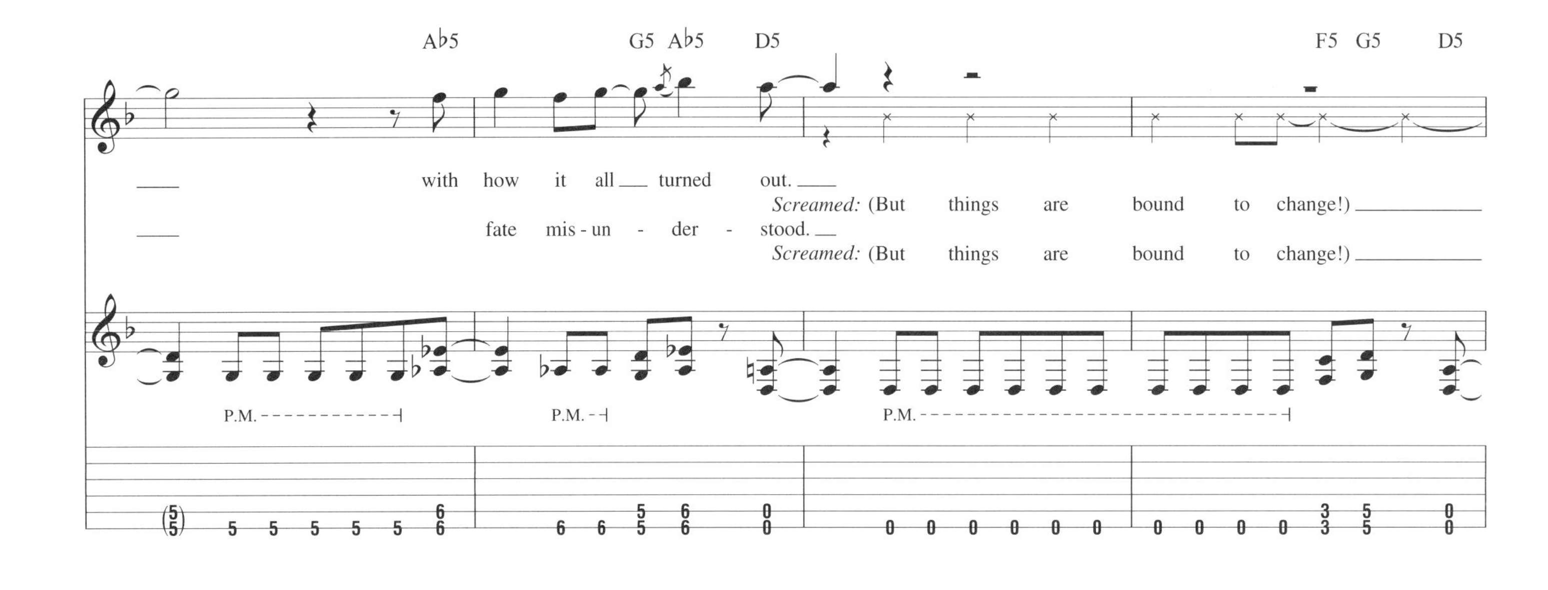

A♭5 G5 A♭5 D5 F5 G5 D5
with how it all turned out.
Screamed: (But things are bound to change!)
fate mis-un-der-stood.
Screamed: (But things are bound to change!)
P.M.
P.M.
P.M.

F5 G5
Un-cov-ered lies, sur-faced through-out,
Swal-lowed the lies, can't blame you for
P.M.
P.M.

To Coda 1
A♭5 G5 A♭5 D5 F5 G5 A5 B♭5
will make you change your mind. Some-
think-ing with your heart. Some-
Gtr. 4
Fill 1
End Fill 1
*w/ wah-wah
*As filter
Gtrs. 2 & 3
P.M.
P.M.
P.M.

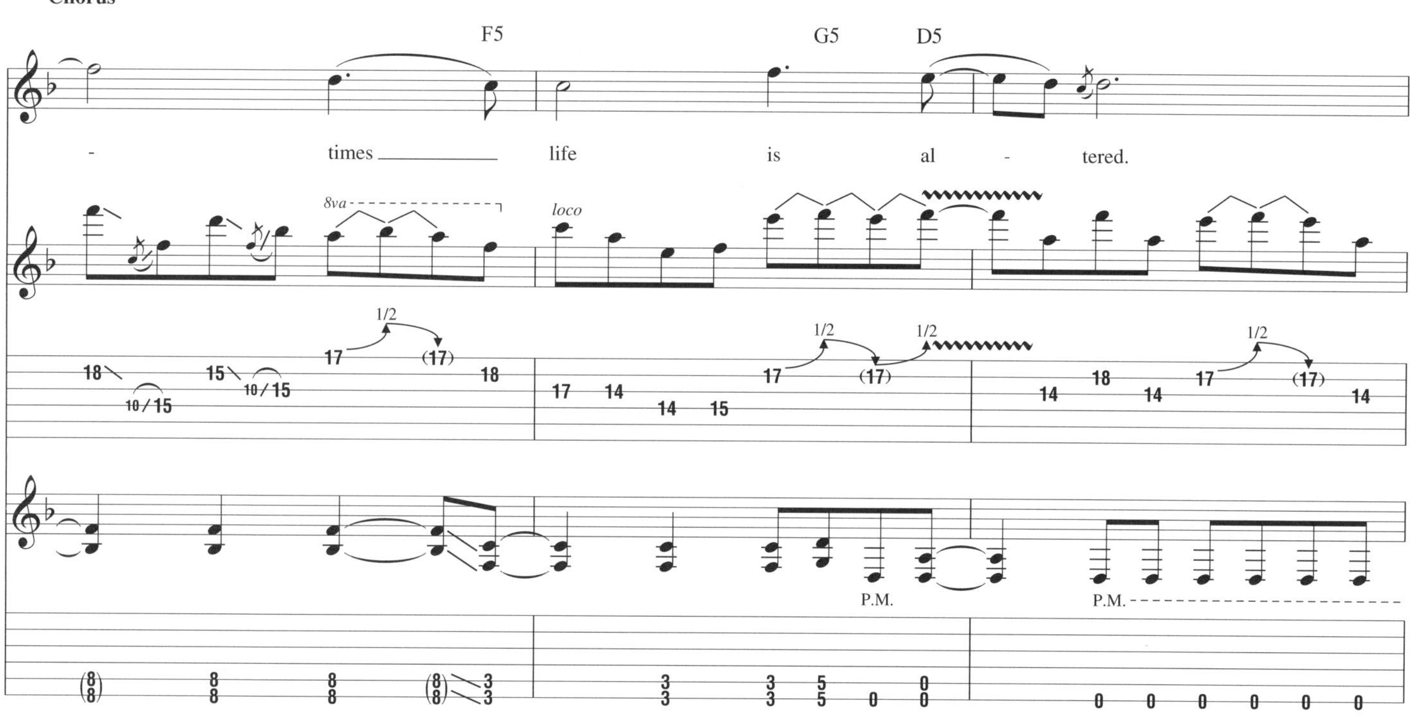

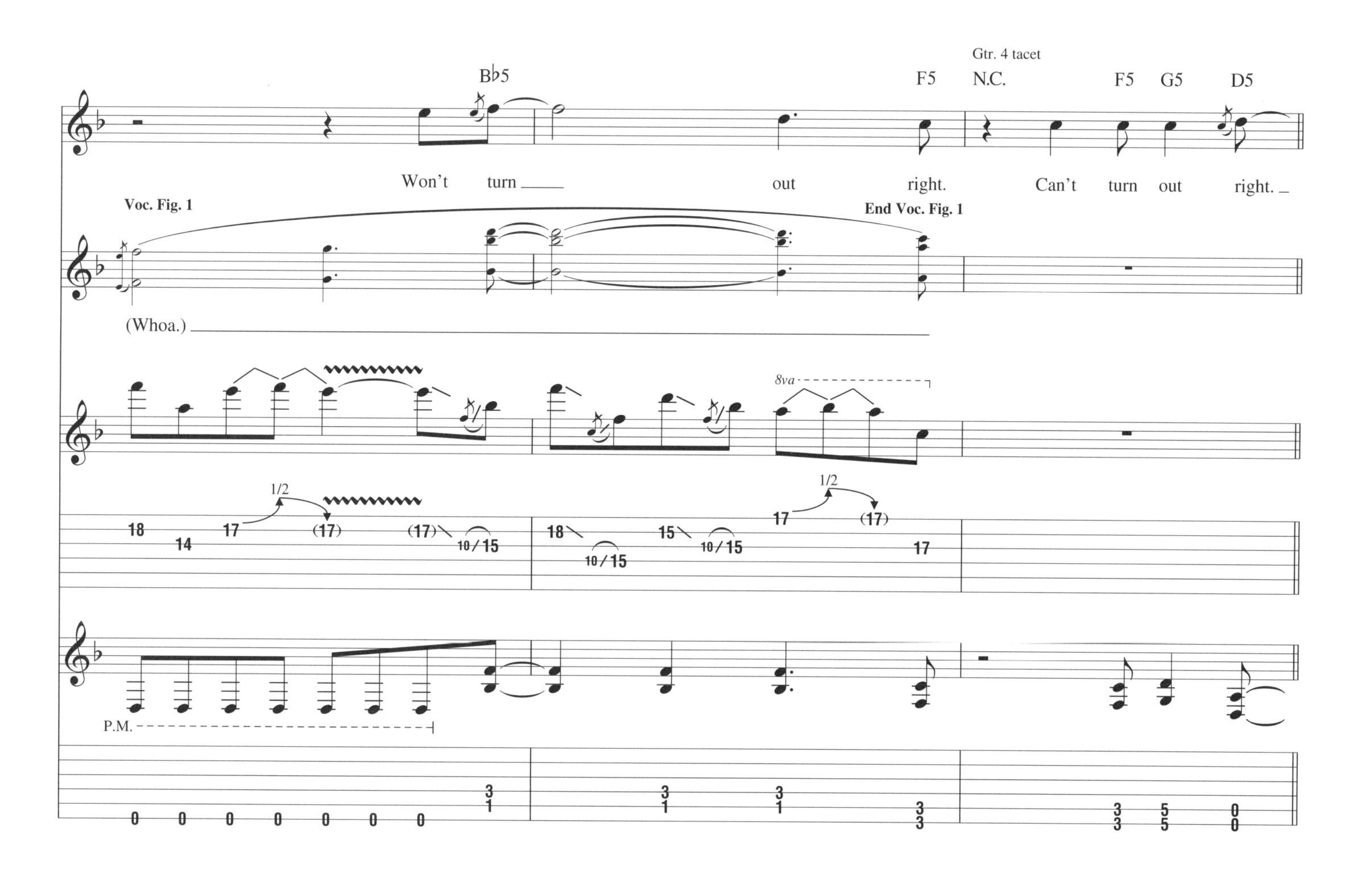

Interlude

Gtrs. 2 & 3: w/ Riffs A & A1

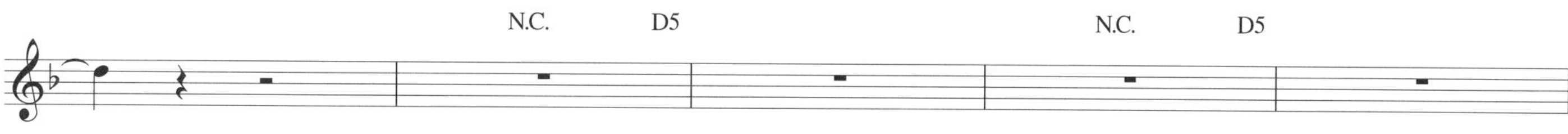

D.S. al Coda 1

Gtr. 5: w/ Riff B

N.C. D5 N.C.

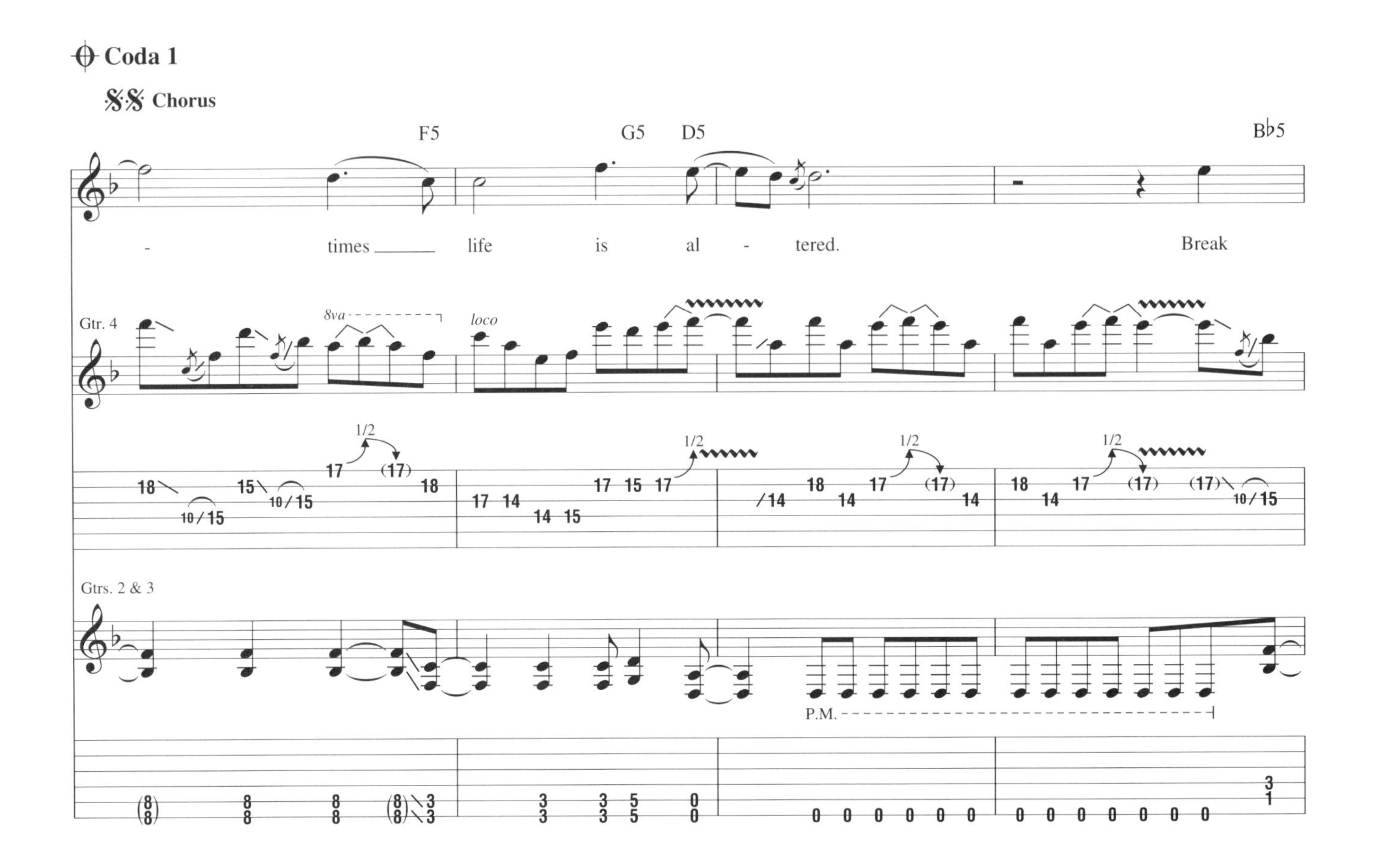

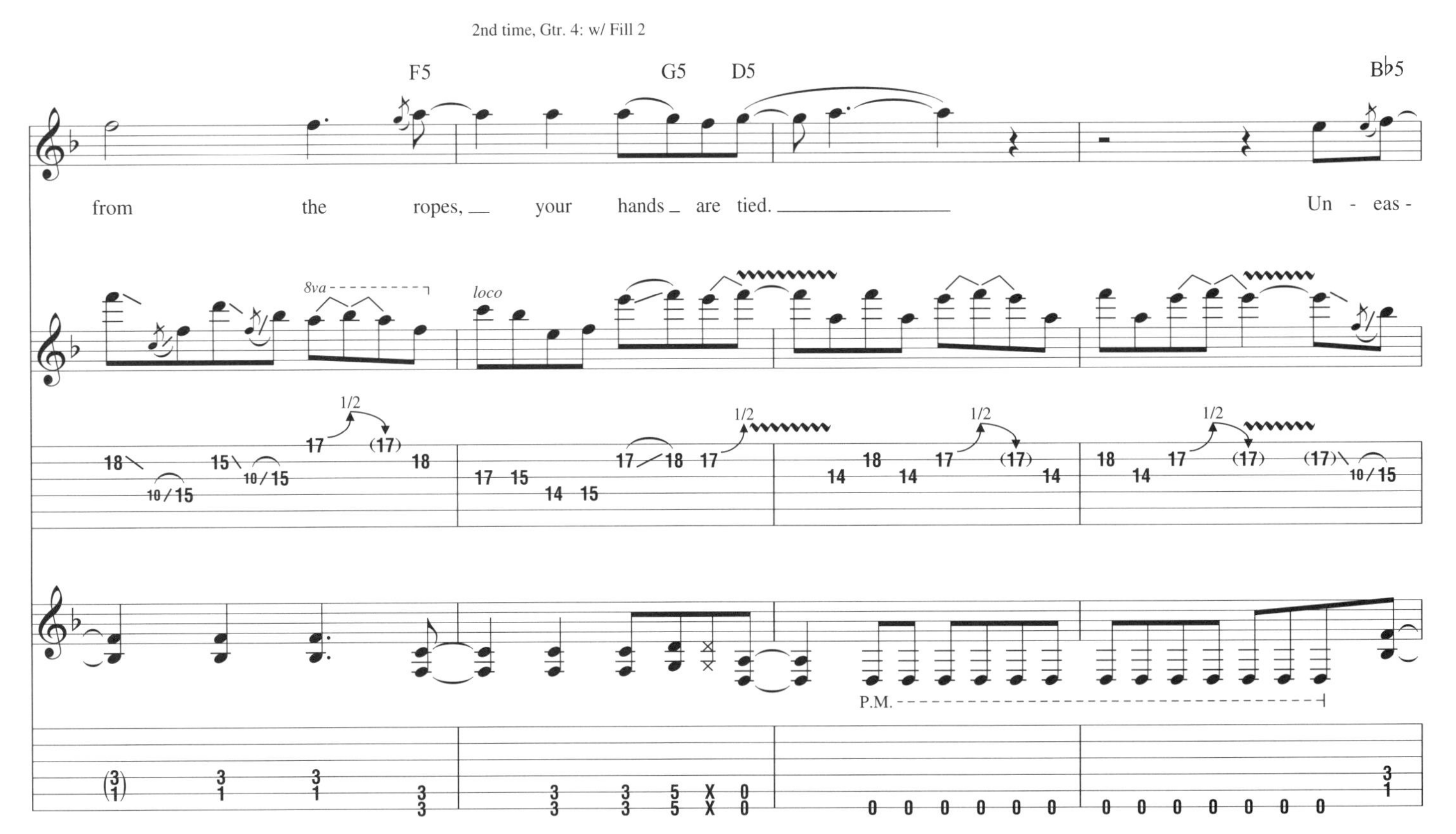

Bkgd. Voc.: w/ Voc. Fig. 1
F5
G5
D5
B♭5
- y with con - fron-ta - tion.
Won't turn
Fill 2
End Fill 2
8va
loco
1/2
P.M.
To Coda 2
Gtr. 4 tacet
F5
N.C.
F5
G5
D5
out right. Can't turn out right.
dim.
Interlude
Tempo I
Dm
C
Gtrs. 2 & 3 tacet
A7♭9/E
Dm(add9)
Gtr. 1
Riff C
let ring
Gtrs. 2 & 3

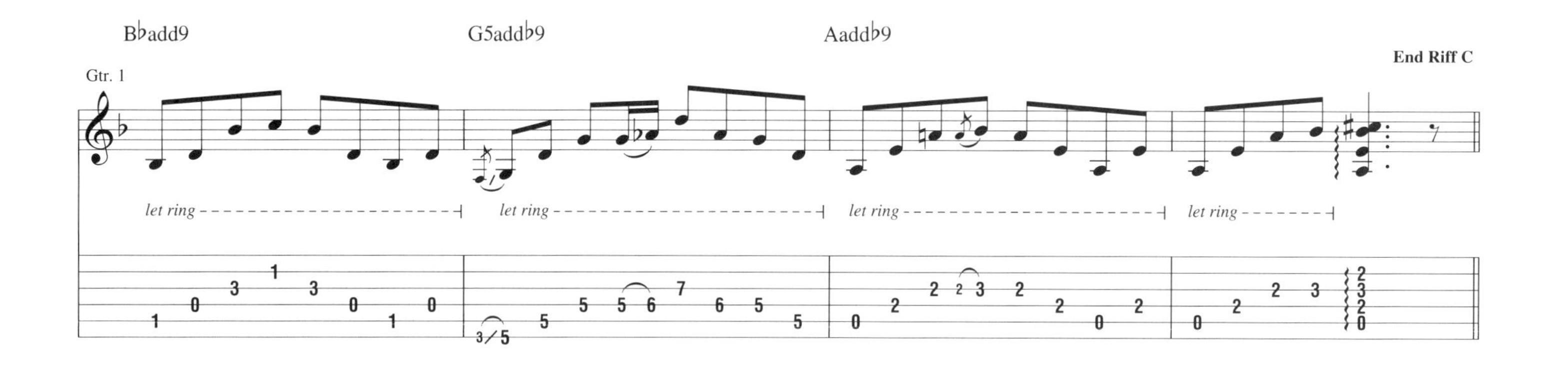

Bridge

Gtr. 1: w/ Riff C (2 times)

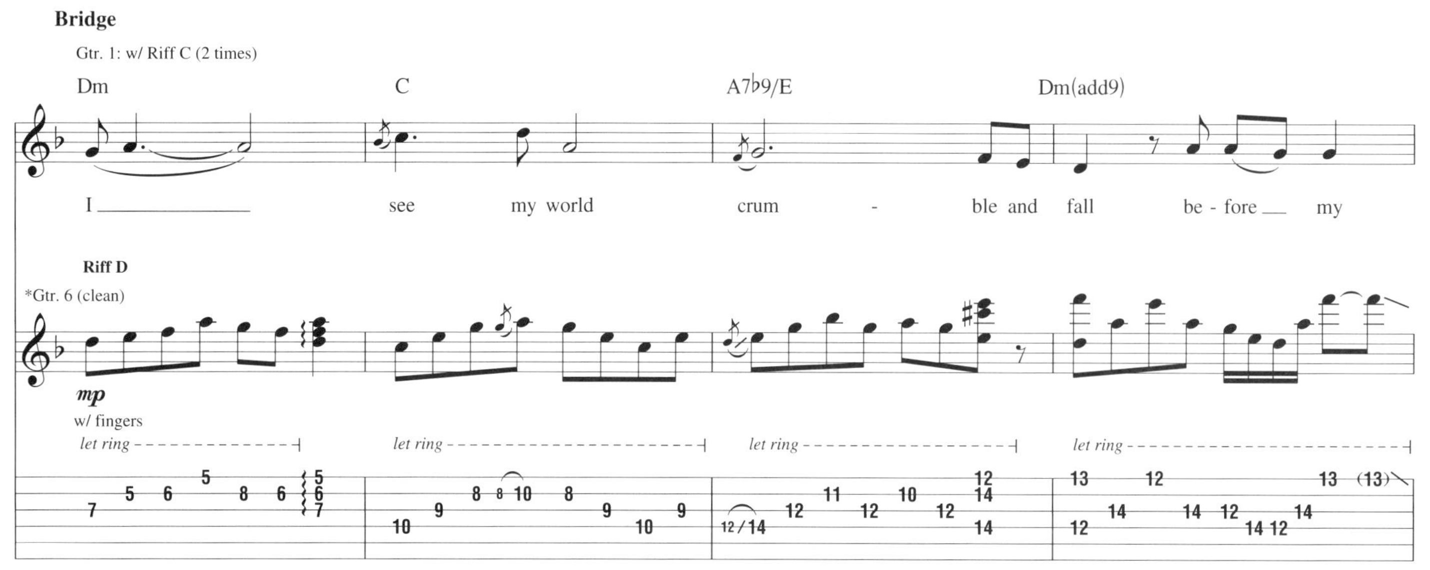

*Two gtrs. arr. for one.

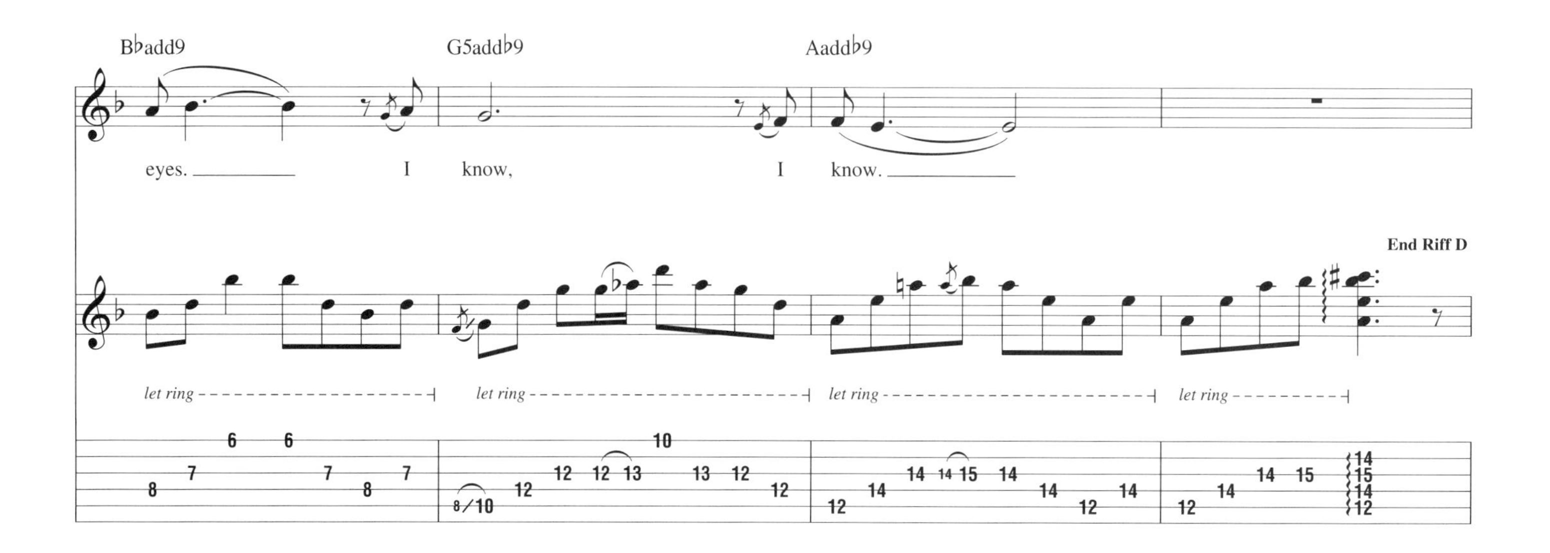

Gtr. 6: w/ Riff D (1st 4 meas.)

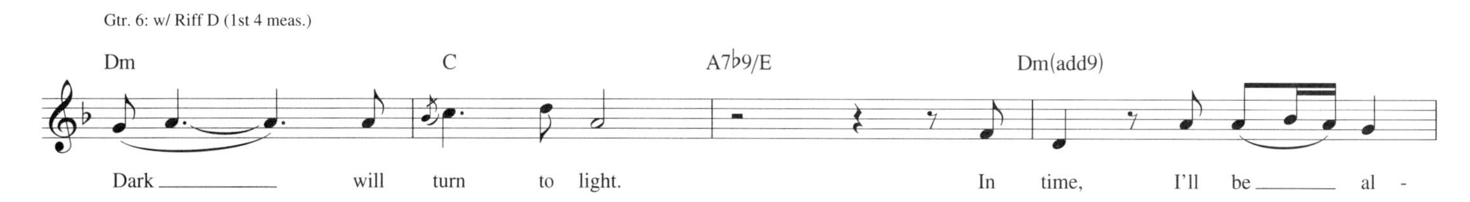

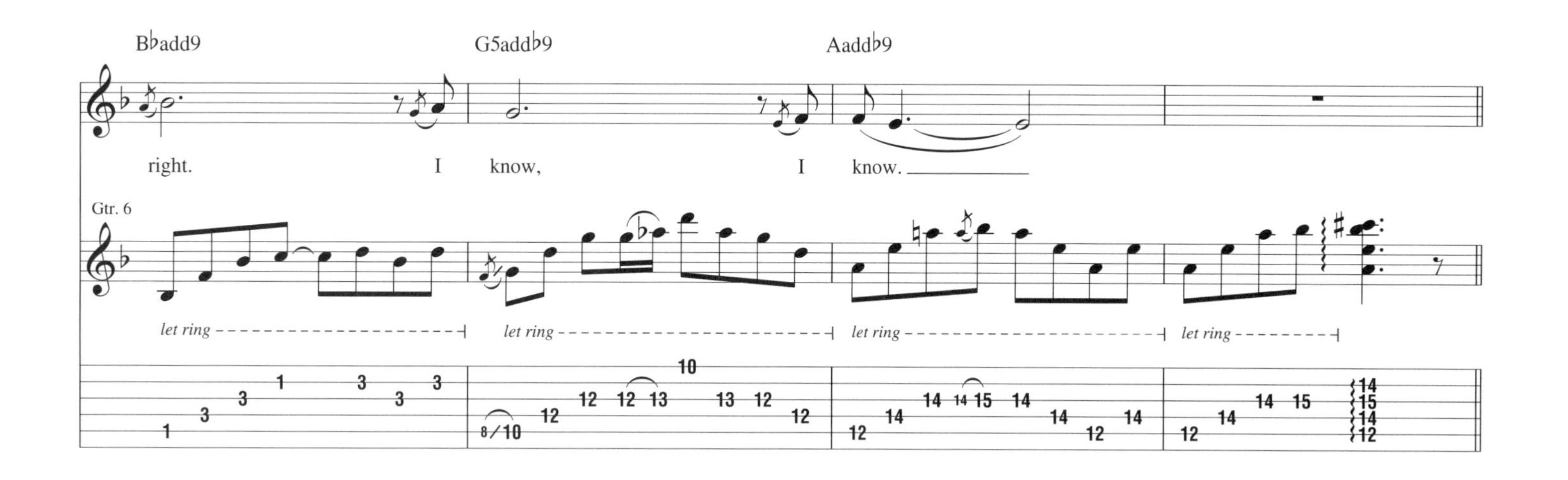
B♭add9
G5add♭9
Aadd♭9
right.
I
know,
I
know.
Gtr. 6
let ring
let ring
let ring
let ring

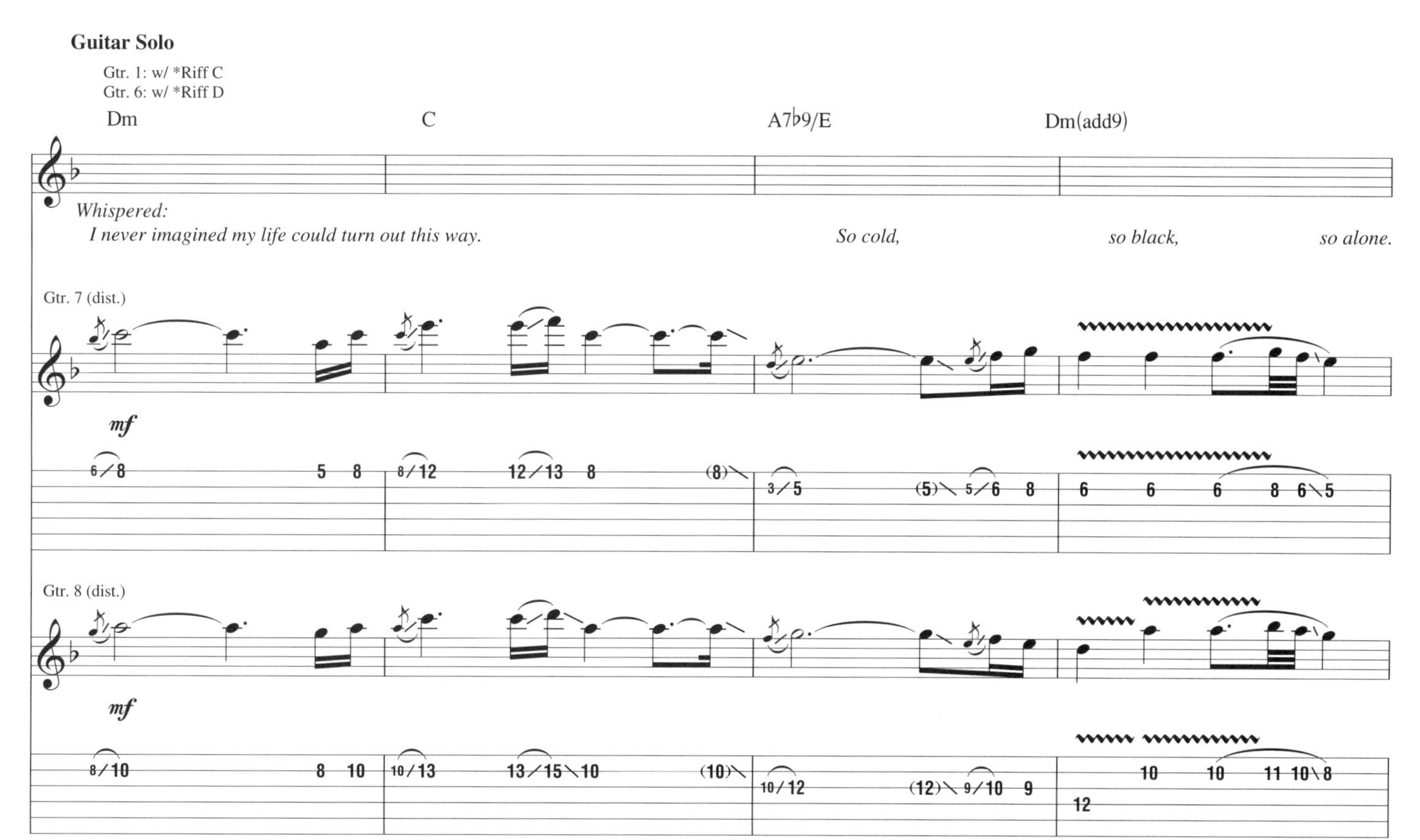
Guitar Solo
Gtr. 1: w/ *Riff C
Gtr. 6: w/ *Riff D
Dm
C
A7♭9/E
Dm(add9)
Whispered:
I never imagined my life could turn out this way.
So cold,
so black,
so alone.
Gtr. 7 (dist.)
mf
Gtr. 8 (dist.)
mf

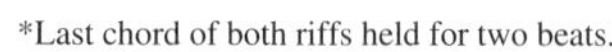
*Last chord of both riffs held for two beats.

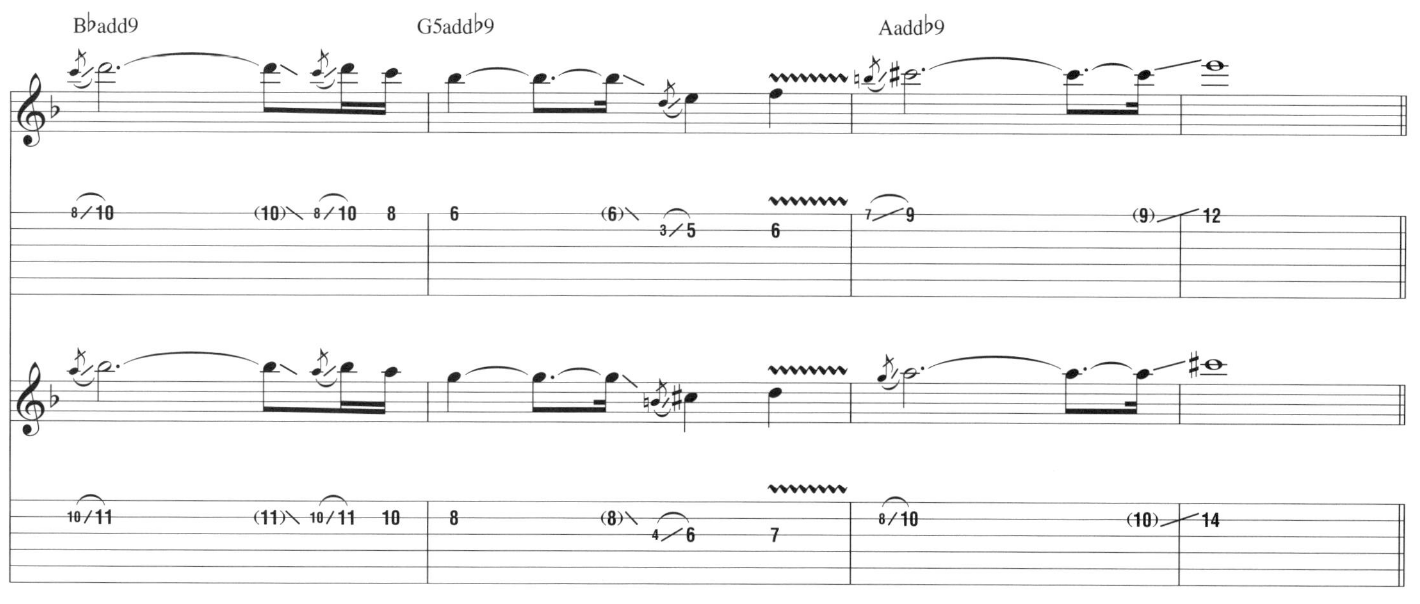
B♭add9
G5add♭9
Aadd♭9

Interlude

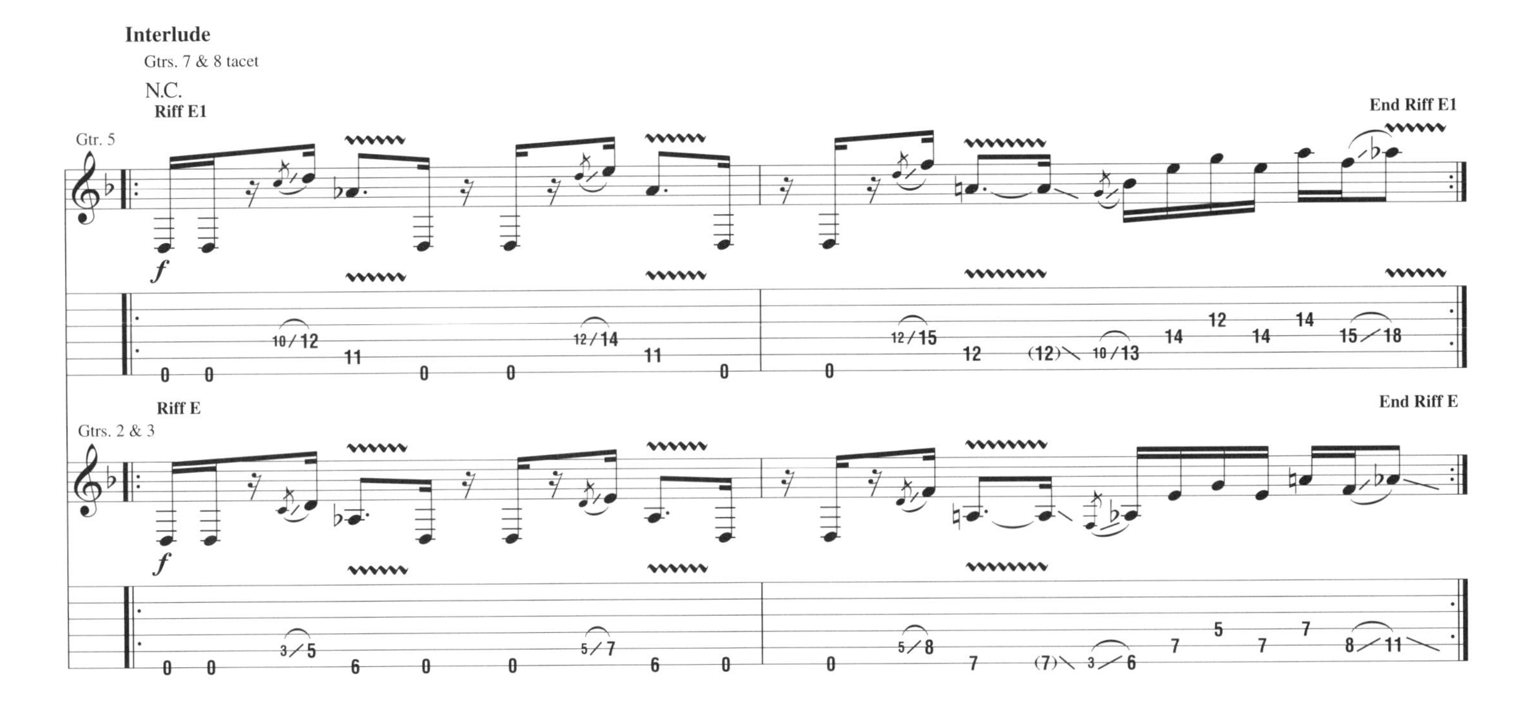

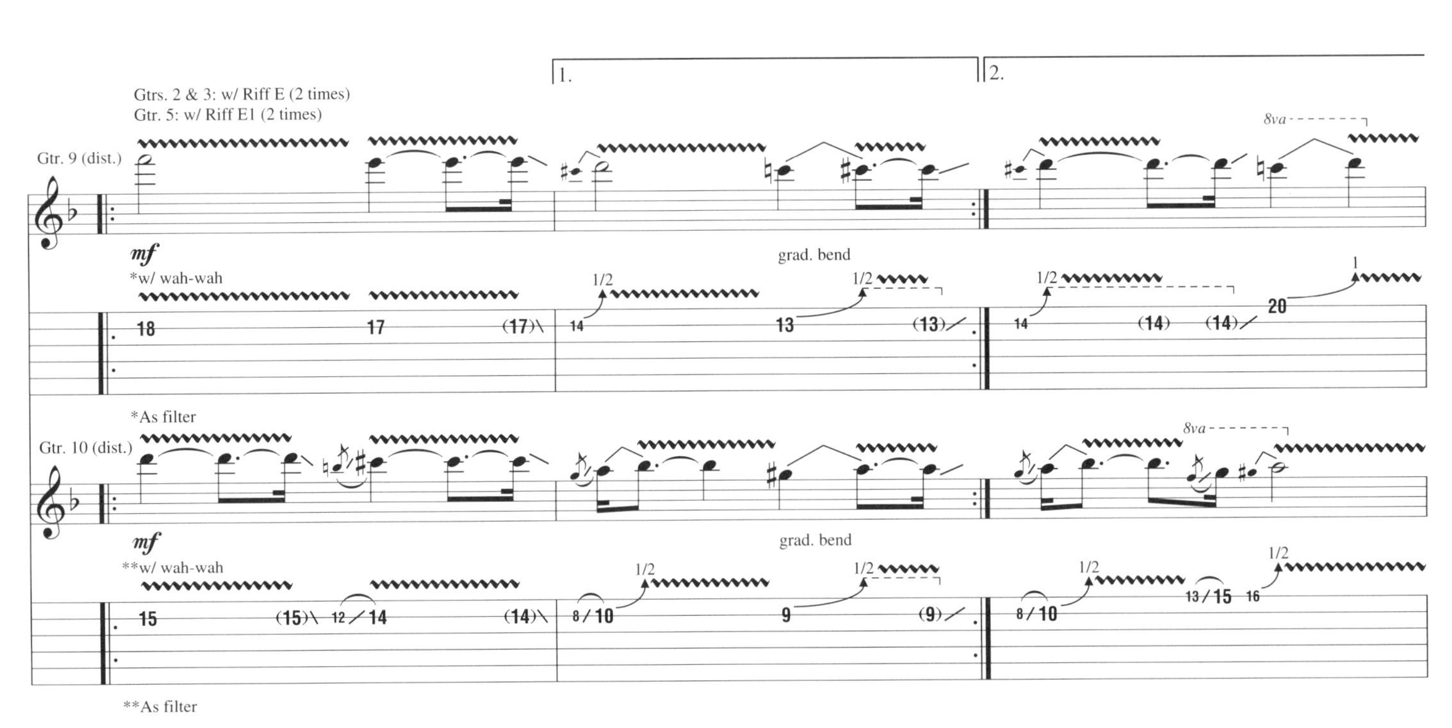

Tempo II

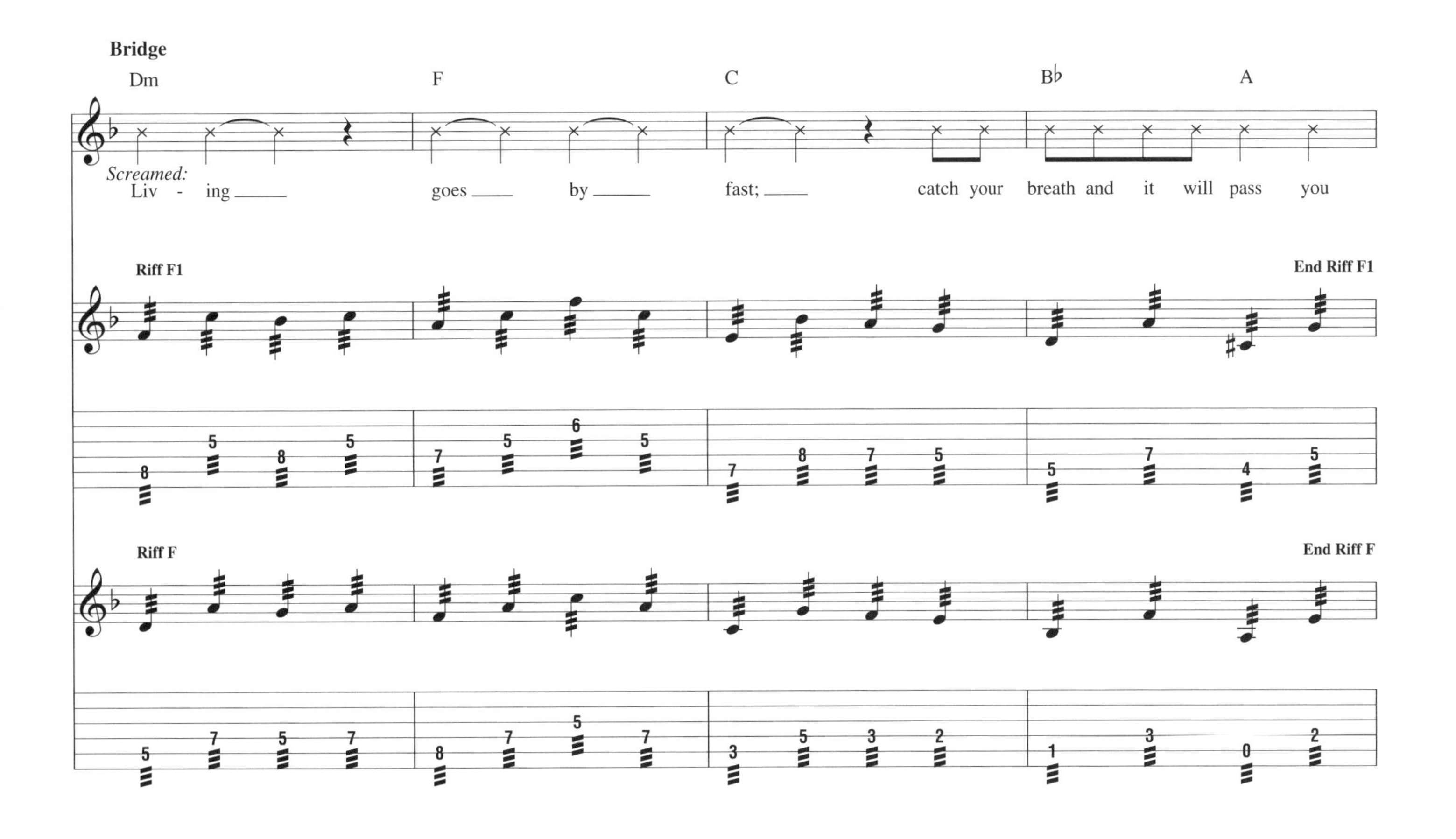
Bridge
Dm F C B♭ A
Screamed:
Liv - ing goes by fast; catch your breath and it will pass you
Riff F1
End Riff F1
Riff F
End Riff F

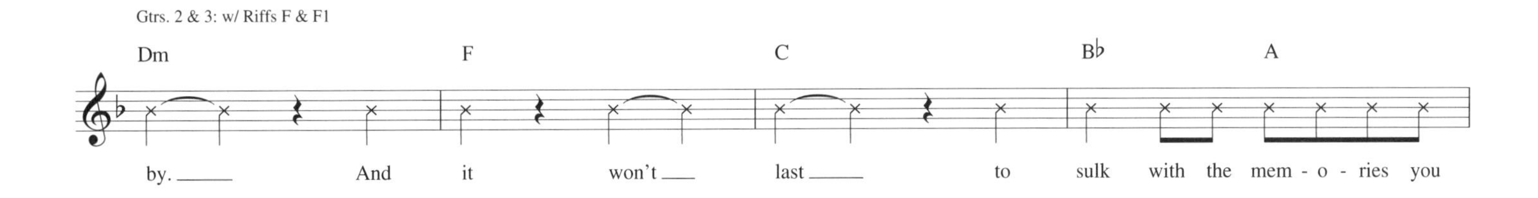
Gtrs. 2 & 3: w/ Riffs F & F1
Dm F C B♭ A
by. And it won't last to sulk with the mem - o - ries you

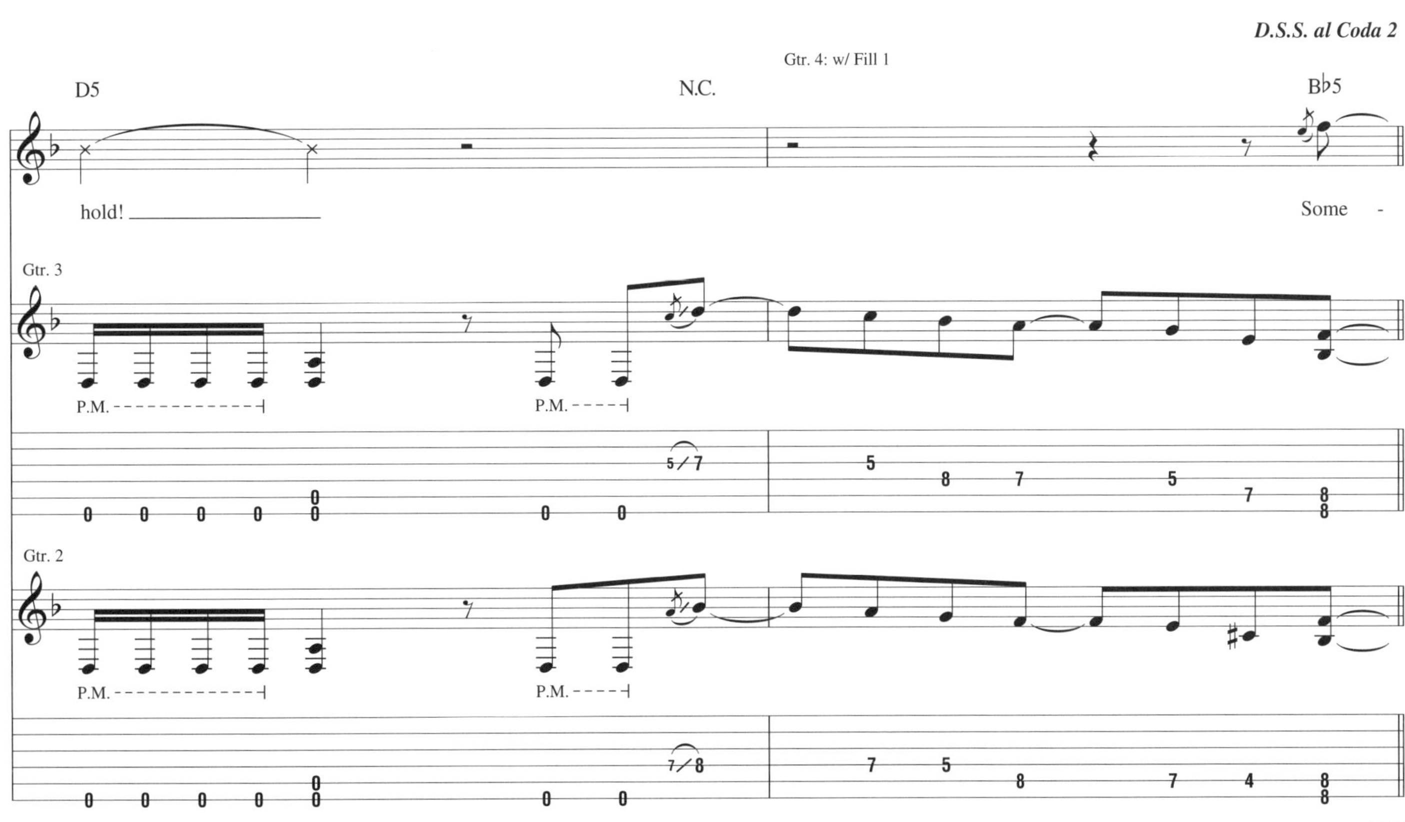
D.S.S. al Coda 2
Gtr. 4: w/ Fill 1
D5 N.C. B♭5
hold! Some -
Gtr. 3
P.M.
Gtr. 2
P.M.

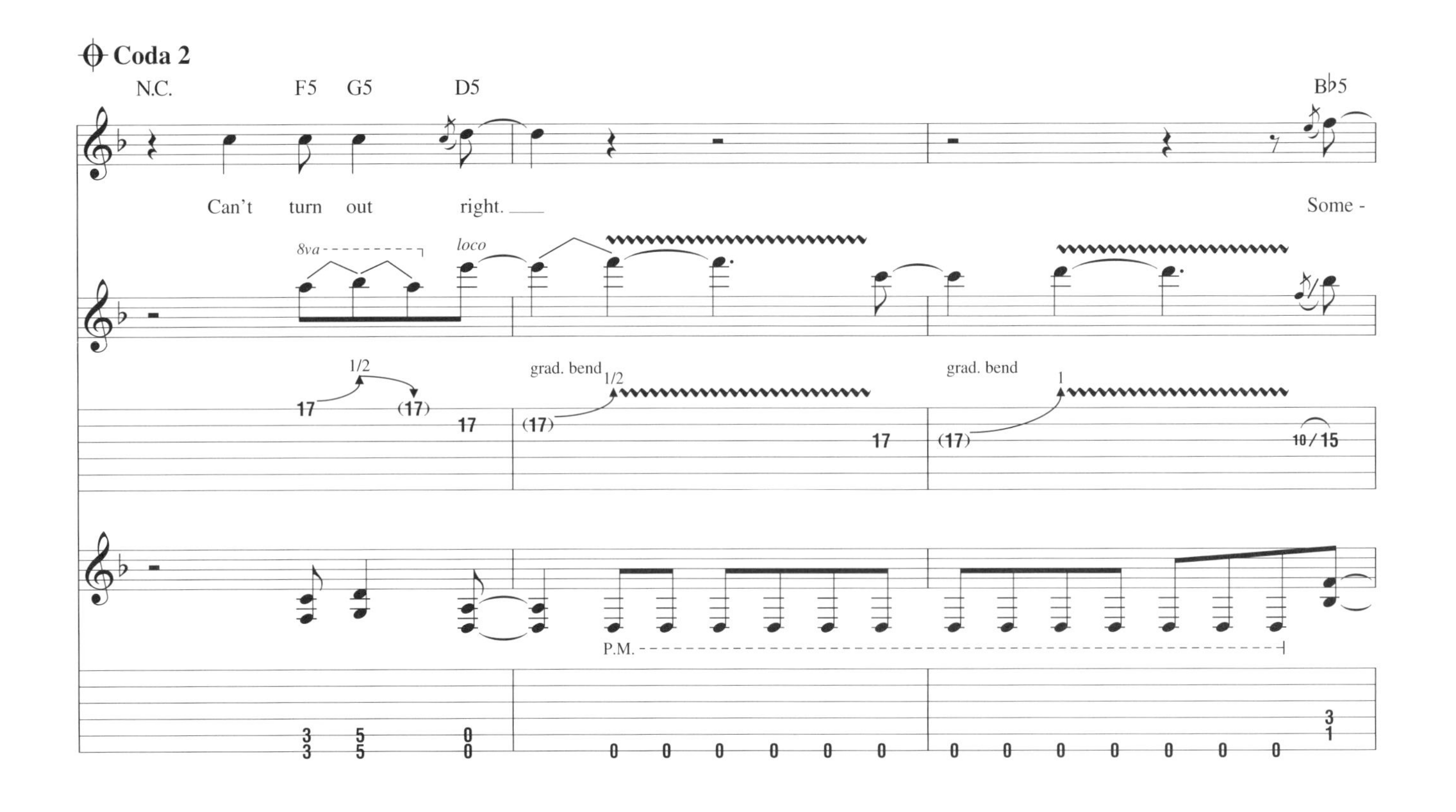
Coda 2
N.C.
F5
G5
D5
B♭5
Can't turn out right.
Some -
8va
loco
1/2
grad. bend
1/2
grad. bend
1
P.M.

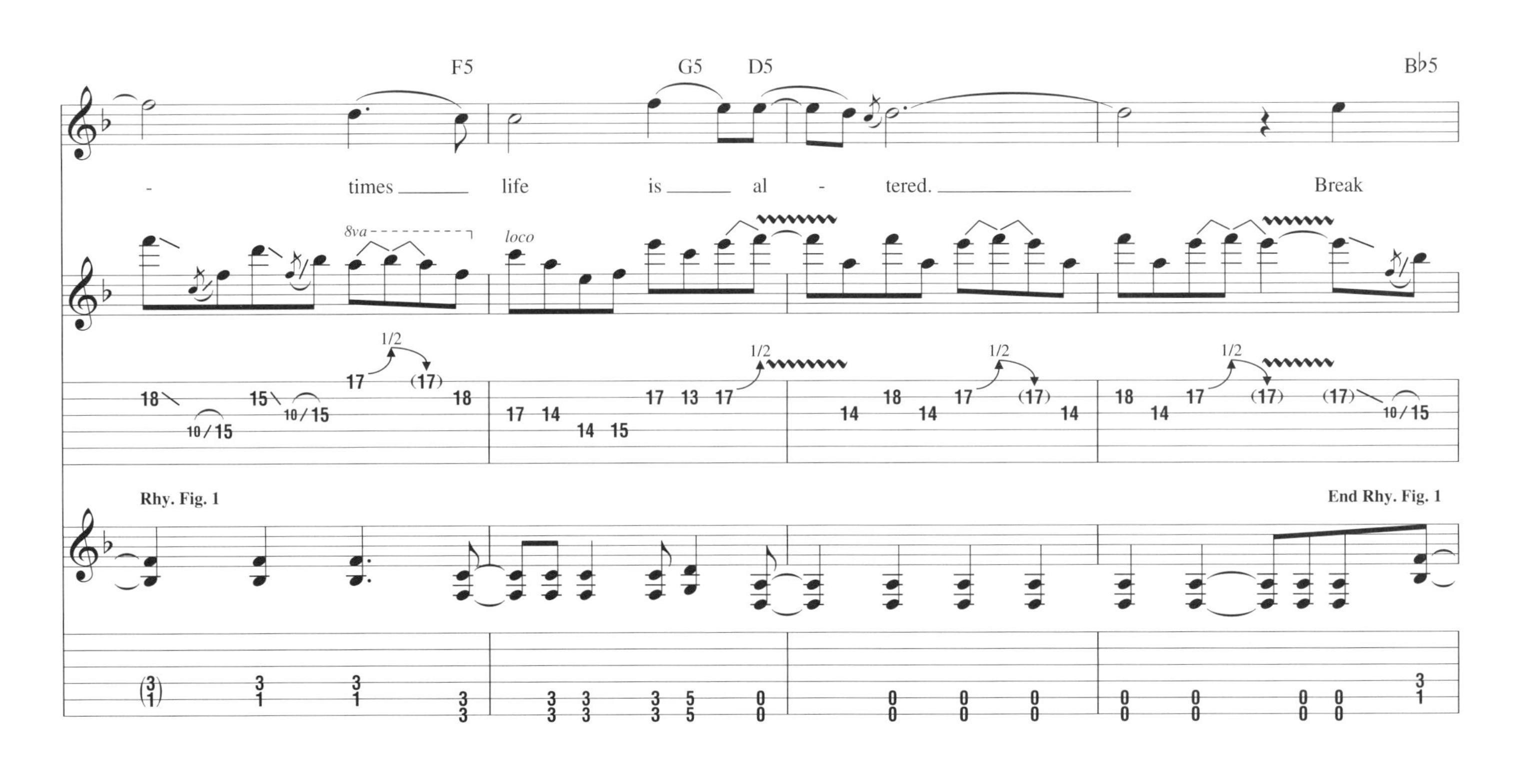
F5
G5
D5
B♭5
- times life is al - tered.
Break
8va
loco
1/2
1/2
1/2
1/2
Rhy. Fig. 1
End Rhy. Fig. 1

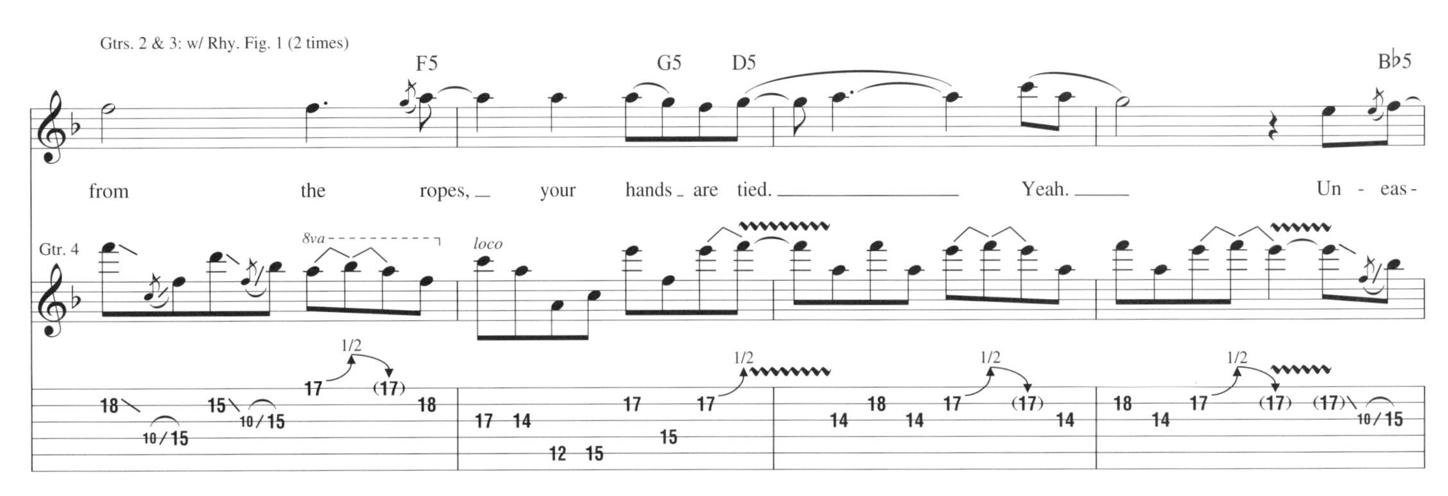
Gtrs. 2 & 3: w/ Rhy. Fig. 1 (2 times)
F5
G5
D5
B♭5
from the ropes, your hands are tied.
Yeah.
Un - eas-
Gtr. 4
8va
loco
1/2
1/2
1/2
1/2

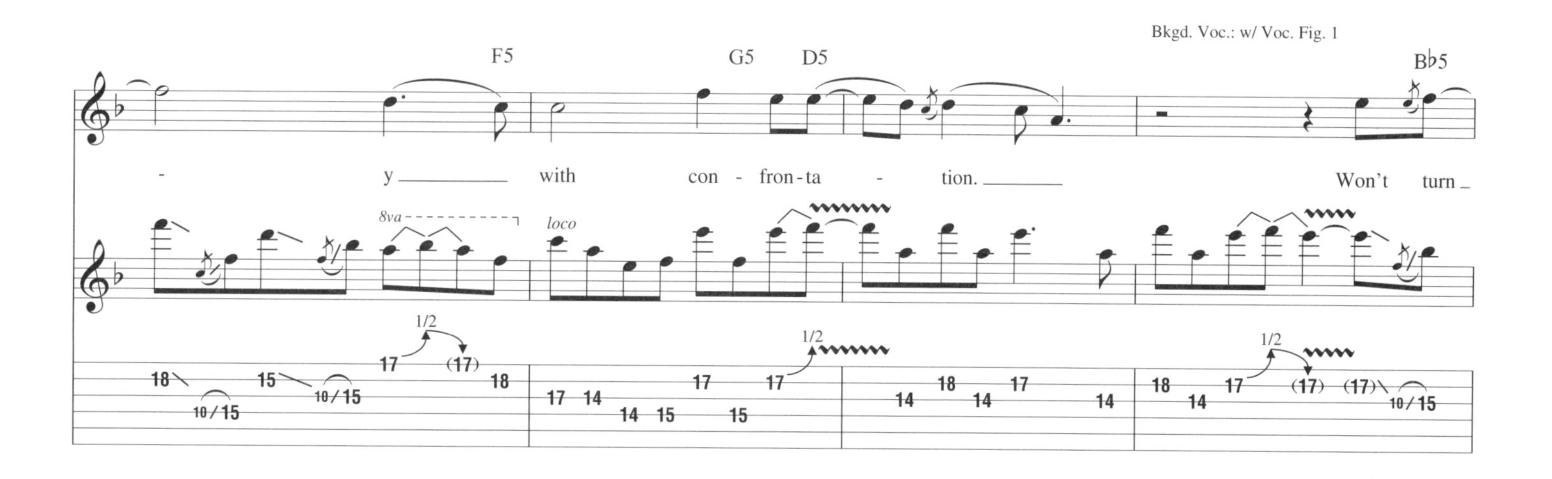
Bkgd. Voc.: w/ Voc. Fig. 1
F5
G5
D5
B♭5
y
with
con - fron - ta - tion.
Won't turn
8va
loco
1/2

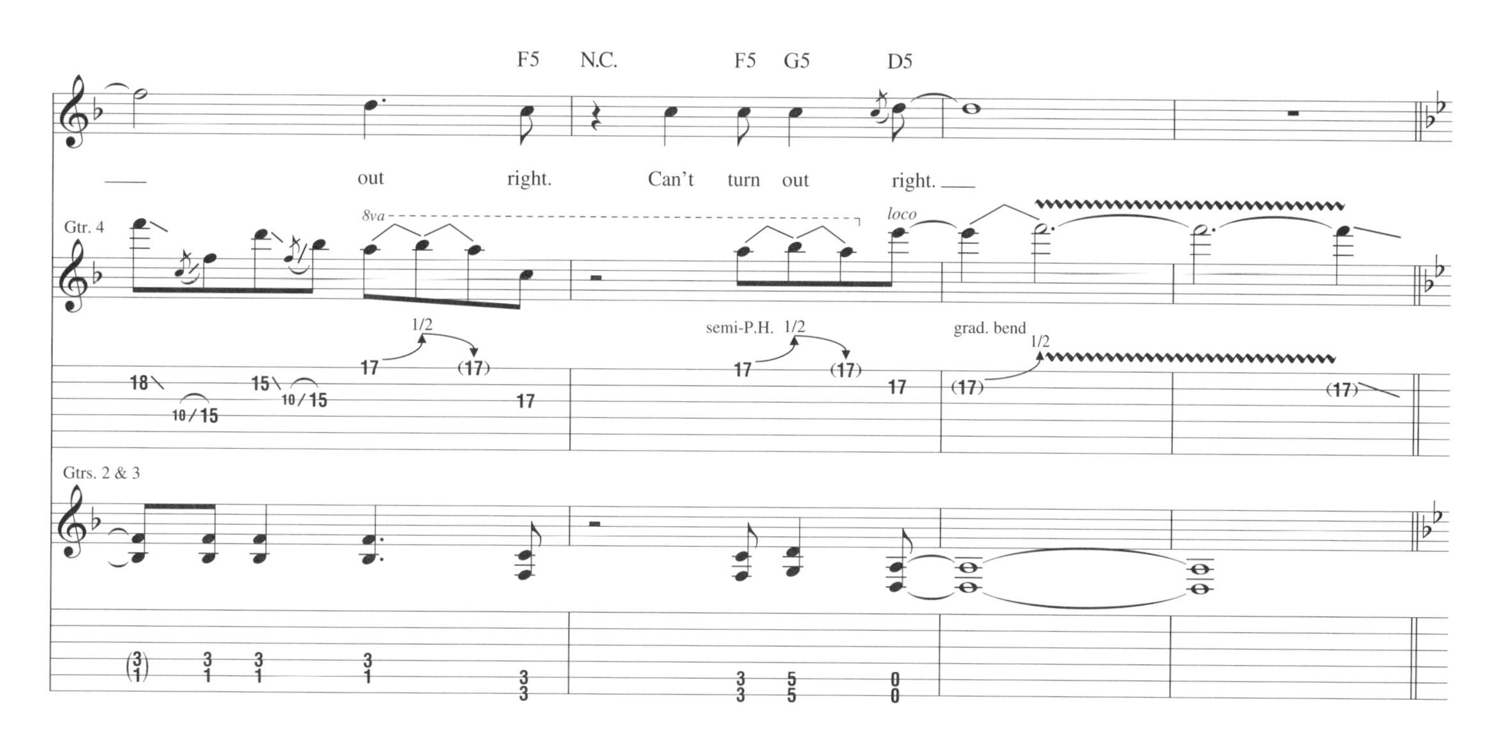
F5
N.C.
F5
G5
D5
out
right.
Can't
turn
out
right.
Gtr. 4
8va
loco
1/2
semi-P.H.
grad. bend
Gtrs. 2 & 3

Outro-Guitar Solo
Tempo I
Gtr. 4 tacet
G5
B♭5
F5
E♭5
D5
Gtr. 7
Riff G
End Riff G
Gtr. 8
Riff G1
End Riff G1
Gtrs. 2 & 3
Rhy. Fig. 2
End Rhy. Fig. 2
P.M.

Gtrs. 2 & 3: w/ Rhy. Fig. 2 (3 times)
Gtrs. 7 & 8: w/ Riffs G & G1 (3 times)

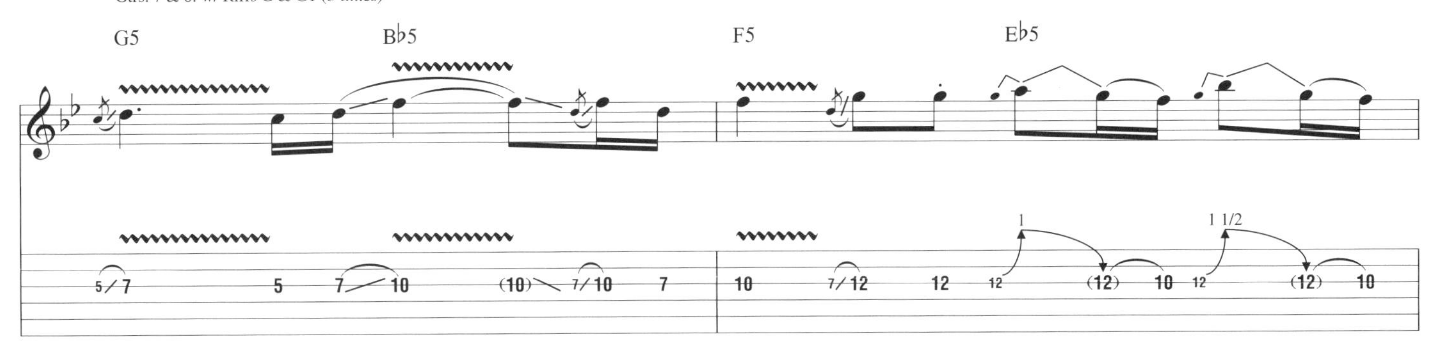

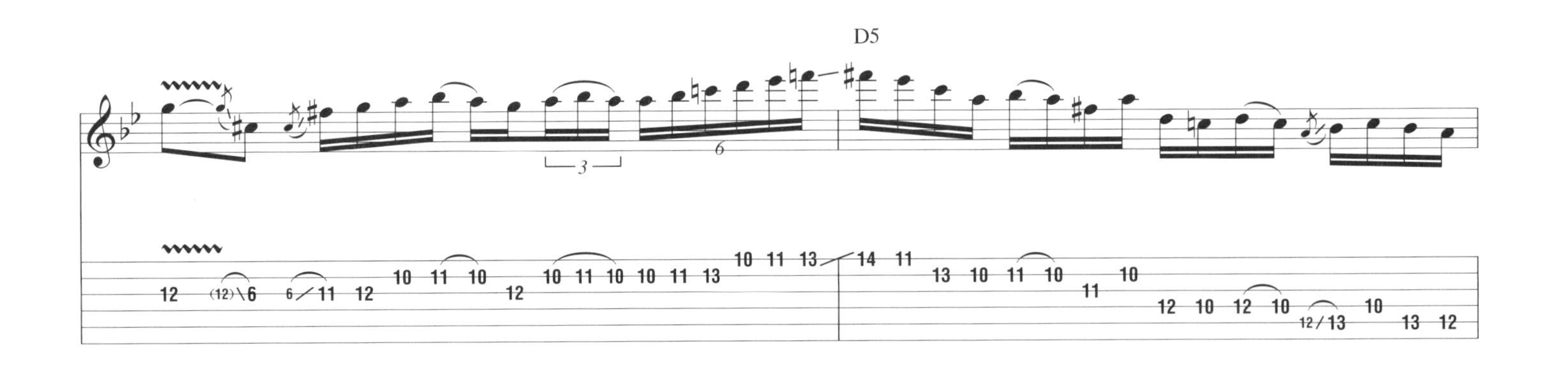

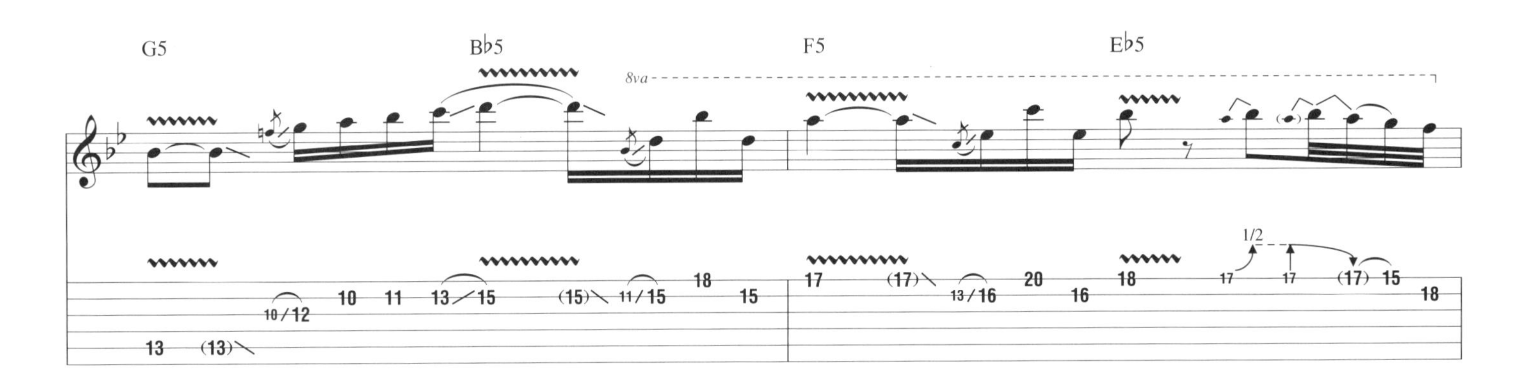

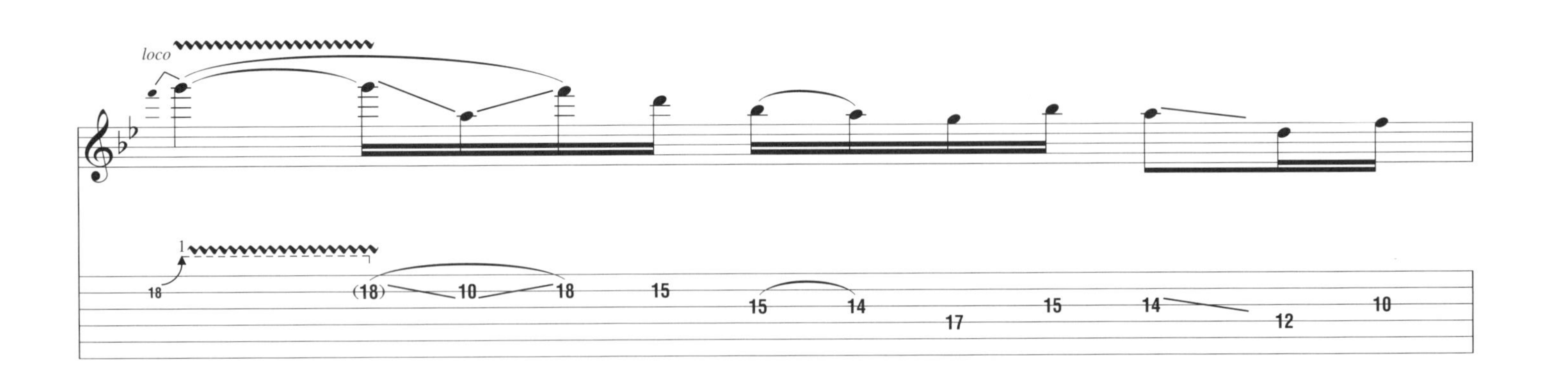

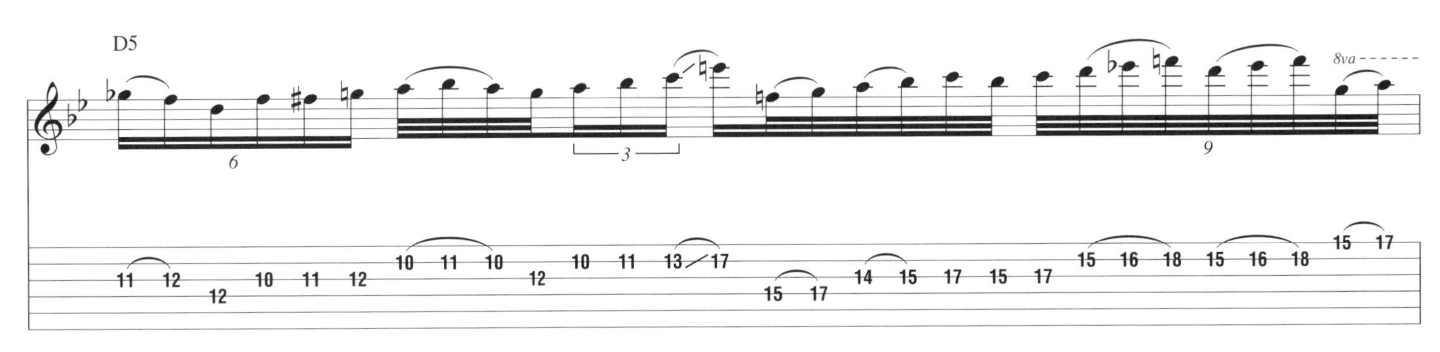

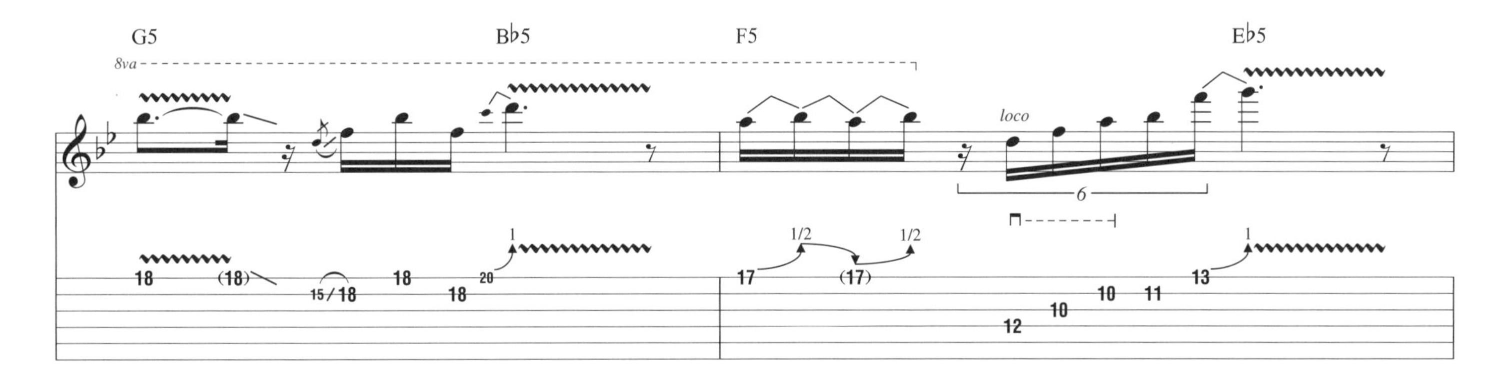

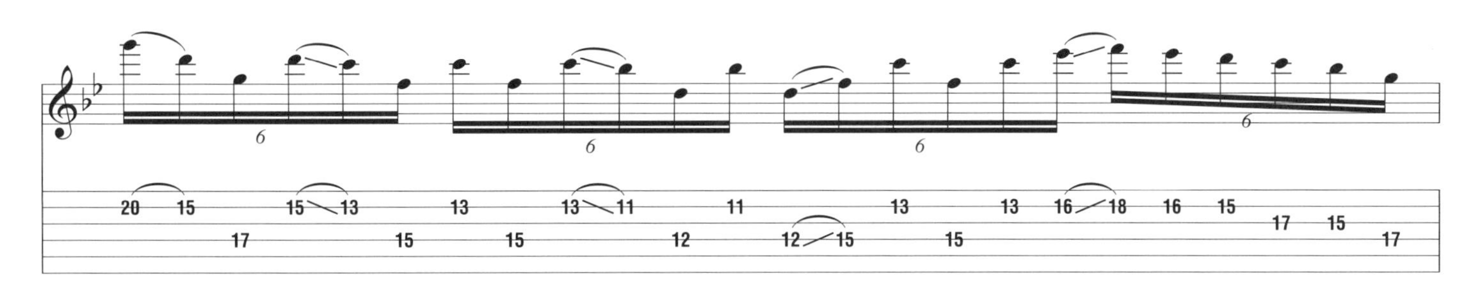

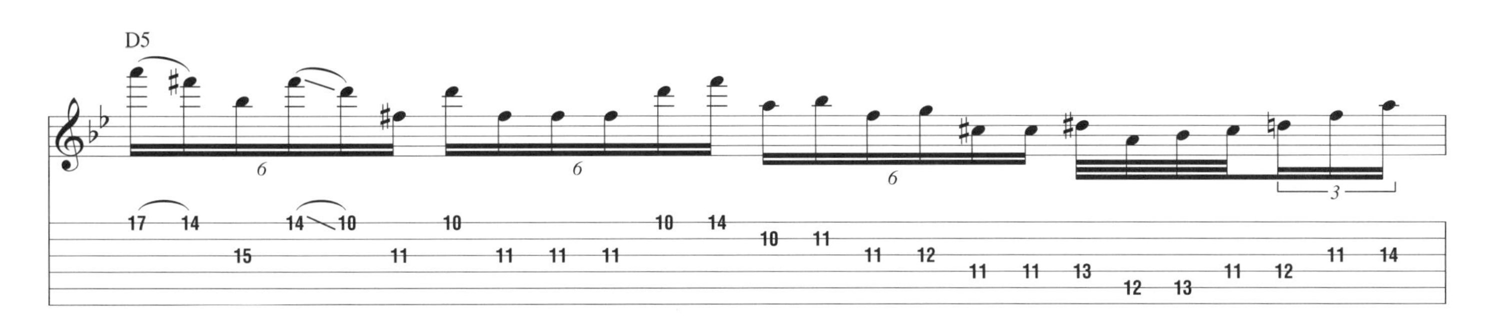

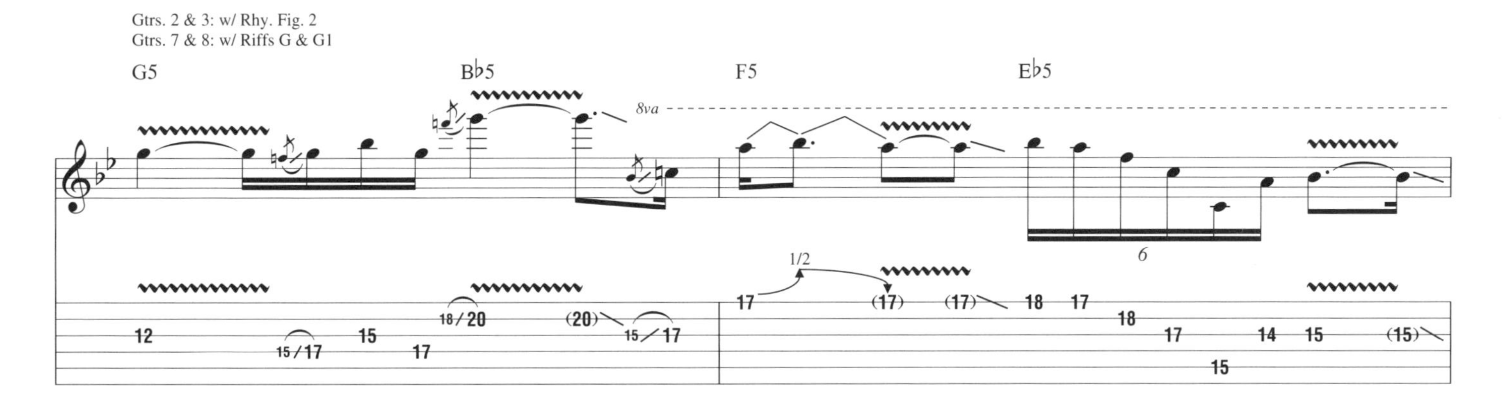

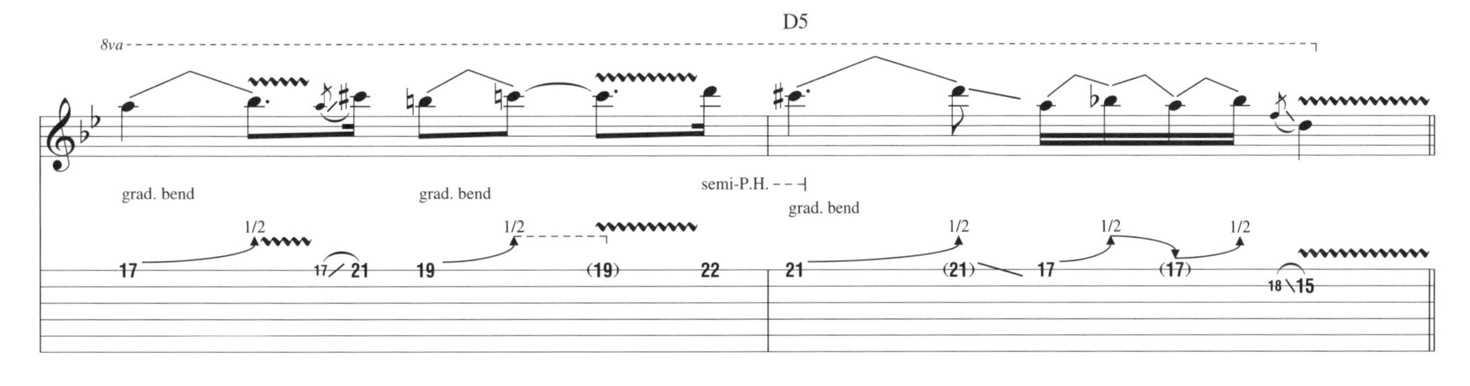

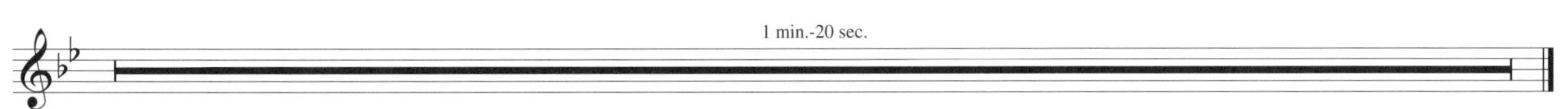

Pitch and tempo gradually decrease while the previous four-measure chord progression repeats and fades.
To approximate the sound of the Master Tape being slowed down, continue shredding while using a
DigiTech Whammy Pedal (set to sweep two octaves below), and gradually depress the treadle while the tempo slows.

GUITAR NOTATION LEGEND

Guitar music can be notated three different ways: on a *musical staff*, in *tablature*, and in *rhythm slashes*.

RHYTHM SLASHES are written above the staff. Strum chords in the rhythm indicated. Use the chord diagrams found at the top of the first page of the transcription for the appropriate chord voicings. Round noteheads indicate single notes.

THE MUSICAL STAFF shows pitches and rhythms and is divided by bar lines into measures. Pitches are named after the first seven letters of the alphabet.

TABLATURE graphically represents the guitar fingerboard. Each horizontal line represents a string, and each number represents a fret.

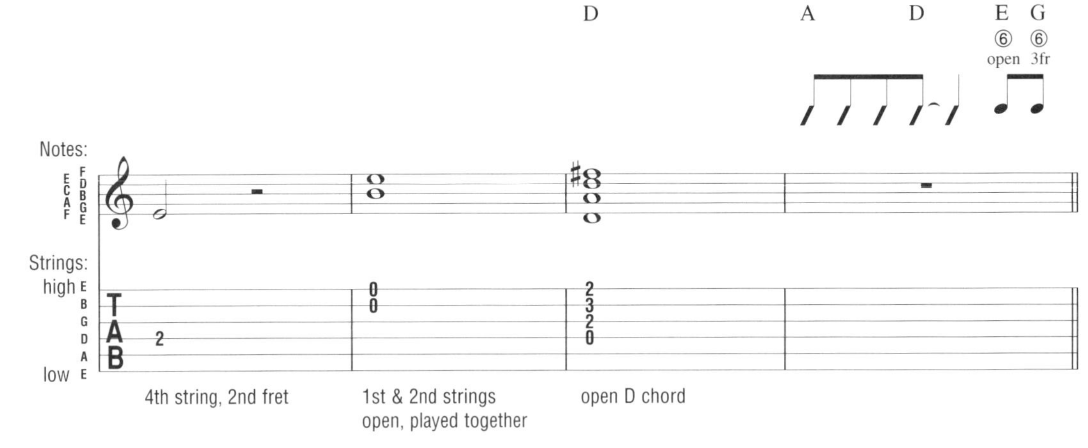

Definitions for Special Guitar Notation

HALF-STEP BEND: Strike the note and bend up 1/2 step.

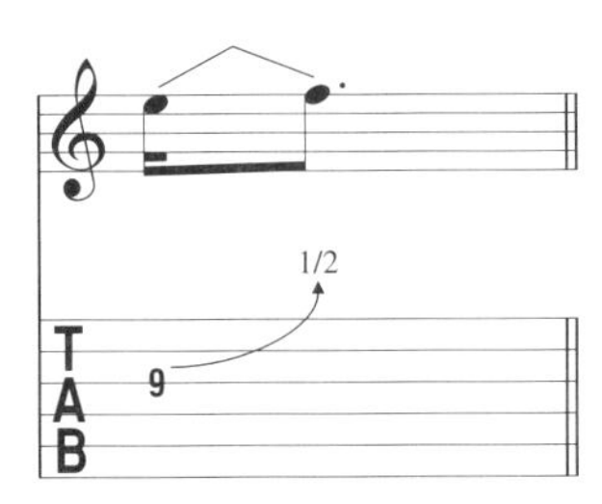

WHOLE-STEP BEND: Strike the note and bend up one step.

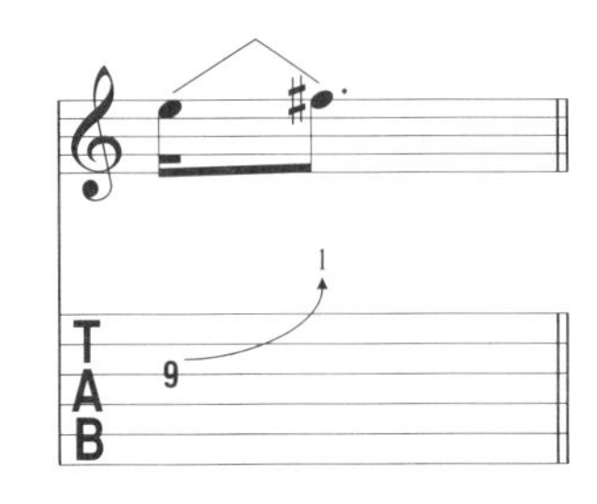

GRACE NOTE BEND: Strike the note and immediately bend up as indicated.

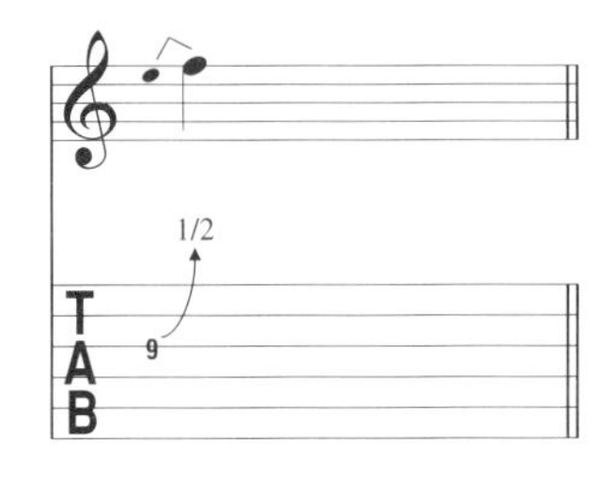

SLIGHT (MICROTONE) BEND: Strike the note and bend up 1/4 step.

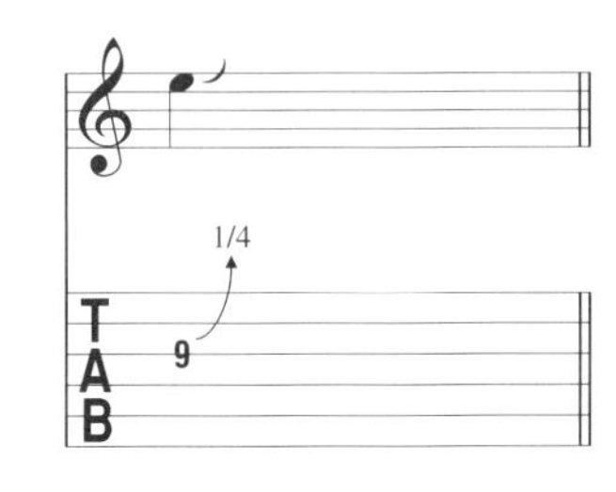

BEND AND RELEASE: Strike the note and bend up as indicated, then release back to the original note. Only the first note is struck.

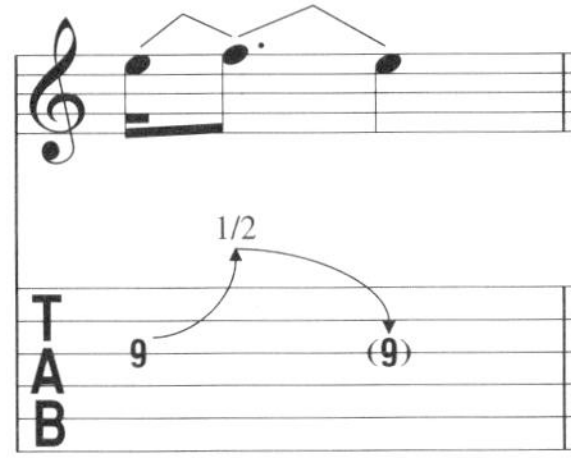

PRE-BEND: Bend the note as indicated, then strike it.

PRE-BEND AND RELEASE: Bend the note as indicated. Strike it and release the bend back to the original note.

UNISON BEND: Strike the two notes simultaneously and bend the lower note up to the pitch of the higher.

VIBRATO: The string is vibrated by rapidly bending and releasing the note with the fretting hand.

WIDE VIBRATO: The pitch is varied to a greater degree by vibrating with the fretting hand.

HAMMER-ON: Strike the first (lower) note with one finger, then sound the higher note (on the same string) with another finger by fretting it without picking.

PULL-OFF: Place both fingers on the notes to be sounded. Strike the first note and without picking, pull the finger off to sound the second (lower) note.

LEGATO SLIDE: Strike the first note and then slide the same fret-hand finger up or down to the second note. The second note is not struck.

SHIFT SLIDE: Same as legato slide, except the second note is struck.

TRILL: Very rapidly alternate between the notes indicated by continuously hammering on and pulling off.

TAPPING: Hammer ("tap") the fret indicated with the pick-hand index or middle finger and pull off to the note fretted by the fret hand.

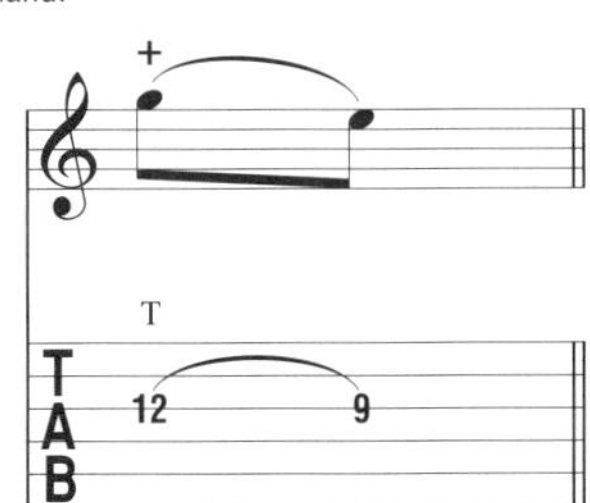

NATURAL HARMONIC: Strike the note while the fret-hand lightly touches the string directly over the fret indicated.

PINCH HARMONIC: The note is fretted normally and a harmonic is produced by adding the edge of the thumb or the tip of the index finger of the pick hand to the normal pick attack.

HARP HARMONIC: The note is fretted normally and a harmonic is produced by gently resting the pick hand's index finger directly above the indicated fret (in parentheses) while the pick hand's thumb or pick assists by plucking the appropriate string.

PICK SCRAPE: The edge of the pick is rubbed down (or up) the string, producing a scratchy sound.

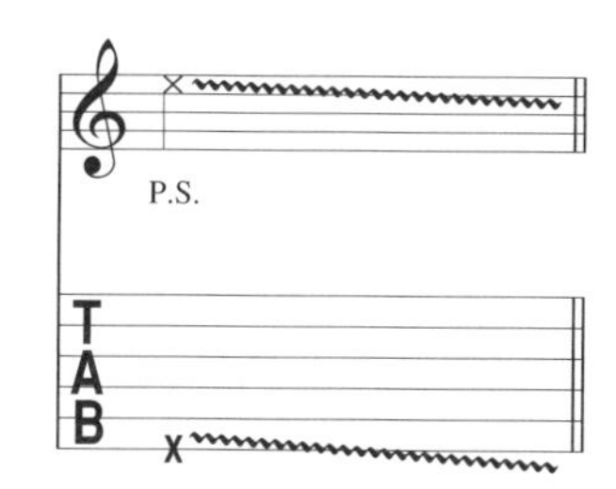

MUFFLED STRINGS: A percussive sound is produced by laying the fret hand across the string(s) without depressing, and striking them with the pick hand.

PALM MUTING: The note is partially muted by the pick hand lightly touching the string(s) just before the bridge.

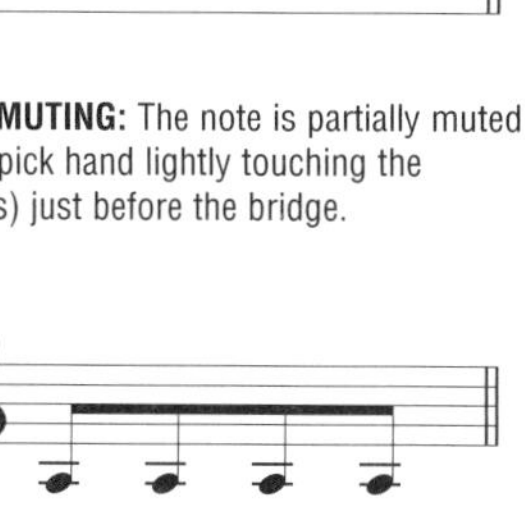

RAKE: Drag the pick across the strings indicated with a single motion.

TREMOLO PICKING: The note is picked as rapidly and continuously as possible.

ARPEGGIATE: Play the notes of the chord indicated by quickly rolling them from bottom to top.

VIBRATO BAR DIVE AND RETURN: The pitch of the note or chord is dropped a specified number of steps (in rhythm), then returned to the original pitch.

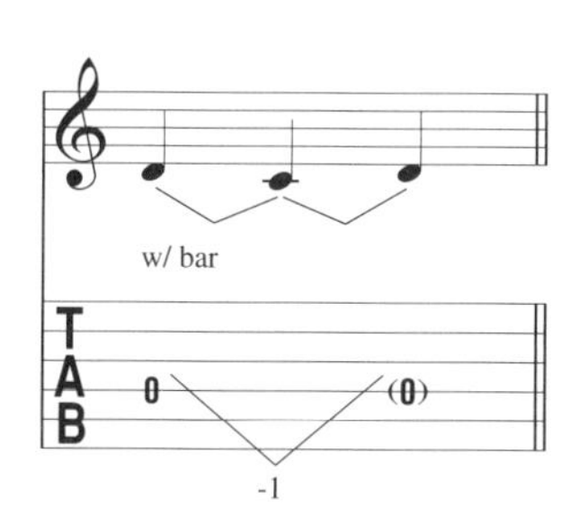

VIBRATO BAR SCOOP: Depress the bar just before striking the note, then quickly release the bar.

VIBRATO BAR DIP: Strike the note and then immediately drop a specified number of steps, then release back to the original pitch.

Additional Musical Definitions

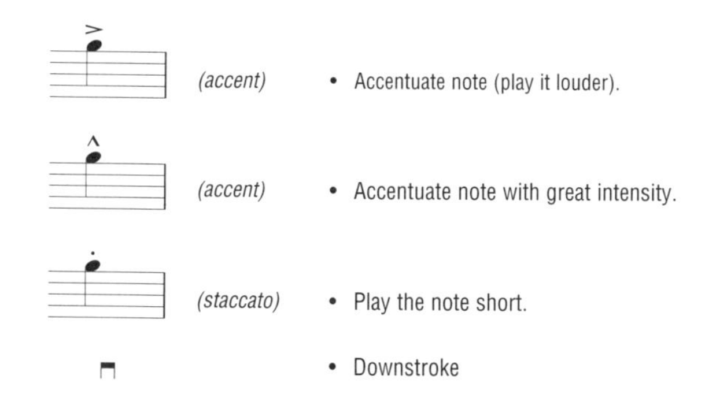

(accent) • Accentuate note (play it louder).

(accent) • Accentuate note with great intensity.

(staccato) • Play the note short.

• Downstroke

V • Upstroke

D.S. al Coda • Go back to the sign (𝄋), then play until the measure marked "***To Coda***," then skip to the section labelled "**Coda**."

D.C. al Fine • Go back to the beginning of the song and play until the measure marked "***Fine***" (end).

Rhy. Fig. • Label used to recall a recurring accompaniment pattern (usually chordal).

Riff • Label used to recall composed, melodic lines (usually single notes) which recur.

Fill • Label used to identify a brief melodic figure which is to be inserted into the arrangement.

Rhy. Fill • A chordal version of a Fill.

tacet • Instrument is silent (drops out).

• Repeat measures between signs.

1. 2. • When a repeated section has different endings, play the first ending only the first time and the second ending only the second time.

NOTE: Tablature numbers in parentheses mean:

1. The note is being sustained over a system (note in standard notation is tied), or
2. The note is sustained, but a new articulation (such as a hammer-on, pull-off, slide or vibrato) begins, or
3. The note is a barely audible "ghost" note (note in standard notation is also in parentheses).

Item	Title	Price
00690814	John 5 – Songs for Sanity	$19.95
00690751	John 5 – Vertigo	$19.95
00694912	Eric Johnson – Ah Via Musicom	$19.95
00690660	Best of Eric Johnson	$19.95
00690845	Eric Johnson – Bloom	$19.95
00690169	Eric Johnson – Venus Isle	$22.95
00690846	Jack Johnson and Friends – Sing-A-Longs and Lullabies for the Film Curious George	$19.95
00690271	Robert Johnson – The New Transcriptions	$24.95
00699131	Best of Janis Joplin	$19.95
00690427	Best of Judas Priest	$22.99
00690651	Juanes – Exitos de Juanes	$19.95
00690277	Best of Kansas	$19.95
00690911	Best of Phil Keaggy	$24.99
00690727	Toby Keith Guitar Collection	$19.99
00690742	The Killers – Hot Fuss	$19.95
00690888	The Killers – Sam's Town	$19.95
00690504	Very Best of Albert King	$19.95
00690444	B.B. King & Eric Clapton – Riding with the King	$19.95
00690134	Freddie King Collection	$19.95
00691062	Kings of Leon – Come Around Sundown	$22.99
00690975	Kings of Leon – Only by the Night	$22.99
00690339	Best of the Kinks	$19.95
00690157	Kiss – Alive!	$19.95
00690356	Kiss – Alive II	$22.99
00694903	Best of Kiss for Guitar	$24.95
00690355	Kiss – Destroyer	$16.95
14026320	Mark Knopfler – Get Lucky	$22.99
00690164	Mark Knopfler Guitar – Vol. 1	$19.95
00690163	Mark Knopfler/Chet Atkins – Neck and Neck	$19.95
00690780	Korn – Greatest Hits, Volume 1	$22.95
00690836	Korn – See You on the Other Side	$19.95
00690377	Kris Kristofferson Collection	$19.95
00690861	Kutless – Hearts of the Innocent	$19.95
00690834	Lamb of God – Ashes of the Wake	$19.95
00690875	Lamb of God – Sacrament	$19.95
00690977	Ray LaMontagne – Gossip in the Grain	$19.99
00690890	Ray LaMontagne – Till the Sun Turns Black	$19.95
00690823	Ray LaMontagne – Trouble	$19.95
00691057	Ray LaMontagne and the Pariah Dogs – God Willin' & The Creek Don't Rise	$22.99
00690658	Johnny Lang – Long Time Coming	$19.95
00690726	Avril Lavigne – Under My Skin	$19.95
00690679	John Lennon – Guitar Collection	$19.95
00690781	Linkin Park – Hybrid Theory	$22.95
00690782	Linkin Park – Meteora	$22.95
00690922	Linkin Park – Minutes to Midnight	$19.95
00690783	Best of Live	$19.95
00699623	The Best of Chuck Loeb	$19.95
00690743	Los Lonely Boys	$19.95
00690720	Lostprophets – Start Something	$19.95
00690525	Best of George Lynch	$24.99
00690955	Lynyrd Skynyrd – All-Time Greatest Hits	$19.99
00694954	New Best of Lynyrd Skynyrd	$19.95
00690577	Yngwie Malmsteen – Anthology	$24.95
00694845	Yngwie Malmsteen – Fire and Ice	$19.95
00694755	Yngwie Malmsteen's Rising Force	$19.95
00694757	Yngwie Malmsteen – Trilogy	$19.95
00690754	Marilyn Manson – Lest We Forget	$19.95
00694956	Bob Marley – Legend	$19.95
00690548	Very Best of Bob Marley & The Wailers – One Love	$22.99
00694945	Bob Marley – Songs of Freedom	$24.95
00690914	Maroon 5 – It Won't Be Soon Before Long	$19.95
00690657	Maroon 5 – Songs About Jane	$19.95
00690748	Maroon 5 – 1.22.03 Acoustic	$19.95
00690989	Mastodon – Crack the Skye	$22.99
00690442	Matchbox 20 – Mad Season	$19.95
00690616	Matchbox Twenty – More Than You Think You Are	$19.95
00690239	Matchbox 20 – Yourself or Someone like You	$19.95
00691034	Andy McKee – Joyland	$19.99
00690382	Sarah McLachlan – Mirrorball	$19.95
00120080	The Don McLean Songbook	$19.95
00694952	Megadeth – Countdown to Extinction	$22.95
00690244	Megadeth – Cryptic Writings	$19.95
00694951	Megadeth – Rust in Peace	$22.95
00690011	Megadeth – Youthanasia	$19.95
00690505	John Mellencamp Guitar Collection	$19.95
00690562	Pat Metheny – Bright Size Life	$19.95
00690646	Pat Metheny – One Quiet Night	$19.95
00690559	Pat Metheny – Question & Answer	$19.95
00690040	Steve Miller Band Greatest Hits	$19.95
00690769	Modest Mouse – Good News for People Who Love Bad News	$19.95
00694802	Gary Moore – Still Got the Blues	$22.99
00691005	Best of Motion City Soundtrack	$19.99
00690787	Mudvayne – L.D. 50	$22.95
00690996	My Morning Jacket Collection	$19.99
00690984	Matt Nathanson – Some Mad Hope	$22.99
00690611	Nirvana	$22.95
00694895	Nirvana – Bleach	$19.95
00690189	Nirvana – From the Muddy Banks of the Wishkah	$19.95
00694913	Nirvana – In Utero	$19.95
00694883	Nirvana – Nevermind	$19.95
00690026	Nirvana – Unplugged in New York	$19.95
00120112	No Doubt – Tragic Kingdom	$22.95
00690121	Oasis – (What's the Story) Morning Glory	$19.95
00690226	Oasis – The Other Side of Oasis	$19.95
00690358	The Offspring – Americana	$19.95
00690203	The Offspring – Smash	$18.95
00690818	The Best of Opeth	$22.95
00691052	Roy Orbison – Black & White Night	$22.99
00694847	Best of Ozzy Osbourne	$22.95
00690921	Ozzy Osbourne – Black Rain	$19.95
00690399	Ozzy Osbourne – The Ozzman Cometh	$19.95
00690129	Ozzy Osbourne – Ozzmosis	$22.95
00690933	Best of Brad Paisley	$22.95
00690995	Brad Paisley – Play: The Guitar Album	$24.99
00690866	Panic! At the Disco – A Fever You Can't Sweat Out	$19.95
00690885	Papa Roach – The Paramour Sessions	$19.95
00690939	Christopher Parkening – Solo Pieces	$19.99
00690594	Best of Les Paul	$19.95
00694855	Pearl Jam – Ten	$19.95
00690439	A Perfect Circle – Mer De Noms	$19.95
00690661	A Perfect Circle – Thirteenth Step	$19.95
00690725	Best of Carl Perkins	$19.99
00690499	Tom Petty – Definitive Guitar Collection	$19.95
00690868	Tom Petty – Highway Companion	$19.95
00690176	Phish – Billy Breathes	$22.95
00690428	Pink Floyd – Dark Side of the Moon	$19.95
00690789	Best of Poison	$19.95
00693864	Best of The Police	$19.95
00690299	Best of Elvis: The King of Rock 'n' Roll	$19.95
00692535	Elvis Presley	$19.95
00690003	Classic Queen	$24.95
00694975	Queen – Greatest Hits	$24.95
00690670	Very Best of Queensryche	$19.95
00690878	The Raconteurs – Broken Boy Soldiers	$19.95
00694910	Rage Against the Machine	$19.95
00690179	Rancid – And Out Come the Wolves	$22.95
00690426	Best of Ratt	$19.95
00690055	Red Hot Chili Peppers – Blood Sugar Sex Magik	$19.95
00690584	Red Hot Chili Peppers – By the Way	$19.95
00690379	Red Hot Chili Peppers – Californication	$19.95
00690673	Red Hot Chili Peppers – Greatest Hits	$19.95
00690090	Red Hot Chili Peppers – One Hot Minute	$22.95
00690852	Red Hot Chili Peppers – Stadium Arcadium	$24.95
00690893	The Red Jumpsuit Apparatus – Don't You Fake It	$19.95
00690511	Django Reinhardt – The Definitive Collection	$19.95
00690779	Relient K – MMHMM	$19.95
00690643	Relient K – Two Lefts Don't Make a Right ... But Three Do	$19.95
00694899	R.E.M. – Automatic for the People	$19.95
00690260	Jimmie Rodgers Guitar Collection	$19.95
00690014	Rolling Stones – Exile on Main Street	$24.95
00690631	Rolling Stones – Guitar Anthology	$27.95
00690685	David Lee Roth – Eat 'Em and Smile	$19.95
00690031	Santana's Greatest Hits	$19.95
00690796	Very Best of Michael Schenker	$19.95
00690566	Best of Scorpions	$22.95
00690604	Bob Seger – Guitar Anthology	$19.95
00690659	Bob Seger and the Silver Bullet Band – Greatest Hits, Volume 2	$17.95
00691012	Shadows Fall – Retribution	$22.99
00690896	Shadows Fall – Threads of Life	$19.95
00690803	Best of Kenny Wayne Shepherd Band	$19.95
00690750	Kenny Wayne Shepherd – The Place You're In	$19.95
00690857	Shinedown – Us and Them	$19.95
00690196	Silverchair – Freak Show	$19.95
00690130	Silverchair – Frogstomp	$19.95
00690872	Slayer – Christ Illusion	$19.95
00690813	Slayer – Guitar Collection	$19.95
00690419	Slipknot	$19.95
00690973	Slipknot – All Hope Is Gone	$22.99
00690733	Slipknot – Volume 3 (The Subliminal Verses)	$22.99
00690330	Social Distortion – Live at the Roxy	$19.95
00120004	Best of Steely Dan	$24.95
00694921	Best of Steppenwolf	$22.95
00690655	Best of Mike Stern	$19.95
00690949	Rod Stewart Guitar Anthology	$19.99
00690021	Sting – Fields of Gold	$19.95
00690597	Stone Sour	$19.95
00690689	Story of the Year – Page Avenue	$19.95
00690520	Styx Guitar Collection	$19.95
00120081	Sublime	$19.95
00690992	Sublime – Robbin' the Hood	$19.99
00690519	SUM 41 – All Killer No Filler	$19.95
00690994	Taylor Swift	$22.99
00690993	Taylor Swift – Fearless	$22.99
00691063	Taylor Swift – Speak Now	$22.99
00690767	Switchfoot – The Beautiful Letdown	$19.95
00690425	System of a Down	$19.95
00690830	System of a Down – Hypnotize	$19.95
00690799	System of a Down – Mezmerize	$19.95
00690531	System of a Down – Toxicity	$19.95
00694824	Best of James Taylor	$16.95
00694887	Best of Thin Lizzy	$19.95
00690671	Three Days Grace	$19.95
00690871	Three Days Grace – One-X	$19.95
00690737	3 Doors Down – The Better Life	$22.95
00690891	30 Seconds to Mars – A Beautiful Lie	$19.95
00690030	Toad the Wet Sprocket	$19.95
00690654	Best of Train	$19.95
00690233	The Merle Travis Collection	$19.99
00690683	Robin Trower – Bridge of Sighs	$19.95
00699191	U2 – Best of: 1980-1990	$19.95
00690732	U2 – Best of: 1990-2000	$19.95
00690894	U2 – 18 Singles	$19.95
00690775	U2 – How to Dismantle an Atomic Bomb	$22.95
00690997	U2 – No Line on the Horizon	$19.99
00690039	Steve Vai – Alien Love Secrets	$24.95
00690172	Steve Vai – Fire Garden	$24.95
00660137	Steve Vai – Passion & Warfare	$24.95
00690881	Steve Vai – Real Illusions: Reflections	$24.95
00694904	Steve Vai – Sex and Religion	$24.95
00690392	Steve Vai – The Ultra Zone	$19.95
00690024	Stevie Ray Vaughan – Couldn't Stand the Weather	$19.95
00690370	Stevie Ray Vaughan and Double Trouble – The Real Deal: Greatest Hits Volume 2	$22.95
00690116	Stevie Ray Vaughan – Guitar Collection	$24.95
00660136	Stevie Ray Vaughan – In Step	$19.95
00694879	Stevie Ray Vaughan – In the Beginning	$19.95
00660058	Stevie Ray Vaughan – Lightnin' Blues '83-'87	$24.95
00690036	Stevie Ray Vaughan – Live Alive	$24.95
00694835	Stevie Ray Vaughan – The Sky Is Crying	$22.95
00690025	Stevie Ray Vaughan – Soul to Soul	$19.95
00690015	Stevie Ray Vaughan – Texas Flood	$19.95
00690772	Velvet Revolver – Contraband	$22.95
00690132	The T-Bone Walker Collection	$19.95
00694789	Muddy Waters – Deep Blues	$24.95
00690071	Weezer (The Blue Album)	$19.95
00690516	Weezer (The Green Album)	$19.95
00690286	Weezer – Pinkerton	$19.95
00691046	Weezer – Rarities Edition	$22.99
00690447	Best of the Who	$24.95
00694970	The Who – Definitive Guitar Collection: A-E	$24.95
00694971	The Who – Definitive Guitar Collection F-Li	$24.95
00694972	The Who – Definitive Guitar Collection: Lo-R	$24.95
00694973	The Who – Definitive Guitar Collection: S-Y	$24.95
00690672	Best of Dar Williams	$19.95
00691017	Wolfmother – Cosmic Egg	$22.99
00690319	Stevie Wonder – Some of the Best	$17.95
00690596	Best of the Yardbirds	$19.95
00690844	Yellowcard – Lights and Sounds	$19.95
00690916	The Best of Dwight Yoakam	$19.95
00690904	Neil Young – Harvest	$24.99
00690905	Neil Young – Rust Never Sleeps	$19.99
00690443	Frank Zappa – Hot Rats	$19.95
00690623	Frank Zappa – Over-Nite Sensation	$22.95
00690589	ZZ Top – Guitar Anthology	$24.95
00690960	ZZ Top Guitar Classics	$19.99

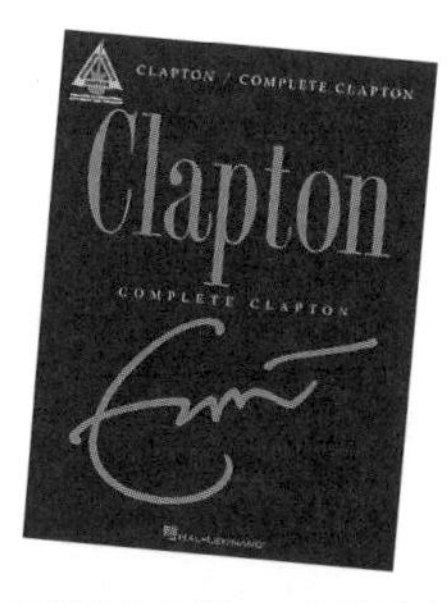

AUTHENTIC TRANSCRIPTIONS WITH NOTES AND TABLATURE

For More Information, See Your Local Music Dealer, Or Write To:

7777 W. Bluemound Rd. P.O. Box 13819 Milwaukee, WI 53213

Complete songlists and more at **www.halleonard.com**

Prices, contents, and availability subject to change without notice.

0611

GUITAR *signature licks*®

Signature Licks book/CD packs provide a step-by-step breakdown of "right from the record" riffs, licks, and solos so you can jam along with your favorite bands. They contain performance notes and an overview of each artist's or group's style, with note-for-note transcriptions in notes and tab. The CDs feature full-band demos at both normal and slow speeds.

ACOUSTIC CLASSICS
00695864 .... $19.95

AEROSMITH 1973-1979
00695106 .... $22.95

AEROSMITH 1979-1998
00695219 .... $22.95

BEST OF AGGRO-METAL
00695592 .... $19.95

DUANE ALLMAN
00696042 .... $22.99

BEST OF CHET ATKINS
00695752 .... $22.95

THE BEACH BOYS DEFINITIVE COLLECTION
00695683 .... $22.95

BEST OF THE BEATLES FOR ACOUSTIC GUITAR
00695453 .... $22.95

THE BEATLES BASS
00695283 .... $22.95

THE BEATLES FAVORITES
00695096 .... $24.95

THE BEATLES HITS
00695049 .... $24.95

BEST OF GEORGE BENSON
00695418 .... $22.95

BEST OF BLACK SABBATH
00695249 .... $22.95

BEST OF BLINK - 182
00695704 .... $22.95

BLUES BREAKERS WITH JOHN MAYALL & ERIC CLAPTON
00696374 .... $22.99

BEST OF BLUES GUITAR
00695846 .... $19.95

BLUES GUITAR CLASSICS
00695177 .... $19.95

BLUES/ROCK GUITAR HEROES
00696381 .... $19.99

BLUES/ROCK GUITAR MASTERS
00695348 .... $21.95

KENNY BURRELL
00695830 .... $22.99

BEST OF CHARLIE CHRISTIAN
00695584 .... $22.95

BEST OF ERIC CLAPTON
00695038 .... $24.95

ERIC CLAPTON – THE BLUESMAN
00695040 .... $22.95

ERIC CLAPTON – FROM THE ALBUM UNPLUGGED
00695250 .... $24.95

BEST OF CREAM
00695251 .... $22.95

CREEDANCE CLEARWATER REVIVAL
00695924 .... $22.95

DEEP PURPLE – GREATEST HITS
00695625 .... $22.95

THE BEST OF DEF LEPPARD
00696516 .... $22.95

THE DOORS
00695373 .... $22.95

TOMMY EMMANUEL
00696409 .... $22.99

ESSENTIAL JAZZ GUITAR
00695875 .... $19.99

FAMOUS ROCK GUITAR SOLOS
00695590 .... $19.95

ROBBEN FORD
00695903 .... $22.95

GREATEST GUITAR SOLOS OF ALL TIME
00695301 .... $19.95

BEST OF GRANT GREEN
00695747 .... $22.95

BEST OF GUNS N' ROSES
00695183 .... $24.95

THE BEST OF BUDDY GUY
00695186 .... $22.99

JIM HALL
00695848 .... $22.99

HARD ROCK SOLOS
00695591 .... $19.95

JIMI HENDRIX
00696560 .... $24.95

JIMI HENDRIX – VOLUME 2
00695835 .... $24.95

JOHN LEE HOOKER
00695894 .... $19.99

HOT COUNTRY GUITAR
00695580 .... $19.95

BEST OF JAZZ GUITAR
00695586 .... $24.95

ERIC JOHNSON
00699317 .... $24.95

ROBERT JOHNSON
00695264 .... $22.95

BARNEY KESSEL
00696009 .... $22.99

THE ESSENTIAL ALBERT KING
00695713 .... $22.95

B.B. KING – THE DEFINITIVE COLLECTION
00695635 .... $22.95

B.B. KING – MASTER BLUESMAN
00699923 .... $24.99

THE KINKS
00695553 .... $22.95

BEST OF KISS
00699413 .... $22.95

MARK KNOPFLER
00695178 .... $22.95

LYNYRD SKYNYRD
00695872 .... $24.95

BEST OF PAT MARTINO
00695632 .... $24.99

WES MONTGOMERY
00695387 .... $24.95

BEST OF NIRVANA
00695483 .... $24.95

THE OFFSPRING
00695852 .... $24.95

VERY BEST OF OZZY OSBOURNE
00695431 .... $22.95

BRAD PAISLEY
00696379 .... $22.99

BEST OF JOE PASS
00695730 .... $22.95

TOM PETTY
00696021 .... $22.99

PINK FLOYD – EARLY CLASSICS
00695566 .... $22.95

THE POLICE
00695724 .... $22.95

THE GUITARS OF ELVIS
00696507 .... $22.95

BEST OF QUEEN
00695097 .... $24.95

BEST OF RAGE AGAINST THE MACHINE
00695480 .... $24.95

RED HOT CHILI PEPPERS
00695173 .... $22.95

RED HOT CHILI PEPPERS – GREATEST HITS
00695828 .... $24.95

BEST OF DJANGO REINHARDT
00695660 .... $24.95

BEST OF ROCK
00695884 .... $19.95

ROCK BAND
00696063 .... $22.99

BEST OF ROCK 'N' ROLL GUITAR
00695559 .... $19.95

BEST OF ROCKABILLY GUITAR
00695785 .... $19.95

THE ROLLING STONES
00695079 .... $24.95

BEST OF DAVID LEE ROTH
00695843 .... $24.95

BEST OF JOE SATRIANI
00695216 .... $22.95

BEST OF SILVERCHAIR
00695488 .... $22.95

THE BEST OF SOUL GUITAR
00695703 .... $19.95

BEST OF SOUTHERN ROCK
00695560 .... $19.95

STEELY DAN
00696015 .... $22.99

MIKE STERN
00695800 .... $24.99

BEST OF SURF GUITAR
00695822 .... $19.95

BEST OF SYSTEM OF A DOWN
00695788 .... $22.95

ROBIN TROWER
00695950 .... $22.95

STEVE VAI
00673247 .... $22.95

STEVE VAI – ALIEN LOVE SECRETS: THE NAKED VAMPS
00695223 .... $22.95

STEVE VAI – FIRE GARDEN: THE NAKED VAMPS
00695166 .... $22.95

STEVE VAI – THE ULTRA ZONE: NAKED VAMPS
00695684 .... $22.95

STEVIE RAY VAUGHAN – 2ND ED.
00699316 .... $24.95

THE GUITAR STYLE OF STEVIE RAY VAUGHAN
00695155 .... $24.95

BEST OF THE VENTURES
00695772 .... $19.95

THE WHO – 2ND ED.
00695561 .... $22.95

JOHNNY WINTER
00695951 .... $22.99

BEST OF ZZ TOP
00695738 .... $24.95

HAL•LEONARD®
CORPORATION
7777 W. BLUEMOUND RD. P.O. BOX 13819
MILWAUKEE, WISCONSIN 53213

www.halleonard.com

COMPLETE DESCRIPTIONS AND SONGLISTS ONLINE!

Prices, contents and availability subject to change without notice.

0811